Baptists in the Balance

Baptists in the Balance
The Tension between Freedom and Responsibility

Edited by Everett C. Goodwin

Judson Press ® Valley Forge

Library of Congress Cataloging-in-Publication Data
Baptists in the balance : the tension between freedom and responsibility / edited by Everett C. Goodwin.
   p. cm.
   Includes bibliographical references and index.
   ISBN 0-8170-1247-8 (pbk. : alk. paper)
   1. Baptists2. Baptists—United States.I. Goodwin, Everett C.
  BX6235.B37 1997
  286'.173—dc21   97-9442

Printed in the U.S.A.
05 04 03 02 01 00 99 98 97
10 9 8 7 6 5 4 3 2 1

To Jane Gray Goodwin

*As a result of our marriage she became a Baptist.
Since then she has encouraged me to celebrate the best
and to endure the worst of being one.*

Contents

Foreword by Bill Moyers xi

Preface xv

Acknowledgments xxi

Introduction: *The Long View: Aspects of the Tension between Freedom and Responsibility*, Everett C. Goodwin 1

Part I. Creations, Connections, and Communities in the Past: Some Aspects of Baptist History

Introduction to Part I 59

Introduction: An Overview, William G. McLoughlin 61

The Rise of the Antipedobaptists in New England, 1630–1655, William G. McLoughlin 72

The Black Baptists: The First Black Churches in America, C. Eric Lincoln and Lawrence H. Mamiya 97

The Southern Baptist Convention, 1979–93: What Happened and Why? Stan Hastey 124

Part II. The Search for Authority: Baptist Use and Interpretation of Scriptures

Introduction to Part II 139

Exercising Liberty of Conscience: Freedom in Private Interpretation, Molly T. Marshall 141

Biblical Authority and Communities of Discourse, Joel B. Green 151

The Authority of the Bible and Private Interpretation: A Dilemma of Baptist Freedom, David M. Scholer 174

Part III. Defining the Boundaries of Baptist Community: Who Are We?

Introduction to Part III 195

American Baptists: An Autobiographical Quest for Identity,
Eldon G. Ernst 197

Being Baptist, James M. Dunn 219

One Denomination, Many Centers:
The Southern Baptist Situation, Bill J. Leonard 228

Reclaiming the Baptist Principle of Associations,
Malcolm G. Shotwell 243

Congregation and Association: Rethinking Baptist
Distinctives for a New Century, Nancy T. Ammerman 260

Part IV. The Boundary of Freedom: Baptists and Church/State Tensions

Introduction to Part IV 273

Responsible Freedom: Baptists in Early America,
Edwin S. Gaustad 275

Back to the Bill of Rights' Beginning, James M. Dunn 286

Baptists and the Establishment Clause: Our Commitment and
Challenge, Melissa Rogers 298

The Ebb and Flow of Free Exercise, Oliver Thomas 306

Part V. The Tensions of Experience and Witness in Contemporary Baptist Life

Introduction to Part V 311

No Room for Bystanders, Bill Moyers 314

Baptist by Choice, Lawrence W. Sherman 319

Why Are We Here? Denton Lotz 326

We Knew What Glory Was, Shirlee Taylor Haizlip 330

The Development of Black Baptists in Virginia, 1867–1882,
Ralph Reavis 333

They Called the Altar "Witness," Norman S. Johnson Sr. 343

Lord, We Are Ready, Daniel E. Weiss 348

Past as Present, Present as Past: Freedom to Read the Self and the World, Vincent L. Wimbush 357

Living under God's Rule: Theological Reflections on Baptist Distinctives, James H. Evans Jr. 371

Afterword: *Looking Backward, Living Forward* 381

Appendix: *The Recent Denominational Development of the American Baptist Churches in the U.S.A.* 387

Baptist History and Identity Resources 397

Index 401

Foreword

Bill Moyers

From their beginning, Baptists have been about faith—faith in which intelligence, the will, and the affections of the heart all have their place. And they have been about freedom. When inspired by these to act in concert, Baptists have often done great works in preaching, teaching, and healing, and they have exercised a powerful influence, directly and indirectly, in the forming of national and world organizations. Today, more than ever, faith and freedom are themes close to the heart of people in America and around the world. Indeed, much of the world hungers for spiritual leadership that can challenge humanity to face the great dilemmas of the new millennium. Why is it, then, that we have such difficulty in bringing faith and freedom together in a common orbit? And why is the fellowship of Baptists so frequently divided in the doing of good deeds and God's work?

These questions are not unique to Baptists. Baptists live in the world, and the world is a confusing and conflicted place, often at odds with our aspirations for it. These days it is marked by moral and social ambivalence as well as economic uncertainty. In such a world, people yearn for freedom—freedom from oppression to be sure, but also freedom from confusion. Sometimes these aspirations can seem mutually exclusive. The late scholar of ancient Greece, Edith Hamilton, wrote that "when the world is storm-driven and the bad that happens and the worse that threatens are so urgent as to shut out everything else from view, then we need to know all the strong fortresses of the spirit which have been built through the ages." Many Baptists are eager, therefore, to reaffirm the fortresses offered by both faith and freedom.

I am impressed by the number of people who tell me they have recently joined Bible study groups, prayer groups, and new church organizations and expressions and by others who have returned to reclaim a spiritual or religious tradition they had once abandoned. Likewise, it is significant how often these same persons and others express in frustration that it is hard to find a truth to live by amid so many expressions or that what once seemed certain to them now appears but one possibility among many. In reaffirming the truth of their experience, Baptists are part of a growing and many-faceted dialogue of a world where no religion can exist in isolation. "How do I hold my truth to be the truth," I recently asked the renowned historian of religion, Huston Smith, "when so many others see truth differently?" He answered, "We listen. We listen as alertly to others' experience of reality as we want them to listen to us."

America faces a new religious landscape. This is not a homogeneous nation, and every day we witness new contributions and confront new challenges to our common life. When I was young, America was often described as a "melting pot." Now it is a mosaic, a "tossed salad." Every American is called upon to examine and respond to these changes in the menu of our cultural life, to hear and engage people who are different.

Nowhere is this more true than in personal faith and institutional religion. And because they often represent the great mainstream of our nation, nowhere is this more true than among Baptists. If it were ever possible to accurately characterize Baptists, it is not so now. Along with others, they are experiencing a rush of the new. This has had a profound impact on their traditions, cherished practices, and even some of their beliefs. In his classic study, *The World's Religions*, Huston Smith writes that when future historians look back on our years, "they may remember them not for the release of nuclear power but as the time in which all the peoples of the world had to take one another seriously, including our quest for meaning." This quest for meaning is, for Baptists, at the heart of faith.

So the secular and spiritual are intersecting with one another in unexpected ways. It is a time when varieties of spiritual traditions and explorations are colliding, conflicting, and, yes, at times cooperating. Painful though the adjustments may be, from the cacophony of voices that speak today will come new ways and new forms of community, new perceptions of the common good, new understandings of God. It is a dangerous time, but grand, too. We are present at a new creation whose shape is impossible to define or ignore.

The scholar James Davison Hunter describes democracy as "the hard, tedious, perplexing, messy and seemingly endless task of working through what kind of people we are and what kind of communities we will live in." This is true for Americans of all stripes, and it is true for Baptists, too. Our associations, churches, fellowships, and missions are being transformed. We see the fissures but the new forms have not arrived in a discernible pattern.

This is a book that reflects the swirling forces of belief and practice. It is about faith and about freedom, and it wrestles with the challenge to all of us in balancing those two powerful forces in responsible community relationships. It is an honest book because it lays open some of the painful dilemmas facing Baptists in the present. It is a hopeful book because it assumes that there will be new common ground from which will rise renewed hope for cooperation. It traces some of the roads we have traveled, asks many of the questions that people of faith must answer, and defines the boundaries of faith, organization, and purpose that sometimes become points of conflict. Here and there it even hints at those contours of a new vision.

In reading these essays we move toward understanding ourselves better as people. By responding to them we participate in the conversation about our future. The new millennium soon to be upon us will be greeted with apprehension and opportunity. I have no doubt that many Baptists, individually and collectively, will play important roles in this new beginning.

Preface

This is a book by, about, and for Baptists. It is also a book for those who desire to understand more about the origins and development of these dynamic people of faith. In both cases there is much to be learned from Baptists' achievements, for they have been many and great. And there is much, too, to be learned from their frustrations and failures. They, too, have been numerous.

Baptists are historic. Although young by the standards of Christian history, their history has been intertwined with the creation of the modern world. Baptists were among the first to colonize the new world and to establish its early traditions. Their spirit of freedom influenced the shaping of the First Amendment to the Constitution of the United States; their passion for mission helped first to bring churches, schools, and colleges to the American frontier; and later that same impulse was formative in empowering the global missionary enterprise that characterized much of the eighteenth and nineteenth centuries and helped shape much of the dynamics of world politics and community to the present.

Baptists are numerous. The largest single denomination of them, the Southern Baptist Convention, is the largest single Protestant denomination in the United States with over fifteen million members. Collectively, Baptists in the United States alone number in excess of thirty million, which is approximately 12 percent of the total population and as much as 20 percent of the estimated church-affiliated population in the United States.

Baptists are influential. Surveys and sociological samples of Baptists frequently identify them to be relatively low on the scale of formal education and social status. Baptists represent the broad middle of American culture, not its elite. Nevertheless, their influence on American religious life has been considerable, affecting the denominational organization, style, and priorities of many other religious groups. Martin Marty, the premier and often quoted observer of American religious life, has popularized their impact with the phrase the "baptistification of American religion." Although the great majority of Baptists are persons of limited means and influence, at the beginning of this century Baptists included Rockefeller, Colgate, and Kraft. At mid-century President Harry S. Truman was a Baptist, as was the nation's then most famous preacher, Harry Emerson Fosdick. And in the 1990s the president, vice president, speaker of the house, and several others in the formal line of succession of national political power are Baptists—as are several others who apparently aspire to the nation's highest offices for the future.

Baptists have been sustained by a high vision of the church. They believe that the church is most vitally formed in the hearts and souls of those who have experienced a redeeming presence in Christ, and who have sought some specific way to give shape to that presence. They believe that no structure or institution is strong enough—or pure enough—to fully contain the presence of the Spirit of Christ, which gives it life. They believe that the church is constantly in a state of renewal and therefore cannot long be contained in any institutional form. In that sense Baptists are extraordinary in their capacity to recreate, renew, and revitalize what they have received and what they have created. For the same reasons, they are not, perhaps, as good at creating consistent, centralized institutions. They seem, therefore, always on the brink of institutional chaos.

Baptists have been guided by an unshakable commitment to certain basic principles: the spiritual freedom of the individual, the autonomy of the local congregation, the primacy of mission over institutions, and the power of the Holy Spirit to conform Baptists and Baptist purposes to the will and work of God. In relationship to the world, they have historically maintained a fierce commitment to the separation of church and state. In short, Baptists do not find it advisable or easy to compromise. Their style and their beliefs are not ones which, in human terms, contribute to long-term stability or smooth, linear development for their programs and institutional life.

Baptists rely on the Word of God as revealed in the Bible. To Baptists that Word is creative, formative, reliable, unshakable, and authoritative. But, because that belief is always mediated by the individual interpretation that individual freedom demands, Baptists in principle find it hard to agree always on what God's Word as revealed in the Scriptures means in practice.

Baptists are experiential. An experience in faith that begins with personal belief and discovers its authenticity in the personal, transforming power of an encounter with the presence of Christ within the believer is, of necessity, individualistic. More, it is by nature inclined to discount unity in favor of individual integrity.

Baptists are, therefore, defined by their freedom. Because of that, defining appropriate responsibility by which they can live and work together has been and is their greatest challenge. The title of this volume, therefore, *Baptists in the Balance: The Tension between Freedom and Responsibility*, is not so much a statement of a proposition as it is a simple observation of reality.

To the degree that a number of Baptist authors can have, collectively, a premise, it is the premise of this volume that Baptist life always hangs in the balance. It is, further, that Baptists are more easily defined by their grand visions and their individual, personal beliefs than they are by their intermediate institutions, programs, and priorities. Baptists find it hard to maintain that balance. Baptists have *always* found it hard to maintain balance.

Nevertheless, the complexity of the world in which Baptists now live makes it urgent that Baptist people, churches, and institutions discover places of common commitment in order that their mission might continue. Observers of religious life in the late twentieth century are unanimous in describing powerful, unalterable changes taking place in American religious and spiritual habits. The most extreme among them predict the death of the church as it has been known. And Baptists, because of their tendency to freedom and division, are occasionally singled out as early candidates for self-destruction. Nonsense. Americans are a fundamentally religious people, and Baptists represent a fundamentally American style of religious expression. Their tribes will increase—and undoubtedly will multiply.

Still, the enormity of the changes that are overtaking present forms of church life and individual faith experiences confront Baptists with the necessity of carefully defining what really matters, and what can be changed, reshaped, or even abandoned without altering their fundamental mission or compromising essential matters of belief. It is the purpose of this book, therefore, to provide perspectives that will encourage that definition and, we hope, greater clarity in commitment.

The idea for this volume grew out of a growing awareness that many contemporary Baptists were uncertain about their institutional origins, the traditions that shaped them, and the principles that had guided their forebears. Almost forty years ago a volume entitled *Baptist Concepts of the Church*, edited by Winthrop S. Hudson (Judson Press, 1959), provided an admirable resource for a similar purpose as Baptists then sought to shape their denominational and mission life. Its contents, articles written by the most able among scholars, clearly defined some of the powerful traditions that had shaped Baptist life in doctrine and in practice. At one stage it was proposed that we reedit and perhaps enlarge that by now classic work. As a result, Judson Press asked if I would be interested in shaping such a task. I was delighted to participate in what seemed an important enterprise, and we began conversations about how to approach the work. But much had changed since 1959. Simple adjustments seemed ultimately to diminish the previous work without adequately dealing with current issues. It seemed therefore better to let a classic remain a classic.

What was proposed, instead, was a volume that adopted the same spirit but would be more fully a description of the issues Baptists are wrestling with in the 1990s. We began to consider what kinds of materials should be included, and it seemed that the style of the nineties—as well as the present character of Baptist life—would be best expressed by a combination of scholarly works, sermons, essays, and personal reflections. A wide variety of material was reviewed, and a number of pieces were selected. At the same time, the tensions—both creative and destructive—that Baptists were commonly experiencing helped form the idea for a conference on Baptist distinctives. That conference, scheduled and held in August of 1996, promised to bring new perspectives to life. We hoped that the conference, titled "Called to Responsible Freedom: A Conference on Baptist Distinctives," might itself provide materials that could be included in this project. We were not disappointed.

What has emerged, therefore, is a volume that contains scholarly, journalistic, personal, dispassionate, intense, reflective, challenging, devotional, reminiscent, and futuristic material. All of it is shaped around the common theme of the tension between freedom and responsibility. The author of each piece is identified as are the circumstances of its original presentation, whether in speech, publication, or conference. Likewise, the contributions are organized into several major categories regarding history, biblical issues, identity, and others. To a different eye this organization may seem arbitrary. It does, however, serve the purpose of our theme and make it possible for brief sectional introductions to provide some order to what otherwise may have seemed a disorienting collection of unrelated contributions.

A rather lengthy introduction precedes the individual contributions. The introduction is provided in order that those who have little knowledge of Baptists and their history might gain at least a summary knowledge of Baptist origins and developments. Alternatively, those who possess an extensive understanding of Baptists are liable to find it woefully inadequate despite its length. It is our hope that it might be considered, however, a helpful refresher and that its perspective on the theme of freedom and responsibility will shape a reflective context from which to approach the materials that follow.

The several contributions that make up this book will reveal much about the life of Baptists in the past and present. By their considerable display of knowledge they clarify much about Baptist beliefs and institutions. Their personal, often confessional, perspectives reveal much about their authors' own faith and hope. It is our common hope that they will stimulate in their readers new visions and new commitments to shape a more faithful, fruitful, and commendable future for Baptists to come.

—Everett C. Goodwin
April 1997

Acknowledgments

Selecting the articles presented here was on the one hand a difficult chore, as there is much material on Baptists and Baptist life available. Yet, in another respect, it was an easy task, for each article represents a high standard of scholarship, expression, or observation. It is a particular pleasure for me to be associated with several of the contributors in this work, because they represent friends, colleagues, and companions in the fellowship of Baptist life or in the work of describing and understanding Baptist contributions. Each work is clearly identified in presentation; therefore I shall not list each contributor individually here. Instead, I will express my gratitude not only for the contributions they have made, but also for their cooperative spirit in making their work available.

Several of the included works have been previously published in another form. Acknowledgments and permissions for republication have been noted with those articles, and we express gratitude here to the many publications that have allowed them to be reaffirmed in this volume.

In developing the material for the introduction, I was guided by a number of standard Baptist histories and works, as well as by my personal observations and interpretations. In that regard I would like to acknowledge especially Winthrop S. Hudson, whose contributions to a predecessor volume, *Baptist Concepts of the Church*, provided a steady guide in helping to shape the introduction to this volume. Likewise, the now classic *A Baptist Manual of Polity and Practice* (Judson Press, 1991) by Norman Maring and Winthrop S. Hudson would be a helpful supplement to this introduction for the reader who wishes to explore in greater detail the workings of Baptist organizational life. Beyond these, the reader is invited to explore the additional resources described in the bibliographical resources section at the end of the volume. Daniel Weiss, general secretary of the ABC/USA, called my attention to documents related to developments in twentieth-century Baptist institutional life, and Beverly Carlson of the American Baptist Historical Society assisted in clarifying several matters of archival detail and interest. James Dunn of the Baptist Joint

Committee on Public Affairs was also greatly helpful in providing insights and suggestions in the development of this volume.

I am especially grateful to two historians whose work and perspectives have inspired my own sense of the importance of understanding the contributions of Baptists both to life in faith as well as in American culture. The first is William G. McLoughlin, with whom I had the privilege of studying at Brown University. His two articles presented in this volume are but samples of a lifetime of contributions to historical scholarship. Their appearance here provided the added personal pleasure of remembering two summers of work with him in the process of developing the corpus of his work on Isaac Backus. The second is Edwin S. Gaustad, also represented in this volume. Baptists are fortunate to have such an eminent historian so dedicated to understanding and clarifying their history. I am particularly indebted to him for his encouragement and suggestions.

To the members of The Baptist Fellowship of Metropolitan Washington, D.C., I express special thanks for their encouragement and support—and for their tolerance of the time required in developing this work. Several of them were particularly helpful in reading and discussing materials included in this volume, and in helping to evaluate their potential contributions. They include Bill Bouschka, Jacquie Calnan, Nancy Blevins, Cordell Smith, and Paul and Sharon Bowen.

I am especially thankful for Kristy Arnesen Pullen of Judson Press, who provided with patience and grace those attributes one hopes for in a publisher and editor. Victoria McGoey, also of Judson Press, was invaluable in her tracking of materials, details, and schedules as the project progressed.

My most heartfelt acknowledgment is noted in the dedication.

Introduction
The Long View: Aspects of the Tension between Freedom and Responsibility

Baptists exist in infinite variety. As one of the contributors to this volume so aptly phrased it, "Jesse Jackson is a Baptist; so is Jesse Helms." Baptists are right, left, and center on almost every issue, and if there are other positions, Baptists are there too. We are high church and low church, liberal, conservative, fundamental, open, closed, restrictive, inclusive— and always in process. We love constitutions and ignore them at every opportunity. We love the Bible and believe its every word to be from God, but there has never been a Baptist who did not feel entitled to edit some of its rougher parts and interpret (authoritatively) some of its more confusing texts. But somehow we are bound together in ways not even our most heated controversies can fully disconnect. Invite us to sing a favorite hymn, remind us of a Baptist witness, call us to a prophetic task, challenge us to an urgent mission, and we will, by the miraculous grace of God, respond in unity and in joy.

Still, Baptists seem to go from crisis to crisis and controversy to controversy. Baptist life seems always to hang in the balance. Why? Who are Baptists, anyway? And how did Baptists come to be who they are? The contributions to this volume help to shape these questions and to propose some answers. They represent some of the most recent and most able scholarship and commentary by and about Baptists. They provide a few images and shadows that will broaden our perspectives. It is our contention that Baptist life hangs in the balance because one of our greatest gifts, *freedom,* is always in tension with our greatest challenge, *responsibility.* Our history began with this tension, and we still find ourselves in the struggle today.

In this introduction I have tried to provide a context for the individual essays, sermons, and narratives this volume includes. Much of what it contains will be well-traveled and familiar ground for some. For others it

1

may be new territory. This introduction is too short to be a real history of any Baptist group in particular, and it is certainly inadequate to describe Baptist experience in general. On the other hand, it is much too long simply to be an introduction to the materials that follow it. It is, rather, an attempt to interpret some major themes of Baptist development, especially with regard to relationships among and between Baptists, as they have shaped our particular theme of freedom and responsibility. From those who are well informed about Baptist history and issues, I beg indulgence for all it leaves out. To those who are unfamiliar with Baptist history, I offer both my sympathy for its considerable length and perhaps overwhelming span of events, and my hope that it will at least open the door to understanding these unique—and sometimes unfathomable—people.

In Search of a Baptist Way

Baptists have a mixed pedigree. They have no patriarch—no Martin Luther to mark the beginning and to shape the future with a single, consistent, and commanding voice, nor a John Calvin to develop a theology by which other views are measured. As a result, they have no standard by which to operate or from which to deviate. Here and there, of course, Baptist history remembers a notable leader who shepherded a flock or championed a particular reform. But to suggest a single example exposes the dilemma: Which one might be exemplified over the others? Each candidate, regardless of his or her own powerful witness, has tended to respond to an acute need or to focus on a single cause. Often such leaders have arisen in response to a crisis. Others have articulated a vision or have been architects of an ecclesiological plan. There have been remarkable leaders and pastors. But none has given rise to a universal theological or ecclesiological benchmark. Because Baptists have no single progenitor, they have followed many leaders. The people who have claimed the Baptist name have, by their nature and experience, often been deeply suspicious of monoliths, systems, and even the leadership of those who have gathered and led them. Therefore, they have often been fragmented, isolated, divisive, and diffused. Instead of a single way, they have been shaped by many influences, have exhibited diverse and sometimes con-tradictory patterns of thought, and have produced a great variety of traditions of church life.

In reviewing the sometimes broad parameters of present Baptist life, it is important to understand that there is strong historical precedent for the tensions that characterize modern Baptists. Historically, Baptists grew out of the "second stage" of the Reformation. The first stage had been marked by sharp division from the traditions of the Roman Catholic Church and by a new vision for the church. This was the era of Luther and Melanchthon and Knox and Calvin. The second stage was characterized by debate and division within the newly emerging church, the so-called Protestant movement. It was a period of political ferment outside the church and of lively theological debate and ecclesiastical experimentation within the emerging church traditions.

From their beginnings, early Baptists drew upon these emerging theologies and experiments. They were shaped by a whirlwind, we might say. It is not surprising, therefore, that early Baptist formations of faith and church life were divergent, sometimes chaotic, and always subject to further change and revision. A consistent theme is the constant tension Baptists have experienced in their encounters with the church universal and its complex community, and their own continuing impulse to define a biblically purer, spiritually freer, and consequently, institutionally more isolated and independent way.

The English Heritage

Baptists in America trace their origins most directly to the continuing Reformation in England. Their leaders were influenced primarily by the Puritan movement of the sixteenth and seventeenth centuries and, to a lesser extent, by the often turbulent reforms of the more extreme reformers on the European continent, including some of the moderate Anabaptists. In England, Baptist habits of thought were divided most clearly between the positions represented by the Particular Baptists and the General Baptists. Both systems followed variant forms of Calvinism: The Particular Baptists derived their name from a doctrine of a "particular" or "limited" atonement, and the General Baptists followed a doctrine of "general" atonement. In each case a complete theological system was involved, and in each case Baptists who followed them were grafting a unique form of church order onto an already existing theology.

The Particular Baptists stood within the traditions of covenant theology, which were ultimately expressed in the Westminster Standards. Particular Baptists were closely related in spirit, therefore, to the more numerous Puritan settlers who dominated the New England colonies. Later, in the colonies, many Baptist churches emerged from Puritan churches shaped by covenant theology. Theologically, it was not a large leap. The General Baptists, on the other hand, adhered to the form of Calvinism commonly categorized as Arminianism. In the long course of time,

Particular Baptists were pushed into the "hyper-Calvinism" camp and exhibited the rigidities of that theology and church practice. Likewise, the notion of general atonement possessed by General Baptists proved not to be sufficiently distinct from Unitarianism, and because of the ill-defined Baptist institutional boundaries of the seventeenth and eighteenth centuries, most General Baptists were first confused with, and then merged into, that movement.

Theology was not the only distinction between General and Particular Baptists. Indeed, the difference in church practices likely proved to be of greater importance. Both branches emerged from the "congregational" church movement. Some congregational churches broke radically with the established Church of England; others sought to maintain at least the fiction of unity, while attempting reforms in church life and practice. General Baptists emerged from among the English Separatists; Particular Baptists were rooted in non-Separatist Independency. Both Separatists and non-Separatists believed that church life should be based on the witness of the New Testament, which meant that they should be self-governing bodies comprised of believers. Where they differed was in their attitude toward the Church of England. Separatists believed that the Church of England was a false church and concluded that a break with it must be complete, final, and uncompromising. Non-Separatists followed a less extreme path: They confessed that even the "purest" churches were subject to error and to the inclusion of some who were not of right belief and perhaps not saved. Their humility on this point made it difficult to conclude that the English church was completely lacking of the true marks of the church. As a result, they were unwilling to break completely with the established church or to renounce the Church of England as apostate. To do so, they believed, might cause the greater sins of lack of charity and the promotion of schism in the body of Christ. Instead, some non-Separatists sought to remain within the church as an active force of reform. Others, in increasing numbers as the reforming path proved difficult, organized their own congregations hoping to establish more correct examples of the church in worship and governance.

General Baptists emerged first, although ultimately they were to nearly disappear as a significant force in Baptist development. In the face of religious persecution, a group of Lincolnshire Separatists sought asylum in Holland in 1608. One group settled in Amsterdam with John Smyth as their minister. The other went to Leyden with John Robinson as their leader. In Amsterdam Smyth resolved that if the Separatist belief that "the churches of the apostolic constitution consisted of saints only" was to be affirmed, baptism could be offered only to those who could provide convincing evidence of grace. He then moved to baptize himself and other members of his community, constituting them into a church. Although Smyth held a firm conviction about believers' baptism, he did not hold to other theological positions as strongly, and as a result, a number of his church members grew restive under his leadership. In 1611 or 1612 a contingent therefore returned to London where they established a small Baptist church. They brought with them the moderate Calvinism of Arminius, which they had embraced in Holland, and established in England a beginning for what became the General Baptist movement. Their growth was slow. By 1640 there were only a half dozen General Baptist churches with a total of two hundred members.

Particular Baptists, arising from the non-Separating stream of Independency, had no need for a sojourn abroad. In 1616 a non-Separatist church was established in Southwark, near London, by Henry Jacob. Then in 1638 many of its members withdrew, peacefully and in good order, under the leadership of John Spilsbury, to form the first Particular Baptist church. Their departure was accomplished with a desire "to depart and not to be censured," and their mother congregation granted their request "with prayer made in their behalf." In this instance, at least, the development of a Baptist congregation was not accompanied by rigid exclusivism. Spilsbury's church was symbolic of much of the early Particular Baptist sentiment. A few of the prominent leaders were willing to organize "mixed" churches so that there would be no overt breach with fellow believers who were distinguished from them only at the point of baptism. Only believers could be newly admitted to the covenant relationship, of course. Other Particular Baptist leaders formed separate churches but practiced open Communion in order to accommodate the variety of specific beliefs and commitments within the extended congregation.

Still others among the Particular Baptist leadership adopted a more rigid view, however, and established congregations in which both membership and Communion was restricted to those who were baptized as believers. This view gained ground and became the dominant practice during much of the eighteenth century. But even these early advocates of a strict view of membership rarely denied the name of Christian to those who did not share their views on baptism, and in the political and social conflicts of the time, they remained in solidarity with the broad stream of Independents in matters of common concern. Later, in the nineteenth century's flood of evangelicalism, particularly as expressed in the leadership of Robert Hall and Charles H. Spurgeon, many Particular Baptist churches adopted the practice of open Communion again. Thus, while English Particular Baptists demonstrated a clear and distinct view of personal belief and response to the inward presence of grace, as well as of the boundaries of church life, they consistently held back from rigid boundaries of church life in practice.

Although both the General and the Particular Baptists experienced a surge of growth following the outbreak of the English Civil War, the latter enjoyed the greatest increase. Also, the Particular Baptists numbered among their adherents some of the leaders of the Cromwellian government. The General Baptists, possessing a more diffused theology, suffered defections into the ranks of the Quakers. And after the restoration of the Stuart monarchy in 1660, both the Quakers and the General Baptists suffered under the application of the Clarendon Code and were driven underground until the 1689 Act of Toleration reduced the danger of their public worship.

Ironically, the sharp theological differences between the General and Particular Baptists led to a situation where both found it easier to maintain cordial relationships with other churches and movements than with each other—a phenomenon that can be generally observed throughout the development of Baptist life. The Particular Baptists, in a variety of ways, were able to maintain fellowship with the Congregationalists, but were unable to tolerate relationships with General Baptists. The General Baptists, on the other hand, with their more closely knit sectarian style, found themselves more often in sympathy with other sectarians with whom they had little in common theologically but much in common experientially. Both groups declined markedly in the eighteenth century. The Particular Baptists withdrew into increasingly defensive theological positions, emerging with a hyper-Calvinist theology that paralyzed their evangelistic outreach. The General Baptists, on the other hand, fell victim to the ravages of skepticism or, conversely, merged imperceptibly into the Unitarian movement.

The Evangelical Revival of the mid eighteenth century brought new energy to the Baptist movement, but rather than renewing existing churches, it broke out in new forms and structures of churches. The New Connexion General Baptists were the most visible product—a Baptist style of church with an explicitly Wesleyan theology. A New Connexion body of churches was organized in 1770. As the revival movement spread to the colonies (later the United States), it emerged in the Freewill Baptist movement. Instead of being narrowly sectarian, these new Baptists were characterized by the indifference typical of evangelicalism regarding outward forms of church life and ritual. The open-membership policy of the modern period was in part the result of the leadership of John Clifford, who came from a New Connexion background. This policy was probably the single most important distinction in spirit of the new developments among General Baptists. Again, however, Baptists within the revival stream found it difficult to remain distinct from other emerging groups.

By the end of the eighteenth century, the mainstream of the English Baptists was therefore occupied by the Particular Baptists, who became as a consequence the forerunners of the modern Baptist movement.

American Beginnings

A similar development took place among Baptists in the American colonies. After an early period of growth in the seventeenth century, the General Baptist churches decayed, disintegrated, or blended into other forms. The handful that survived never entered the mainstream of emerging Baptist life in the American colonies and exerted no real influence on later development.

One notable exception was the church established at Providence, which was something of a hybrid. A mixed gathering of Baptists there were reconstituted into a church by Roger Williams in 1639—the year after John Spilsbury had formed a Baptist church out of the old non-Separatist church founded by Jacob in Southwark. Williams's own general theological position was similar to that of Spilsbury, but he had also adopted the narrower Separatist view of the church before he became a Baptist. As Edwin Gaustad has succinctly described him, Williams "loved Christianity but hated Christendom." True to this characterization, Williams soon came to the conclusion that all churches, including his own at Providence, lacked proper scriptural foundation. It was, he believed, a problem that could only be solved when a new apostolic dispensation with new apostles, authoritatively commissioned and divinely authenticated, appeared to start a new church. Williams therefore left the Providence church. Because the church had no strong traditions beyond his own leadership, the vacuum created by his departure was filled with the arrival of three General Baptists who took charge and in 1652 reconstituted the church along General Baptist lines.

There is evidence of scattered General Baptist church life elsewhere in the colonies from an early date, but the only real concentration of General Baptist churches was in Rhode Island. Those churches have the distinction of forming the earliest Baptist association in America. In 1670 four

General Baptist churches united in a yearly meeting, established a mechanism for sending elders and messengers, and defined their purpose as "setting in order the things that are wanting" in the churches. They also sought to resolve "any difficulties that might arise."[1] By 1729 this association embraced thirteen churches including five or six in Massachusetts, Connecticut, and New York. Although General Baptists in the colonies were not subject to the theological diffusions that led to their disintegration in England, their isolation, failure to receive new immigration, and lack of new leadership from England caused them to degenerate into confusion and decay. The General Baptists gradually diminished in subsequent years, until by the mid twentieth century they listed five churches with a total membership of approximately 325.

When the Providence church veered away from an analogous Particular Baptist position and was reconstituted as a General Baptist church, a small minority withdrew to maintain the former witness of the church. This group never gained much strength and went out of existence in 1720. The only other strong Particular Baptist center was in Newport, where sometime between 1641 and 1648 the church gathered by John Clarke adopted Baptist views. Clarke stood squarely in the center of Particular Baptist tradition with respect to his theology and churchmanship. He was aided and supported by Mark Lucar, who had come out of the old Jacob church with John Spilsbury and who had been associated in London with William Kiffin. Only two other Particular Baptist churches can be identified during this period. Both were in Massachusetts. One was the Swansea church formed in 1663 by Welsh immigrants under the leadership of John Myles. Myles had been a noted Baptist leader in Wales and had served as one of the Triers in Cromwell's voluntary national establishment. The other was the Boston church, organized in 1665 by Thomas Goold and two others from Kiffin's London congregation. There was, in addition, one Particular Baptist church in Charleston, South Carolina, founded in 1683 or 1684.

The Particular Baptist future in the colonies did not belong to any of these churches, however. That center was located in the Middle Colonies. A Baptist church was founded at Cold Spring, in what became Bucks County, two years after William Penn arrived with his first settlers in 1682. Its founder was Thomas Dungan, a member of the Newport church. Dungan died in 1688, and by 1702 the church became extinct. But by then Elias Keach and Thomas Killingworth were present. Both men were characterized by a marked evangelistic zeal, and they were instrumental in laying the foundation for Baptist expansion in the years to come.

Killingworth was apparently a Baptist minister in England who migrated to the Delaware Valley from New Hampshire and Long Island. Keach was the son of Benjamin Keach, the most active leader of the Particular Baptists in England. Elias Keach had responded to Penn's appeals for colonists and had left home to establish himself in the colonies. Both humor and evidence of divine persistence mark his contributions to Baptist development. Arriving in Philadelphia at the age of nineteen, he sought for some reason—perhaps as a prank—to impersonate a minister. He was, as he might have expected, invited to preach. During his sermon he was struck with the pangs of conscience and confessed his imposture. Shaken, he traveled to Cold Spring to seek the counsel and care of Thomas Dungan, who soon thereafter baptized and ordained him in 1688. Later that year Keach gathered a church composed of Baptists from England, Ireland, and Wales at Pennepek. Killingworth, meanwhile, had already formed a church at Piscataway in New Jersey. Both of these energetic young men preached at a number of centers in the area, and soon their mutual labors produced churches at Middletown and Cohansey. Another church, the Welsh Tract Church, was organized in Wales in 1701 by a group preparing to emigrate to Pennsylvania. This group and their church settled briefly near Pennepek but moved on to the present state of Delaware and settled on a large tract of land they had secured. These became the five churches that united to form the Philadelphia Baptist Association in 1707.

From these establishments, later powered by the enthusiasm and zeal of the Great Awakening, significant growth developed. By 1760 the Philadelphia Baptist Association embraced churches in Connecticut, New York, New Jersey, Pennsylvania, Delaware, Maryland, Virginia, and West Virginia. Its missionaries had labored up and down the coast from South Carolina to Nova Scotia. The Charleston Baptist Association was formed on the Philadelphia model by Oliver Hart after he traveled there from Philadelphia. The Ketocton Baptist Association in Virginia and the Warren Baptist Association in Rhode Island and southeastern Massachusetts had emerged as extensions of the Philadelphia Association. Baptist growth continued to the degree that, by the close of the American Revolution, Baptist churches and associations modeled on the Philadelphia Association were being established everywhere. By the time of the formation of the United States' Constitution in 1789, Baptists were a significant force demanding religious liberty and strong advocates for freedom from taxation for religious purposes.

Shaping Influences in Early Baptist Life in America

Baptist life in America was strongly shaped by the broad social and political events that defined the mid and later years of the eighteenth century. Chief among them were the establishment of institutional structures, the leveling and energizing effects of the powerful religious movements of the Great Awakening, and the emergence of a powerful philosophy of individualism. We have already noted the strong institution-shaping influence of the Philadelphia Baptist Association. Henry C. Vedder once proclaimed that this influence "fixed the character of the denomination for all time."[2] The issues of the late twentieth century have proved this to be an overstatement, but it is true that the mainstream of Baptist life developed its principles of polity, matters of style, and basics of doctrine under the Philadelphia Baptist Association's influence. Nevertheless, the associational principle was not easily established among Baptists and Baptist congregations, and its general reception came at the cost of significant weakness in the specific connectional character it exhibited.

As we have noted, the Baptists who led in shaping Baptist institutional life identified themselves as Particular Baptists; their leaders and early members came from the Particular Baptist churches of England, Wales, and Ireland. For purposes of instruction, they utilized a catechism written by Benjamin Keach, and they kept up regular correspondence with the board of Particular Baptist ministers in London. They also adopted the Particular, or Philadelphia, Baptist Confession of Faith, which was itself an adoption of the London Confession of the English Particular Baptists. The London Confession, in turn, represented a slight modification of the Savoy Declaration of the English Congregationalists; and it, in turn, was a slightly altered reproduction of the Westminster Confession of Faith. The Baptists even incorporated into the body of the confession the statement concerning "The Institution of Churches and the Order Appointed in Them by Jesus Christ," which the Congregationalists had appended to the Savoy Declaration.

As further evidence that these Middle Colony Baptists perceived themselves firmly within the general non-Separatist tradition of Independency, we note that they appealed frequently to the writings of major non-Separatist theologians and writers, such as William Ames, Thomas Goodwin, Thomas Hooker, and John Owen to support their views and positions. The minority emphasis on open Communion had mostly disappeared among the English Particular Baptists, and it did not reemerge in the colonies. However, a general spirit of ecumenism prevailed, and they were willing to commune with others in worship, if not in the Lord's Supper; and, as had been the tradition in England, they were eager to cooperate in matters of common interest.

It was the influence of the Great Awakening, however, particularly as personified in the Presbyterian preacher and teacher Gilbert Tennent, that was responsible for the renewed zeal and missionary activity among Baptists in the 1740s and 1750s. This revival movement created great and sometimes disabling controversies among the Presbyterians and within the Anglican Church. It did not create such ecclesiological concerns for Baptists and, in fact, propelled them to greater growth and activity. It did, however, introduce the first real penetration of "evangelical" spirit and emphasis among Baptists. An even more radical result of this dynamic movement derived from the schisms that took place within the Standing Order of New England Congregationalism. In short, many zealous participants in the revivals of this period became critical of their Congregational churches and the leadership within them and withdrew from the Standing Order to seek a more purified church. In some cases whole churches withdrew to become "Separate," and in other cases significant segments of churches withdrew to form "Separate" churches. Many of these Separate churches later became Baptist and thus added greatly to the numbers and strength of Baptists in the North. They brought with them, however, a deep suspicion of authority and connection. Indeed, they often confused the two—perhaps an understandable difficulty in light of the oppression and humiliation many of them endured from the Standing Order of Congregationalist churches and leaders.

Baptists in the South, on the other hand, had been relatively weak and disorganized prior to the Great Awakening. There, however, Shubal Stearns, originally a Connecticut Separate, led a remarkable development of Baptist strength. Having moved south as an itinerant preacher in 1755, he settled in Sandy Creek, North Carolina. In a brief time he had gathered a number of converts, gathered several churches, and established the Sandy Creek Association with churches that extended into Virginia and South Carolina. As this vigorous movement grew, one major issue kept southern Separate Baptists apart from the older tradition of Regular Baptists of Virginia and the Carolinas: the unwillingness of the Separates to subscribe to the Philadelphia Confession. The matter was not one of dissent from the doctrines the confession articulated; rather, it was that they insisted as a matter of principle that faith must be grounded on the Scriptures and not on a confession. Ultimately the dispute was compromised in what became a frequent Baptist solution: written verbal compromise that established the purpose but avoided the appearance of external authority. The Philadelphia Confession of Faith was adopted in 1787 as the point of union between Separate and Regular Baptists in Virginia but with the understanding that

> to prevent its usurping a tyrannical power over the consciences of any, we do not mean that every person is bound to the strict observance of everything therein contained, yet that it holds forth the essential truths of the gospel and that the doctrine of salvation by Christ and free unmerited grace alone ought to be believed by every Christian and maintained by every minister of the gospel.[3]

It is interesting—and perhaps an indication of Baptist awareness of the activities of Congregational church strivings with similar issues—that the same problem had been solved by similar strategies when the Congregationalists in the Cambridge Platform accepted the Westminster Confession "for substance of doctrine."

The debate regarding the exact authority of confessions of faith would continue until the present time. But in the late eighteenth century an even more significant and lasting issue began to take shape: individualism. It first came into focus between churches and church organizations as new and old Baptists sought to lengthen and strengthen their ties. For example, in 1766 the Philadelphia Baptist Association proposed that a subsidiary association be formed at Warren, Rhode Island, composed of Rhode Island and Massachusetts churches. For many Baptist churches this posed no problem. It was supported by many—including James Manning and Hezekiah Smith, both Philadelphians who had settled in New England. Some older Particular Baptist churches were reluctant, however, perhaps because they had been suspicious of revivalism from the beginning, and no doubt wished to avoid unity with the Separate Baptists as a matter of taste as well as doctrine. It was not an issue for the Connecticut Separates turned Baptists. But it was an issue for Massachusetts Separates. They articulated strong suspicion for any connectional or associational body. Their reluctance spread to other Baptists in America during a long and frequently heated exchange regarding the propriety of such fellowship in association.

Specifically, the insistence of the Massachusetts Separate Baptists on the complete, individual autonomy of the local church was due to their connection to the peculiar history of Congregationalism in Massachusetts. The General Courts there had never permitted the churches to develop a regularly constituted body that would link individual churches together. On the one hand, this was because the churches legally represented the spiritual and moral arm of the government and were considered already to be linked through the General Court itself. And on the other, the autonomy of local parishes was jealously guarded by the leaders of local communities who were eager to control the affairs of the local parish without outside interference. In time the churches themselves became used to their prerogatives and developed an ideology that guarded against any intrusion of an ecclesiastical framework. Ironically, even the Separate Congregationalists preserved this prejudice against ecclesiastical institution building and sought instead to be done with any form of intrusive connection. It was from these Separate Congregationalists that many of the Baptist churches were born. Their experience as minorities within the parishes had forced them into an arduous struggle to gain the freedom to control their own churches. They were not eager to give it up again in any form to councils or connections of churches or leaders. They feared both politics in religious garb and religious motivation in political activity. Sometimes it is not clear whether, with regard to institutional development, they could discern the difference between government, politics, and religion.

This tension became evident in the creation of the Warren Association. Eleven churches responded to an invitation to send representatives to a meeting at Warren, Rhode Island, on September 8, 1767, for the purpose of forming an association. The Philadelphia Association delegated three representatives to participate in the process, and they presented a letter that stated the case for association in general. The letter further argued the benefits of linking association into a larger union, thus proposing a denominational structure. The argument in both cases focused on the unity, strength, and utility to be discovered in forming such associations.[4]

Despite the assurance of "the exercise of the greatest tenderness and moderation," the letter proved ultimately not to be persuasive. Those who were eager for association joined the proposal. The Massachusetts Separates did not. Isaac Backus, soon to become the Massachusetts Separates' most conspicuous leader, wrote in his diary, "I did not see my way clear to join now, if ever I do."[5] Nevertheless, the new Warren Association began to take the lead in securing relief from the persecution and oppression to which Baptists were subjected in Massachusetts, and the Philadelphia Association joined them in seeking redress for them there and in gaining the cooperation and support of associations in Virginia and Carolina. Backus moderated his position. His fear that associations would "assume jurisdiction over the churches" was not abated, but he became persuaded that some of its functions might be useful in serving the cause of freedom for Baptist churches. Therefore, in 1770, he led his church to join the Warren Association, but did so only "upon the express condition that no complaint should ever be received by the Association against any particular church that was not of the Association, nor from any censured member of any of our churches."[6]

Thus Backus's leadership on this issue established a model Baptists would often replicate in establishing connections beyond a local congregation: Organization and affiliation to accomplish common purposes or to defend against common enemies was acceptable and effective. But organization for the purpose of ordering a common institutional life was not acceptable and, more, was to be defended against.

Backus was a tireless leader and communicator among Baptists. His writings and propagandist activities with the Continental Congress and later with the Constitutional Convention exerted a strong influence among and for Baptists. And while associational connection served an immediate political necessity in his view, he never overcame his opposition to all but the weakest associational formation. Except for the possibility of associations serving the specific needs of Baptists against limiting or oppressive power, Backus's views were in harmony with the spirit of Lockean individualism, which was popularized by Thomas Jefferson. John Leland, also a leader among the Separate Baptists of Massachusetts, held even more extreme views as an individualist. Leland questioned whether church order and discipline were desirable. Leland's work among the Separate Baptists of Virginia was at least one reason why the Baptists there reversed their previous views on associationalism. While they had originally assented even to grant the powers of ordination and excommunication to the Sandy Creek Association, they ultimately were to strenuously oppose the formation of any sort of general association in Virginia.

The Paradox of Baptist Style

The nineteenth century in the United States was a time of rapid expansion, development of institutions and ideas, and the often pragmatic combination of once unique and isolated experiences. In Baptist life the old Particular Baptist tradition, the newer evangelicalism, and the radical individualism embraced by the Massachusetts Separates gradually became inextricably intermingled. The prevailing temper of the era gave strong support to the individualism that had been articulated by Isaac Backus and John Leland. By mid-century it was being carried to new and eloquent expression by Francis Wayland, theologian, educator, and president of the Baptists' first and most established university, Brown University.

Further, the New Hampshire Confession of Faith, popularized by the American Baptist Publication Society, affirmed this development by omitting any reference to the idea of the church universal in its texts and by publishing a variety of manuals and directories for Baptist use that reflected Wayland's articulate views. The most extreme expression of a hyperindividualistic position was the driving force of the Landmarkist Movement in the South—a movement given life by another New England individualist, James R. Graves.

The Particular Baptist tradition, which underlay the Philadelphia Association and those modeled after it, continued in the actual practices of local churches and associations. This older, more institutionally hospitable tradition still represented the mainstream of Baptist life throughout the nineteenth century. It was, however, continually being modified by evangelicalism, which had become the engine of Baptist growth. Evangelicalism was almost completely focused on conversion experience and "heart religion." It was compatible with almost any ecclesiastical system, even one that functioned with a strong system of centralized controls such as Methodism, which, perhaps even more than the Baptists, grew from evangelical origins. But evangelicalism itself was essentially indifferent to church order. Its sole focus was the proclamation of the gospel in such a way that individuals would respond and become believers, and its sole standard was growth.

Therefore, because Baptists had few well-established doctrinal positions, the effect of evangelicalism among Baptist churches was to further disperse and diffuse the theological and ecclesiological foundations on which the first practices and traditions of Baptist churches were based. Thus, while individualism was not the ideal of evangelicalism itself, it was the practical result among Baptists. It made Baptists slow to develop a clear denominational identity even while it made them unusually able to adapt and take advantage of shifting cultural and social circumstances in a rapidly expanding society. Winthrop Hudson suggests that this same development later made it possible for Baptists in the twentieth century to indulge in unlimited experimentation and improvisation, often with the result of schism, division, and a resulting multiplication of Baptist bodies and institutions.[7] The ecclesiological result of this was the gradual disappearance of an awareness of central traditions and a growing irrelevance for any attempt to explain church life theologically or historically. If anything, by the end of the century, evangelicalism itself was the central theme of Baptist life in a majority of Baptist churches.

The truth of this can be seen in the difficulty Baptists in the North and Midwest experienced in attempting to develop a workable denominational identity. It was a challenge made more complex by the sympathetic cooperation and fellowship of churches that eventually carried the Baptist name but joined the stream from different origins. For example, the Freewill Baptists who united with the Northern Baptist Convention in 1911 provide an informative case study. They represented a different tradition for the major Baptist groups in the United States. In origin and practice they were quite explicitly Wesleyan in theology, and their form of church government demonstrated strong affinities with Methodism, especially nonepiscopal Methodism.[8] Freewill Baptists also embodied a characteristic of the evangelical Christian "movement" style of church development that had been introduced by the Great Awakening. It was, in one sense, an early form of ecumenism, the goal of which was to achieve Christian unity by attempting to restore the New Testament church and by rejecting sectarian and party names in favor of general Christian terminology. Many Freewill Baptist churches were named something other than Baptist, such as the Church of Christ, or used the Baptist designation in parentheses or as a subheading in their title.

The founder of the Freewill Baptists, Benjamin Randall, embraced believers' baptism and as a result joined forces for a time with the Regular Baptists, until his unorthodox Wesleyan positions became a divisive issue and he and his followers were disfellowshiped by the Baptists. Similarly, members of a group gathered by Abner Jones in Vermont were popularly known as Unitarian Baptists because, while they embraced believers' baptism, they rejected the doctrine of the Trinity as a postbiblical imposition. Abner Jones's followers were generally successful in claiming the name *Christian* for their churches so that, ironically, the Randall group later accepted the designation of Freewill Baptist—one originally ascribed to them by their critics rather than created by them—as a way of distinguishing themselves from the Unitarian Baptists or Christian Connection of Abner Jones.

Randall's Freewill Baptists were firm in their Trinitarianism. But their pursuit of Christian unity led them to encourage the practice of open Communion and to diffuse the significance of doctrinal distinctions. By the close of the nineteenth century, increasing numbers of Freewill Baptist churches were no longer even insisting upon believers' baptism as a prerequisite to church membership, again in an attempt to foster unity among Christian believers of all varieties. The inclusion of the Freewill Baptists within the infant Northern Baptist Convention in 1911, without causing debate or controversy on what might, in retrospect, seem significant issues of difference, is an indication of the general lack of well-defined Baptist habits and principles. Similar tendencies within the churches of the Northern Baptist Convention were simply hastened by these additions. In the South, the same spirit of evangelicalism so infused the spread of the Baptist movement across the southern states that evangelicalism, combined with the tenets of Southern cultural identity, was in truth the central and defining character of Baptist churches. The almost complete lack of distinction between evangelical Christianity and the Baptist movement in the South led to the reality that the name *Baptist* was applied to virtually all Christian churches of evangelical spirit with the exception of the Methodists, whose strong central authority kept them separate.

It is fair to say, therefore, that the Baptist style was first a style of freedom and independence. It was a considerable gift to American religious understanding and, to borrow Martin Marty's phrase, this development of strong, local congregational control and individual personal freedom of doctrine was to result in the "baptistification of American religion." But the gift that Baptists gave others was costly to their own ability to maintain a corporate core and an institutional tradition. The dark side of this development, the abiding mistrust and fear of institutions that might transgress the boundaries of individual or congregational prerogatives, made it virtually impossible for Baptists to gather, shape, and exercise the responsible authority necessary to define, guide, and direct the institutions they created.

Pathways into the Twentieth Century

Although Baptists have never been shaped by the thought of a single theologian or church leader, they have rarely lacked for leadership. By the beginning of the twentieth century, Baptists in the United States possessed a remarkable collection of theologians and church leaders. Alvah Hovey was completing a distinguished career at the Newton Theological Institution, where Frederick L. Anderson was also rising in reputation. William Newton Clarke was at Colgate, and Augustus Hopkins Strong and Walter Rauschenbusch were strong voices at Rochester. At Crozer Theological Seminary, Henry G. Weston, Elias H. Johnson, Milton G. Evans, Henry C. Vedder, and Alvah S. Hobart were well recognized. The greatest concentration of distinguished Baptist scholars was at the Divinity School of the University of Chicago. There, in addition to the university president, William Rainey Harper, there were Ernest DeWitt Burton, Shailer Mathews, Ira M. Price, Edgar J. Goodspeed, J. M. P. Smith, Charles R. Henderson, Shirley Jackson Case, Gerald Birney Smith, George Burman Foster, Theodore G. Soares, and others.[9]

"Giants also walked the land" in many churches and colleges. When Rauschenbusch left New York City he was but one of a notable group of young ministers that included Leighton Williams and Nathaniel Schmidt. Ahead even of them in stature were Cortland Myers, Cornelius Woelfkin, P. S. Henson, W. H. P. Faunce, R. S. MacArthur, George C. Lorimer, Edward Judson, and William C. Bitting. Every major city—and many minor ones—had similar stars: in Philadelphia, George Dana Boardman and Russell H. Conwell; in Rochester, J. W. A. Stewart at First Baptist Church and Clarence A. Barbour at Lake Avenue Baptist Church. In short, in a time when local gatherings of ministers often outnumbered the majority of local intellectuals and visionaries, Baptist preachers, writers, and educators, not to mention political and community leaders, were to be counted among the leaders and luminaries in innumerable cities and towns throughout the country. But they were first of all strong individuals, and their activities were most often expressed through individual achievements in the pulpit, in publications, and in the variety of professional work they accomplished. Less were they seen—or did they see themselves—as part of a united purpose or common community.

They should have been—and some were—those who shaped the world of Baptists to come. But in addition to the individualistic style they both inherited and exhibited, the social, political, and cultural environment in which these and others exercised their leadership contained enormous challenges that were just then coming into focus. They were challenges that further diffused Baptist self-consciousness and reinforced individualism and localism as normative for Baptist life.

The Challenge to Theology

The promise of leadership apparent in such a galaxy of theological stars was never fully realized. The preachers and teachers of the waning nineteenth century and the rising twentieth century were confronted with a massive variety of new challenges and influences that were to question both their view of the world and their theology. These new developments were to alter the role and purpose of the church in ways they never imagined. And despite their considerable gifts, they individually and corporately were ill-prepared to meet the challenges that confronted them.

It was, in the first place, an age of enormous intellectual ferment and change. New scientific hypotheses, notably Darwin's theory regarding the origin of species and Freud's introduction of psychological dynamics, raised towering questions regarding the nature of humankind. New methods of textual and historical study, first developed for the study of human literature, were quickly adapted and focused on the origin and meaning of sacred Scriptures. These techniques raised fundamental questions regarding the nature of God and of God's relationship to humankind. By themselves these ideas were laying a minefield that would disrupt the experiences of even the most nonintellectual in faith. But just as the implications of scriptural criticism were being recognized, a whole new field, the psychology of religion, combined forces with a new historical approach that relegated religion to a less monolithic role in the course of recorded events. This development nudged the role of religion from its place at the pinnacle of scholarship and authority. Psychology, for example, identified conversion as only one kind of human experience and thereby questioned theological concepts such as the grace of God and the active role of the Holy Spirit. In the early twentieth century William James took its assumptions to articulate expression in his book *The Varieties of Religious Experience,* which expressed a new perspective that viewed a range of religious and spiritual experiences as equally valid, equally conditioned by culture, and directly related to personality and personal experience. Historical interpretations, likewise, began to perceive the church as but one among many of civilization's institutions, and suggested that its contributions were as often political as spiritual and its results as often negative as positive. Sociological studies emphasized that human experience is shaped by human decisions, manipulations of external environments, and social organizations. Therefore, while historical analysis treated the church as an institution, psychology and sociology began to encourage religious leaders—Baptists and others—to consider new ways to meet human needs and to develop new techniques for shaping religious environments and experience.

Thus, while Baptist leaders at the century's crossing were unusually talented, able, and distinguished, they were ill-prepared to cope with the intense and rapid changes that were overtaking them. They were earnest and devoted in faith, but their faith had been shaped by a spirit of opposition to a theological world of the past. Their energies were focused on preserving faith and freedom against religious oppression. Little did they understand that the new forces would not seek to control them, but would instead declare them irrelevant. Several dynamics made them particularly vulnerable.

First, their whole religious outlook, from their understanding of Scripture to their view of the world around them, was shaped by evangelicalism's essential anti-intellectualism. Evangelicalism was grounded in the primacy of personal religious experience, and its effective appeal was to the emotions, not the intellect. Matters of doctrine and intellectual exploration of scriptural meaning were less important than a posture of conviction and conversion. The language of faith therefore remained the language of an earlier day, and doctrines, while honored in principle, were mostly ignored in practice.[10] This encouraged a grassroots ecumenism among those of evangelical spirit, but it also left them unprepared to address emerging currents of thought and especially the rising tide of scientism.

Second, Baptists had thrived in rural, small-town contexts, where life was more simply integrated. In previous eras Christians had lived in a unified world where work, worship, and leisure were integrated by doctrine, vocation, and daily life. As the twentieth century came into focus, Christians, and Baptists in particular, began to live in several life contexts: the context of daily life, the context of their religious experience, and the emerging culture of an inherited matrix of faith, traditions, and values now cohabiting in a disorienting arena of new, challenging, and life-changing ideas and practices. The intellectual, spiritual, and social forces emerging in the 1890s would reshape the world faster and more completely than any period of change that preceded it. But instead of stimulating Christians to rethink their positions and reevaluate their experiences, the inherent contradictions of the several worlds in which they lived were simply ignored. More, it was assumed that any energy expended in dealing with contemporaneous issues and thoughts would only divert attention from the primary agenda, which was the building of the coming kingdom by urging simple, clear-cut, emotional decisions to be Christian. Virtually all Christians, and certainly Baptists among them, were fixed on the coming of the Christian century. And a phrase that later came to title a specific, liberal Christian magazine articulated for Baptists a unified view that an evangelical spirit could not fail to overwhelm and shape the time to come.

But even by the 1890s the new intellectual currents presented such a sharp challenge to old doctrines that conflict was inevitable. Compelled by the need to articulate the Christian faith in intellectually convincing terms, theologians and preachers failed to assert that faith and its articles of belief had any claim to truth on their own merit and could meet and interact with new theories of both the universe and humankind without unusual defense. Even more, having assumed that the subtleties of theological discussion were the pastimes of idle intellectuals and were therefore distasteful, they seemed ill-prepared to do anything more than to reclaim and restate the work of past scholars and leaders. The theologians and professors in seminaries recognized the need to join in the emerging dialogue. But unfortunately, they confused the new style of organizing thought with the changing assumptions about the substance of knowledge. Therefore, they became systematizers of religious thought and not creators of new perspectives and wisdom regarding God and God's work in the world. It became, therefore, an age of systematic theology built on a structure of theological understanding that seemed, even to a broad range of Christians, increasingly archaic, irrelevant, and unworkable. This error, in particular, led to the great cleavage that both defined and disabled Christian witness in the twentieth century. This great gulf ultimately became a division between conservatives and later "fundamentalists," who perceived that the best response to new thoughts was to defend the absolute authority of Christian truth by underlining the absolute certainty of both its origins and its documentation, and others, categorized from "moderate" to "liberal," who variously perceived that the best way to reinvigorate Christian experience was to reinterpret it using the categories of emerging thought without much reference to its ancient roots. Few, if any, apprehended that what was emerging was a whole new age with remarkable possibilities for new experience and new understanding.

The crisis of the approaching new century was therefore underlined by complacency. Organizationally, the religious enterprise had been wildly successful. The frontier had closed, and the country had effectively been "churched." Churches in settled communities were well attended as centers of moral direction and social activity, and as the stimulus of the western frontier lost its attraction, churches and church people looked for practical new goals to accomplish. It was the age of the growth of booming new cities, and while the migration of people from town to city caused disruptions, it also brought the opportunity to refocus evangelical energy on the establishment of urban churches to accommodate new populations. "Kingdom" theology was therefore fed by opportunities for new growth in numbers and institutional formation, as well as by the apparent challenge of the world beyond the shores of the United States, which seemed to invite a renewed emphasis on evangelical missions to make new converts and to establish new churches. In short, the future of the church was perceived to be bright, especially among Baptists who were confident that they were called to claim it.

Baptists claimed among their number not only bright lights of theology and history, but wealthy industrialists and entrepreneurs. John D. Rockefeller founded and funded his vision for a world-class university at the University of Chicago under the leadership of a Baptist president, William Rainey Harper. Augustus H. Strong told the students of Stetson University that there was no room for "gloomy views," and Russell H. Conwell was confident that every man could and ought to be a millionaire.[11] Among Baptists, a new focus on history seemed to demonstrate that they were destined to be chief among the leaders of a new world order and that the emerging techniques of psychology, sociology, and even science could be subdued to serve as assistants in ushering in the age of the new Christian, increasingly Baptist, century. It is no wonder that they did not perceive that they needed first to attend to what it was that defined their theological understanding, or how they might shape their ecclesiological order to meet the challenges of the new age as it arrived.

The gap between theology and faith and practice was to become especially apparent as Baptists confronted their inherited pattern of institutional life and the needs of the emerging order. No theological support was effectively marshaled to integrate a new establishment of order. Instead, familiar pragmatic connections focused on the accomplishment of common goals were substituted. Baptists had begun with a high view of the church and had developed a well-articulated view of church life expressed in faithfulness and obedience to what were perceived to be the clear commands of Christ as encountered in the Scriptures. To be sure, Baptists were strong advocates of freedom and individual prerogative, but this focus was sharpened more by the necessity of their battles with government and religious authorities who sought to impose church practices or obligations on them than by conflict between churches and individuals. Within church life, individual freedom was always tempered by the discipline of scriptural admonitions for both individual behavior and relationships within the church. The authority of the pastor, the discipline of the corporate body, and both the rights and responsibilities of members were clear. Matters of conflict were not unusual, of course, but when they arose, they were dealt with seriously by seasons of prayer and dialogue, and, when they were unresolved or where clear violations were established, it was not unusual for individuals to be dismissed or for factions within the congregation to separate and to form new, equally structured, church bodies.

This tradition of church practice continued in form almost until the twentieth century. But even at the beginning of the nineteenth century the theological assumptions that supported it were becoming frayed. In the first place, the vigorous growth of individualism broke the balance between the body of the church and its individual members. Then the general individualism of the frontier, enshrined in both the real and the mythical labors of those who conquered it, made the "rugged individualist" a national ideal. The intellectual individualism sponsored by the Enlightenment found political and cultural expression in Jeffersonian democracy and utilitarian effect in Jacksonian populism. Both weakened the underpinnings of Baptist church life, especially because it had neither doctrinal nor ecclesiastical authority to counter it. Evangelicalism redefined Christian life in terms so purely individualistic as to render almost irrelevant any sense of mutuality between and among Christians except for social and pragmatic purposes.

These trends caused most Baptist institutional and corporate life to remain undeveloped or to become weak. The associational life that had begun in high concept in the eighteenth century was now relegated to only the most basic and utilitarian functions. And in reality, no associational life was permitted to grow beyond only the narrowest geographical limits. Even the justification for such corporate life as existed was framed on individualistic grounds. It was articulated, essentially, on the basis that "we do together those things which we cannot do separately." Missions, especially, became the stated purpose and the underlying reason for Baptist connections; and only rarely were matters of belief, relationships, or corporate life a significant priority. Otherwise, Baptist life continued in form, it seemed, for a century, content that it was doing what was prescribed by the Scriptures, and was therefore faithful.

It was, ironically, when the authority of the Bible in a literal or legal sense was questioned as a result of the introduction of critical methods that the substructure of Baptist life began to dissolve. Externally, Baptists generally denied the validity of scriptural criticism. Internally, however, it seemed as if these new practices almost immediately seemed directly to affect the value of church order. Rather than the practices and procedures that had been characteristic of Baptist order being affirmed, they began to diminish. Discipline was relaxed, covenants fell into disuse, the role of the pastoral office was diminished in theory and practice, while, at the same time, boards and committees proliferated without clear unifying purpose. It was as if the legitimate purpose of the church itself was in question: Admission procedures and baptismal practices became uncertain or indiscriminate; the boundaries that defined the integrity of the Lord's Table were abandoned; the practice of covenant meeting was discarded, and its replacement, the church meeting, became preoccupied with trivialities and obsessions.

For some the older conception of the church as an expression of covenant was abandoned for a new understanding of the church in almost completely utilitarian and instrumental terms as a missionary society or a social agency. For others the response was a retreat into the church as a purely sacramental institution into which others might be gathered in the hope that, by association, an experience of grace might be encouraged. And most evident of all, what might have seemed a mounting battle between the defenders of faith against an attack of skepticism or a battle between the champions of the church against the doubts of the world never really materialized. Instead, within the Baptist tradition itself a division soon took place. The challenge to the scriptural basis of the church's authority did not result in a conflict between the church and the world. Instead, it occasioned a battle between churches and church leaders that would occupy much of the energy of the next century. This battle was about the limits of freedom and the claims of responsibility. It was couched in the language of theology and piety—piety because it was the language of individual belief and theology because it was the language of the church, and it had been too long neglected.

Reinterpreting the Authority of the Bible

The most obvious challenge to Baptists in this period was the challenge to the authority and meaning of the Scriptures.[12] In general, American Baptist scholars and leading pastors responded with a cautious conservatism. The most vehement rejection of new criticism was expressed in the South, while in the North, response ranged from outright rejection to a cautious acceptance of certain of the new principles. Most scholars and many pastors were, however, preoccupied with the challenge new forms of biblical analysis and new currents of scholarship in general had brought. For the most part they were demoralized and confused by the impact of the new ideas, and in many ways their responses contributed to loosening the bonds between the church and Scripture.

Augustus H. Strong represented the most valiant attempt to confront new currents of thought without abandoning the authority of Scripture. Strong accepted the doctrine of evolution and the methods of biblical criticism. He boldly asserted the possibility that the Pentateuch had multiple authors, that Isaiah might well be two books, not one, and that some biblical material might better be understood as allegory than as literal narrative. The Bible, he contended, is the record of a progressive revelation "shaped in human moulds and adapted to ordinary human intelligence." It was, therefore, a book of "human composition." At the same time, he maintained, it was also "God's Word" because it presented "divine truth in human form."[13]

Strong's approach was to accept the scholarly validity of criticism but to question the approach of those who applied it. "The 'historical method' of Scripture interpretation," he wrote, "ends without Christ because it begins without him." It ignored the relationship of the Scriptures to Christ, who alone furnished the key to its meaning. In that sense, he claimed, sponsors of the critical method were guilty of "treating Scripture as it would treat any unreligious or heathen literature." To properly interpret the Bible, he maintained, one must adopt a confessional stance that acknowledges as its beginning the authority of Christ and the inspiration of the Scripture. At that point, he asserted, the "historical method" becomes a "servant" and not the "master," showing "not how man made the Scripture for himself, but how God made the Scripture through the imperfect agency of man."[14]

Strong was correct in claiming that the effect of the historical method improperly used as a method of biblical interpretation in Baptist churches was to "cut the taproot of their strength and to imperil their very existence." He understood that such doctrines as regenerate membership, the church ordinances belonging only to believers, and other "marks" of the church were based on an authoritative rule of faith and practice as defined by the New Testament. And he understood that without a comprehensive doctrine, creed, or authoritative structure, Baptist churches were dependent on Scripture as an arbiter in controversy. In that sense he repeatedly argued that the authority of the Bible was essential. Yet, for Strong, it was also important not to deny the most obvious and compelling contributions of the new scholarship. "Inspiration," he confessed, "did not guarantee inerrancy in things not essential to the main purpose of Scripture." The writers of sacred truth had performed their task obediently and faithfully, delivering the message they were commissioned to proclaim. Yet they were neither omniscient nor infallible.

Strong wanted it both ways: an authoritative Scripture, yet a Scripture that could be honestly admitted to be flawed, inaccurate, or otherwise less perfect than Baptists had desired it to be. "In spite of its imperfections in matters nonessential to its religious purposes," when properly interpreted the Bible could be assumed to be a "rule of faith and practice" that was

trustworthy. Worse, Strong, like most others wrestling with the implications of critical methods, focused on the matter of authority rather than on
the more fruitful issue of how sacred tradition might be redefined or its
truth even enlarged by the new methods. Instead, by admitting that some
of the text was flawed or dependent on a correct interpretation, Strong had
confirmed the worst fears and the confusion created by critical methods.[15]
As a result, Baptists were in danger of being cut loose from their one
anchor: the authority of the Scriptures.

Other Baptist scholars, such as Alvah Hovey, Elias H. Johnson, and
Henry G. Weston, took similar positions, although the latter two hinted
that Strong's approach was too easy a solution to the problem raised by
the new methods. At Crozer Seminary, for example, Johnson sought to
restate the case for biblical authority so as to avoid the debate about
inspiration. In his case he argued that the Bible's central significance was
that it bore witness to God's revelation in Christ, a witness clear enough
to make preoccupation with inspiration unnecessary. Weston, essentially
agreeing with Johnson, went a step further in arguing that the Bible was
first a book of principles rather than rules or laws. And while he was ready
to defend Baptist patterns of church order, he was convinced that such a
defense could be grounded only on the principles the Bible contained,
rather than on specific precedents or examples. From the principles at
hand, therefore, both focused on the implications for specific Baptist
practices, such as closed Communion or the nature of authority within the
church, while hedging about some of the conclusions raised by critical
methods.[16] Cut off from the authority of Scripture, Baptists developed
uncertainty about the marks of their churches and the precedent for some
of their practices.

William Newton Clarke approached the dilemma with a more radical
proposal. His strategy was to conclude that all theories of a unique biblical
authority were irrelevant. In his view the living Christ was his own
witness, transcending both the accuracy and the authority of Scripture.
"Christ was saving sinners before the New Testament was written, and
could do the same today if it had not been written." Clarke viewed the
relationship between Christ and the disciples as one by which Christ
trusted his followers to enact a mission but not to guarantee its origin. That
is, "he trusted his gospel in the world to the keeping of the Holy Spirit,
who was to abide with men. He never promised an infallible church, or an
infallible book, or any infallible visible guide, but committed his kingdom
to the Spirit and the divine life." In Clarke's scenario the Scriptures were
a "valuable help" provided by Divine Providence, but they were not to

take the place of "the abiding Spirit."[17] He proposed that what was really needed was a truth expressing itself, not in words, but in life. Theologically, Clarke was skimming close to universalism, perhaps spiced with elements reminiscent of gnosticism.

Practically, by narrowing the authority of Christ in the contemporaneous activity of the Holy Spirit, Clarke reduced almost all outward forms and marks of the church to irrelevance, or at least to indifference. In his system all concepts of the church were dissolved, and what remained was a global and diffused concept of the church universal—a communion of saints created and sustained by the vicissitudes of an untamed Holy Spirit "blowing as it listeth," as Winthrop Hudson cringed to say. Clarke's theology has an appeal for mystics. It did not serve to define churches or to sharpen dynamics of relationship within and among them. Instead, it intellectually legitimated the extreme reliance on personal, internal "faith experiences" that the broad stream of evangelicalism had already established.

Still another approach, decidedly different from either the mysticism of Clarke or the accommodationism of Hovey and his colleagues, was evident in several of the faculty at the University of Chicago and in the work of Shailer Mathews in particular. The Chicago faculty was conspicuous for its great contributions to biblical study and the new critical methods. Yet the school of "scientific modernism" that arose there steadily deemphasized the Bible as normative in religion. It was deemed suitable for historical study, but truth was to be found in the sciences, both the natural sciences and the more recent "social" sciences. Their working assumption was, therefore, that the normative intellectual discipline for individual religious experience was psychology, and for the church, sociology. The focus of the Chicago faculty was increasingly on the church as a social agency, and the sharp focus of mission was on the strategic outreach of the settlement house. This approach neatly removed any real anxiety about biblical "authority" and recast the church in the role of a change agent and catalyst in human community. With the role of the Scriptures, the traditions of the church, and even the efficacy of Christ having been eroded, the Chicago school responded by redefining grace as a socio-psychological expression of good works.

Unwittingly, the majority response to the new sciences among Baptist scholars thus served to devalue scriptural authority and, thereby, the security of Baptist churches. By attempting to maintain the importance of the role of the Bible, and at the same time accepting the scientific method of both biblical study and intellectual investigation, they were forced to create an artificial synthesis in order to allow both to exist. But by keeping them apart, they neither reaffirmed the underlying truth of the Scriptures nor allowed new methodology to reformulate their fundamental meaning as an interpretive tool of human experience. The result was that Baptist churches began to function by paying respects to a remembered myth of biblical authority while shaping their future with the utilitarian principles established by the social and political dynamics of the rapidly changing age.

The Bible and the New Dynamics of Church Order

It was the nature and future of the church, therefore, that drew increased attention in the 1890s and early 1900s, not theology. There were two powerful reasons for this. First, while the new academic disciplines and approaches brought confusion to biblical studies and forced theology on the defensive, they, in the second place, brought a new vocabulary and a new form of analysis, which in fact stimulated, rather than retarded, the work of ecclesiology. So while theology maintained classical form and was increasingly presented in systematic packages, the role of the church, particularly the church as a defined, institutional entity, was subjected to increasing reformulation.

Of all the Baptists who addressed the church in this period, Augustus H. Strong and Henry G. Weston provided the most thorough and articulated statements of Baptist ecclesiology. Strong, for example, recognized that the word *church* was used with two distinct meanings in the New Testament. On the one hand, he understood its larger meaning as "the whole company of regenerate persons in all times and ages." This is "the church universal, the organism to which Christ gives spiritual life and through which he manifests the fulness of his power and grace." But on the other hand, he recognized that the New Testament distinguished between the invisible church universal and the individual church in which the universal church takes specific, local, and temporal form. The sole object of the local church, he proposed, "is the glory of God in the complete establishment of his kingdom, both in the hearts of believers and in the world."

Strong saw the matter of difference between the universal church and the local congregation as a presence of boundaries and connections. There is a transcendent element in the church, he stated, and because "it is the great company of persons whom Christ has saved, in whom he dwells, to whom and through whom he reveals God," the church "cannot be defined in merely human terms as an aggregate of individuals associated for social, benevolent or even spiritual purposes." No single, specific church, therefore, could claim to be the whole church. Yet, unlike other divinely proposed institutions, such as the family or the state, membership in the church is neither hereditary nor compulsory, but is rather an expression of an "inward and conscious reception of Christ and his truth." That expression had to be identified in a particular and personal way through the lives and activities of individual Christians. The local church is, therefore, a voluntary society. But that is not the end of it: It is a voluntary society that is, nevertheless, formed from within. "Christ, present by the Holy Ghost, regenerating men by the sovereign action of the Spirit and organizing them into himself as the living center, is the only principle that can explain the existence of the church."[18]

Turning to the outward character of the church, Strong rejected the most extreme notion that the church was exclusively a spiritual body, devoid of organization and "bound together only by the mutual relation of each believer to his indwelling Lord." He also rejected the theory that "the form of church organization is not definitely prescribed in the New Testament, but is a matter of expedience, each body of believers being permitted to adopt that method of organization that best suits its circumstances and condition." Instead, he believed that church order had been prescribed "in all essential particulars" in the New Testament. Christ, he insisted, is the only giver of laws, and thus the government of the church is of the nature of an absolute monarchy. In practice, however, this power did not devolve to a single person, but to the process of consultation and mutual consideration: "In ascertaining the will of Christ, however, and in applying his commands to providential exigencies, the Holy Spirit enlightens one member through the counsel of another and, as the result of combined deliberation, guides the whole body to right conclusions."[19] There were two implications for the local church: With Christ at its center, it was sovereign with respect to relationships with all other institutions, and with regard to its carrying out the will of Christ, the church was a democracy.

When Strong turned to focus on the relationship between local churches, he saw the issue in terms of sovereignty and cooperation rather than authority and connection. Still, he also perceived that it is the duty of ministers to teach the members of their churches "the larger unity of the whole church of God." On one side, he maintained the "absolute equality of the churches" and yet, on the other, he was convinced there must be "fraternal fellowship and cooperation." This fraternal fellowship of churches had a parallel to the way in which members within the local church were to relate to one another in that they had a "duty of special consultation with regard to matters affecting the common interest." And this duty included "the duty of seeking advice" and the "duty of taking advice."

Winthrop Hudson asserts that Strong had moved more clearly in the direction of the connectionalism than was characteristic of the early Baptists and quotes him as saying, "The polity of the New Testament is congregational rather than independent." Yet Strong was not settled in his understanding about the form a closer connectionalism should take. Some of his uncertainty was based on practical developments. The old associations had lost many of their functions to the voluntary societies (for missions, education, publication, and other purposes) that had been formed in the intervening years and by the substitutions of councils, formed often on an ad hoc basis to handle matters of ecclesiastical concern. Concerning one proposal to replace both special councils and associations with a permanent council form of association, Strong was of two minds. Such a standing, powerful council structure could create, revise, and rescind actions, unlike temporary councils that met once and then had no continuing life or status. Such councils could be created with considerations of representation, balance, and equity, thus mitigating the tendency toward "packing" a council on matters of high contention. Still, Strong had several objections toward the creation of such a body. First, it did not possess the authority and example of the New Testament. Second, it tended toward a Presbyterian form of government. And again drawing on the new science of politics and institutions, he said, "All permanent bodies of this sort gradually arrogate to themselves power; indirectly if not directly they can assume original jurisdiction; their decisions have altogether too much influence, if they go further than personal persuasion."[20]

Henry G. Weston's view of the church was, in most material respects, very similar to that of Strong. Two contributions are illustrative of the currents of ecclesiological consideration of the time, however. The first is a statement of the nature of the church that contains language that clearly identifies the currents of thought against which any definition of the church had to swim—the perspectives of sociology, political analysis, and human dynamics that had begun to perceive the church in strictly human terms. Of the church Weston said: "It is not a development of the moral, religious, or social nature of man; it is not a product of the human intellect; it is not a school of opinion, nor a voluntary association of persons of similar tastes or pursuits. It is a supernatural and vital union, a new creation, a divine organism."[21] Weston did adopt the new sciences of social and institutional analysis in pursuing the relationship between theology and practice, however, and in doing so, gives clear evidence of the growing influence of these disciplines in considerations of the church:

> A given theology and a given polity are rarely dissociated. The external constitution of a church is the fruit and exponent of its inner principle of belief, while "the outward form and constitution of a church, its worship and discipline, its offices, its ritual, react with great force on its inner life and on the doctrine which it teaches." A scheme of doctrine leads to a cognate theory of the church.[22]

Convinced that it was the principles of theology that would shape the church in form and practice, Weston offered four theological principles that "must be conserved and developed in all church polity."

1. The vital relation of Christ to each member and of each member to Christ. Each member sustains as close a relation to Christ as any other member; there is an essential and vital equality of the members, so that there can be no sacerdotal class, no class with special privileges, or permitted any special access to Christ, or endowed with any special function. The members of the church are all kings and priests.

2. The living and continuous relation of Christ to the church. The life of the church is not something deposited, a store of grace to be distributed by the officers or received in the sacraments; it is a living Christ, a person and a presence to whom the church is united as the body is united to the head; as the branches are united to the vine.

3. The organic relation of members to one another and to the body. They are one, not by voluntary combination, but by a common birth, a common nature, and a common life.

4. The completeness of each church; first, as related to Christ; second, as related to one another; third as related to the world.[23]

These principles are familiar to modern Baptists. In Weston's formulations we find a tension. There was, and is, a conflict between his third and fourth principles. If the church is organic and not, therefore, strictly dependent on voluntary association, connections between and among congregations might seem to be natural and required. Yet if each church is complete with respect to other churches, the world, and Christ, no real connection can easily be defined. Therein lies a fundamental tension—a tension between church and church, church and organization, church and individuals, a tension between freedom and responsibility.

Toward an Ecclesiology of Individualism

The concept of a structured church life had been undermined already by the evangelicalism and frontier developments of the nineteenth century. Now changes in assumptions about scriptural authority, and especially the effect of the reformulations and the reflections on the role of the church, were to dissolve any concept of the church as distinct from a social institution and to reduce all questions of church order to pragmatic and utilitarian considerations.

In fact, the older Baptist understanding of church order had been much more seriously weakened than the writings of Strong, Weston, or any of their colleagues described. The radical individualism of Jeffersonian democracy that had its parallels in the writing and leadership of Backus, Leland, and Wayland had deeply penetrated Baptist life and had been reinforced by the goals and successes of evangelicalism. And the push to establish Baptist churches on the frontier had placed a premium on hearty, self-sufficient church styles in claiming the hearts and habits of people on the edge of civilization. These influences, we have seen, were clear in the writings of Strong and Weston and had been given new intellectual status by them. But the attrition to which the older concepts had been subjected by individualism is even more apparent in the thoughts of Alvah Hovey, who exerted considerable influence on a rising generation of pastors and church leaders.[24]

In his *Manual of Christian Theology*, Hovey dismissed the concept of the universal church. He noted that the word was used a "few times" in the New Testament to denote "all Christians in heaven and on earth," but he insisted that this was an "exceptional" usage that had no bearing on the constitution or government of the church. Even in terms of a particular church, Hovey's perspective is permissive. "The members of a Christian church, fully organized for growth and service, may be divided into three classes, laical, diaconal and clerical," but it is the body alone that is essential, and not the body and its duly appointed officers.[25] Hovey's treatment of the role of officers revealed a high degree of flexibility and even diffusion regarding leadership and authority. His view of discipline within the church is demonstrated when he agrees that the lay members of the church are required "to see that their pastor has reasonable compensation for his official work," but in the event that such members fail to contribute, Hovey did not propose that the congregation had much right to discipline financially irresponsible members.

With regard to Hovey's view of church connections or relationships with one another, he proposed that churches are "organically separate" but that they "ought to respect the action of one another." Under some circumstances they may seek advice from several churches gathered by their representatives in a council, and upon a voluntary basis they "may combine their resources and influence for the furtherance of religious or benevolent enterprises."[26] But on the whole Hovey's view of interchurch connection always preserved the rights of both individual churches and individual members.

Hovey's views were closely related to what E. Y. Mullins identified as the constitutive principle of Baptist church life—that is, the competency, under God, of the individual soul in religion—soul competency. If there is to be summarized a Baptist position, an apologetic in dealing with other denominational influences and theologies, it is on the basis of this highly individualistic principle. And it is clearly apparent that this principle was derived from the general cultural, political, and religious climate of the nineteenth century rather than on any particular position based on biblical sources. It proved, however, an inadequate basis for church life. Not only did it fail to provide detailed guidance for questions of church order beyond generalized axioms such as "all believers have a right to interpret the Bible for themselves" and "all believers have a right to equal privileges in the church," but it also served to dissolve any real concept of the church primarily because it consistently interpreted faith experience as a one-to-one relationship between God and the individual.

The practical effect of the continuing affirmation of the idea of soul competency as the primary Baptist doctrine was, as Winthrop Hudson phrased it, "to make every man's hat his own church."[27] W. R. McNutt, professor of practical theology at Crozer Theological Seminary from 1928 to 1944, made this position both explicit and formative for the twentieth century. In his popular and much quoted book, *Polity and Practice in Baptist Churches*, he affirmed that the "directive life principle" of Baptist polity is "the creative idea that the individual is competent in all matters of religion" and "has within himself by divine gift and right those capacities that make him competent to meet all the demands with which genuine religion confronts him." The individual, therefore, "has no inescapable need of the church to bring him salvation or to mediate to him divine grace." Instead, he stands alone since "competency reposes authority in religion within the individual."

Competency and freedom "cannot be separated in thought, and must not be divorced in organized religion," McNutt confidently proclaimed. And any abridgment or denial of "the exercise of soul liberty" can only serve "to strangle man and fly into the face of God."[28] A church therefore exists only as a subordinate principle: the principle of "the free association of believers." While an individual may not abdicate either authority or freedom, "he may call to his side those who have counsel to give" and "from them take little or much, as seems good in his sight." Free association may also be useful "to keep their hearts warm in allegiance to him, their Lord, to culture their souls in his graces, and to spread the good news about him through all the earth."

A church is, then, merely a voluntary association "constituted by the individuals who believe themselves endowed with competency in religion," and it is "brought into being for the furtherance of their purposes." Such a church, believed McNutt, "by the very logic of its nature, must behave democratically," and any other type of organization would violate its "inherent constitution." "Polity is made for man and not man for polity. He that was created in the image of God must not be bound by the cords of organization."[29] As each individual is "competent," so each church is "competent in and of itself." Each church is regarded as a "law unto itself." The only way a church can be connected with others is as "an independent unit" that functions voluntarily and democratically "in cooperation with other groups of disciples to enlarge the reign of God in the hearts of men everywhere."[30]

McNutt recognized that his position was not without difficulty. And in drawing upon the emerging work of sociology and psychology, he revealed an interesting perspective that is an anomaly in light of his persistent view of independence. In light of such emerging work, he said, "clear thinking reveals no such thing as the individual in society, neither can it discover the strictly independent church." Even more, he observed that churches themselves had "found it impossible to live, much less to grow, in isolation." Nevertheless, regardless of the arrangements that might be required by circumstance, necessity, or opportunity, McNutt did not sway from his basic ideal that churches and individuals are alone in their relationship to God and that all right polity and practice derives from that principle.

Even by the time McNutt was publishing in his long and well-established career, circumstances and opportunities were leading Baptists to experiment with and to create new forms of connections. These rising denominational structures, along with sorting out the relationships within them and among them that would allow them to function, were to become the dominant theme of Baptist life in the twentieth century. But they arose not from any basic understanding of biblical principle or commitment to an articulated polity of shared life in faith by and among Baptists. No, they were in part the creation of a new era. But the old era did not fade without its work being accomplished. The rise of evangelicalism; the new disciplines of scholarship and thought; the work of Baptist scholars and writers such as McNutt, Hovey, Hiscox, Strong, and Weston, to name a few; and the rambunctious opportunism of the late nineteenth century had brought most Baptists to a common conclusion: They were free and independent, and in that independence they had opportunity to experiment and to improvise on an essentially pragmatic basis quite apart from theological or biblical considerations, whether from their own past traditions or from the traditions of the Bible as presented by others. In that sense freedom stretched and distorted the bounds of responsibility to such an extent that common life among Baptists would be increasingly impossible to define.

Shaping the Boundaries of Church and Denominational Connection

The reaction to the developments of the late nineteenth century set the Baptist agenda for much of the twentieth. It developed in two broad directions. First, Baptists of all theological perspectives sought to reclaim the authority, if not the meaning, of Scriptures. Second, they expended enormous energy in establishing ecclesial corporate structures, hoping thereby to unite churches in mission.

With regard to the Scriptures, some Baptists continued to assert scriptural authority by underlining their essential accuracy as revealed by God. The trouble with this approach was that it made every discussion and activity regarding the Scriptures to be first an act of faith. This approach therefore did not engage those persons for whom issues of faith were uncertain but who otherwise were open to experience the truth and personal transformation of scriptural testimony. As this position hardened, it ultimately came to espouse the "fundamentalist" and later an "inerrant" view of Scriptures as not only divinely revealed, but divinely edited as well. The alternative approach was to beg the question of the origin of the Scriptures themselves and instead to advocate the compelling wisdom and logic they demonstrated. Baptists in this stream focused particularly on ethics, on public and social policy, and on establishing a role for Scriptures that was consistent with the emerging certainty of the new sciences and philosophies. This approach made discussions and activity regarding the Scriptures first a matter of the intellect. It, therefore, did not persuade or influence those who did not find scriptural logic compelling but instead desired to engage the truth of Scriptures as an experience of spiritual encounter.

While Baptists were increasingly divided in their reaction to the crisis of Scripture, they were, however, united in the assumption that the great task of the new century was to build up God's kingdom. The twentieth century became, therefore, a century of corporate institution building.

Historical Precedents for a New Baptist Order

Associations of Baptists, as we have seen, were rooted deep in the past. The London Baptist Confession of 1644 had stated, "Though we be distinct in respect of particular bodies . . . [we] are all one in communion, holding Jesus Christ to be our head and Lord." In 1652 the Berkshire Baptists carefully articulated that "there is the same relationship betwixt particular churches each towards [the] other as there is betwixt particular members of one church."[31] Among English Baptists, associations served to facilitate the distribution of benevolences, start new churches, resolve disciplinary problems, settle questions of theology and polity, and even supervise ordination. Baptists in England envisioned national organizational structures—called General Assemblies—as early as the seventeenth century. And, as discussed earlier, the associational principle among Baptists was also established early among General Baptists in Rhode Island and then in the Philadelphia Baptist Association first organized in 1707.

Although the associational principle was always challenged by the individualism and congregational independence characteristic among Baptists in America, there were, nevertheless, even early advocates of a national connection. Morgan Edwards of Philadelphia, for example, suggested that a national body could be advantageous: "It introduces into the visible church what are called joints and bands whereby the whole body is knit together and compacted for increase by that which every part supplieth. And therefore it is that I am so anxious to render the same combination of Baptist Churches universal upon this continent."[32] Such views were supported by a few others, especially James Manning, the first president of Rhode Island College (Brown University).[33] But such sentiments were slow to gain support because of the fear of loss of freedom and also because there were not as yet urgent, practical agendas to motivate Baptists to establish organizations on a national scale.

The nineteenth century, however, became a time for creating associations between and among Baptist churches in many areas. And the evangelical spirit pushed churches to reach beyond themselves. Baptists in many areas, therefore, sought the means to advance the church and its mission beyond local limits. As a result, the early and mid nineteenth century was a time that spawned a broad variety of voluntary associations among Baptists for missions, Christian education, dissemination of Bibles and Christian literature, and the raising of financial resources to support these causes. The logical development might have been to strengthen the loosely organized regional and state associations by linking them nationally. Fear of encroachment on the part of a centralized authority encouraged the alternative development of separate regional or national societies to accomplish these goals. These voluntary societies were composed of individuals, groups, churches, and other societies, and membership was primarily dependent on the payment of dues or the contribution of funds. As the societies proliferated, there were early attempts to create a national Baptist organization. The notable attempt at creating such an organization was the Baptist Missionary Convention—more popularly called the Triennial Convention—which was brought into being by Luther Rice, Thomas Baldwin (Boston), and others. As with the societies, membership in the Triennial Convention was based on contributions and dues for many purposes similar to those supported by smaller societies. It was forthrightly a "stopgap organization" whose purposes, its supporters hoped, would be taken over by a more clearly defined national Baptist organization.

At the 1826 Triennial Convention, however, a delegation from New York heavily influenced by the Hamilton Missionary Society and Hamilton College, who did not wish to lose control of their new college or of the work and name of the society, influenced delegates to abandon their movement toward a national organization. Localism, particularism, and independence were victorious, but at an unanticipated cost: the same independence that guaranteed that local churches would not be controlled by a larger organization also had the effect that the voluntary societies would not be accountable to local churches.[34]

This 1826 decision to continue a society arrangement rather than to seek a more fully developed national structure had several effects. Clearly the societies accomplished great and good works, but the pattern of organization now firmly adopted also drastically influenced Baptist life for the future. First, the Triennial Convention henceforth restricted its work primarily to that of foreign missions. Second, it developed a structure for Baptist organization that endured into the next century. And, most of all, it discouraged any further linkage between and among Baptist churches beyond local associations. As Maring and Hudson observed:

Direct responsibility for mission outreach was removed from the churches bit by bit, as societies composed of dues-paying members took over the work of missions, publication, Christian education, and other functions. The association route would have likely kept alive a vision of the wider church, acted as a check to an exaggerated autonomy of local churches, and involved churches more directly in mission.[35]

Over time the bonds that had united Baptists in association were replaced by a more and more articulate spirit of independence that denied that there was any such thing as "interdependence" between or among Baptist churches. Instead, communication and cooperation among churches was maintained on a largely individual or ad hoc basis. The teaching, writing, and counsel of many Baptist leaders helped to deeply ingrain the habits of independence and isolation. The popular writing of E. S. Hiscox, for example, whose widely influential 1859 manual, the *Baptist Church Directory,* gave practical guidance and advice to churches and church leaders, contained a strong prejudice against Baptist connections and cooperation.[36]

Throughout the nineteenth century the associational principle emerged in a variety of structures, notably establishing gatherings and fellowships of churches in new areas where Baptist churches were developed to meet the needs of new and migrating populations. Although some associations attempted to establish strong connections and program emphases in addition to support of mission and evangelism activities, their primary lasting activity was fellowship and mutual support among churches. In no case were such local or regional associations effectively able to subsume and coordinate the work of the voluntary societies. Instead, they often served overlapping constituencies, provided parallel support for the same or similar work, and essentially conducted separate, isolated institutional programs. As the number of concerns and causes multiplied, so did the number of independent societies dedicated to accomplishing them. Over time, Baptist life became cumbersome.

One consequence of the proliferation of societies and mission organizations was increasing conflict. Confrontations emerged over issues of "boundary" between societies, between associations of churches, and between associations and societies. These conflicts were most often focused on territorial issues or on the protocols for raising funds, because many Baptist organizations were asking for financial support from the same people. Another source of tension was the authority to determine policy. As theological and ecclesiological perspectives differed among Baptists, so did the relative weighing of priorities for work to be accomplished and methods for accomplishing it. Churches and individuals who imagined they were working with others of "like faith and order" were forced frequently to recognize a wide disparity in priorities and choices.

But the biggest conflict emerged at mid-century over the same issue that shattered the country as a whole: slavery. In the South the church, like much of the rest of the culture, had in many cases adapted both theology and practice to accommodate the institution of slavery. In addition, the localism and individualism that characterized Baptist life also was a natural ally of the emerging "states rights" philosophy upon which the South built its bid for regional political independence. Thus, when the moral discussion regarding slavery reached a high pitch among Baptists at the Triennial Convention, Baptists in the South elected to withdraw from the Triennial Convention and as well from many of the societies in which they had been involved. Then they began to construct voluntary societies and associations that would accomplish the same or similar purposes, but which would reflect their regional concerns and priorities. Chief among them was the Southern Baptist Convention.

Baptists in the South organized the Southern Baptist Convention in 1845 for the purpose of "eliciting, combining and directing the energies of the whole denomination."[37] In theory the constitution provided for a convention with boards for missions and other purposes. In reality, however, for seventy-five years it followed the general pattern of the Triennial Convention and was based on the payment of money by individuals, churches, or other groups and existed corporately only when it was in actual meeting.[38] Then in 1917 the SBC moved decisively toward developing a centralized corporate model by establishing an executive committee with powers to guide and direct the work of mission boards, schools, publications, and other programs. In 1925 the Cooperative Program was established to provide a common treasury for all Southern Baptist purposes. In 1927 the Executive Committee was given oversight of the funds gained by the Cooperative Program. As a result, the SBC moved toward strong denominational organization.

Despite the relatively early move by Southern Baptists to establish a strong and comprehensive national structure, in many ways it did not confront the issue of individualism and local independence earlier or more effectively than any other group of Baptists. For example, it was not until 1931 that the basis of membership in the SBC was modified to specify that membership would be comprised of messengers sent to the convention by individual cooperating and contributing churches. This was a reversal from the generally ad hoc assemblage of individuals, church representatives, and organizational affiliates that previously defined it. The SBC experienced phenomenal growth during the twentieth century, increasing from approximately five million members in 1940 to over fifteen million members by 1990. But represented within that membership was an increasingly broad diversity of theological opinion and ecclesiological practice. The denomination effectively maintained peace and was able to aggressively pursue its missions and purposes precisely because, with a few notable exceptions, it refrained from confronting diversity and division among its churches and people. Instead, it focused almost exclusively on the advancement of its cooperative missions programs. In effecting what Bill Leonard calls this "Grand Compromise," Southern Baptists were continuing the spirit and practice of the voluntary society method of organization among Baptists.[39]

Beginning in 1979, self-consciously "conservative" leadership within the denomination began to change the historic institutional dynamics of the Southern Baptist Convention by focusing much more on unity expressed around a theological position rather than on missions alone. This group effectively took control of denominational priorities and institutions by gaining control of the strong Executive Committee through a well-organized and orchestrated use of established protocols in annual convention elections. But institutional control was only the first step. Having consolidated their institutional power, conservative forces within the SBC have turned to confront what had long been studiously ignored: the establishment of a central, articulated doctrine to identify and guide Southern Baptists and SBC churches, and programs that reflect this unified doctrine. In one sense the SBC has seemed to reclaim the spirit of the old Particular Baptist view of unity in belief and connectionalism in purpose. But in another, conservatives among Southern Baptists have broken new ground in Baptist denominational development.

Other groups of Baptists have effected denominational organization around theological, regional, racial, or ethnic identities. African American Baptists, particularly since the late eighteenth century, for example, have developed several strong national denominational structures focused on fellowship, mutual support in church development, and missions.[40] After the development of the Northern Baptist Convention (later the American Baptist Churches in the U.S.A.) in 1907, two groups of Baptists in particular, the North American Baptist Conference (German Baptist in background) and the Baptist General Conference (Swedish Baptist in background) established separate denominational identities in part to maintain a conservative theology and to maintain their historic ethnic identities.[41] Still a third, the Seventh Day Baptist General Conference, traces its roots to the seventeenth century and is distinguished from other Baptists primarily by belief that the Seventh Day (Saturday) is the scripturally defined day of worship. Each of these conference-style denominations is small in size and maintains close, collegial relationships among their churches. They function as voluntary societies in style but are in reality united by common cultures and histories. They have developed effective mission and education organizational structures but have not developed large national bureaucracies or programs.

One additional precedent, also established at a relatively late date in Baptist life, is the structure of Conservative Baptists. Their departure from the ABC/USA in 1947 was motivated by two concerns. Like the Swedish and German Baptists they identified with strong, conservative theological positions. Even more, however, they perceived a growing threat to the independence of local churches in the development and progress of the Northern Baptist Convention. Conservative Baptists have been reluctant to think of themselves as a denomination and instead prefer the word *movement*. Their structure is essentially comprised of the Conservative Baptist Foreign Mission Society, the Conservative Baptist Association, the Conservative Baptist Home Mission Society, and seminaries. They have developed no unified budget but instead effect their common programs through the individual work of their mission societies. In this sense they are true to their name: They represent a direct and continuing reliance on the voluntary society method of Baptist cooperation but have resisted stronger ties.

Shaping Forces in Denominational Life: Toward More Evident Unions

In the twentieth century the struggle to define the point of balance between individual freedom and corporate unity has developed along three distinct and parallel lines. These included:

1. Institutional tensions concerning the balance of power and privilege between individuals and churches, between churches and denominational structures, and between denominational structures and agencies.

2. Doctrinal and biblical tensions concerning the establishment of orthodox theological positions and the ability of minorities to disagree with them.

3. Social or political tensions in which Baptists became divided as

the result of divergent choices as Baptist persons or groups identified with one or another side of significant matters of public policy or social direction.

Although each of these balance points was at issue in virtually every Baptist denomination, each Baptist denomination was to some degree dominated by one of them.

Among Baptists in the North, for example, the primary point of tension has been focused on the development of institutional structures. In the South it has been more clearly a struggle to balance personal and congregational freedom against a prevailing sense of biblical and doctrinal orthodoxy. Among African American Baptists, the common struggle to gain social and political freedom against racist traditions helped to maintain a sense of corporate and community unity. Nevertheless, African American churches and denominations have wrestled with the point of tension created by diverging perspectives regarding the role of African Americans in the culture at large.

After the withdrawal of Baptists in the South in 1845 around the issue of slavery, the first real move in searching for an institutional alternative to the fragmented societal method was the organization of the Northern Baptist Convention in 1907. The defects of the societal method—complexity, duplication, and little or no coordination—were obvious. But the growing spirit of independence made anything more than a cautious step toward denominational structure unadvisable. Thus, in 1907 the Northern Baptist Convention was devised as a compromise between a church-style organization with strong central authority and the loosely affiliated societal methods already in existence.

Its central features were simple. The societies that were related to it—mission, publication, and education—remained legally separate, and termination with the convention arrangement could be made with one year's notice. Administrative policy was coordinated by holding annual meetings of the societies simultaneously with the meeting of the Northern Baptist Convention. The delegates to the annual convention were considered to be voting members of each separate society. A coordinating function was given to an executive committee comprised of the convention's officers, its past presidents, and thirty other members elected by the convention. However, the effectiveness of this committee in carrying out its coordinating function was often frustrated by a lack of communication and cooperation between the denominational societies in practice.

By 1907 a range of Baptist associations of churches had gained considerable stature, if not power, and had also to be included in the formation. These state conventions and city societies were cast as "affiliating organizations" in an attempt to move toward greater central coordination while, at the same time, preserving both the independence and functioning power of the associations. In fact, following the organization of the convention, the affiliating organizations generally increased their functions by adding divisions and departments for stimulating and leading youth work, men's and women's activities, and campus ministry, and assisting churches both in program development and in finding new pastors. These affiliating organizations also played an increasingly critical role in the development and encouragement of funding by churches and individuals for the support of the societies at the national level. One result, however, was enormous duplication. Much of the relationship between national and associational structures was built on custom and on effective personal relationships among leaders. Practically, this resulted in almost incomprehensible duplications in officers and program board leadership at local, regional, and national levels and a Byzantine array of treasurers, presidents, officers, and other personnel charged with effecting the same or similar programs.

In 1925 a report issued by a team of management consultants, approved by the Northern Baptist Convention in 1923 and funded by a grant from John D. Rockefeller, drew attention to the proliferation of Baptist agencies and offices in the Northern Baptist Convention. Its introduction summarized the thrust of the report: "The Committee did not find as much uniformity as seems necessary, considering that these organizations are agents of a common principal."[42] In making its recommendation for greater administrative efficiency, it pointed out "the amounts expended for raising money and for administration are excessive." It underlined the lack of cooperation by noting that "each organization considers itself autonomous and therefore not an agent. Those having surpluses consider that they have a vested interest in them, while those with deficits feel that they are entitled to call upon the denomination as a whole, or upon their constituencies in particular, to make up the deficits," and that "as there are 58 different corporations, at least 58 separate sets of books are now maintained."[43] They underlined that "no effectual means exist for exercising the degree of coordination and control of denominational activities now necessary" and listed a lengthy variety of other issues related to representation, communication, coordination, management, and reporting,[44] which they found consistently inadequate and frequently inaccurate. Ominously, they reported:

The apathy of the average church member toward the work of the denomination profoundly impressed your Committee. They criticize the Northern Baptist Convention as not representative, and they also feel that it is a mere mass meeting. . . . they repeatedly inquire whether an unreasonable proportion of amounts contributed is expended for overhead at the expense of the direct field work. Moreover, they insist that the number of financial appeals must be reduced, and that cooperative financing must be improved.[45]

They recommended, therefore, stronger central authority and control and urged the Baptists to adopt a more streamlined method of organization.[46] The report was received, it is reported, as too radical and listened to "with little grace." Its recommendations were ignored. It is interesting that following that report, Rockefeller family and foundation support, once generous to Baptist causes, radically declined.[47]

By the mid twentieth century the corporate inadequacies of a decentralized, loosely federated system of societies with unclear relationships both to individual churches and to "affiliated" associations and societies had become very clear. In addition, despite continued commitment to independence and local church autonomy, there was a perceived desire for greater unity. In part the desire for unity and harmony had been heightened because the departure of churches from the Conservative Baptist movement, the Baptist General Conference, and the North American Baptist Conference had weakened confidence in the present system. Ironically, the departure of these same churches made a quest for unity theologically and ecclesiologically more possible. Also, across a broad American cultural range, the period following World War II generally encouraged the development of institutions and social organizations. And, as we have seen, evangelical ambition lay at the heart of Baptist outreach, and Northern Baptists were generally unsatisfied with the growth rates of their churches and organizations. Southern Baptists, on the other hand, were experiencing continuing stages of strong numerical growth. Therefore, Northern Baptists sought to build a more effective well-defined and united denominational organization while the Southern Baptists proceeded to strengthen and define their denomination by rallying around the Cooperative Program and by increasing reliance on the Executive Committee of the convention to provide a firm leadership hand.

Beginning in 1950 with both a change in structure and a change in name, the Northern Baptists moved toward greater centralized cooperation among mission and program boards. In the 1960s and 1970s a succession of special commissions studied and brought recommendations to the convention, which, as enacted, gradually produced a more rational system of representation and cooperation in governing the variety of societies and organizations that comprised the American Baptist Convention and, later, the ABC/USA.[48]

Southern Baptists, having already established the basic form of a unified convention structure governed by a strong executive committee, engaged in a rapid expansion of programs and agencies in home and foreign missions activities, in educational and publications programs, and in the establishment of new churches. Southern Baptists seemed to have a more evident cultural sense of identity. Therefore, newly established churches bore evident marks of a Southern Baptist "style," and both homogeneity and loyalty to the convention seemed stronger. Because of the relative strength of the Executive Committee in coordinating the affairs of the convention, internal institutional division was not a frequent problem. Nevertheless, beginning in 1960, Southern Baptists were faced with what many perceived to be critical challenges to fundamental truths and practices. Whereas the focus of disagreement in other Baptist organizations was most often in churches and in organizational bodies where policy was determined, in Southern Baptist structures the challenge more often came from seminaries. What were received as "liberal" theological points of view among several seminary faculty members and a few other leaders were quickly met with resistance. Beginning in 1960 with Ralph Elliott's publication of materials on Genesis, which many Southern Baptists believed to rely on repugnant "critical" methods, and culminating in the actions of the 1980s when seminary boards reflected the concerns of a growing conservative majority, a number of professors either were removed from positions of teaching or preaching responsibility or left voluntarily to seek new denominational affiliations.

Beginning in 1979 with the election of the first of a succession of self-identified "conservative" convention presidents, Southern Baptists entered a round of division and debate focused not on organizational disagreement, but on the essential meaning of doctrine, the authority of the Bible, and the role of those serving in the name of the Southern Baptist Convention. As one result of this period, the convention structure was actually strengthened, with the power of institutional leaders and trustees affirmed. The ability to establish tests for theological orthodoxy and to determine unified policy was greatly enhanced. Another result, however, was the shearing away from Southern Baptist corporate unity by the Southern Baptist Alliance (later named the Alliance of Baptists) that represented a "progressive" emigration from Southern Baptist ranks, and the Cooperative Baptist Fellowship, a larger group, but one less willing to abandon ties to Southern Baptist identities and purpose. It is, to be sure, too early to predict the final institutional forms these two groups will ultimately take. Both are examples of the difficulty of finding balance between freedom and theological orthodoxy within the southern branch of Baptist life. The significance of biblical and theological orthodoxy as important connections for the unity of Southern Baptists and their derivatives is evident in the proliferation of new seminaries that has resulted from the tensions in their midst.

Like their sister denominations that struggled against the tides of independence and autonomy to preserve united denominational structures, African American Baptists divided and multiplied during the first half of the century. By mid-century the largest of these bodies had developed strong leadership and cohesive patterns of institutional unity and had developed structures of boards and commissions to carry out programs and missions. However, the wrenching stresses of the Civil Rights movement of the 1950s and 1960s brought unique challenges to the internal workings of these denominational structures, even as it did to American society as a whole. One common theme was a growing disagreement between an older style of accommodation to separation and segregation and the new agenda of emerging leaders who advocated a confrontation of racism and its social and legal implications. An example was the National Baptist Convention, U.S.A., Inc., in which a challenge to the leadership of the president, Rev. Dr. Joseph H. Jackson, was in part a reaction to his desire for continuing office and in part a response to his apparent resistance to Martin Luther King's strategy of civil disobedience and nonviolent protest. This challenge, led by Dr. Gardner C. Taylor as an alternative candidate to lead the NBC, U.S.A., and supported by Martin Luther King, Ralph Abernathy, Benjamin Mays, and other African American clergy and leaders committed to social change strategies, was ultimately unsuccessful. However, the latter group left to form a new denominational structure, the Progressive National Baptist Convention, which was more uniformly committed to King's social change leadership and which more homogeneously reflected a new style of Baptist engagement in social and political policy.[49]

Between 1920 and 1970 Baptist denominations worked to develop stronger, more centrally coordinated structures to support local and world missions and to effect leadership for programs and the delivery of resources for use in local churches. Divisions, when they occurred, were the result of a process of self-definition along theological, political, ethnic, and racial lines. As a result, Baptist structures had become more defined and, it seemed, more homogeneous.

Baptists in the Balance: Present Tensions

Just at the point of achieving what would appear to be new structures of unity, denominations, Baptist and others, began to experience internal stress and general decline in both participation and financial resources. It is doubtful that these phenomena are specifically related to organizational developments. Rather, tensions and changes within American culture at large may define many of the tensions within Baptist institutional life, as in other Christian denominations. These include:

- A declining sense of loyalty to specific traditions, denominations, and traditions among many people,
- A declining number of participants in established church life at the same time that new church organizations and new religious expressions have established alternatives for spiritual connections and fellowship,
- Growing points of cultural polarization around several issues of policy and morality, particularly regarding the role of women in both church and family life, "reproductive issues" such as abortion, marriage relationships, school prayer, issues of public morality, and others,
- A growing tendency to establish political preferences and agendas as determinative in choosing a religious affiliation and also to advocate on behalf of specific political and legislative action as a matter of faith and witness,
- The increasing isolation of classes, racial and ethnic populations, and others into distinct communities and geographical locations,
- The emergence of conflicts between competing values, styles, ambitions, and entitlements within the American culture at large,
- An erosion of the significance of theology as a discipline and an increase in the importance of theological and managerial style in developing successful church organizations.

In addition, it is interesting to note that at present there are strong tendencies toward localization and independence in many social and cultural institutions. Many new and often successful churches, while they demand much in loyalty and commitment from individual members, retain fierce independence for the church. Likewise, in education, health care, and a wide variety of other traditional community services, localism and

individual choice are currently presenting challenges to attempts to solid-
ify and unify at national levels.

In Baptist life recent tensions have emerged around several specific,
critical issues. One is the issue of biblical authority. First raised in the late
nineteenth century, this issue remains confusing, challenging, and potentially divisive for Baptists. Another is the tension experienced by the
gradual but persistent erosion of a sense of homogeneity in American
community life. As new patterns of immigration, social mobility, and other
forces have changed community dynamics, churches and denominations
have been affected also. These changes have exposed many patterns of
worship and church order as "culturally bound" traditions. Because some
have sought to preserve traditions while others have desired new forms
and new directions, conflict has emerged. As a result, churches and
denominations have sought effective ways to manage conflict by establishing new and more inclusive visions for church life and mission and
have also explored experiences from which to develop common traditions
and practices.

The application of biblical belief and ethical perspective to issues of
public policy has also proved to be a particular source of conflict, especially in the context of annual or biennial meetings of Baptists. For
example, the general issue of sexuality, and in particular homosexuality,
has often proved recently to be a source of serious tension for Baptists. In
the broad sense this issue includes a wide range from dating and marriage
relationships to birth control and abortion. Together these two intensely
felt and debated concerns have been the focal point for determining moral
authority and identity in many churches. Some have argued that not since
the slavery debate in the mid nineteenth century has an issue proved as
potentially divisive in both denominational structures and in local
churches.

Human sexuality has always been a difficult subject for the church in
general and Baptists in particular. Neither a discussion of its moral
challenge nor an understanding of its variety of patterns and expressions
has been easy for churches to accommodate. During the so-called sexual
revolution of the 1960s, for example, Baptists and Baptist churches
struggled to cope with a sudden revision of public standards for dating,
mating, and the variety of heterosexual relationships. These changes were
enhanced by the parallel changes of the role of women in church, home, and
the workplace. With specific regard to sexual issues, new and more open
practices of premarital sex and cohabitation by sexual partners in antici-
pation of marriage, in preparation for marriage, or instead of marriage

proved to be a great embarrassment for Baptist families and congregations and were most often dealt with by silence—even when they affected church families. New social trends including frequency of divorce and remarriage, and the prevalence of single parenting both as the result of divorce and as the result of choice by single persons desiring to adopt or give birth without a marriage partner, destabilized traditional moral certainties regarding family life and family values. As a result, churches often experienced great confusion in attempting to keep differing opinions regarding moral issues separate from understanding new needs and opportunities for outreach and ministry resulting from new family or living relationships. The result was a frequently paralyzing tension.

Because homosexuality most directly confronts longstanding assumptions about relationships and family order, discussion about it has been especially inflamed. In the 1980s most Baptist churches were unprepared for open discussion of homosexuality. Some homosexuals within Baptist churches, however, were supported by a few heterosexuals in desiring a more public acceptance of homosexual identity and relationships. By the late 1980s, partly as the result of a growing recognition that churches needed to consider appropriate ministry responses to HIV infected persons and those suffering with AIDS, which was perceived as an illness largely within the homosexual population, open conflict on this subject appeared in some churches, and sublimated tensions were evident in others. At the extremes, some Baptists rejected any toleration of homosexual living relationships or expressions and urgently called for repentance from homosexuality as one of the greatest of sins. At the other extreme, a few churches seemed willing to support pastors in their consideration of blessing "same-sex unions" and to welcome homosexual partners fully into church fellowship. In between were a number of churches able to incorporate some level of public and open acceptance of gay or lesbian persons, and some of these were also able to affirm their leadership in churches as lay leaders and, in a few cases, as pastors. Many churches, however, experienced open conflict and tension in the process of determining (or even deciding whether to participate in the process of determining) whether to become, officially, an "open and affirming" congregation.[50]

Some Baptist organizations remained silent on the issue. Others, notably the Southern Baptists, maintained a uniform position of condemnation of homosexuality as a sin. Still others reflected the division of opinion regarding homosexuality within American society at large. At the denominational level among American Baptists, for example, a moderately "open" policy statement with regard to homosexual inclusion in church and denominational life met with rising opposition from a significant number of more conservative churches. As a result, amid much tension and debate at the 1991 Biennial, a new Statement of Concern was passed. This resolution, which was brought to the Biennial by the signature process, rather than by the deliberation of the Statements of Concern Committee, adopted the text of Romans 1:24-27 as its guide and affirmed that the "church should love and minister to the homosexual, but condemn the sin of the practice of homosexuality." It further explicitly rejected homosexual marriage, ordination of homosexual clergy, and the establishment of "gay churches" or "gay caucuses." It urged the General Board to adopt the Statement of Concern as its new position on homosexuality. In subsequent months, by internal action, the General Board established a new, more conservative stance that explicitly rejected homosexuality as a biblically approved manner of life.[51]

In several local and regional associations similar conflict soon became apparent. Between 1991 and 1996, controversy on homosexuality issues developed between local churches and the regions or associations to which they belonged. In at least two regions churches were disfellowshiped by the region because of their affirming or open stance toward homosexuals in their own congregation—or because of encouraging such positions in others. In one case, at least, the action to break relationships with the churches in question was couched in terms of conflicts in covenant—a conflict in the covenant between the churches and the association, and also a conflict resulting from the churches having become affiliated with an association of "welcoming and affirming churches" and therefore having placed themselves in a position of conflict of loyalty. These actions precipitated a crisis in American Baptist Church denominational practice. Although the subject was as new as the late twentieth century, its dynamics were familiar. At issue were the interpretation of the Scriptures, the autonomy of the local church, "soul freedom," varying interpretations of Baptist heritage and practice, and understandings of covenants, real or implied, between Baptist churches and associations.[52]

Homosexuality is a lightning rod for broader issues. Interpretation of the Scriptures is often at the center of immediate controversy. Resolution of its dilemma for the church may still require both considerable time and continued discussion. But for Baptists the larger conflict is the one it exposes: the fragility of common assumptions, connections, and covenants that make corporate denominational life possible for Baptists.[53] Because beliefs and feelings about homosexuality are deep and tend to be expressed with passion, individual Baptists and churches experience severely strained relationships as a result. In discussions about these issues the matter of freedom is often squarely juxtaposed against the obligation of responsibility. No party to these discussions denies that a church has the autonomy to do whatever it perceives as God's will—or to do its own will and call it God's—as the case might be. What some argue is that once entered into, a covenant between and among churches cannot be broken, and that autonomy must be tolerated, even if by that autonomy a position is taken by a local church that is not the prevailing or popular one. Others believe that individual churches must walk in deference to the prevailing understanding of the whole—that is, they must conform to the majority position on critical matters around which the association is organized. If a church, in affirming its autonomy, violates the prevailing assumptions by affirming or taking actions counter to it, does the association (region, state, or city) have the right—perhaps even the obligation—to break its ties with that church? In the case of the churches that were disfellowshiped around the issue of homosexuality, the region obviously believes that it does.

A further question arises following the breaking of ties between a church and its regional association: Does a church have the right to retain a corporate relationship with the American Baptist Churches in the U.S.A. or the Southern Baptist Convention at the national level, even if it ceases to be a member of a geographical region or association? If so, how might that relationship be defined, and what is the pathway for such a connection? At the heart of that question, of course, lies a potential revision of the specific or implied covenants by which a particular denomination exists. Among American Baptists, for example, until the question was raised, the only way a local church could relate to the national organization was through its local or regional association. A Southern Baptist Church, however, could retain membership in the national convention even if it did not have membership in a local association. As a result of the trends and changes of the last several years, the role and identity of associations have therefore been raised for redefinition. Must associations be based on geographical identity, or may they be created and defined by mutuality regarding theological, ecclesiological, ethical, or social concerns?

As we have seen, Baptists have approached this issue before. In the early eighteenth century the formation of independent societies was the result, in part, of the need to circumvent the established geographical associations as they existed. Those societies, or their heirs, later were included in the ultimate formation of the denomination. These are, to be certain, issues that expose the still unresolved challenges of living both in freedom and with responsibility: individual independence, local autonomy, the priesthood of the individual believer (including the right to life choices even when potentially offensive to others), and the interpretation of Scriptures. Parallel to these, of course, is the right of regional associations likewise to order their affairs internally, even if it means ejecting an offending church, and the right of churches to form new associations if those to which they might otherwise belong are unwilling or unwelcoming. In the past, these have been the issues for which Baptists have had no recourse except to abandon principle, or else to choose schism and division. Is it possible that Baptists can establish an alternative where freedoms can be maintained but where moderation of their specific activities can allow them to live within the communal expectations of corporate responsibility.

Virtually every Baptist church, denomination, agency, or organization is, at present, striving to maintain or achieve harmony, peace, and cooperation: the quality that, for want of a better word, we have called "balance." In seeking to achieve it, several familiar and perplexing questions have returned for discussion within Baptist life. Against the tradition of "priesthood of all believers," what does it mean for an individual, or a small group, within the larger fellowship of a church, to possess and advocate a different understanding of the Scriptures or a different framework of acceptance or tolerance for everything from cultural norms to social practices to sexual behavior? And, given the powerful tradition of the autonomy of the local congregation, how does a congregation—whether conservative or liberal, open or defined by clear boundaries, racially homogeneous or racially diverse—maintain confidence regarding spiritual nurture and connection when it becomes aware that it is not in full agreement or sympathy with other churches with which it is in official fellowship? How does a Baptist congregation that enjoys a sense of being but one expression of God's people with interdependent relationships not only with other Baptists, but with God's people in other denominations—or even other religious expressions—still affirm a primary fellowship with Baptist congregations that are convinced that Baptists are God's only true and faithful people?

These are not new questions. They are, in fact, questions that Baptists have wrestled with for the entirety of their individual and corporate history. Nor are they the only questions. The pace with which contemporary life is changing surely brings both variations and whole new questions as quickly as we can define ones that have already confronted us. It is perhaps the intensity of the time that gives urgency to these and the other questions already forming. Most Baptists, while publicly proclaiming confidence in God's purpose for them in the future, have dark moments of private anxiety when it appears that Baptist life and traditions hang in the balance. The issues of freedom and responsibility—in spirit, in biblical interpretation, in mission activity, in ordering corporate church life, and in private, personal conviction—define the fulcrum upon which that balance is determined. It is the purpose of this volume, if not to answer the questions, at least to share them so that we can deal with them together. And, we confess, it is our hope in offering this volume that it will facilitate the development of more effective ways by which Baptists might live in the freedom that has traditionally defined Baptist life and, at the same time, live in responsible commitment to corporate life in Christ.

Notes

1. Richard Knight, *History of the General and Six Principle Baptists in England and America* (Providence, R.I., 1827), 327. William H. Bowen, "Six Principle Baptists," a paper read before the Backus Historical Society in Boston, February 24, 1896. Typescript in the Samuel Colgate Baptist Historical Collection of the American Baptist Historical Society. Works cited in Winthrop S. Hudson, ed., *Baptist Concepts of the Church* (Valley Forge, Pa.: Judson Press, 1959), 18.

2. Henry C. Vedder, *A History of the Baptists in the Middle States* (Philadelphia, 1898), 93. Cited in Hudson, *Concepts*, 21.

3. A. D. Gillette, ed., *Century Minutes of the Philadelphia Baptist Association: 1707-1807* (Philadelphia, 1851), 233. Cited in Hudson, *Concepts*, 21.

4. See R. A. Guild, *Life, Times, and Correspondence of James Manning, and the Early History of Brown University* (Boston, 1864), 76-77, for a partial text of the letter from the Philadelphia Baptist Association. See also the citation in Hudson, *Concepts*, 25-26.

5. Isaac Backus, *A History of New England with Particular Reference to the Denomination of Christians Called Baptists*, 2 vols. (Newton, Mass., 1871), 2:409n, as cited in Hudson, *Concepts*, 26.

6. Ibid. See also William G. McLoughlin, *Soul Liberty: The Baptists' Struggle in New England, 1630-1833* (Hanover and London: Brown University Press, 1991), sections of which are reprinted in this volume, and McLoughlin, *New England Dissent, 1630-1833: The Baptists and the Separation of Church and State*, 2 vols. (Cambridge: Harvard University Press, 1971).

7. Hudson, *Concepts*, 28.

8. It is important to note that Methodism was usually weak in the centers of Freewill Baptist strength.

9. The founding of the University of Chicago is an effective example of diffusion and ambiguity as Baptists established institutions. While the university was built out of the ashes of an earlier Chicago university and drew upon the resources of the Baptist seminary previously located in the Morgan Park area of Chicago's south side, it was in reality a creation of the vision and resources of John D. Rockefeller. Rockefeller, a Baptist layman, essentially put his resources behind the leadership of a unique

individual, William Rainey Harper, whom he charged with building a great university. (Indeed, his pattern was later repeated when he similarly placed confidence and resources behind Harry Emerson Fosdick in establishing the Riverside Church in New York.) And while the divinity school of the university was established under the guidance of Baptist trustees, its relationship with other Baptist organizations and institutions has always been unclear and often uneasy. As a consequence, a century after its founding, the University of Chicago has more than fulfilled the vision to become a great university, while its relationship to Baptists, past or present, is often a nearly forgotten footnote. While this example may be clearer than some, it is the rule rather than the exception in the development of Baptist institutional life.

10. Doctrine, or its absence, has always been problematic for Baptists. To the Baptist spirit, any doctrine that claimed the status of authority has been anathema because it would seem to violate cherished principles of freedom of conscience, priesthood of the believer, soul liberty, and others. Yet the lack of doctrine has left Baptists peculiarly vulnerable both to sudden shifts and to gradual erosions of theology and principle. Ironically, however, it has been in Baptist intellectual life that the absence of a general, clear doctrinal position has been most costly. Without an agreed upon, historic, well-developed statement of theology, principles, and belief, Baptists have not generally been required to do the intellectual work of remembrance, restatement, and reinterpretation that is required for habits and traditions to continue both as conserving forces as well as creative resources to shape new directions.

11. Augustus H. Strong, *Miscellanies,* 2 vols. (Philadelphia, 1912), 1:172-96. See also Winthrop S. Hudson, *The Great Tradition of the American Churches* (New York, 1953), 182-85.

12. Shifting views regarding biblical authority among Baptists are discussed by Norman Maring in *Foundations* 1, no. 3 (July 1958): 52; and 1, no. 4 (Oct. 1958): 30.

13. Augustus H. Strong, *Outlines of Systematic Theology* (Philadelphia, 1903), ix, 55, 58ff. See also Augustus H. Strong, *Tour of Missions* (Philadelphia, 1918), 186; and Hudson, *Concepts,* 202.

14. Strong, *Outlines*, xi, 55-60. See also Hudson, *Concepts,* 203.

15. Strong, *Outlines,* 59-60, 62. See also Hudson, *Concepts,* 203.

16. See, e.g., Alvah Hovey, *Manual of Christian Theology* (New York, 1900), 83, 85; and E. H. Johnson, *An Outline of Systematic Theology* (Philadelphia, 1895), 34, 350. See also Hudson, *Concepts,* 203-4, 206.

17. William Newton Clarke, *An Outline of Christian Theology* (New York, 1898), 38, 46, 381-85; also 41-45, 49ff. And see Hudson, *Concepts,* 204.

18. Strong, *Systematic Theology* (Philadelphia, 1907; 20th printing, 1958), 3:887-89, 893. See also Hudson, *Concepts,* 206-7.

19. Strong, *Systematic Theology,* 3:895-97, 903; Hudson, *Concepts,* 207-8.

20. Strong, *Systematic Theology,* 3:926-29; Hudson, *Concepts,* 209.

21. Henry G. Weston, *Constitution and Polity of the New Testament Church* (Philadelphia, 1895), 17-18, 20; Hudson, *Concepts,* 210.

22. Weston, *Constitution and Polity,* 47-48; Hudson, *Concepts,* 211.

23. Weston, *Constitution and Polity,* 48ff.; Hudson, *Concepts,* 212.

24. The varied writings of Edward S. Hiscox are published under a variety of titles, but notably *The Standard Manual for Baptist Churches* (1890) and *The New Directory for Baptist Churches* (1894), and the earliest of his efforts, the popular *Baptist Church Directory* (1859), also contributed greatly to the individualistic bent of pastors who relied on his work as a model for church leadership and ministry.

25. Hovey, *Manual,* 347, 351-54, 357.

26. Ibid.

27. Hudson, *Concepts,* 216.

28. W. R. McNutt, *Polity and Practice in Baptist Churches* (Philadelphia: Judson Press, 1935), 21-24. See also Hudson, *Concepts,* 215-17.

29. See McNutt, *Polity,* 25-29; Hudson, *Concepts,* 217.

30. McNutt, *Polity,* 25-29.

31. E. A. Payne, *The Baptists of Berkshire through Three Centuries,* app. 1, pp. 147ff. (London: Carey Kingsgate Press, 1951). Cited by Hugh Wamble, "The Beginnings of Associationalism among English Baptists," *Review and Expositor,* Oct. 1957, 547. See also Norman H. Maring and Winthrop S. Hudson, *A Baptist Manual of Polity and Practice,* rev. ed., Norman Maring, ed. (Valley Forge, Pa.: Judson Press), 174.

32. Quoted by W. W. Barnes, *The Southern Baptist Convention, 1845-1953* (Nashville: Broadman, 194), 9.

33. Maring and Hudson, *Polity,* 179-80.

34. For a more complete treatment of this episode and its several effects, see Maring and Hudson, *Polity,* 180-87.

35. Ibid., 187.

36. The Hiscox work had a profound influence on Baptist churches and leaders that continued well into the twentieth century. Two volumes emerged from his early manual: *The Standard Manual for Baptist Churches* (1890) and *The New Directory for Baptist Churches* (1894). In 1964 these were merged by Frank T. Hoadley (then book editor for Judson Press) into a single volume entitled *The Hiscox Guide for Baptist Churches.* In that volume the strong emphasis on local church independence was eliminated, a new section headed "The Wider Fellowship of Baptists" was added, and much of Hiscox's outdated advice was revised. More recently a rewritten and expanded volume sensitive to the challenges and concerns of the late twentieth century was written by Everett C. Goodwin under the title *The New Hiscox Guide for Baptist Churches* (Valley Forge, Pa.: Judson Press, 1995).

37. Maring and Hudson, *Polity,* 198.

38. For more extensive treatments of the origins and development of the Southern Baptist Convention see R. A. Baker, *The Southern Baptist Convention and Its People, 1845-1972* (Nashville: Broadman, 1974), esp. 164-76, 308-18, 400-406. See also H. Leon McBeth, *The Baptist Heritage: Four Centuries of Baptist Witness* (Nashville: Broadman, 1988), and Bill Leonard, *God's Last and Best Hope: The Fragmentation of the SBC* (Nashville: Broadman, 1990), for comprehensive treatments of issues of organization, tension, and purpose in Southern Baptist institutions.

39. Bill Leonard, *Best Hope,* 38-39.

40. For effective treatments of the development of the black church see Leroy Fitts, *A History of Black Baptists* (Nashville: Broadman, 1985), and more recently, C. Eric Lincoln and Lawrence H. Mamiya, *The Black Church in the African American Experience* (Durham: Duke University Press, 1990), of which one particularly relevant chapter is reprinted in this volume.

41. See Frank H. Woyke, *Heritage and Ministry of the North American Baptist Conference* (Oakbrook Terrace Ill.: North American Baptist Conference, 1979), and Adolph Olson, *A Centenary History Related to the Baptist General Conference of America* (Chicago: Baptist Conference Press, 1952). See also Maring and Hudson, *Polity,* 200.

42. "Report on a Survey of Fifty-Eight Organizations of the Northern Baptist Denomination (For Private Distribution Only)" (New York: Wynkoop Hallenbeck

Crawford Company), 108 pages. Item 286.17302; qN75R of the Samuel Colgate Baptist Historical Collection, American Baptist Historical Society, Rochester, New York, 11. The report was accompanied by a letter to the "Finance Committee, Northern Baptist Convention" and dated June 1, 1925. The chair of the study committee was Raymond B. Fosdick. I am grateful to Daniel E. Weiss, general secretary of the ABC/USA, for calling my attention to this document.

43. Ibid., 12, 20, and 23.

44. Ibid., 35-43.

45. Ibid., 41.

46. It is interesting that, in reviewing their analysis of problems of coordination, lack of cooperation, and independent—even to say jealous—guarding of boundaries and priorities, they concluded that "in most of these matters, the attitude of the women showed greater sympathy with, and a better understanding of, a sound basis of relationships, than was shown by the men." Therefore, it was not surprising that in making a variety of recommendations to improve coordination, communication, administration, and general efficiency in Northern Baptist operations, they recommended that "there should be a nucleus of controlling members in each Board, supplemented by associate and advisory members located throughout the United States. Each group should have carefully defined responsibilities, and *provision should be made for the substantial representation of women on the International Program Council, and on its Boards and Societies"* (emphasis added). Ibid., 42, 56.

47. Rockefeller support of Baptist churches, missions, and concerns had been considerable prior to that date. In addition to many local church, association, and regional institutional and educational programs, John D. Rockefeller had generously created and endowed the University of Chicago as a "Baptist" enterprise, had built and endowed the Riverside Church in New York also as a Baptist church, and had prompted the establishment of the Ministers and Missionaries Benefit Board with a significant contribution that enabled its effectiveness in providing both retirement and insurance services to Northern—later American—Baptist ministers, missionaries, and lay employees.

48. For a more complete discussion of the development of American Baptist changes, see the appendix on the American Baptists and also Maring and Hudson, *Polity,* 204-25.

49. Denominational developments among Southern Baptists and African American Baptists are treated in articles published in this volume.

50. The phrase "open and affirming" generally implies an attitude not only of acceptance, but of commendation for homosexuals living in committed, long-term relationships with persons of the same sex. A loose-knit "association style" of network among "open and affirming churches" was developed by American Baptist and other Baptist churches adopting that perspective. It should be noted that many more churches were able to be "open"—implying at least an ability to welcome and include homosexual persons, than were able also to be affirming—implying approval of homosexual relationships, particularly physical ones.

51. The rejection of gay caucuses, for example, immediately effected a rejection of American Baptists Concerned, a homosexual support and dialogue organization, from official connection to ABC/USA processes and later resulted in a similar disconnection of the Baptist Peace Fellowship, a common interest association of Baptist churches in several denominations, from ABC/USA funding or official contact as a result of their refusal to distance themselves from the American Baptists Concerned. Because non-ABC/USA affiliated groups were not granted

the privilege of exhibition space at Biennials, Baptists Concerned and the Peace Fellowship, as well as others, established an alternative exhibition site at the 1993 and 1995 Biennials.

52. Many of the issues of principle and practice regarding this issue, particularly relating to the unity and order of denominational life, were articulated in a document entitled "Open Letter to American Baptist Congregations and Pastors from Some Former Leaders of ABC/USA—January, 1996," signed by several dozen former ABC/USA presidents, executive ministers of regional, state, and city society organizations, ABC/USA national agency leaders, and others. Having articulated an interpretive position regarding scriptural interpretation, heritage, church autonomy, and other aspects of Baptist heritage, this document counseled a commitment to continued dialogue and restraint in the face of diversity, praying for continued unity in things of agreement, with tolerance regarding matters of disagreement. A letter from the executive minister of the American Baptist Churches of the Pacific Southwest, John Jackson, dated January 23, 1996, apparently in response to the "Open Letter" of former leaders and mailed individually to them, rebutted many of the positions of the "Open Letter" and spoke of recovering a "biblical vision for ministry, a passion for mission, and a clear sense of our identity as a movement of God." Copies of this letter were sent to members of the Regional Executive Ministers Council and to the members of the General Executive Council of the ABC/USA.

53. The January 23 letter signed by John Jackson, executive minister of the ABC of the Pacific Southwest, put the unspoken concern in clear relief: "The local churches, the associations (regions), and the national program boards all existed before the denomination . . . and they maintain their missional purposes in the midst of, in spite of, and/or in partnership with the denomination. Covenants can be seriously entered into, and can be prayerfully exited from."

Introduction to Part I.
Creations, Connections, and
Communities in the Past:
Some Aspects of Baptist History

Baptists have a relatively short history. In the Americas, Baptist history can be stretched to encompass 350 years, or almost 400 if we reach across the Atlantic to claim our British heritage. But during that short period several specific principles and events established precedents and pathways that have guided most Baptists as surely as if they were following ancient traditions. And given the great diversity among Baptists, the same short history contains a broad array of experiences. In the introduction we have sought to provide an overview of some of these developments.

In such a work as this, it is simply not possible to record even a sampling of the stories and activities of the Baptists that have brought us to the present. But it is important to be reminded of some of the strains that established our character. The four essays presented here define several of the mileposts along our journey. They represent some of the earliest Baptist work in the American experience and the establishment of the unique institutions of the African American church in the United States, and help us understand some of the tensions within the largest Baptist group, the Southern Baptist Convention. They lead us to a better comprehension of some Baptist principles and also to view some of the forces at work in Baptist development.

William G. McLoughlin, though not himself a Baptist, developed a scholar's love and appreciation for his subject. As a consequence, he has provided us with a great record of the mind, heart, spirit, and activities of Baptists in the first two centuries of their American experience. The two essays presented here are from his *Soul Liberty: The Baptists' Struggle in New England, 1630-1833*. The first provides a succinct and eloquent overview of the labors of the tiny Baptist minority in New England to define themselves as distinct from the established churches of New England and to achieve justice and equality in their effort to be free from the taxation that supported the church establishment. He argues that as minority became majority in spirit, the tension between their past and their present was intensified. In the second piece, McLoughlin describes the biblical, social, and political dynamics involved as Baptists worked their way through a previous controversy in their church life: the rejection of infant baptism. Though it is hard to believe, at one time this firmly established principle was a source of great tension in the Baptist family.

The third piece is, likewise, a re-presentation of significant work, in this case a chapter from C. Eric Lincoln's *The Black Church in the African American Experience.* It makes clear the kinship all Baptists share as people who invariably arose out of minority, often oppressed, and frequently despised circumstances. The black church, of course, has deep roots in the darkest moment of American experience—slavery. And in a future day when the history of how the American people have dealt with the rough edges of their diversity is written, the black church will play a central role in it. All Baptists, especially African American Baptists, have reason to be encouraged by the strong role of leadership black Baptists provided. Nevertheless, African American Baptists, like all others, will have wrestled with the balance between the individual and the corporate in establishing church and denominational life.

Finally, Stan Hastey provides a clear description of the remarkable events that reshaped and redirected the Southern Baptist Convention from 1979 through 1993. Dealing with theology, issues of power and control, and also the social context of this classic Baptist conflict, Hastey provides a means not only of understanding it, but of assessing it in light of other Baptist tensions, past and present.

Individually and collectively, these works provide a point of reference for the tension between freedom and responsibility, which is an ever-present theme among Baptists of all varieties.

Introduction: An Overview

William G. McLoughlin

Humbly hoping your Honours will consider that they are utterly unable to maintain their own way of worship and pay taxes to the Presbyterians [Congregationalists].
—BAPTIST PETITION TO THE CONNECTICUT LEGISLATURE, 1729

The Baptists of New England played an important role in American religious history from their first emergence as a group of dissenters in Massachusetts Bay in the early 1630s. Only grudgingly were they granted limited toleration in 1691. The Massachusetts authorities continued to tax them, distrain their property, and jail them throughout the eighteenth century. Finding little help at first from their Puritan neighbors or their legislators, the Baptists occasionally turned to the king and his counselors for assistance. But although the kings provided some help against the Congregationalists, they were hardly advocates of separation of church and state. Essentially, the Baptists had to rely on themselves.

Baptist grievances and complaints became louder in the 1760s, when new ideas about "the rights of Englishmen" and "inalienable natural rights" became popular. However, their fellow colonists did not like or trust them. On the eve of the colonial rebellion against the king and Parliament, many American patriots in New England doubted whether the Baptists would be on their side. The leading Congregational minister in Rhode Island (later the president of Yale), the Reverend Ezra Stiles of Newport, said of one of the foremost New England Baptists on July 16, 1776:

William G. McLoughlin, prior to his death in 1994, was Annie McClelland and Willard Prescott Smith Professor of History and Religion at Brown University. His several contributions to understanding Baptist development in America include the three-volume *Diary of Isaac Backus,* which opens the lives, minds, and spirits of eighteenth-century Baptists for modern understanding. This article is from *Soul Liberty: The Baptists' Struggle in New England: 1630-1833* (Brown University Press, 1991), pages 1-12, and is reprinted with permission.

Mr. Manning, President of the Baptist College [in Rhode Island] is a
Tory affecting Neutrality. He never prayed for the Congress or [for]
Success to our Army till Gen. Washington, returning from Boston last
Spring, being at Providence on Lordsday, he went to Mr. Manning's
meeting [at the First Baptist Church]—then, for the first time, he prayed
for the Congress and Army. But he and most of the Heads of the Baptists,
especially Ministers, thro' the Continent are cool in this Cause, if not
rather wishing the King's side Victory. . . . [Mr. Manning lately made]
some sneering reflexions on the public affairs—he suggested that this
was a Presbyterian [Congregational] War—the Congregationalists to
the Northward had prevailed upon the [Anglican] Churchmen to the
Southward [in Virginia] to join them—and that it was worth considering
[whether] the Baptists would be crushed between them both if they
overcome [the king]. This is the heart of the bigotted Baptist Politicians.[1]

Most of the doubts about Baptist patriotism grew out of the fact that the
Congregationalists and Anglicans had been anything but fair toward the
Baptists. Nevertheless, when the Revolution got underway, the Baptists
enlisted overwhelmingly on the side of the patriot cause.

But something happened to the Baptist movement in America after the
Revolution. The Baptists became the victims of their own success. With
the victory of Thomas Jefferson (for whom most Baptists voted) in the
election campaign of 1800, the Baptists entered the mainstream of American life. Though they did not succeed in overthrowing the remnants of the
Congregational establishment in New England until 1833, they grew so
numerous and popular that they were one of the two major denominations
in the United States. They were no longer a small sect of outcast and
downtrodden martyrs. It is not too much to say that the Baptists (especially
in the south and west) embodied the basic outlook of the American people
for most of the nineteenth century.

By entering the mainstream the Baptists ceased to be critics of American society; their piety relaxed, and they became the captives of the culture
against which they had fought for so long. As the embodiment of American
values, they were guilty of what Reinhold Niebuhr called "absolutizing
the relative." That is, they came to believe that because the American
social order had accepted their evangelical views, then America must be
the equivalent of a Christian society. They concluded that the United States
was, in fact, the most Christian society the world had ever known and that
the Baptist cause must sink or swim with America. To be a good Baptist
one should be a good American, and to be a good American one should
be a good Baptist. Which meant, in effect, that the Baptists began to act
as though they were the establishment. In short, between 1630 and 1833

the Baptists went through the classical evolution from a dissenting sect to an established church. In a way, the history of the Baptists is a paradigm of the American success myth: from rags to riches, from outcast to respectability, from pariah to pillar, from heresy to orthodoxy, from criminal deviant to authoritarian standard-bearer.

Although the first Baptist church in America still exists in Providence, the history of Rhode Island does not hold the key to either the history of the Baptists or the history of "soul liberty" in America. Rhode Island's "lively experiment" in freedom suffered from being at least 150 years ahead of its time. Rhode Island was called "rogues's island"—a scandal to decent order and propriety. It was not a model the other colonies wanted to imitate. The key to the history of religious liberty in New England lies in the story of the Baptists who did not run away to rogue's island but who stuck it out in Massachusetts, Connecticut, and Plymouth colonies. In some of those early battles for soul liberty the Baptists had to join forces with the Quakers (a sect that Roger Williams considered the worst form of heresy) because the Quakers in the early eighteenth century had powerful allies in England who had the ear of the king, which the Baptists did not. In the seventeenth century the Quakers suffered far crueler persecution in Puritan New England than did the Baptists. No Baptist was ever hung on Boston Common.

The Baptists were saved from the cruelties meted out to Quakers because they were not so different from their neighbors and did not invade the colony suddenly from outside. Most Baptists started as good Calvinistic members of the Puritan congregations. Some of them were deacons in the Puritan churches. Because the Puritans were themselves very uncertain about the question of infant baptism, the Baptists were able to argue with them pretty much on their own terms. In fact, it was the view of the earliest Baptists in Massachusetts, like Thomas Goold, that the mode and subject of baptism was a minor and "non-essential" matter about which good Puritans might differ without splitting the churches. We know that John Cotton and Charles Chauncy, two outstanding Congregational ministers, both agreed that baptism by immersion was as proper a mode as baptism by sprinkling. We know that the Puritans believed in gathered churches of baptized believers and in a congregational autonomy. We know that at first the Puritans favored voluntary support of the ministers and churches, not compulsory taxation. Hence, the early Baptists had much common ground on which to stand with their neighbors.

But if the Baptists had the advantage of arguing from within the Puritan system as respectable, hardworking, pious farmers and churchgoers, they also had several disadvantages. There was no college-educated Baptist who could stand up and speak for them (Henry Dunster, the president of Harvard, tried to do so briefly in 1654, but he was immediately silenced and left for Plymouth Colony). Second, their opponents were quick to associate their views with the wild and revolutionary Anabaptists of 1535, who took over the city of Munster, Germany, and practiced polygamy and rebellion against their rulers. Third, some of these early Baptists were not the most tactful and reasonable of men, and when the Puritans tried to tell them to shut up, some of them got very angry and raised a great fuss. One early Baptist in Charlestown was sentenced to pay a fine of ten pounds or be openly whipped ten stripes because he stomped to the front of the meetinghouse one Sunday morning when an infant was being baptized and threw the baptismal basin on the floor. A Rhode Island Baptist who had the temerity to enter Massachusetts to baptize a believer by immersion in 1651 was given thirty-nine lashes with a three-corded whip.

Despite these and other early examples of contumely and persecution, the Baptist faith persisted. In 1665 a small group of Baptists in the town of Charlestown, just across the river from Boston, formed a little church in the home of Thomas Goold. Goold and his friends were threatened with banishment and fled to Noddles Island in Boston harbor until things cooled down a bit. Then, in 1679, these Baptists secretly built a meetinghouse in the very center of Boston, telling those who asked what they were building so close to the millpond that it was to be a brewery. When it was completed and they tried to worship in it, the authorities boarded up the doors. But by that time Massachusetts was under considerable pressure from Puritans in old England to go easy on the Baptists. English Puritans were themselves being persecuted under the Restoration government of Charles II. Fearing that the king might revoke their charter, in 1682 the Puritans of Massachusetts finally relented to the point of allowing the Baptists to worship freely in their Boston meetinghouse.

So the first stage of Baptist martyrdom ended, and toleration was obtained. It is worth noting that in none of the early debates with the Puritan authorities did the Baptists argue against the system of compulsory religious taxes to support the Congregational churches (a system Massachusetts adopted in 1646). Under this practice every town in the colony (and in those of Plymouth, Connecticut, New Hampshire, and Vermont) was required to levy taxes on all inhabitants to pay the salary of the Congregational minister in that town and also to build and maintain the Congregational meetinghouse (where town meetings were also held). There were no exemptions from this tax. But not until they first obtained sufficient toleration to worship as they pleased did the Baptists try to take the next step toward soul liberty by demanding that they be excused from paying these ecclesiastical taxes.

The main scene for this stage of their development was in southeastern Massachusetts in the area of the old Plymouth Colony. Plymouth had been somewhat more tolerant toward dissenters than had Massachusetts, and many Baptists and Quakers had settled in towns like Rehoboth, Swansea, Dartmouth, and Tiverton as well as on Cape Cod. In some of these towns the Baptists and Quakers constituted a majority of the residents, and they refused to pass laws levying taxes to support Congregational ministers. When, after 1691, Plymouth Colony was merged into Massachusetts Bay Colony, the legislature in Boston tried to force the Baptist and Quaker towns to hire Congregational ministers and to lay taxes for their support. At the instigation of the Quakers in Dartmouth and Tiverton an appeal was carried to the king in 1723, claiming that this was contrary to the Toleration Act that had been passed by Parliament in 1689. The king agreed and demanded that the Congregationalists stop taxing other dissenters for the support of their churches. Although the king had no objection to Anglican churches taxing dissenters, he saw no grounds for Congregationalists to assume this right.

In 1728 Massachusetts began passing a series of laws that eventually granted the right of Anglicans, Baptists, and Quakers to tax exemption for the support of Congregationalism. Strangely enough, this seemed to satisfy the Baptists. They quietly agreed to the idea of an established church as long as they did not have to support it. During the 1730s the Baptists in Massachusetts did everything they could to gain the respect of their Congregational neighbors. As early as 1708 they had begun to send some of their young men to Harvard to be educated. Moreover, they agreed not to spread the Baptist cause by evangelizing among the Congregationalists. And some of the Baptists around Boston began to lose interest in Calvinistic theology; they adopted the Arminian doctrines that were popular among Rhode Island Baptists and becoming popular at Harvard. As a result, the Baptist movement ceased to grow after 1710.

It might well have died out entirely had it not been for the Great Awakening, which occurred in the 1740s. For obvious reasons the Arminian Baptists were not interested in that revival. In the first place most of the revivalists were, like Jonathan Edwards and George Whitefield, strict Calvinists in their theology. Second, the Awakening was seen in New England as essentially a Congregational movement. George Whitefield, for example, never preached in a Baptist meetinghouse when he toured New England, and Jonathan Edwards, Gilbert Tennent, and other revival preachers had nothing but scorn for Baptists.

Ultimately, however, the Awakening did revive the Baptist movement. Many of the Congregationalists who were converted during the revival of the 1740s became dissatisfied with their ministers either because they were not sufficiently ardent in their preaching or because they admitted unconverted persons into the churches or because they allowed ecclesiastical councils to interfere with the congregational autonomy of the churches. These newly converted or reawakened Congregationalists were called New Lights. They were ardent believers in voluntarily gathered churches of converted believers. Thwarted in their efforts to reform the Old Light conservatives, they separated from the established churches and began what historians now called the Separate movement. Scores of new Separate churches were formed throughout New England, creating, in effect, a new denomination (sometimes called Strict Congregationalists or Separates). By the middle of the 1750s there were more than 125 Separate churches in New England. The town and colony magistrates refused to recognize them as a new denomination and continued to lay taxes on their members to support the "old light" churches from which they had separated.

These devout and earnestly pious New Light Calvinists began to study their Bibles more carefully, and they tried to make their churches as free of corruption as possible. Many of them came to the conclusion that the source of corruption within the Puritan churches was the unscriptural practice of infant baptism. Within a few years, more than half of the Separate churches had adopted the principle of believers baptism by immersion. The churches that did so were then called Separate-Baptist churches. Their growth provided a new impetus to the Baptist movement and a return to Calvinist theology for the denomination. By 1760 the Baptists and their principles were spreading far and wide across the Puritan colonies; Baptist principles found new popularity, and because the Separates and Separate Baptists opposed being taxed to support corrupt Old Light churches, they began to agitate for tax exemption. New leaders, such as Isaac Backus, Ebenezer Smith, and Thomas Green, arose out of the Separate-Baptist movement. They wrote petitions and memorials for religious freedom and lobbied against the "certificate system" through which the old Baptists had obtained tax exemption.

The rise of a large Baptist movement in New England attracted the attention of Baptists in the middle colonies. Men from Pennsylvania and New Jersey, who were themselves learned ministers—Hezekiah Smith,

Samuel Stillman, David Howell, John Davis, and James Manning—came to New England to urge the founding of a Baptist college in Rhode Island, where Baptists could train pastors for their growing churches. They also urged the Baptist churches to unite in an association or confederation to provide stability, unity, and order to the denomination in New England. From this point on, the Baptists of New England combined their efforts for soul liberty with their efforts at institution building.

The founding of the Baptist College in Warren, Rhode Island, in 1764 was one of the first major achievements of the reinvigorated Baptist movement. It would never have been founded without the Great Awakening, the Separate movement, and the influx of leadership from the Baptists to the south. It had to be founded in Rhode Island because none of the Puritan colonies would grant a charter to a Baptist institution. James Manning became its first president. In 1767 Manning also drafted a constitution for the first permanent Baptist association in New England, the Warren Association. Many Baptists were at first suspicious that such associations would assume power over the individual churches, and Elder Peter Werden (the Baptists preferred the term "Elder" to "Minister") of the Baptist church in Coventry, Rhode Island, explained that his church would not join such an association because it could not find anything in the Bible that "supports a classical government over the churches of Christ." Werden's church members also said that an association would "overthrow the independence of the churches of Christ."[2] Elder Isaac Backus of the First Baptist Church in Middleborough, Massachusetts, a trustee of the new college, wrote to Manning saying that he and his church did not believe "that the rights and liberties of particular churches are sufficiently secured by what is said in your plan."[3]

There is little doubt that Manning did want the association to exercise some measure of order and regulation over the constituent churches. Some of them were tending toward heterodoxy and perfectionism. He also wanted to assure that all Baptist churches were Calvinist in theology and to give the association the power to adjudicate disputes between or within churches. But he had to make some concessions before the majority of Baptist churches agreed to join the association. Over the next twenty years some forty-five churches, most of them in Massachusetts, joined, but many others did not. Eventually, new associations were formed: the Stonington, Connecticut, Association in 1772; the New Hampshire Association in 1776; and the Shaftesbury, Vermont, Association in 1781.

Despite the strength that this new unity gave the Baptist cause, the established (or Standing) order continued to lay taxes on Separate Baptists, who, they said, were wholly different from the Baptists exempted from taxation in the law of 1729. Isaac Backus wrote a history of the Baptists in 1776 in which he gave dozens of examples in which Separate Baptists were sent to jail or had their property distrained and sold at auction for refusing to pay ecclesiastical taxes. He told the story of an elderly widow, Esther White, in his own church who spent thirteen months in jail because she would not pay the eight-penny tax levied on her. In the face of this continued persecution, the members of the Warren Association agreed in 1769 to create a Grievance Committee, which would assist any Baptist unfairly taxed, distrained, or jailed. Elder John Davis was its first chairman; in 1773 Isaac Backus succeeded him. The members of the Grievance Committee collected affidavits from the persecuted and their friends, wrote petitions to the courts and legislature, appeared before the legislative committees to lobby for revision of the exemption laws, and in some cases carried appeals to the king of England. In 1773 this committee organized a campaign of massive civil disobedience in an effort to fill the jails with Baptists who would refuse to cooperate in any way with the tax laws. This effort failed, but it indicated a new turning point in the evolution of the New England Baptists' position on separation of church and state. Hitherto, they had worked only to make tax exemption through certificates of Baptist membership more workable; now they concluded that ecclesiastical taxes in any form were contrary to the higher principle of separation of church and state. It is significant that until this date no Baptist had ever cited Roger Williams as an authority on this point.

The Revolution brought a temporary lull in Baptist agitation as they joined in the fight for political liberty. They assumed that one of the principles of the revolutionary cause was freedom of religion. To their astonishment, when Massachusetts adopted its first constitution as a state, in 1780, it included the right and duty of every town to lay taxes for the support of religion. Although the majority in almost every town was Congregational, the constitution of Massachusetts stated that "every denomination of Christians . . . shall be equally under the protection of the law and no subordination of any one sect or denomination to another shall ever be established by law." What Massachusetts intended by this apparent contradiction was that the churches of every denomination in every township should also have the right to support from ecclesiastical taxes. The taxes for religious support in each town were to be divided up among the denominations in proportion to the number of members in each. The writers of the constitution, assuming that most citizens were too stingy to provide adequate support for religion, wished to use the power of the state for that purpose. This same procedure was advocated in Virginia by Patrick Henry and others in the 1780s and was called "a general assessment for the support of religion." In Virginia the people rejected the general assessment bill and adopted instead the bill for religious freedom drafted by Thomas Jefferson and sponsored by James Madison. In 1785 Virginia abolished the tax-supported system for religion, but in New England the general assessment compromise was tried with disastrous results for over half a century.

The difficulty arose from the fact that few towns could devise or sustain a fair and nondiscriminatory means of dividing up the ecclesiastical tax. Some towns tried to reinstate the old certificate system (though it was no longer on the law books). Some were dominated by stubborn Congregationalists who required dissenters to sue the town before they would return their taxes. The courts inclined toward the view that dissenting congregations could not legally obtain a share of the ecclesiastical taxes in their township until they had applied to the state legislature for incorporation: only corporate bodies were "public" and thus entitled to a share of ecclesiastical taxes under the constitution. On this point, however, juries often disagreed with the judges. Dissenters who tried to give in certificates found that, as before, they were not always honored. Those who refused to pay such taxes continued to be distrained and jailed. As for seeking incorporation, many dissenters (like Isaac Backus among the Baptists) fiercely opposed any such obeisance to "Caesar" in order to worship according to conscience; they continued to struggle for total disestablishment and voluntary support for religion.

The final phase in the history of disestablishment (discussed more fully in chapter 15 [referring to the book *Soul Liberty*]) involved the complex efforts by various court decisions, legislative acts, and dissenting protests to discover whether a general assessment system could be made fair and workable. Some Baptists were willing to accept the system, but only a minority. Those who did so sought incorporation and made the most of the taxes raised for them by the state. But this was not the only inconsistency in the Baptist struggle for religious freedom in these years. In 1781, at the very time when Backus and the Grievance Committee were making their most eloquent pleas for religious equality, a prominent Baptist minister in the town of Pittsfield, Elder Valentine Rathbun, helped to write (and then signed) a statement urging the selectmen to arrest, imprison, or drive out of the town all of those irregular and disorderly persons called Shakers.[4] In Massachusetts, Vermont, and New Hampshire there were instances in which the Baptists, finding themselves to be a majority in a

town, paid taxes for the support of their Elder and then forced Congregationalists and others to give in certificates or sue for their share. Although
Isaac Backus wrote some of the most stirring tracts on religious liberty of
the eighteenth century, nonetheless he supported the test oath in the
Massachusetts Constitution, which discriminated against Roman Catholics.[5] He also proclaimed fast days and thanksgiving days from his pulpit
at the request of the governors, knowing full well that failure of any citizen
to attend church on such days was punishable by law. In fact, he never
thought it necessary to oppose the existing New England laws that required
church attendance on the Sabbath, nor did he oppose inculcating the
Westminster catechism in the public schools. The Baptists never opposed
state-supported legislative chaplains, and several Baptist elders served in
that capacity. The Baptists in Rhode Island ardently sought license from
the state to issue lottery tickets to raise money for their college in 1795.
And in 1792 Backus joined with the Congregationalists of New England
in petitioning Congress to establish a committee to license the publication
of Bibles (though the right to license would seem to include the right to
censor). All of which indicates that it was as difficult then as now to draw
a precise line between church and state, especially when the Baptists, like
most Christians in the early nineteenth century, considered that the United
States was, and of right ought to be, a Christian nation.

When Isaac Backus died in 1806, the fight for separation of church and
state was still far from over in New England. Vermont did not disestablish
its Congregational churches until 1707; Connecticut followed in 1818,
New Hampshire in 1819, and Massachusetts in 1833.[6] But the political
power of dissenters grew steadily after 1776, making disestablishment
ultimately necessary. The institutional growth of the Baptist denomination
hardly needs documenting. In the year 1740 there were only twelve Baptist
churches in New England (outside the colony of Rhode Island). Between
1740 and 1800 these had grown to one hundred. By 1830 there were more
than 250. In addition to Rhode Island College (after 1805 called Brown
University), the Baptists founded Colby College in 1820, Hamilton College in 1821, and Newton Theological Seminary in 1825. In 1802 the
Baptists founded their first home missionary society and in 1814 their first
foreign missionary society. They began their first monthly magazine in
1802 and their first weekly newspaper in 1819. In the 1820s they organized
state conventions to unite the various associations, and with the formation
of the Triennial Baptist Convention in 1814 they tied the New England
movement into the even larger Baptist movements in the middle, southern,
and western states. By 1830 they were engaged in all kinds of voluntary

reform societies and had eminent national leaders like Francis Wayland and Thomas Baldwin in New England.

As they became one of the most prominent denominations in the nation, the Baptists assumed the right to speak for the nation and even for the city of Boston. In an editorial in their Boston newspaper in 1828, they deplored the fact that the radical British lecturer Frances Wright "has been permitted to come into the heart of our city with the avowed object of contesting the dearest principles of our social state."[7] Three hundred years after the law banishing them from Massachusetts, the Baptists were claiming that the city upon a hill was "our city" in "our state." Victory seemed to have gone to their heads.

On the long route to this victory, the Baptists presented a colorful and valiant panoply of defiance and protest in the name of disestablishment and the free exercise of religion, one that needs to be better known. The mighty and respectable should not forget their own humble origins.

Notes

1. Ezra Stiles wrote a good deal about the coolness of the Baptists toward the Revolution prior to 1776. His diary is cited in W. G. McLoughlin, *New England Dissent* (Cambridge, Mass., 1971), 1:561-62, 576-82, 585. This quotation is on p. 579 in vol. 1. One reason Stiles and others in New England suspected the Baptists of being Tories was that Isaac Backus, James Manning, and Chileab Smith, among others, went to the Continental Congress in Philadelphia in September 1774 and accused John Adams, Robert Treat Paine, and other delegates (all Congregationalists) from New England of denying freedom of religion to the Baptists. New Englanders considered this an effort to create dissension in the colonial ranks at a very crucial moment. Ibid., 1:552-62.

2. Ibid., 1:505.

3. Ibid., 1:505-6.

4. Ibid., 1:664-65.

5. For the important role of Isaac Backus in the Baptist movement for separation of church and state, see W. G. McLoughlin, *Isaac Backus and the American Pietistic Tradition* (Boston, 1967).

6. See chapter 15 of McLoughlin, *Soul Liberty,* for a discussion of this final phase.

7. *The Christian Watchman* (Boston), 1 August 1828, p. 122; 14 August 1829, p. 130.

The Rise of the Antipedobaptists in New England, 1630–1655

William G. McLoughlin

It is no more possible to speak of "the Baptists" than it is to speak of "the Indians" in seventeenth-century America because there were too many different kinds of them. Lumping varieties of peoples together is usually a way of stereotyping them under certain pejorative characteristics. Just as all Indians were considered pagan, savage, cruel, and untrustworthy, so early New Englanders tended to lump all Baptists (or in their term, "Anabaptists"—meaning "rebaptizers") under the heading of heretics, schismatics, troublemakers, and fanatics. Once such a stereotype takes hold, it is easy to rouse the populace against such "enemies" of good order and Christian truth and then to pass discriminatory laws or to tolerate popular harassment of these deviants from decency. Persecution then becomes respectable.

The wide variety of Baptists in the early nineteenth century indicates something else equally important here. They were a comparatively new group, still seeking self-definition, coherence, and uniformity even among themselves. The Puritans of New England suffered from the same incoherence as part of a general dissatisfaction among Englishmen with the beliefs and practices of the Church of England. Pilgrims in Plymouth Bay thought a good Puritan should separate himself from that polluted sepulcher. Puritans in Massachusetts Bay thought they ought not to separate but to reform the Anglican church from within. The whole of England became a seething mass of new sects and schismatics in the mid-seventeenth century. It is well to start any discussion of religious liberty by understanding

William G. McLoughlin, prior to his death in 1994, was Annie McClelland and Willard Prescott Smith Professor of History and Religion at Brown University. His several contributions to understanding Baptist development in America include the three-volume *Diary of Isaac Backus,* which opens the lives, minds, and spirits of eighteenth-century Baptists for modern understanding. This article is from *Soul Liberty: The Baptists' Struggle in New England: 1630-1833* (Brown University Press, 1991), pages 13-36, and is reprinted with permission.

*the variety of Baptists who claimed that title. This will help us to remember
that the Baptists were themselves part of the Puritan movement against
the Anglican establishment.*

When they first arose in the early part of the seventeenth century, those
who eventually were to be known as Baptists did not know whether to
advocate complete or partial separation from the churches they left,
whether they wanted open or closed communion with other Reformed
Protestants or among themselves, whether they believed in baptism by
sprinkling or immersion, whether they should worship on the seventh or
the first day of the week, whether there were five or six principles
fundamental to their faith, whether they should stand for pacifism, communism, faith healing, antimagistracy, the priesthood of all believers, or,
after all, for only a slightly modified form of Puritanism. In England and
in Rhode Island they did not even know whether they stood for Calvinism
or Arminianism. Ultimately, it proved to be the most conservative wing
of the movement, that closest in principle and practice to the Puritans from
whom they separated, who dominated the denomination and carried the
day.

Because the Baptists did not know at first who they were or what they
stood for, it is not surprising that the Puritans also misunderstood them.
At first the Puritans looked upon them as eccentric fanatics—a dangerous
resurgence of sixteenth-century Munsterite Anabaptism. At other times
they equated them with Brownists, Antinomians, Levellers, Familists,
Quakers, and even "Papists." In the battle of words and whips that the
Puritans of Massachusetts waged to extirpate these dissenters between
1635 and 1682 the basis of the differences between them was slowly
hammered out. The truth was that both the Puritans and the Baptists
changed gradually with the times and with experience. Yet each group was
convinced that it, and it alone, constituted the vanguard of the "new
Reformation" that was to carry forward in the realm of Britain the work
begun a century earlier by Luther and Calvin on the continent. They argued
not in terms of denominationalism but in terms of which of them had the
clearer insight into the revealed will of God and which of them, therefore,
knew best how to establish and maintain the true church and the true faith.
As there was only one true church and one true faith, those who were not
with God were against him.

In addition to religious principles there were certain pragmatic problems raised by the claim of the minority to be tolerated. Regardless of the
theological merits of the Baptists' claim, the Puritans were convinced that

Massachusetts Bay was not big enough for two rival groups of true believers. Those who did not agree with the principles of the founders and leaders of the colony had "free liberty," as Nathaniel Ward put it in *The Simple Cobbler of Agawam* (1647), "to keep away from us." After all, the plantation was a private company. It had the right by royal charter to establish its own rules of church and state as long as they did not contradict those of England; and until Oliver Cromwell came to power, no Baptist could claim he was tolerated in England. Throughout Christendom the policy of *cuius regio, eius religio* prevailed. The Puritans were convinced that if the Baptists ever became a majority they would not tolerate deviants from their way. Even when, under Cromwell's regime, England did tolerate Baptists, the New England Puritans pointed out that what might be allowed in an ancient, large, and well-established country like England would be a grave danger to a small, unstable young frontier plantation like Massachusetts Bay or Connecticut. The Baptists, adding their own pragmatic arguments, replied that nothing was less conducive to peace and order than persecution of respectable persons for conscience. Abstract and absolute principles of religious faith and order thus mingled indiscriminately with questions of expediency, law, custom, and majority rule.

Because religion was so deeply imbedded in the social and political principles of the era, the quarrel involved more than toleration or the separation of church and state. It displayed all of the fundamental antinomies of human social behavior and private belief. It could be roughly subsumed under such headings as church versus sect, conservatism versus radicalism, corporate welfare versus individual freedom, aristocracy versus democracy, in-group versus out-group. The solutions that were worked out in colonial New England to settle this struggle (insofar as it can ever be settled) were those that, for better or worse, shaped the history of liberty in modern America.

Although evolution of the Baptist persuasion was simultaneous in old England and New England, direct connection between the two groups was relatively slight. The first so-called Baptist church was founded in England in 1611 or 1612, when Thomas Helwys and John Murton returned to London from Holland (where they had gone in 1608 as Separatists). In Holland, Helwys and Murton had been influenced by the Mennonites to the extent of giving up infant baptism, but they did not agree with the Mennonites in rejecting oaths, war, and civil magistracy. Nor did they believe that baptism should be by immersion. But they did follow the Mennonites in adopting an Arminian revision of Calvinism, notably in believing that Christ died to save all men who would accept him on faith, not just the predestined or particular elect. Hence, the Baptist church of Helwys and Murton began the wing of the Baptist movement known as the General Baptists, as differentiated from the Calvinistic or Particular Baptists. During most of the seventeenth century there were more General Baptists than Particular Baptists, though their relationship with the New England Baptists was even more tenuous, except among those in Providence Plantations.

The founding of the first Particular Baptist church in England is usually dated from 1638, though its members did not practice baptism by immersion until 1641—two years after the Baptists in Providence, Rhode Island, appear to have adopted it. Significantly, the Particular Baptists in London, led by John Spilsbury, derived from the Non-Separatist Congregational church founded by Henry Jacob in Southwark in 1616.

Jacob was an Oxford graduate and a Puritan minister within the Anglican church. He is credited with being among the founders of that branch of Congregationalism that contributed most to the settlement of Massachusetts. He also persuaded John Robinson, whose followers settled the Plymouth Colony, to modify his early Separatism after 1612 to the extent of sanctioning open communion with the Church of England, at least in preaching and prayer.

The fact that John Spilsbury and his antipedobaptist congregations derived directly from Jacob's Non-Separatist Congregational principles is characteristic of the whole Calvinistic Baptist movement in England and New England. Yet the Anglo-American relationships even with this Calvinistic wing of the movement were minimal. Several individuals baptized in Spilsbury's church and in other Baptist offshoots from Jacob's church found their way into New England Baptist churches. One of these was Hanserd Knollys, who had a stormy career as a minister in New England from 1638 to 1641, returned to London, and became a Particular Baptist in 1644. That same year Spilsbury, William Kiffin, and several other Calvinistic Baptist ministers drew up the first confession of faith for the Particularists and thus gave the beginning of unity to the movement. The adherence of several college-educated former Puritans to the Baptists in the 1640s (men like Knollys, Henry Jessey, and John Tombes) gave the denomination some able scholarly apologists whose books were quoted in New England. In 1645 Tombes sent one of his books to the magistrates of Massachusetts in the hope of persuading them to reconsider their recent law banishing Anabaptists from the colony. Knollys and Jessey (though not Kiffin) adopted a policy of open or mixed communion with the Independents and Presbyterians who would accept it, and over the years (especially after 1660) the open-communion Congregationalists in England urged toleration for Baptists in New England. But except for this kind of general encouragement and example, the English Baptists provided little help or stimulus to their New England brethren. Knowledge of intolerance in Massachusetts prevented any mass exodus of Baptists to the Puritan colonies even after the Clarendon Code led to their persecution in England. Only one leading Baptist minister, John Myles of Wales, ever came to New England to provide the leadership sorely needed for the movement there, and he settled in the Plymouth Colony in 1663.

In short, the Baptist movement in New England was essentially an indigenous, parallel movement to that in England and not an offshoot or extension of it. It stemmed from a common source in the theological and ecclesiological principles of the general Puritan movement and needed no other source or stimulus than the ideas the Non-Separatist Congregationalists brought to New England.

The spectrum of the seventeenth-century pietistic movement, which Increase Mather called "the new Reformation," went from Presbyterianism on the right to Quakerism and Seekerism on the left. Roger Williams ran the spectrum from right to left, as did many other Englishmen. To the Anglicans and Presbyterians the settlers of the Massachusetts Bay Colony "were separatists and would be Anabaptists." For the New England Puritans, however, the difference between their own views and those of all varieties of the antipedobaptists was the difference between the civilized frontier of the true Reformation and the wilderness of anarchy and chaos: "the briars of Anabaptisme," Cotton Mather called it. He added, "Most of the Quakers that I have had occasion to converse with were first Anabaptists." Once a man began to have scruples about infant baptism, he had started down the slippery road to Antinomianism, Familism, Ranterism, Quakerism, and all of the other heresies to which Satan lured the ignorant, the arrogant, and the self-righteous. The Reverend William Hubbard of Ipswich, writing his history of New England in 1680, concluded, "It is too often seen that these new sectaries that go about to unchurch all other Christian societies do at last unchurch themselves and from anabaptists become sebaptists then seekers and at last ranters"—all "out of a giddy unstable mind."

In one sense the fight for toleration that the Baptists waged in New England in the seventeenth century was an attempt to prove that they were not ignorant, irresponsible enthusiasts like the Munsterites or the Quakers, that they were in fact just as respectable and law-abiding and correct in their interpretation of Scripture as were the Puritans. Because they were former members or adherents of the Puritan churches and generally respectable inhabitants of the commonwealth—not wild invaders like the Antinomians and Quakers—they had one advantage that these immigrant sects lacked. As offshoots from the Puritan churches they had the additional advantage of being orthodox Calvinists who argued within the accepted philosophical and social framework of the community. And finally, because the New England Puritans themselves could not make up their minds precisely what the correct practice of baptism involved, the Baptists had a third advantage: they waged their fight for reform on the most controversial and unsettled ground in the whole Puritan system. Increase Mather went so far as to say that "the right to baptism" was to "the new Reformation" of the seventeenth century what the argument over transubstantiation was to the Reformation of the sixteenth century. The question of baptism reached not only to the heart of the complex problem of the true form of church policy but also to the church's relationship to the state. It challenged the very structure and purpose of the Puritan social and political order. Was the Massachusetts Bay Colony a corporate, collectivist, Christian order in which, as John Winthrop said, "the care of the publique must oversway all private respects"? If so, were the magistrates, as nursing fathers to the church, obligated primarily to follow the will of God rather than the will of those who elected them? Or was it essential for the purity of the churches, and ultimately for the prevalence of Truth, that the magistrate keep scrupulously out of religious affairs and confine himself basically to the role of an umpire in public affairs? Was every man to be free, not only in his conscience but also in his actions (insofar as he caused no direct harm to the body or property of others), to follow his own judgment in all of the affairs of this world because ultimately he alone must answer to God in the next?

The questions were not phrased precisely in these terms in the seventeenth century, and the Baptists often denied that they were trying to raise them. Yet they lay at the heart of the controversy, and Americans were a long time finding answers to them.

Roger Williams began the struggle for separation of church and state in 1635 with a magnificent failure. His inability to define his own beliefs or to remain for long in any church or denomination is symbolic of the amorphous quality of religious dissent in old and New England during his lifetime. Williams, like the Baptists, whose claims he accepted for only a few months in 1639, knew better what he was against than what he was for. Soul liberty, as he explained it, was a negative, not a positive ideal. It asked the state to stop interfering in religious affairs because interference had, as experience demonstrated, led to the oppression of true saints and the persecution of true churches. But precisely what true saints and true churches, Williams spent the whole of his life seeking unsuccessfully. Some of those who came to share the freedom of his "lively experiment" in Rhode Island and Providence Plantations found the answer in mysticism, others in Socinianism, some in Quakerism, and still others in the several varieties of the Baptist persuasion.

Roger Williams's experiment was a failure because of the inability of Rhode Islanders to shape, by example or evangelism, the destiny of either New England or any of the other colonies. Despite the valiant efforts of Williams, almost no one in colonial New England ever praised his experiment, sought his advice, quoted his books, or tried to imitate his practices. Even in Rhode Island he was often assailed as unsound—and to the other New England colonies, Rhode Island was always the prime example not of the virtues but of the horrors of religious liberty. Those who fought hardest for religious freedom in Massachusetts, Connecticut, Vermont, and New Hampshire considered Rhode Island an embarrassment rather than an asset to their cause. During and after the colonial period, Rhode Island, "the licentious Republic" and "sinke hole of New England," was an example to be shunned.

Hence, Rhode Islanders were always on the periphery of the battle for religious liberty. What happened in their precariously held corner of New England counted for little unless the citadel of Puritanism was taken. The Rhode Islanders rightly saw themselves not as the center of an expanding crusade but as a wilderness shelter for outcasts, a precarious experiment in nonconformity, a furtive supplier of succor for those who waged the real fight within the gates of the enemy. Because they had separated themselves from the corruptions of the Puritan system (or had been banished for their separatism), they went their way alone. The lump of compulsory conformity from which they separated had to be leavened from within by the saving remnant who stayed behind—the non-separating dissenters.

In the fight for separation of church and state in New England, the Baptists were only one of several battalions of dissenters. Ultimately, however, they proved to be the most consistent, the most numerous, and the most effective. During the seventeenth and early eighteenth centuries they often received valuable assistance from the parallel (but seldom cooperative) efforts of Presbyterians, Anglicans, and Quakers. In the middle and latter parts of the eighteenth century and the early nineteenth century they received similar assistance from the Separates during the

Great Awakening and from the Methodists and Universalists afterward. Without this help they could not have won the fight for religious liberty. Generally, however, the Baptists bore the brunt of the fighting from 1635, when Roger Williams was banished, to 1833, when compulsory religious taxation was abolished.

Because the term Anabaptist was so loosely applied to a wide range of dissenters from Puritan orthodoxy, it is impossible to assess with any accuracy the generation and growth of the Baptist movement in the seventeenth century. Almost any person to the left of the Puritan position was termed an Anabaptist or said to be "tinged with Anabaptistry."[1] Contemporary private and public records mention some forty to fifty incidents in New England between 1635 and 1680 involving "Anabaptists" or Persons "with anabaptistical tendencies"; but since these terms were used to describe Antinomians like Anne Hutchinson, as well as Separatists, these incidents tell us more about Puritan fears than about Baptist growth. Baptism was a controversial issue, but it was difficult at the outset to distinguish Baptists as a sect. Charles Chauncy was called a Baptist by some simply because he advocated the baptism of infants (and adults) by immersion, though he differed from his colleagues in the Massachusetts ministry on nothing else. Henry Dunster was called a Baptist though he was never excommunicated from the Puritan church in Cambridge and never was more explicit in his dissent than to oppose infant baptism.

There is no record of many forerunners of the Baptist movement because they feared to reveal themselves. The promptness with which ecclesiastical and civil authorities pounced on suspected Anabaptists gave pause to any who leaned in that direction. However, the fact that the First Baptist Church of Boston grew from its nine original founders in 1665 to more than eighty members by 1680 indicates that an inert potential existed for the movement.

The authorities usually discovered an incipient Anabaptist by his own action—his refusal to have a child baptized or his unwillingness to participate in the baptismal services for the infants of others. The certainty of punishment for such overt acts of nonconformity undoubtedly led many to prefer emigration from the colony. No doubt some who were punished for failing to attend church regularly were covert Baptists who chose that alternative to the more severe penalties they could have received had they attended a baptism and felt obligated in conscience to turn their backs on it or to walk out of the church rather than participate. Once a Baptist church

was formed, many admitted that they had long held antipedobaptist views
but had not dared express them.[2]

By the end of the seventeenth century there were six Baptist churches
in Rhode Island, three in the old Plymouth Colony area, one in Boston,
and none in Connecticut.[3] Rhode Island and the towns on its indeterminate
boundaries (Seekonk, Dartmouth, Tiverton, and Little Compton on the
east and New London and Westerly on the west) acted as safety valves for
the dissenters from the Puritan colonies. Even after 1682, when Baptists
and other dissenters in Massachusetts ceased to be subject to civil punishments, social discrimination continued to drive them off to unsettled areas
between villages, to the frontier, or to other colonies. Toleration, as it
turned out, did not lead to any rapid increase in dissent. Intolerance after
1682 merely became secularized. Not until the Great Awakening did the
Baptist movement in New England really attain sizable proportions.
According to the best estimate that can be made, not more than one in one
hundred persons in New England (including Rhode Island) was an acknowledged Baptist in the year 1700. Not more than two in one hundred
belonged to any other dissenting denomination—Quakers, Anglicans,
Presbyterians. Most of the ten thousand people living in Rhode Island at
that time, however, may be considered as opponents of the Puritan system,
and many silent dissenters still existed within the Puritan colonies.

The first group openly advocating antipedobaptism in New England,
and the first to adopt baptism (for them, rebaptism) of adult believers by
immersion as the only proper basis for church membership, was the small
band of exiles from Salem who formed the First Baptist Church in
Providence in 1639. Roger Williams and Ezekiel Holliman baptized each
other and then ten more persons, most of them former members of the
Salem church. According to John Winthrop, Williams was led to adopt
"anabaptism" by the wife of Richard Scott, a sister of Mrs. Hutchinson,
who had come to Providence with her husband that year.[4] But it is just as
likely that Williams's own incessant search for the true form of the true
church led him to adopt Baptist views at this time. Four months after his
baptism Williams left the Baptist church because he doubted the validity
of adult immersion, and in subsequent trips to England he found the
friendship of Congregationalists like Harry Vane and John Milton more
congenial than that of Baptists.[5] In 1652 the Baptist Church in Providence
split over two questions: the "laying on of hands" upon all believers ("the
sixth principle") and Arminianism. The Six Principle and Arminianism
both prevailed, and the Five Principle Calvinists in Providence soon died
out. The lack of strong leadership among the Providence Baptists and their

break with Calvinism prevented their playing a significant role in the spread of Baptist views among the Puritan colonies thereafter, for the Baptist movement outside the Rhode Island area, especially around Boston, was Calvinistic.

Thus, it was the First Baptist Church in Newport, which had good leadership and remained Calvinistic, that had the closer relationship with the Baptists of Massachusetts Bay. Founded by John Clarke in or about 1644, it lost some members in a schism over the laying on of hands in 1656, and others became Seventh Day Baptists in 1671. But these schisms failed to stem its growth. Clarke, born in Suffolk, England, in 1609 and educated as a physician (possibly at the University of Leyden), arrived in Boston in the fall of 1637.[6] He appears to have sympathized with the Antinomians and was among those disarmed by the Puritan leaders out of fear of insurrection. He left Boston after a few weeks, spent the winter with a group of Antinomian emigrants in New Hampshire, and moved to Portsmouth, Rhode Island, the next spring. Why Clarke assumed religious leadership over the church founded in Portsmouth is not known. It does not appear that he was a Baptist at this time, and the church that he led in Portsmouth (and after 1639 in Newport) probably was a Separatist Congregational church until 1644. That some of the Antinomians became Baptists and others became Quakers after 1641 can be explained only in terms of their own intense pietistic striving (through the help of the Holy Spirit) to discover or to recover the basic doctrines of divine revelation and the basic policy of the primitive church. It may be that the immigration of some Baptists from London, like Henry Lukar, influenced Clarke's decision to found a Baptist church, but there is no record of this.[7]

While the Baptist (and later the Quaker) movement flourished in the tolerant antinomian atmospheres of Providence, Portsmouth, Newport, and other Narragansett Bay settlements, the dissenters in Massachusetts Bay found life very difficult in the seventeenth century. One of the proudest claims of the New England Puritans was that their system retained its uniformity and its stability, simultaneously maintaining a strict division between the things that are God's and those that are Caesar's. Not only did they have no bishops or ecclesiastical courts but no creeds, no rituals, no liturgies, no disciplines, no book of common prayer imposed on their autonomous churches by the state. One of their claims to being a more purified Christian commonwealth lay in their careful attempt to maintain a rigid line between the rights of the churches and the duties of the magistrates. Though they were accused of establishing a theocracy, they called their establishment a coordinate system, and they laid down careful regulations to keep the ministers and the magistrates within their respective spheres. These two spheres, said John Cotton, were not to be confused "either by giving the Spiritual Power which is proper to the Church into the hands of the Civil Magistrate . . . or by giving Civil Power to church officers, who are called to attend to Spiritual Matters and the things of God."[8] When a Baptist published a list of what he called the "Ecclesiastical laws" of the Bay Colony in 1652, he was firmly corrected by the Reverend Thomas Cobbett, who said, "We profess against any such title or thing . . . for Civil Power to make laws properly ecclesiastical, were an usurped power."[9] What seemed like ecclesiastical laws to dissenters were simply laws for keeping Christian peace and order. The Puritans had had sufficient experience with ecclesiastical interference in religious affairs in England to make every effort to avoid this in New England. "It is not so long since our own Necks bled under an intolerable yoke of Imposition on conscience as that we should forget what it is to be so dealt with," said Increase Mather.[10] "God's institutions (such as government of church and commonwealth be)," John Cotton concluded, "may be close and compact, and coordinate to one another and yet not be confounded."[11]

But if Puritans have received too little credit for the step they took toward separating church and state in their opposition to Erastianism, prelacy, and sacerdotalism, they have nevertheless been rightly charged with failing to maintain in practice the sharp division that they advanced in theory. Many times the Puritans quarreled among themselves over whether the clergy and the magistrates were not still too closely inter-twined in New England, a problem that grew out of the firm belief of the leaders of Massachusetts Bay that the principal duty of the magistrates was to act as "nursing fathers to the churches," preserving the churches from disorder and the commonwealth from offending God. But did this mean that the magistrates could decide when a church had chosen an improperly qualified minister? Could they prohibit any new church from being formed without their permission? Could they lay taxes on all inhabitants for the support of the churches? Could they command the ministers to hold a synod? There was less quarrel, however, over the assumption, universal then in Christendom, that the magistrates were duty bound, as the Cambridge Platform put it in 1648, to suppress all "Idolatry, Blasphemy, Heresy, venting corrupt & pernicious opinions, that destroy the foundation, open contempt of the word preached, prophanation of the Lord's day, disturbing the peacable administration & exercise of the worship & holy things of God."[12] As for those who would separate from the existing churches and seek to lead souls into error by challenging the uniformity and conformity to truth that God required of his people in "the new Jerusalem," the "modern Canaan," the "new Israel" of New England, the Cambridge Platform, sustaining a law of 1631, declared: "If any church one or more shall grow schismaticall, rending it self from the communion of other churches, or shall walke incorrigibly or obstinately in any corrupt way of their own, contrary to the rule of the word; in such case the Magistrate is to put forth his coercive power as the matter shall require."[13]

Fighting a desperate battle to prove to Episcopalians and Presbyterians in England that the congregational polity could be sustained in good order and orthodoxy, the Puritans' coordinate system necessitated a delicate balance that they could not always maintain. But the effort had to be made, for life itself was a delicate balance between good and evil, and it required that every man be made to abide by Truth and be subject to lawful authority, that he know his place and mind his duties lest Satan make use of him to cause evil to church and state and arouse the wrath of God against those who tolerated such delinquents. In an era of pietistic ferment the Puritans took a practical view: "While the liquor is boiling it must needs have a scumming." The banishments of Roger Williams, Anne Hutchinson, Robert Childe, and the Quakers are simply the best-known incidents of scumming—the Puritans' attempt to maintain at least outward conformity and uniformity in faith and worship. Their effort was praised by most contemporaries but condemned by their descendants.

What differentiated the Baptists from the other dissenters in Massachusetts was their disorganized and sporadic evolution. Until the First Baptist Church was organized in Charlestown in 1665, they had no leader or spokesman, no coherence or unity of purpose. The history of the movement, if it can be called that, during the first thirty-five years of the colony is a history of scattered individuals maintaining a furtive hole-in-the-corner existence, occasionally bursting out in mild or vigorous dissent only to be summarily dealt with and then lapsing back into obscurity. Those who might have provided leadership (Williams, Clarke, Obadiah Holmes, Henry Dunster) were bludgeoned into silence or exile. Nor did the Baptist movement in England, which had many leaders, send any significant disturbers of the peace to Massachusetts or Connecticut. What force the Baptist persuasion developed in New England in the early years derived largely from internal disagreements among the Puritans themselves.

Although the dynamic personality of Roger Williams seems to have left a decided mark on the inhabitants of Salem and Lynn, which had more than their share of dissenters from 1630 to 1655, antipedobaptist views were not limited to any area. Cases of prosecution that reached the courts occurred in almost a score of towns at one time or another in the seventeenth century, though there appear to have been a few that occurred prior to 1639. William Wickenden and William Wolcott of Salem were accused of antipedobaptist views in 1639; they left that same year for Providence.[14] During the next five years, as the revolution in England loosed a flood of dissent, declared Baptists increased rapidly, first in one place and then another in Massachusetts. But wherever the Baptist movement raised its head, the authorities proceeded vigorously to lop it off.

First the delinquent was presented to the county court by the grand jury for failing to present his child for baptism or for turning his back on God's ordinance; then he was warned or fined by the court (or whipped if he was too truculent in defending his views or too poor to pay his fine). If he persisted, he was again presented, warned, fined, or whipped. Refusal to pay the fine meant imprisonment for an indeterminate period. Meanwhile, if he was a church member, as many of them were, he was warned, censured, and ultimately excommunicated by his church. The prosecution was unrelenting unless the Baptist either left the colony or publicly repented, confessing his sinfulness and humbly asking forgiveness, promising to sin no more. There are records of some individuals in the Middlesex County Court who were brought to trial at least twenty times in as many years for persisting in their Anabaptist views. But the majority of these early Baptists either left the colony very quickly once the authorities hailed them in or else they recanted—at least to the point of conforming and keeping their views to themselves.

There is no doubt that the social persecution by their neighbors and fellow church members was at least as potent a force in their suppression as the punishments meted out by the courts. Throughout the colonial period Baptists were the pariahs of New England society. Known Baptists could not attain the rights of freemen in the seventeenth century; thus, they could not vote or hold office. Their children were the butts of childish malevolence, their sons and daughters were considered unfit for marriage to the orthodox (after a time the Baptists defensively refused to have their children "unequally yoked with unbelievers," thereby making a virtue of necessity). Adults were shut out from the closed circle of social, political, and economic control. Even after 1682, when they dared to build a few meetinghouses, they did so in an outlying corner of their township, far from the Puritan meetinghouse on the village green. Baptists were to the respectable churchgoers of the colonial period what the Mormons and Adventists were to respectable Baptists and Methodists in the nineteenth century and what the Holiness and Pentecostal sects are to respectable Presbyterians and Episcopalians in the twentieth century: eccentric, fanatical, ignorant enthusiasts. Prior to 1682 they were deemed even worse—they were subversives, dangers to civil and political safety, threats to the peace and order of the commonwealth, men whose presence was apt to bring down the vengeance of God upon the community. Denouncing the Baptists as un-American subversives, a convention of Massachusetts ministers told the legislators in 1668, "if once that party becomes numerous and prevailing, this country is undone, the work of reformation ended."[15] As a result, the Baptists pursued such a *sub rosa* existence that it is still difficult to discern their activities. To the descendants of the Puritans who wrote the history books, they were little more than a distasteful footnote.

Among the more notable cases of Anabaptism in the 1640s was that of Lady Deborah Moody, one of the few persons of education and wealth in the colony to take up the persuasion. In 1649 she settled in Salem and was admitted to the church. But in 1642 she came to the conclusion that infant baptism was not justified by Scripture and began to persuade other women in the church not to have their children baptized. After the minister and elder were unable to dissuade her from this error, the church censured her and two of her friends, and she was brought before the quarterly court of sessions in Salem and admonished publicly. She would not give up her views, but not seeing any way to make them prevail, she left for Long Island in 1643, where her wealth and intelligence brought her considerable influence among the more tolerant Dutch. But as the Puritans would have predicted, her Anabaptism eventually carried her into Quakerism.[16]

More typical of the early advocates of antipedobaptism in Massachusetts was Thomas Painter, a poor, stubborn laborer in Hingham. Painter, said John Winthrop, "on the sudden turned anabaptist" in 1644: "having a child born, he would not suffer his wife to bring it to the ordinance of baptism, for she was a member of the church, though he himself was not."[17] Painter was taken to court, where he told the judges he thought infant baptism was "antichristian." The judges, with "much patience," tried to dissuade him from this view, but he persisted. Whereupon "because he was very poor, so as no other but corporal punishment could be fastened upon him—he was ordered to be whipped, but not for his opinion, but for his reproaching the Lord's ordinance, and for his bold and evil behavior both at home and in the Court." Painter soon left the colony for Newport, where he joined John Clarke's church.

Whipping, as Winthrop said, was a last resort with the more obstinate and stubborn fanatics and with those who were so poor that it was impossible to fine or distrain them. The court record for the case of Christopher Goodwine of Charlestown reveals more clearly the type of behavior that warranted whipping. Goodwine,

> being convicted of contempt & violence to ye publ: dispensac[io]n of ye ordinance of Baptisme at Charlestowne, throwing done [down] the Basin of Water in the meeting house & strikeing the constable in ye meeting House & kicking him on ye Lords day & expressing himselfe in Court with High contempt of ye Holy ordinance, justifying himselfe in his former acc[i]ons & highly contemning the Court, is sentenced to pay ten pounds or to be openly whipt 10 stripes.[18]

It is doubtful whether Goodwine had ten pounds in cash or property to pay the fine.

More than once, whole families were brought into court for Anabaptism. Benanual Bowers, his wife, and his son George of Charlestown and Cambridge were among those who refused to be suppressed and yet who would not leave the colony. Between 1655 and 1682 the Bowerses were brought into court at least a dozen times on various charges, including absence from worship, "abetting vagabond quakers," and turning their backs on infant baptism at worship. The Bowerses were poor, vociferous, and irascible. Bowers himself went insane in his old age, but his various petitions to the courts indicate that he was neither ignorant nor stupid. When they were first whipped for their actions is not known, but in 1683 Bowers complained that he and his wife had been whipped several times for their religious views.[19] Bowers's petition to the Court of Assistants in 1673 reveals the extent to which the Massachusetts authorities were prepared to go when faced with a particularly stubborn and outspoken opponent of the system:

> I have been formerly sentenced at Cambridge & Charlestowne Court much after this manner of proceeding five or six times, fined imprisoned and three times whipt privately at the house of correction at Cambr. My hands being put in the irons of the whipping post for the execution, which hard usidge did cause my neighbours hearing it to be so much [disturbed that they] did desire me to let them see the signs of the stripes which I did, at which they were much troubled and grieved for my sore sufferings, and my imprisonment was in ye dead & cold time of the winter and in seed time, and they kept me in prison two weeks, and after that whipt me and sent me [away?] . . . and my maid servant which was hired for one year was forced away from my wife when she had five small children, one of them sucking, and against the maids own will and threatened by Capt. Gookin if she would not go away he would send

her to the house of correction and also my wife have suffered much when I was in prison by coming to me in the extremity of winter having noe maid, being destitute of any assistance or other help, and also my wife have bine forced to come to Court when she had lain in bed but three weakes and condemned for contempt of authority in not coming to Court when she had laine in but three daies and my wife have bine likewise whipt upon the same account or pretense as I have bine and all this hath not satisfied the will and desires of some of my judges but do still continue their cruel proceedings against me mostly every Court still; & magistrate Danforth expressing his fury yet further in open Court against me saying unto me, if I be not hanged he would be hanged for me.[20]

This was probably the most extreme case of Baptist persecution. The extant records indicate that only a few of those prosecuted for Anabaptist views were whipped.[21] Nor were the whippings as vicious as those given to the Quakers in this same period.

The case of William Witter is more typical than those of Painter, Goodwine, or Bowers, though he appears to have been just as contemptuous of authority. Witter, born in 1584, was a farmer who lived in Swampscott and was a member of the Salem church until he was excommunicated for being rebaptized in 1651. He was presented to the county court in Salem in February, 1643/4 "for entertaining that baptism of infants was sinful" and for calling the ordinance "a badge of the whore." The court sentenced him to confess his fault before the church and to apologize to Thomas Cobbett, the minister in Lynn, whose services he had interrupted to make these blasphemous statements. But Witter neither changed his opinion nor confessed his fault. Two years later he was again presented to the court, this time for saying "that they who stayed while a childe was baptised doe worshipp the dyvill." He was again sentenced to make a public confession of his error, and again he refused. In May 1646 he was ordered to appear before the General Court, but he did not. Probably old age and increasing blindness, plus greater reticence, saved him from continuing harassment, for there is no further record of his being prosecuted, though he was censured by the Salem church for his views. At some time between 1646 and 1651 he apparently was immersed and joined the Newport Baptist church. He continued to live in Lynn, however, and evidently the Salem church was not aware of his rebaptism until after he became involved in one of the most celebrated cases of American Baptist martyrology. This occurred in the summer of 1651, when Witter requested the church in Newport to send some brethren to visit him in Lynn, presumably because he had some friends who wished to be immersed.[22]

John Clarke knew that he was courting trouble when he acted on
Witter's request, but he and his church believed that God had called them
to make this trip into the Puritan citadel and to bear witness for the Baptist
persuasion. Perhaps he was deliberately testing the authorities. On Saturday, July 19, 1651, Clarke and two leading members of his church,
Obadiah Holmes and John Crandall, arrived at Witter's home late at night.
The next morning they held a private religious service there that was
attended by several of Witter's friends. Apparently, the Rhode Islanders
had planned to attend the services at Thomas Cobbett's church in Lynn
and there make a more public witness against infant baptism, but, said
Clarke, we did not have "freedom in our Spirits for want of a clear Call
from God to goe into the Publike Assemblie to declare there what was the
mind and counsell of God concerning them."[23]

Almost at once, knowledge of the invasion from Rhode Island reached
the local magistrate, Robert Bridges, and during the service in Witter's
home two constables arrived to arrest the three visitors. That afternoon the
constables compelled the visitors to attend the service at the church in
Lynn. When they walked in, Clarke and Holmes refused to remove their
hats, which were "plucked off" by the constable. After the sermon Clarke
stood up to rebuke the Puritan churches publicly, saying that they were
not instituted "according to the visible order of our Lord" because they
were based on infant baptism. The next day, having somehow escaped the
surveillance of the constables, the three men conducted another service at
Witter's home at which Holmes administered the Lord's Supper and
baptized two or three persons, including Mrs. William Bowditch (Bowdish), a member of the Salem church.[24]

On Tuesday, July 22, the three Rhode Islanders were taken to Boston
and imprisoned. A week later they were tried by Governor John Endecott
and the Council with several ministers in attendance (one of whom, John
Wilson, angrily struck Holmes). They were found guilty of holding a
private meeting on the Lord's Day, showing disrespect to God's ordinance
by keeping their hats on in church, disturbing the congregation during
worship, denouncing the basis of church organization, administering the
Lord's Supper to persons not entitled to it, rebaptizing persons, and
denying in court the lawfulness of baptizing infants. "All of this," said the
court, "tends to the dishonour of God, the despising of the ordinances of
God among us, the peace of the Churches, and seducing the subjects of
this Commonwealth from the truth of the Gospel of Jesus Christ, and
perverting the strait waies of the Lord."[25]

Holmes was sentenced to pay a fine of thirty pounds; Clarke, twenty;

and Crandall, five, "or else to be well whipt." They were to remain in prison until the fines were paid or the whipping executed. The three men refused to pay their fines, but some friends paid Clarke's, and Crandall was released after he paid bail. Holmes persuaded his friend that he would be offended if they paid so unjust a fine for him.[26] Clarke and Crandall returned to Rhode Island. Holmes remained in prison until September, when the court decided that he should receive thirty lashes with a three-corded whip. The sentence was executed, the executioner "spitting on his hand three times" to get a good grip on the whip.[27] Holmes said that God sustained him through the ordeal: "You have struck me as with roses." The bloody public spectacle aroused the sympathy of several bystanders who offered afterward to assist Holmes. Two, known to be Baptists, shook his hand saying, "Blessed be the Lord"; they were fined and imprisoned for implicit contempt of the justice of the sentence.[28]

This incident received wide notoriety when John Clarke published a detailed account of it in London a year later under the title *Ill-Newes from New England* in which he tried, unsuccessfully, to persuade Parliament to force a policy of toleration on New England. It was the last time Baptists from Rhode Island invaded Massachusetts to immerse converts; the movement continued to lack organization and leaders for another fifteen years.

Still the incidence of Baptist tendencies increased. The most significant involved Henry Dunster in 1654. Dunster's case had far more serious implications for the Massachusetts ministers and magistrates than the invasion from Rhode Island. When the president of Harvard College, a graduate of Cambridge University, refused to have his child baptized and publicly stated his disbelief in the ordinance, it was no longer possible for the Puritans to argue that antipedobaptism was simply a fanatical delusion held only by ignorant enthusiasts. Nor was it possible to treat Dunster with the same summary justice given to less important men. The shock to the community called for more extraordinary action.

Jonathan Mitchell, the pastor of the Cambridge church, first tried to persuade President Dunster of his error. But the learned Dunster almost succeeded in shaking his young pastor's faith. The General Court then instructed nine ministers and two ruling elders to meet with Dunster in Boston to try by private conference and debate to correct him. Dunster wrote an account of this futile two-day discussion in which he defended himself by insisting that "all instituted Gospel Worship hath some express word of Scripture. But pedobaptism hath none."[29] Nor did Dunster find any precedent for it in the practice of the primitive church: "John the

Baptist, Christ himself, & [the] Apostles did none of them baptize children." The crux of the matter to Dunster was the *"Soli visibiliter fideles sunt baptizandi,"* and since infants were not, in his view, "visible believers," they should not be baptized.

Since the conference proved fruitless, the General Court in May 1654 passed a law requiring that all teachers at Harvard or in the public schools who were "unsound in the faith" should be relieved of their offices. Dunster compounded his crime by openly stating his views during a baptismal service at the Cambridge church on July 30, 1654. For this he was sentenced to receive a public admonition by one of the magistrates on a lecture day in the Cambridge church, to which he submitted. Not only was he also required to give bond for his future good behavior, but his resignation from Harvard was demanded; it took effect in October of the same year.

Dunster evidently recognized the consequences it would have for the colony if he were to assume leadership of the Baptist movement; he chose instead to view the dispute as a private matter of conscience. Unlike Roger Williams and Anne Hutchinson, he saw no need to conduct an ecclesiastical revolt. Consequently, he held his peace, and in March 1655 he left Massachusetts Bay for the more tolerant atmosphere of Plymouth Colony, where he spent the remaining four years of his life. He seems to have preached occasionally to some members of the Standing church in Scituate, though he was never ordained over them. His preaching evidently did not touch on the controversial aspects of the Baptist persuasion, which even the Plymouth authorities would not have permitted. Nor did he leave any known Baptist followers behind in Scituate at his death. But he did express his distaste for the persecution of the Quakers.[30]

Dunster's significance for the Baptist movement was considerably diminished by his failure to seek rebaptism for himself. He neither advocated his antipedobaptist views in print nor attacked the tolerance of the Massachusetts system. He was not excommunicated from the Cambridge church, and he continued to own property in Cambridge. His desire to be buried in the Cambridge burial ground was granted. Like many Congregationalists in England at this time, he may have approved open or mixed communion between pedo- and antipedobaptists, but he never said so. By holding his peace he probably proved an embarrassment rather than a help to the Baptists, for he gave truth to the Puritan claim that uniformity and conformity were not insisted upon by them so long as dissenting opinions were "not vented." According to Cotton Mather,

Dunster "died in harmony of affection with the good men who had been the authors of his removal from Cambridge."

The failure of Dunster, Holmes, Clarke, Williams, Witter, Painter, Bowers, Lady Deborah, and many others to advance either the organization of Baptist churches or the toleration of Baptist views within Massachusetts Bay indicated the coherent strength of the Puritan community and its conviction that "he that corrupteth a soule with a corrupt religion, layeth a spreading leaven which corrupteth the state."[31] Nothing reveals more clearly the radical danger that the Puritans sensed in these sporadic Baptist outbursts than the laws they wrote to eradicate them. When the first Baptists appeared in the colony in the 1630s and early 1640s, they were tried under the existing general laws requiring civil order, subjection to authority, and preservation of the churches. Under these laws many Puritan deviants or malcontents were also tried for one reason or another: failure to attend church, contempt of religious authority, reading heretical books. But when, as Winthrop noted in 1644, "Anabaptistry increased and spread in the country" and when Baptist tracts and sermons began to arrive in large numbers from England, the Puritans recognized the beginnings of a distinct new movement in their midst. And so, in November 1644, the General Court passed the following act to name, define, and stamp out this heresy:

> Forasmuch as experience hath plentifully and often proved that since the first arising of the Anabaptists about a hundred years since they have been the incendiaries of the commonwealths and the infectors of persons in main matters of religion and the troublers of churches in all places where they have been, and that they who have held the baptizing of infants unlawful have usually held other errors or heresies together therewith though they have (as hereticks use to do) concealed the same till they spied out a fit advantage and opportunity to vent them, by way of question or scruple; and whereas divers of this kind have since our coming into New England appeared amongst ourselves, some whereof (as others before them) denied the ordinance of magistracy, and the lawfulness of making warr, and others the lawfulness of magistrates, and their inspection into any breach of the first tables; which opinions, if they should be connived at by us, are like to be increased among us, and so must necessarily bring guilt upon us, infection and trouble to the churches, and hazard to the whole commonwealth; it is ordered and agreed that if any person or persons within this jurisdiction shall either openly condemne or oppose the baptizing of infants or go about secretly to seduce others from the approbation or use thereof, or shall purposely depart the congregation at the ministration of the ordinance or shall deny the ordinance of magistracy or their lawful right and authority to make

warr or to punish the outward breaches of the first table, and shall appear
to the Court willfully and obstinately to continue therein after due time
and means of conviction, every such person or persons shall be sentenced to banishment.[32]

There is no record that any of the early Baptists in Massachusetts
opposed the lawfulness of making war or the lawfulness of magistrates or
even the enforcement of the first table by the civil authorities, but there
were some in old England and a few in Rhode Island who did so. The
concept of toleration, however, was implicit in the Baptists' requests to be
indulged or connived at.

In addition to this law to protect the civil peace by banishing antipedobaptists, another law was passed in 1646 to maintain the dignity of the
ministers and the good order of the churches by punishing those who
turned their backs on infant baptism or who walked out of the churches or
stood up to speak against the ordinance when it was performed. Though
it did not specifically mention Anabaptists, it had them clearly in mind.
By this law, anyone who

> shall contemptuously behave himself toward ye word preached or ye
> messengers thereof . . . either by interrupting him in his preaching or by
> charging him falsely with error . . . or like a sonn of Corah, cast upon
> his true doctrine or himselfe any reproach . . . and making God's wayes
> contemptible and ridiculous . . . shall for the first scandall be convented
> and reproved openly by ye magistrates at some lecture and be bound to
> their good behavior [and for the second offense pay a fine of five
> pounds] stand two howres openly upon a block for foote high on a
> lecture day with a paper fixed on his breast with this: A WANTON
> GOSPELLER, written in capitall latters.[33]

Thus, social opprobrium and humiliation were added to the more drastic
law of banishment.

The existence of open dissent constituted an affront to the uniformity
and conformity of the Standing Order even though it was not until 1648
that the doctrines and practices of that order were codified in the Cambridge Platform. The need to codify their own position, like the need to
define the position of the dissenters, is indicative of an increasing formal-
ism in Puritan New England. A consensus could no longer be taken for
granted. Yet the mere act of defining the Baptists as a distinct group
(however unfairly or inaccurately) undoubtedly served to give coherence
to a formless malaise among certain pietistic colonists who had previously
considered themselves part of the community. Even to deny that to be an
antipedobaptist was also to be a pacifist or an opponent of magistracy

helped to give these nonconformists a new coherence. As the frontier community codified its own beliefs and structure, so it simultaneously formalized dissent. Massachusetts was forced to profess and develop a homogeneity it had assumed but had not possessed. The spontaneity of the new reformation was slowly congealing in New England, and it continued to do so through the ensuing century.

Notes

1. Elder William Brewster of Plymouth predicted of Roger Williams in 1633 (two years before he was banished from Massachusetts and six years before he temporarily adopted Baptist views) that "he would run the same course of rigid separatism and Anabaptistry which Mr. John Smith the Sebaptist of Amsterdam had done." Nathaniel Morton, *New England's Memorial* (Cambridge, Mass., 1669), p. 78. Geoffrey Nuttall (*Visible Saints* [Oxford, 1957]) quotes Francis Cheynell on the loose use of the term *Anabaptist* in 1643: "Every man is now counted an Anabaptist if he does not maintain Monarchy to be *iure Divino*" (p. 2).

2. John Cotton and Cotton Mather both claimed to know persons who held Anabaptist views in the colony during its early years but who were tolerated because they did not openly express them. The Cambridge Platform specifically forbade the magistrates from punishing "erroneous opinions not vented."

3. The origins of these churches are discussed below. The best history of the Baptist movement in New England is Isaac Backus, *History of New England.* It was originally published in three volumes between 1777 and 1795; however, I have cited throughout the more useful two-volume edition edited by David Weston and published by the Backus Historical Society, Newton, Mass., 1871. Some accounts list the Rogerenes of New London, Connecticut, among the early Baptists because they originated in 1674-1675 as a branch of the Seventh Day Baptist Church in Newport. But by 1685 this eccentric group had "declined into Quakerism" and was excluded from fellowship by the Baptists. See John R. Bolles and Anna B. Williams, *The Rogerenes* (Boston, 1904) and chapter 15 in this volume [*Soul Liberty*].

4. Mrs. Scott, who, like many of the other Hutchinsonians "declined" into Quakerism, was whipped in Boston in 1658 when she returned there to express her new views (Joseph B. Felt, *The Ecclesiastical History of New England* [Boston, 1862], 2:202).

5. In 1649 Williams stated of the Baptists, "I believe their practice comes nearer the first practice of our great Founder Christ then other practices of religion doe, & yet I have no satisfaction neither in the authorities by which it (baptism) is done nor in the manner [immersion]; nor in the prophecies concerning the rising of Christ's Kingdome after the desolation of Rome &c" (Letter to John Winthrop, Jr., 9 December 1649, in Massachusetts Historical Society, Collections, 4th ser., 6 [1863]: 274). Williams's views are discussed more fully below [in source volume, *Soul Liberty*].

6. For John Clarke, see Thomas W. Bicknell, *The Story of John Clarke* (Providence, 1915); John Callendar, *An Historical Discourse . . .* (Boston, 1739), pp. 27, 63ff.; Clarke's autobiographical remarks in *Ill-Newes from New England* (London, 1652); Backus, *History,* 1:77-78, 97; and I. E. Richman, *Rhode Island* (New York, 1902), 1, chapter 4.

7. Lukar split off from Henry Jacob's Non-Separatist Congregational Church in

London in 1633 and joined John Spilsbury's Separatist group. In 1641 he was rebaptized by immersion along with Spilsbury and others. Shortly after that he went to Rhode Island, where he joined Clarke's church and became a ruling elder in it. He died in 1676 (A. H. Newman, *A History of the Baptist Churches in the United States* [New York, 1894], p. 50). John Winthrop states that as early as the summer of 1641 some of Anne Hutchinson's followers "turned professed Anabaptists," but his description of them indicates that they were not the predecessors of Clarke's group. See his *History of New England*, ed. James Savage (Boston, 1828), 2:38. Unfortunately, there are no extant records for either the Providence or the Newport Baptist churches in the seventeenth century, and what little is known of them comes from indirect sources, many of them hostile.

8. For the best discussions of the Puritan theory of church and state, see George L. Haskins, *Law and Authority in Early Massachusetts* (New York, 1960) and E. S. Morgan, *The Puritan Dilemma* (Boston, 1958). Cotton's remark is quoted in Perry Miller, *Orthodoxy in Massachusetts* (Cambridge, Mass., 1933), p. 240.

9. Thomas Cobbett, *The Civil Magistrates Power in Matter of Religion . . . Together with a Brief Answer to a Certain Slanderous Pamphlet Called 'Ill-Newes from New England'* (London, 1653), p. 34.

10. In Samuel Willard, *Ne Sutor Ultra Crepidam* (Boston, 1681), Preface.

11. C. M. Andrews, *The Colonial Period in American History* (New Haven, Conn., 1934), 1:450, n. 1. In the Body of Liberties adopted by the General Court in 1641, section 95 was devoted to "the Liberties the Lord Jesus hath given to the churches," and the fifth among these indicates clearly the anti-Erastianism of the New England Puritans: "No injunctions are to be put upon any Church, Church officers or members in point of Doctrine, worship or Discipline whether for substance or circumstance besides the Institutions of the Lord" (W. W. Whitmore, ed., *The Colonial Laws of Massachusetts Reprinted from the Edition of 1660* [Boston, 1889], p. 57).

12. Williston Walker, *The Creeds and Platforms of Congregationalism* (New York, 1893), p. 237.

13. Walker, *Creeds and Platforms*, p. 237.

14. Backus, History, 1:88; Felt, *Ecclesiastical History,* 1:403-4. In 1772, Elder John Davids, pastor of the Second Baptist Church in Boston, tried to discover who was the first Baptist in Massachusetts. In a letter to Isaac Backus, August 3, 1772, Davis claimed that Seth Sweetser of Charlestown deserved that title. According to Davis, Sweetser and his family came from Tring, in Hartford, England, in 1638. Because of his Baptist views he was denied the right of inhabitant and could not share in the common land, yet he was required to pay taxes for the support of the Congregational ministers in Charlestown. His son, Benjamin Sweetser, became an early member of Thomas Goold's Baptist church in Boston. Davis's letter is among the Backus Papers, Andover Newton Theological School, Newton Center, Mass.

15. Felt, *Ecclesiastical History,* 2:427.

16. Winthrop, *History*, pp. 123, 136. "Many others infected with anabaptism removed there also," Winthrop adds. See also Backus, *History,* 1:486; Alonzo Lewis and J. R. Newhall, *History of Lynn* (Boston, 1865), p. 187; George E. Ellis, *The Puritan Age* (Boston, 1888), p. 381.

17. Winthrop, *History,* 2:174-75. Winthrop also noted under this entry, July 5, 1644, that it was at this time that "Anabaptistry increased and spread in the country which occasioned the magistrates, at the last court, to draw up an order for banishment such as continued obstinate after due conviction."

18. See David Pulsifer's transcript of the Middlesex County Court Records, 1:232,

287, in the Middlesex County Court House, Cambridge, Mass. Hereafter referred to as Pulsifer Transcript.

19. Ibid. 1:301, 3:205; Nathan E. Wood, *The History of the First Baptist Church of Boston* (Philadelphia, 1899), p. 113. See the loose files of the Middlesex County Court in the courthouse under dates April 6, 1666; October 3, 1663; April 5, 1681; 1(2) 1655; April 6, 1693. Bowers appears to have held Quaker views in 1661, but in 1666 and thereafter he attended the Baptist Church in Charlestown, though he is not recorded in its records as a member. It is not clear why he was never banished.

20. Wood, *History,* pp. 113-14. See also Bowers's petition of April 5, 1681, in the loose files of the Middlesex County Court.

21. One of the few other cases of whipping involved William Baker, first mate of a London ship, who was whipped in Cambridge in 1657; see Backus, *History*, 1:400; and Jonathan Sprague, *The Answer of Jonathan Sprague to a Scandalous Libel . . .* (Providence, January 24, 1722/23), a broadside in vol. 155, p. 3 of the Providence Town Papers, Rhode Island Historical Society.

22. For Witter's arraignments, see Felt, *Ecclesiastical History,* 1:482, 568; Ellis, *Puritan Age,* pp. 381-82; and Lewis and Newall, *Lynn,* p. 231. For his excommunication on July 24, 1651, see Felt, *Ecclesiastical History,* 2:46. Isaac Backus is the authority for the fact that he was "a brother of the church" in Newport before the summer of 1651 (*History,* 1:178), although the Newport church records that Backus cites are now lost. It is possible that he was not yet a member when he requested a visit from the Newport church and that he was asking to be immersed in order to join the church at that time. Although those who visited him in July, 1651, did perform some baptisms at his home, it is not clear whether Witter's was one of them, and all contemporary accounts are obscure on this point.

23. For Clarke's version of this incident, which seems reliable, see his *Ill-Newes from New England* (London, 1652); for the Puritan side of the story, see Cobbett, *Civil Magistrates.* John Gorham Palfrey, the nineteenth-century historian of New England, claimed that Clarke had ulterior political motives in staging this invasion of Massachusetts at that particular moment. For an examination and refutation of Palfrey's claim, see H. J. King, *A Summer Visit of Three Rhode Islanders to the Massachusetts Bay in 1651* (Providence, 1896).

24. There is no way to clear up the confusion regarding the precise sequence of events. Clarke states in his account that after being apprehended on Sunday they were watched by constables overnight "as theeves and robbers" and the next day were arraigned and taken to jail in Boston. But the date of the order committing them to jail is Tuesday, June 22. Moreover, the sentence of the court states that "upon the day following" their arrest, "being then in the custody of the law," they did "meet again at the said William Witters . . . and did there receive the Sacrament" and "Baptize such as were Baptized before." See also Cobbett, *Civil Magistrates,* p. 39. Obadiah Holmes, in his account of the incident in Clarke's tract, admits to having baptized "Goodwife Bowdish" and defends himself against the charge that he baptized her naked—a common canard against the Baptists. Mrs. Bowditch had been presented to the county court for Baptist views in 1646. Felt, *Ecclesiastical History,* 1:576. In November 1651 Witter was brought before the Salem County Court on charges of denying infant baptism and "being re-baptized" (H. L. Osgood, *The American Colonies in the Seventeenth Century* [New York, 1904], 1:266).

25. Clarke, *Ill-Newes,* pp. 5-6.

26. As in most of the details, there is confusion over the payment of these fines. Clarke says that he did not want anyone to pay his fine, but the court accepted the

money tendered for him despite his wishes. Why the court would not accept the fine money offered by Holmes's friends is also unclear. Clarke's account says that Crandall's jailer later had to pay his fine. Other accounts say that Crandall's fine was paid for him over his objection at the time he was released. Undoubtedly, the authorities wanted to make an example of someone and Holmes was the most likely candidate.

27. Clarke, *Ill-Newes,* p. 122.

28. Ibid., p. 22; Backus, *History,* 1:184ff. The two men involved, John Spur of Salem and John Hazel of Rehoboth, had both been admitted as freemen in Boston in the 1630s and had been admonished before the courts for openly venting their Baptist views in the 1640s (Backus, *History,* 1:195, n.2). Spur was excommunicated from the Salem church for antipedobaptism on July 13, 1651 (Felt, *Ecclesiastical History,* 2:46).

29. For an account of this debate and selections from it, see Jeremiah Chaplin, *Life of Henry Dunster* (Boston, 1872), pp. 122-31. See also *Pulsifer Transcript,* 1:74-75, 132.

30. There has been considerable debate among historians as to whether Dunster actually preached to a group of antipedobaptists in Scituate—perhaps they were some whom Charles Chauncy had indoctrinated with the necessity for baptism by immersion. There is no concrete evidence for this, and it appears more likely that on occasion he preached before perfectly orthodox members of the regular Congregational church there.

31. John Cotton, *The Bloudy Tenent Washed and Made White in the Bloud of the Lambe . . .* (London, 1647), p. 64.

32. This law is quoted in Backus, *History,* 1:126. In the revised edition of the General Laws published in 1660 this law was combined with a law of 1646 against heresy; see Whitmore, *Colonial Laws of Massachusetts,* p. 154. It should be noted that John Winthrop was not enthusiastic about this law (probably because it made Massachusetts seem too intolerant in the eyes of many friends in England). He appears to have favored a petition asking for its repeal, which was sent to the legislature in October 1645. That the Commissioners for Plantations had ordered toleration in the West Indies and Bermuda that year and had advised New England to follow suit may also have encouraged this petition. However, the following year an even stronger petition called for strengthening the law, and the legislature decided to let it stand unchanged. See Winthrop, *History,* 2:250-51; Ellis, *Puritan Age,* p. 386; Morgan, *Puritan Dilemma,* p. 188; Backus, *History,* 1:145.

33. This law is quoted in David B. Ford, *New England's Struggles for Religious Liberty* (Philadelphia, 1896), pp. 34-35; it was slightly revised in the book of General Laws in 1660. See Whitmore, *Colonial Laws of Massachusetts,* p. 148.

The Black Baptists:
The First Black Churches in America

C. Eric Lincoln and Lawrence H. Mamiya

The cultural origins of the black Baptists are to be found in the South rather than the North as was the case with the founding of the mother congregations of the African Methodist Church and the African Methodist Zion Churches in the mid-1790s. This basic difference still holds true for the black Baptists—even though they now dominate the urban scene. Regardless of this preponderance, these churches are still characterized by a distinct Southern religious milieu which stresses enthusiastic and demonstrative worship. *

Overview

The first independent black Baptist congregations were organized in the last half of the eighteenth century, at a time when the American colonies and black Methodists alike were issuing their respective declarations of independence. The black Baptists were pursuing no overt political revolts but rather were struggling to carve out a religious space in the midst of the southern plantations that defined their lives as slaves. During the antebellum period, however, fugitive slaves and free Blacks in the

C. Eric Lincoln is Professor of Religion and Culture at Duke University and is the author of numerous books, including *The Black Muslims in America, The Black Church Since Frazier*, a book of poetry, and an award-winning novel. He is also the editor of the C. Eric Lincoln Series in Black Religion. Lawrence H. Mamiya, Mattie M. Paschall Davis Professor of Religion and African Studies at Vassar College, has published widely in the sociology of religion and African American religious studies. This chapter is from Lincoln and Mamiya's book *The Black Church in the African American Experience* (Durham: Duke University Press, 1990), pages 20–46, and is reprinted with permission.

*James M. Washington, *The Origins and Emergence of Black Baptist Separatism, 1863-1897* (Ann Arbor, Mich.: University Microfilms, 1983), 257.

North did form abolitionist missionary associations and societies, the leaders of which then organized the first regional black Baptist conventions. Many of the participants in these associations and conventions were for a long time simultaneously involved in white Baptist organizations. Miles Mark Fisher reports that:

> After Nat Turner's insurrection in 1831 one must define anew a Negro Baptist church. That movement sent hot hate back and wide consternation all over the Southland. Generally, what independence Negro churches had enjoyed was taken away. A revised black code was enacted . . . silencing . . . colored preachers. A [white] church . . . [and] association . . . would take a Negro church as a branch; and thus the independence of the Negro church was further postponed. . . .[1]

Early in the Reconstruction era, however, an emergent ideology of separatism gave impetus to the organizing of a national black convention.[2] While this first national organization lasted but a dozen years, it established a critical precedent for subsequent efforts.

Today there are eight identifiable black Baptist communions in the United States, the largest ones being the National Baptist Convention, U.S.A., Inc.; the National Baptist Convention of America; and the Progressive National Baptist Convention, Inc. These three conventions, along with the Lott Carey Baptist Foreign Mission Convention share a common ancestry and are the principal focus of Baptist development. Of the remaining four, the largest is the National Primitive Baptist Convention, U.S.A., which originally withdrew from the white Primitive Baptists in 1865 and organized formally in 1907. The National Primitive Baptists have an estimated 250,000 members. The United Free Will Baptist Church began in 1870, but did not formally organize as a denomination until 1901. It has an estimated membership of 100,000.

The National Baptist Evangelical Life and Soul Saving Assembly of the U.S.A., a group originally formed in 1920 as part of the National Baptist Convention of America and becoming independent in 1937, has some 50,000 members. The Free For All Missionary Baptist Church, Inc., formed in 1955, has perhaps 10,000 members. In addition to the predominantly black groups, at least 75,000 blacks belong to the Southern Baptist Convention, and at least 150,000 to the American Baptist Churches in the U.S.A.[3] The American Baptist Churches of the South, an initially integrated but now predominantly black regional unit of the ABC, organized in the early 1970s.

Emergence of Black Baptists

The formal Baptist movement, like the Methodist, has its origins in England, although the Baptists antedate the Methodists by a century. The first Baptists evolved from a group of Puritans compelled to take refuge in Holland as a result of persecution in their homeland. While in Holland, these Separatist Puritans became persuaded that only baptism of adult believers and baptism by immersion were doctrinally correct. They also came in contact with Anabaptists, the radical wing of the Protestant Reformation who, among other convictions, gave primacy to the separation of church and state. In this milieu the exiles established the first English Baptist church in 1609. Upon their return to England, members of this group organized a Baptist church in London around 1612. This was followed by a second church in 1616, which split over doctrinal differences in 1638. The resultant new church in turn split in 1641, giving rise to a third variation of the proliferating Baptist movement.

The American Baptist movement emerged in the colonies during the same period as the movement in England, and is generally dated from the arrival in America of Puritan Roger Williams in 1631. Exiled from the Massachusetts Bay Colony because of his fierce opposition to the intermingling of church and state interests, Williams obtained a charter from the British monarch to establish the Rhode Island colony, and the first Baptist Church in America was established by Williams in Providence in 1639. A second church was organized by John Clarke in Newport, Rhode Island, in 1641. A few congregations were subsequently established in Massachusetts, but the inhospitable reception there caused Rhode Island to develop as the Baptist stronghold. Throughout the seventeenth century the Rhode Island churches were typically known as "General" Baptists, a reference to their Arminian inclinations.[4] In 1670 these congregations organized the first Baptist association, but thereafter gradually declined.

In the eighteenth century the orientation of the Baptist churches in Rhode Island and throughout the Middle Colonies became more rigorously Calvinistic in contrast to the earlier General churches. These new churches were known as "Particular" Baptists, and by 1707 five such churches in New Jersey, Pennsylvania, and Delaware united in the formation of the Philadelphia Baptist Association. By 1767 associations had also been organized in New England, Virginia, and the Carolinas. This growth in the Baptist movement was attributable in part to the mission work of the Philadelphia Association, but even more to the impact of the Great Awakening which made large numbers of people receptive to the Baptist appeal. At the same time, however, the Awakening led to a division of

Baptists into two distinct groups. The "New Light" or Separate Baptists, initially concentrated in New England, became even more extreme in their Calvinistic emphases and the intensely emotional tactics of revivalism. The "Old Light" or Regular Baptists, consisting largely of the Philadelphia Association, were more moderate in their doctrinal requirements and more traditional and decorous in their rituals of worship.

Before the end of the century Old Lights and New Lights had set aside their differences in the interests of cooperative mission efforts, and by 1800 some twelve hundred churches were organized in nearly fifty local associations. The first step toward denominational structure was taken in 1814 with the formation of the General Missionary Convention of the Baptist Denomination in the United States of America for Foreign Missions. This fellowship subsequently was known as the American Baptist Missionary Union, and was joined by two complementary organizations, the American Baptist Home Mission Society, and the American Baptist Publication Society. But long before this degree of unity and organization was achieved, both the New Light and the Old Light Baptists had extended their missionary efforts to southern states where slaves attending revival services were introduced to evangelical Christianity.

The first known black Baptist, identified only as Quassey, was listed as one of fifty-one members of the Newton, Rhode Island, church in 1743. The Providence, Rhode Island, Baptist Church had nineteen black members in 1762, and blacks were first received into membership in the First Baptist Church of Boston in 1772. But by far the preponderance of black Baptists were in the South.

The National Baptists

The ancestry of the National Baptist Convention reaches back to the first known black churches in America, generally acknowledged to have been the African Baptist or "Bluestone" Church on the William Byrd plantation near the Bluestone River in Mecklenberg, Virginia, in 1758, and the Silver Bluff Baptist Church, located on the South Carolina bank of the Savannah River not far from Augusta, Georgia.[5] Although historical records indicate that the Silver Bluff Church was established by a slave named George Liele sometime between 1773 and 1775, the cornerstone of the present church building claims a founding date of 1750.[6] Like many other slaves, Liele embraced Christianity during the evangelistic revivals that followed the Great Awakening. He was subsequently licensed as an exhorter to perform mission work among other slaves on neighboring plantations, which included the Galphin plantation and trading post at Silver Bluff. The church was short-lived, as a consequence of conflicts associated with the Revolutionary War. After being freed by his master, however, Liele went to Savannah where he preached for some time. He emigrated to Jamaica in 1782 or 1783, leaving behind him a baptized group of slaves, among whom was Andrew Bryan who organized the First African Church of Savannah around 1788. Bryan was assisted by another slave, Jesse Peters (also called Jesse Galphin), who was previously a member of the Silver Bluff Church and had become a preacher as a result of Liele's work. Peters became the pastor of the Springfield Baptist Church of Augusta, Georgia, which was organized around 1787.[7]

As these early churches grew and multiplied in the Savannah area, other independent black churches were established in cities such as Williamsburg, Richmond, and Petersburg, where there were greater numbers of blacks and proportionately more free blacks. Two black ministers, Josiah Bishop at Portsmouth and William Lemon at Gloucester, are known to have pastored white Baptist churches in Virginia. Nor was it uncommon for black churches to have white pastors. Robert Ryland was the white pastor of the First African Church of Richmond for twenty-five years.[8] Baptist churches were also established early in North Carolina and South Carolina. At the turn of the century the number of black Baptists was estimated to be in excess of 25,000.

The degree of independence diminished, however, as the number of slave members increased despite the strict regulations requiring that they have written permission to leave the plantations for worship. Many of the slaves were permitted to attend only the white churches of their masters or black churches pastored by white clergymen. Very often the slave members of nominally white churches outnumbered the white membership. In 1846 a church in Georgetown, South Carolina, had thirty-three white members compared to 798 black, while a church in Natchez, Mississippi, had sixty-two white members and 380 black.

Many slaves were obliged to worship clandestinely in hidden enclaves on the plantations as units of what came to be called the "invisible institution." But even when secrecy was not mandated, under no circumstances were the scattered independent churches allowed to develop formal black associations, though some of them did seek to join with existing white Baptist organizations. Miles Mark Fisher has summarized the situation with sensitivity when he observes that:

A Negro Baptist church was somewhat independent in the North, although associations like those in Philadelphia and New York could appoint preachers for Negro churches. In the South a large congregation of colored people could lay no claim to sovereignty apart from the white people. This point is illustrated in the First African Baptist Church, Savannah, whose membership of seven hundred was divided into three churches by the Savannah Association in 1802. . . . Only after emancipation can complete autonomy be called a distinguishing mark of a Negro Baptist Church.[9]

As the spirit of the Revolutionary era waned and tensions were aggravated by incidents such as the planned slave uprising by Gabriel Prosser in 1800, the Denmark Vesey revolt of 1822, and the Nat Turner rebellion of 1831, increasingly severe restrictions were imposed on religious activities until "independent" became a misnomer where southern black congregations were concerned. The status of blacks grew even more tenuous when the Baptists split in 1845 over the issue of slavery. Nevertheless, the number of black Baptists continued to grow, reaching 150,000 by 1850, and nearly 500,000 by 1870 as independent churches proliferated with the demise of slavery.

In the early nineteenth century organized black Baptist activity became a distinguishing feature of the northern churches. In northern states, as in the South, the move toward racially separate churches was not a matter of doctrinal disagreement, but a protest against unequal and restrictive treatment. Out of this interest emerged such historic institutions as the Joy Street Church in Boston, originally organized as the African Baptist Church by Thomas Paul in 1805; the Abyssinian Baptist Church, also founded by Thomas Paul, in 1808; and the First African Baptist Church in Philadelphia, organized by Henry Cunningham in 1809.

The separation of northern black Baptists from white churches was made easier by the nature of Baptist polity. In contrast to the elaborate connectional structure of the Methodists, the hallmark of Baptist polity is the absolute independence of each local church. A group of churches may join together in an "association," that is, a cluster of congregations within a given geographical area which may encompass several towns or counties, or only a portion of one city. Similarly, states with a substantial Baptist population invariably have one or more "state conventions." But the affiliation of a given local church with larger organizations is strictly voluntary and may be terminated at any time on the vote of the local congregation. Similarly, it is the prerogative of a state convention to affiliate or not with one of the national conventions. Furthermore, a local church may vote to affiliate directly with one or more of the national conventions, completely bypassing the state structure. So jealous are local churches of their independent status that many Baptists take exception to the very use of the word denomination in describing their loose-knit structures. This sensitivity has historically been in tension, however, with the struggles of black Baptists to create and maintain regional and national organizations.

While the departure of black Baptists from white churches in the late eighteenth and early nineteenth century was easier than for the black Methodists, the formation of a national denomination was more difficult. Indeed, that effort preoccupied the better part of a century. From 1815 to 1880, many black Baptists worked through existing national white Baptist organizations via the African Baptist Missionary Society. The ABMS was first under the auspices of the American Baptist Union. After the 1845 division of the white Baptists over slavery, the Society became associated with the Southern Baptist Convention. The primary objective of the African Baptist Missionary Society was mission work in Africa, and the best known of its representatives was Lott Carey, one of its founders who established the First Baptist Church in Monrovia, Liberia, in 1821.

The earliest all-black Baptist associations were organized not in the South, but in the "West": Providence Association in Ohio in 1834; Union Association, also in Ohio, 1836; Wood River Association in Illinois in 1839; and Amherstburg Association in Canada and Michigan in 1841. In contrast to the white associations, the black groups generally assumed a strong abolitionist posture, and many of their members were active in the Underground Railroad in Ohio and Canada. In 1844 the Wood River Association organized the Colored Baptist Home Missionary Society, whose efforts resulted in the formation of the Western Colored Baptist Convention. The WCBC was an expanded association with representatives from seven states, and it endured from 1853 to 1859. In 1864 this effort was revitalized by the Wood River Association with leadership assistance from the other three associations. Out of this relationship emerged a regional grouping known as the Northwestern and Southern Baptist Convention, with representatives from eight states.

The Northwestern and Southern Baptist Convention was actually the second regional convention to be formed. The first, the American Baptist Missionary Convention, had been organized fully two decades before emancipation at the Abyssinian Baptist Church in New York City in 1840, for purposes of evangelization, education, and general racial uplift. This convention was restricted in its activities to the New England and Middle Atlantic areas until after the Civil War, when it sent black ministers to the South as missionaries.

In 1866 in a meeting of the Plan of Union Committees held in Richmond, these two regional conventions merged in what was the first attempt to create a national convention. The Consolidated American Baptist Missionary Convention, as it was called, held its first official meeting in August 1867 in Nashville, and in 1868 reported a constituency of 100,000 black Baptists, with 200 ministers. The Consolidated Convention, consisting of six subdivisions called district conventions, lasted for twelve years. It held its final meeting in 1879, by which time it was already fragmenting into separate regional conventions.

Partly as a result of heightened race consciousness, partly in reaction to the discrimination of southern white Baptists and the paternalism of northern white Baptists, the independent church movement initiated among black Baptists in the antebellum period intensified during the Reconstruction and its aftermath. Though in tension with a competing school of thought which favored working on a cooperative basis with whites within the existing northern Baptist organizations, the separatist ideology prevailed and ultimately culminated in the establishment of an independent Baptist denomination. The first national effort at consolidation, the Consolidated American Baptist Missionary Convention, foundered on the shoals of inadequate financial support and internal class conflicts between the educated northern blacks and the southern ex-slaves on such issues as emotional fervor and political activism. Upon the demise of this convention, however, three new organizations came into existence.

The Baptist Foreign Mission Convention of the United States of America was formed at a meeting of 151 delegates from 11 states convened by Rev. W. W. Colley in Montgomery, Alabama, on November 24, 1880. It was originally headquartered in Richmond, with Rev. Mr. Colley serving as corresponding secretary. The convention not only sent missionaries to Africa, but concerned itself with such domestic social issues as the use of alcohol and tobacco.

The American National Baptist Convention was organized August 25, 1886, at a meeting of 600 delegates from churches in 17 states convened in St. Louis, under the leadership of Rev. William J. Simmons, who became its first president. This convention, which claimed over one million constituents in some 9,000 churches with 4,500 ministers, represented the most ambitious effort to date to create a black Baptist denomination, an initiative pursued in spite of resistance from northern white Baptists.

The third convention, the National Baptist Educational Convention of the U.S.A., was formed in Washington, D.C., in 1893 under the leadership of Rev. W. Bishop Johnson for the primary purpose of educating and training clergy and missionaries.

At the 1894 annual meeting of these various bodies in Montgomery, a motion was made proposing their merger into one convention, whereupon a joint committee was appointed to report on the proposal the following year. The merger was accomplished at a meeting convened in Atlanta on September 28, 1895, and attended by over 500 delegates and observers. The resulting organization was the National Baptist Convention, U.S.A., with subsidiary Foreign Mission, Home Mission, and Education boards, to which a publishing concern was added in 1897. Rev. E. C. Morris was elected the first president of the new convention.

The display of unity was timely because African Americans had entered into an era of intensified repression. From 1890 to 1910 legislation was passed by all southern states which effectively disenfranchised African Americans, and gave license to lynchings and other forms of racial suppression. The Supreme Court also ratified the Jim Crow segregation by approving "separate but equal" railroad cars and, by extension, in all other public facilities in *Plessy v. Ferguson* in 1896. In the process, the ranks of the black churches, which constituted the sole place of sanctuary, expanded accordingly. Between 1890 and 1906 the number of black Baptist ministers increased from 5,500 to over 17,000.

Baptist unity was short lived, however. When a new corresponding secretary was appointed to the Foreign Mission Board and its headquarters moved from Richmond to Louisville, some of the original members of the board declined to cooperate and withdrew in 1897 to form the Lott Carey Foreign Missionary Convention. The issues involved loyalties to the old Foreign Mission Convention which had been based in Richmond (as had the original African Baptist Missionary Society) and resentment of the publishing activities of the new convention, which jeopardized the relations of the Richmond group with the white Baptist organizations.

Withdrawal of the Lott Carey contingent, made up of better educated members from Virginia, North Carolina, and the District of Columbia, was an expression once again of the class and ideological differences that had long plagued the movement for denominational independence.

In 1905 the Lott Carey Convention and the National Baptist Convention were ostensibly reconciled. Today they continue to function as independent bodies, although most of their members and officers have a dual affiliation. The National Baptist Convention, U.S.A., meanwhile, became a distinctly black denomination but internal conflicts persisted. The convention was to experience schism twice more in the next century, once in

1915 with the formation of the National Baptist Convention of America, and again in 1961 with the organizing of the Progressive National Baptist Convention.

To some degree, these divisions are transcended, if not obscured, in efforts supported cooperatively by the different conventions. A number of black institutions of higher learning have Baptist origins and maintain Baptist affiliations. They are not, however, generally under the direct jurisdiction of one particular convention. They may receive support from the various black conventions, as well as from one or both of the major white conventions, or they may be sponsored principally by a state convention. Many of these institutions were founded in the years immediately following emancipation (often as secondary schools) by the white American Baptist Home Mission Society. Others were established by black Baptists around the turn of the century. A dozen of these schools survive today as junior colleges, and another dozen as four-year colleges. Among them are Benedict College, in Columbia, South Carolina; Virginia Union University, Richmond; Shaw University, Raleigh, North Carolina; and Morehouse College and Spelman College in Atlanta. Some schools like Tuskegee Institute were closely aligned with the Baptists due to the influence of leaders like Dr. Booker T. Washington. The American Baptist Theological Seminary in Nashville is jointly operated by the Southern Baptist Convention and the National Baptist Convention, Inc.

National Baptist Convention, U.S.A., Inc.

After the schism in 1915 which produced the National Baptist Convention of America, the NBC, U.S.A., incorporated and its other boards became subordinate to the convention.[10] Rev. E. C. Morris, who had first been elected president when the NBC was created in 1895, continued in that capacity with the incorporated body until 1922. Following the loss of the publishing concern in 1915, a new board was created, the Sunday School Publishing Board of the National Baptist Convention. The Foreign Mission Board, however, replaced the publishing concern as the center of the convention's operations.

The convention also involved itself in domestic interests. Even before the turn of the century the NBC was active in education, supporting nearly 100 elementary and secondary schools and colleges, as well as providing for the education of African missionaries. In the first decade of the new century the NBC spoke out against racial violence and waged campaigns against segregation in public accommodations and discrimination in the armed service, education, and employment. These and other activities were generally carried out within the prevailing ideological framework of self-help. While both Booker T. Washington and W. E. B. Du Bois were frequent speakers at the annual conventions, it was Washington's program which the convention formally endorsed in 1909. The NBC, Inc., strongly supported the NAACP, however, and was vocal on such matters as the right to vote and to serve on juries.

At the time of the split in 1915 the National Baptist Convention represented nearly 3 million black people in over 20,000 local Baptist churches. Spurred by the northern migration of African Americans over the next several decades, both conventions experienced a shift from rural to urban churches, and a rapid growth in membership.

E. C. Morris was succeeded as convention president by W. G. Parks, who served only one year before L. K. Williams took office in 1924. D. V. Jemison was elected president in 1941 and served until 1952. In 1953 J. H. Jackson became president and held that office for a record twenty-nine years.

At the time of Rev. Dr. Joseph H. Jackson's election, the NBC, Inc., had nine boards and commissions. To these the new president added an additional thirteen. The program expansion was not reflective of social concerns, however, as the convention took a decidedly conservative turn. Jackson represented a strong vocal opposition to Martin Luther King and King's strategy of civil disobedience and nonviolent protest. Under his slogan of "from protest to production!" he located himself in the patriotic, law and order, anticommunist, pro-capitalist, school of gradualism. Although his was a position out of favor with most younger African Americans, Jackson succeeded in blocking the participation of the convention as an institution in the civil rights movement. King, for his part, left the NBC, Inc., as one of the leaders of the Progressive National Baptist Convention, a splinter group founded in 1961.

In contrast, Jackson's successor, Rev. Dr. Theodore J. Jemison, was a veteran of the civil rights movement, having organized a bus boycott in Baton Rouge, Louisiana, in 1953, and having served as the first general secretary of the Southern Christian Leadership Conference. Upon his election in 1982 Jemison pledged his support for social action in pursuit of civil rights, and initiated a nationwide voter registration drive.

The National Baptist Convention, U.S.A., Inc., is by far the largest of all the black denominations, and is considered the largest organization of African Americans in existence. The NBC, Inc., reports about 7.5 million members, of whom all but 100,000 are in the United States. The membership thus encompasses nearly one-fourth of the entire black population of the United States, and at least one-third of the estimated number of black members of Christian churches. Over 29,000 clergy and 30,000 local churches are affiliated with the convention, as are 4,700 associations and 59 state conventions. The annual budget of the National Convention in 1989 was about $4.5 million.[11]

NBC, Inc., convenes once a year, at the same time in September as the National Baptist Convention of America. Local churches, associations, and state conventions are required to pay a fee of from $10 to $50 for representative delegates, depending on the size and type of the sponsoring group, except that state conventions pay $200 for the first two messengers. Individuals may join the convention by paying an annual membership fee of $10, but they are not entitled to vote. Life membership is awarded upon payment of $200.

The officers of the convention are elected annually. Offices specified in the constitution include president, vice president-at-large, four vice presidents, vice presidents from each of the states represented, general secretary, four assistant secretaries, treasurer, statistician, historiographer, executive editor, and attorney. The convention is governed by a board of directors, which consists of fifteen members-at-large elected by the convention in addition to the named officers. The board of directors and its nine-member executive committee are responsible for conducting the business of the convention when it is not in session.

Traditionally, the purpose of the National Convention has been to carry on work in areas such as education, mission, and publishing which could not be done effectively by individual churches and would be done less efficiently by multiple regional bodies. More recently the national body has also assumed responsibility for matters such as ministerial pension plans. Current information on the organization of the convention is restricted inasmuch as no literature setting forth the president's program has been published since the change in administration in 1982. (The convention is empowered to create each year whatever boards are deemed necessary to carry out its work.) The scope of its activity is suggested by the auxiliary conventions and boards officially reporting at the 1980 session of the convention. These included Foreign Mission, Home Mission, Sunday School Publishing, Baptist Training Union (B.T.U.), Education, Evangelistic, and Benefit boards, and Usher's and Moderator's Auxiliaries. The Laymen's Movement Auxiliary, Women's Convention Auxiliary, and Congress of Christian Education (formerly Sunday School and B.T.U. Congress) are specifically provided for in the constitution. A

Young People's Department, operated as a subsidiary of the Women's Convention, is subdivided into several units based on age and marital status of the girls and young women. The Laymen's Auxiliary has a department for boys. Various commissions appointed from time to time address such matters as social service, rural life, theological education, theology, church-supported schools, ecumenical Christianity, the United Nations, civil rights, and intercultural relations.

According to the constitution, each board is to be made up of one member from each state and territory represented at the convention, plus an additional eight members from the state in which the board is located. Each board determines its own laws and regulations, nominates its own officers, and selects its own employees, who are then subject to ratification by the convention or its board of directors. Several of the boards have counterpart departments to implement the various programs. The auxiliary conventions generally meet in session at the same time as the National Convention. They have their own officers and committee structures, and in some instances a separate constitution and their own publications.

The convention presently has no permanent national headquarters, although it has plans to complete a new $12 million National Baptist World Center in Nashville in 1990, adjacent to the American Baptist Theological Seminary (jointly supported by National Baptists and Southern Baptists). Its current president, T. J. Jemison, pastors the Mount Zion First Baptist Church in Baton Rouge, Louisiana, while the general secretary resides in Mount Vernon, New York, and its publishing house, the Sunday School Publishing Board, is located in Nashville.

National Baptist Convention of America

The National Baptist Convention of America (NBCA), originally called the National Baptist Convention, Unincorporated, is a product of the 1915 split in the National Baptist Convention, U.S.A., which was founded in 1895. The central issue in this conflict was the publishing concern, which had also been a factor in the 1897 schism resulting in the Lott Carey Convention. This time the dispute involved the "Boyd faction" led by R. H. Boyd, secretary of the Publishing Board, and the "Morris faction," led by E. C. Morris, president of the convention. Ultimately, the Boyd faction took the name "National Baptist Convention of America" and remained unincorporated. The Morris faction retains the original name of the convention, but incorporated to become the National Baptist Convention, U.S.A., Inc.

Both groups claim to be the original parent body. Both claim the founding date of 1880. In fact, no unified National Baptist Convention existed in 1880, which was the founding date of the oldest of the three entities that merged in 1895. In short, while three Baptist bodies went into the funnel in 1895, two emerged from the other end in 1915.[12]

The conflict was set in motion shortly after the NBC, U.S.A. was created, when the American Baptist Publication Society, upon complaints from Southern Baptists, withdrew its invitation for black leaders to write articles for one of its publications. As a result of this impasse, the National Baptist Convention determined to establish its own publishing capabilities. The new Publishing Board was initially placed under the Home Mission Board of which R. H. Boyd (who introduced the resolution proposing the printing committee) served as corresponding secretary.

Under Boyd's leadership and on the basis of his personal credit the Publishing Board quickly became a successful business venture. New facilities were built on land owned by Boyd in Nashville, who had the agency incorporated in the state of Tennessee, and materials produced by the publishing house were copyrighted in his name. When in 1905 the Rev. Mr. Morris acted to separate the publishing house from the Home Mission Board, Boyd and the other members of the board resisted, and a decade-long controversy ensued centered around the question of ownership and control of the publishing interest. Ultimately the conflict was resolved in Boyd's favor by the courts of Tennessee. The convention itself was unincorporated and so unable to own property in its own name and although it had created the Publishing Board, it had neglected to make proper provisions for legal claim to it.

The National Baptist Publishing Board became the nucleus of a separate National Baptist body, which was organized in Chicago on September 9, 1915. As this convention moved to establish additional boards, an agreement was struck whereby all foreign mission work of the new group would be conducted through the Lott Carey Convention. The latter thereby strengthened its hand in missions, while the NBCA gained an enlarged audience for its literature. Over the years, however, this working relationship declined and NBCA ultimately organized an independent Foreign Mission Board. In addition to the issues of prohibition, evangelism, and education, the NBCA gave early support to civil rights organizations, urban social service programs, and the antilynching campaign.

The Boyd family continues to be prominent in the NBCA publishing concern. Henry Allen Boyd succeeded his father, R. H. Boyd, in 1922, and he in turn was succeeded by his nephew, T. B. Boyd, Jr., who led the publishing house from 1959 to 1979. Since 1979 the Publishing Board has been headed by T. B. Boyd III, in his capacity as executive director.

Rev. E. P. Jones was elected president of the convention at the time of its organizing. His successors were E. Woods, 1923; J. W. Hurse, 1930; G. L. Prince, 1933; C. D. Pettaway, 1957; J. C. Sams, 1967; and E. E. Jones, 1985.[13]

The National Baptist Convention of America is the second largest of the three black Baptist conventions having a national constituency, and the third largest of all the black denominations. In 1989 its estimated membership of 2.4 million in 7,800 local churches indicates an average congregation of about 280, which is somewhat larger than the average congregation of the National Baptist Convention, Inc. (235), but far smaller than that of the Progressive National Baptist Convention (a thousand). These churches are served by from 2,500 to 3,000 clergy, suggesting a substantial number of small rural churches. Some four hundred associations, ranging from five to a hundred local churches, and thirty-five state conventions in twenty-seven states, are affiliated with the convention.[14]

The NBCA convenes every year on the Wednesday following the first Sunday in September. Convention delegates called "messengers" include lay and ministerial representatives from local churches, associations, and state conventions. Each church is assessed a minimum of $50, or $1 per member for the first messenger, and $10 for each additional messenger. Each district association pays $50 for the first two messengers, and $10 for each additional messenger; each general association and state convention pays $100 for the first five messengers, and $10 for each additional messenger.

The officers of the convention are elected annually and include a president; first, second, and third vice presidents; recording secretary; first, second, third, and fourth assistant recording secretaries; corresponding secretary; statistical secretary; treasurer; auditor; director of public relations; historian; and secretary of youth activities. The presidents of the state conventions and moderators of the general associations are associate vice presidents. The Executive Board, which conducts the business of the convention when it is not in session, consists of the elected convention officers and presidents of the state conventions. The constitution provides for five administrative committees: Registration, Budget, Finance, Bills and Accounts, and Credentials.

The NBCA has seven program boards: Home Mission, Foreign Mission, Baptist Training Union, National Baptist Publishing, Evangelical,

Benevolent, and Educational. The membership of each board consists of one member from each state convention and general association. The auxiliaries of the convention include two Women's Missionary auxiliaries, Junior Women's Auxiliary, Brotherhood Union, Ushers, Nurses' Corps, and Youth Convention. Each board and auxiliary elects its own officers, although the officers of the latter are subject to ratification by the convention. The constitution also specifies four commissions: Transportation, Christian Education, Social Justice, and Army and Navy Chaplains.

The NBCA does not have centralized national headquarters. The publishing house is in Nashville. The principal officers do not ordinarily relinquish their offices as local pastors.

In 1988 a new schism occurred in the NBCA over the question of the Boyd family's control of the Publishing House. With an estimated 25 percent of the membership, the Boyd faction styled itself the National Missionary Baptist Convention of America (NMBCA). It remains to be seen whether this group will emerge as the fourth major black Baptist denomination.

Progressive National Baptist Convention, Inc.

The Progressive National Baptist Convention, U.S.A., Inc., (PNBC) came into existence in 1961 as a result of conflict within the National Baptist Convention, U.S.A., Inc. The dissension began in 1957 when ten pastors were expelled from the NBC, Inc., for challenging the president, J. H. Jackson, in court on his ruling that an amendment setting a four-year limit on tenure was invalid, inasmuch as it had been adopted in 1952 in a manner that was procedurally unconstitutional. Jackson's position was upheld by a federal court.[15]

His opponents, reacting to the larger issue of what was perceived as autocratic rule, subsequently organized around the candidacy of Rev. Dr. Gardner C. Taylor.[16] The "Taylor team," as it was called, included Martin Luther King, Sr., Martin Luther King, Jr., Ralph David Abernathy, Benjamin Mays, and a number of other clergy committed to King's social change strategies which Jackson condemned as inadvisable and injurious to the cause of racial advance and harmony.

At the 1960 convention in Philadelphia, the nominating committee unanimously presented Jackson's name for another term, whereupon he was declared reelected. When the Taylor team protested, demanding a roll call vote by states, the convention was declared adjourned. The delegates remained, however, and conducted an election in which Taylor won. When the Jackson faction refused to acknowledge the vote results, the Taylor team proceeded to conduct a sit-in at the convention. The Taylor faction claimed throughout the following year to be the rightful officers of the convention, but the courts again ruled in Jackson's favor.

The next year, in Kansas City, Missouri, the Taylor delegates, who had been meeting in separate session, were initially denied admission to the larger assembly. When they were admitted, physical confrontations erupted as they moved to take control of the platform. Ultimately, a court-supervised election was held, and Jackson emerged victorious. Taylor acknowledged the results, and he and King both called for unity. Before the convention was ended, however, Martin Luther King, Sr., Martin Luther King, Jr., D. E. King, Marshall L. Shepard, C. C. Adams, and others were removed from any offices they held, including membership on the board of directors.

Rev. L. Venchael Booth assumed leadership of the opposition and, as the chairman of the "Volunteer Committee for the Formation of a New National Baptist Convention," called for a meeting in November 1961 at his church, Zion Baptist Church, in Cincinnati. The thirty-three people who attended from fourteen states voted to start a separate convention. The first annual meeting was held in Philadelphia the following year. Rev. T. M. Chambers was elected the first president; he was succeeded in 1967 by Gardner Taylor.

The new convention adopted as its motto: "Unity, Service, Fellowship, Peace." PNBC was actively involved in the civil rights movement, was supportive of the black power movement, and was one of the earliest groups to publicly oppose the war in Vietnam.[17] In more recent years it has given emphasis to black political development, economic development, education and job training, and strengthening of the black family. Around 1970 several white churches established dual affiliations with PNBC. Conversely, many PNBC churches today maintain dual affiliations with one of the white conventions.[18] The Progressive National Baptist Convention, Inc., is the smallest of the three National Baptist conventions. In 1989 the denomination claimed 1,000 clergy with 1.2 million members in 1,000 churches, giving it an average congregation of 1,000. Its estimated budget was $1.2 million for that year. The unusually large size of the congregations is attributable to the fact that the convention's membership consists primarily of churches in major metropolitan areas, many of which have memberships of from two to three thousand, while including relatively few rural churches.[19] Unlike the other two conventions, PNBC is divided into regions. Within the four regions, a total of thirty-five state conventions are affiliated with the convention; the number of associations is not known.

The departments of PNBC include Women, Laymen, Youth, Ushers and Nurses, Moderators, and the Congress of Christian Education. Other agencies include the Board of Christian Education and Publication, Home Mission Board, Foreign Mission Bureau, Progressive Pension Plan Board, and Chaplaincy Endorsing Agency. Committees and commissions are Program, Convention Arrangements, Internal Affairs, Cooperative Christianity, Civil Rights, and Community Economic Development.

For several years PNBC met in September at the same time as NBCA and NBC, Inc. In the mid-1970s the convention began convening during the week following the first Sunday in August to accommodate school schedules and encourage the participation of families. The constitution calls for affiliated churches to pay membership fees equivalent to 1 percent of their previous year's operating budget, with the number of official messengers or delegates from each church determined by the size of the church. Each state convention, upon payment of $200, is entitled to two messengers. Fellowships must pay $150 for two messengers, and associations $50 for one messenger. Any member of an affiliated church may attend the convention; however, only representative members so designated by the churches, associations, or state conventions may vote. Individuals may secure life memberships, with voting privileges, upon payment of $500.[20]

In a departure from the other conventions, PNBC presidents since 1967 have been limited to two consecutive one-year terms. Thus, in its twenty-five-year history the convention has already had a dozen different presidents. Most of the other officers including first and second vice presidents, regional vice presidents, general secretary, recording secretary, assistant recording secretaries, treasurer, historian, and editor are subject to the same tenure rule.

The sixty-member Executive Board, which is responsible for oversight of the convention when not in session, consists of the elected officers, the heads of the departments, chairpersons of all boards and commissions, past presidents, the general secretary, and one representative chosen by each state convention. An executive committee, consisting of the president, vice presidents, general secretary, recording secretary, treasurer, and five additional members, may be empowered to act on behalf of the Executive Board. Standing committees of the Executive Board are Personnel, Planning and Evaluation, and Finance and Property.

National headquarters with a permanent staff are located in Washington,

D.C. In another departure from the other conventions the general secretary of PNBC is a full-time employee responsible for the day-to-day administration of the convention's program. Consequently, the role of the president, aside from presiding at official sessions, is largely that of ambassador to the larger world. PNBC has no publishing house of its own.

Baptist Polity and Ministry

As noted previously, in addition to the national conventions, many Baptists are also organized into state conventions and associations. Like the national conventions, most state conventions convene once a year, with delegates participating from all associations and local churches within the jurisdiction who have elected to affiliate. The North Carolina General Baptist State Convention, for example, involves 1,666 churches, with a membership of nearly 400,000 individuals. The state conventions may be legal corporations in their own right, and thus commonly maintain permanent offices with paid staffs. The business conducted at the annual session includes electing messengers to national conventions, if any, with which it may choose to affiliate, whether formally or informally; raising funds for national mission efforts; and receiving reports from its various auxiliaries. These may include such units as Laymen's League, Sunday School Congress, Training Union, Usher's Convention, Young Adult and Youth departments, and Woman's Convention.

State conventions may support various institutions such as colleges or orphanages, provide training for local ministers and lay officers, assist college and seminary students, contribute to retirement plans, administer community social service projects, and issue publications. The governmental structure of the conventions varies from state to state, but generally consists of a president, Executive Committee, and Administrative Board, which includes the heads of the various auxiliaries. The conventions frequently contain the word "General' in their title, which distinguishes them from white state conventions.

Associations, consisting of churches within a smaller geographical area, are independent entities which may be legally incorporated.[21] Many associations, particularly in the South, date back more than a century, and have a long tradition of service to the community and to its member churches. The more elaborate associations may have a number of subsidiary units, such as a Parent Body (Pastors) or Ministers, Deacons, and Deaconesses Union; Woman's Federation, Department, or Auxiliary; Youth or Young People's Department; Church Training Department or

Baptist Training Union; Sunday School Convention or Christian Education Department or Congress; Nurses' Department; and Laymen's League.
Many of these auxiliaries have their own constitutions, officers, departments or committees, and budgets, and meet independently of the annual
or semi-annual meetings of the association itself.

Officers of the association, who may be either ministers or lay persons
and are elected annually, include a moderator, vice moderator, recording
secretary, treasurer, financial secretary, members of the Executive Board,
and presidents of the auxiliaries. All pastors and members of the churches
belonging to the association are members of the association; however,
each church and auxiliary is allotted a given number of delegates, and only
the delegates may vote for officers.

In addition to the auxiliaries, an association may have a number of
committees, such as Finance, Budget, Time and Place, Nominations,
Resolutions, Recommendations, Admission of New Churches and Members, and others as needed. Of particular import is the Ordaining Council,
which in some associations is the standing subunit of the Ministers and
Deacons Union responsible for establishing qualifications for ordination,
and for examining candidates for the ministry within the association. Other
associations convene an ordination committee or council as needed. Local
churches, however, are not bound by association guidelines.

As might be expected given the autonomy of the associations, the
theological and ideological orientations vary from one to another. In
some parts of the country, for example, ministers who ordain women
or admit them to association membership are subject to reprisal and
retribution. In contrast is this resolution adopted in 1984 by a North
Carolina association:

> Whereas, ours has been a history of oppression from all institutions
> including the white religious institutions; therefore: Be it resolved that
> the East Cedar Grove Association publicly disassociate itself from the
> decision of (the) Southern Baptist Convention in their rejection of
> support for the ordination of women,
> Be it further resolved that we inform the General Baptist State Conven-
> tion that our position is one of ordaining and supporting called and
> qualified women in their attempts to pastor.

At the same session, this association passed a second resolution which to
a substantial degree typifies black Baptist churches—their diversity notwithstanding—and, indeed, is characteristic of the Black Church as a
whole: "Whereas, all of our lives are affected by the political process, be
it hereby resolved, That the Association urges our churches to impress

upon their members the sacred duty of registering to vote and to vote in the upcoming election."[22]

The motive for coming together in these associations and conventions is fellowship and mutual support; no "book of discipline" or any other denominational authority makes participation obligatory. Because Baptists do have a congregational polity, local members often are less concerned or informed about the national organization than is the case in connectional denominations. In many areas the state convention, rather than the national, serves as the principal arena of activity. Involvement is primarily by the ministers, with only marginal lay participation. Characteristically, the preferences of the local pastor determine largely whether there will be any external affiliation or activities and how they will be expressed.

Most ministers participate in an additional Baptist form of organization called ministerial conferences or fellowships. These conferences, made up of the pastors in a given city or metropolitan area, generally meet once a week and serve as forums for teaching, preaching, in-service training, evaluation and endorsement of candidates for political offices, addressing current community and civic issues, and general mutual support.

In the Baptist churches there are but two categories of official ministry, the one being preliminary to the other. Candidates are first licensed by the local church, usually in consultation with an association, upon the satisfactory preaching of a trial sermon. The "licensed preacher," to become a minister, must satisfy the study requirements of the local association, if any; be examined by a group or council of ministers and lay persons convened by the local church; and experience the ritual of ordination which is performed by the laying on of hands by ministers who usually are members of the local association. Great emphasis is placed on being "called" to the ministry, while less significance is attached to formal education and training, although this varies from one locale to another. Those ministers who are responsible for a local church are called pastors, (that is, all pastors are ministers; but not all ministers are pastors). In contrast to other denominations, Baptist pastors are not appointed to a church by a higher ecclesiastical authority, but are elected by majority vote of the local congregation. Unlike the Methodist churches, deacons in the Baptist churches are lay persons. Traditionally, deacons were to be ordained, and that practice continues in most black churches, but they remain lay persons, and are not considered to be in preparation for a higher ministry.

Once ordained and called to pastor a particular church, ministers

generally are granted considerable autonomy in conducting the affairs of
the church. As one observer put it over sixty years ago, "These separate
(black Baptist) churches are a law unto themselves. They vary widely
in doctrine and method. In government they may be absolute monarchs
ruled by a strong pastor who, in fact, is responsible to nobody. Usually,
however, some power is in the hands of the trustees and in many cases
they acquire dominating power, making the church a little oligarchy."
Still, the power ultimately redounds to the membership, for "always
there exists the power of secession to curb the tyranny of the pastor or
trustees or as a method of expelling them. In nearly every city or town,
one will have pointed out 'the First Baptist' and then one or two splits or
withdrawals, making a 'Second Baptist' or a 'Siloam' or 'Shiloh.'"[23]

However much or little this characterization may apply today, Baptists
do in fact share a common doctrinal foundation, and local churches
manifest much the same pattern of organization, which often is set forth
in a church constitution and bylaws. The Board of Trustees is responsible for financial matters and maintenance of church property. There
may be a finance committee as well. The duties of the deacons vary
from church to church. In some instances deacons and trustees are
combined in one board, but in general they are to assist the pastor in
maintaining the quality of the spiritual life of the church. They assist with
communion, visit the sick, care for the needy, conduct devotional services,
and administer the affairs of the church in the absence of a pastor. In
some churches these duties are shared with deaconesses. Other church
auxiliaries commonly include Missionary societies or circles; Sunday
School, and a board or committee of Christian education; Youth Department, Pastor's Aid, several choirs, Benevolence Committee, Usher
boards, and various men's and women's clubs. There may also be
committees on stewardship, evangelism, nominations, music, flowers,
and social concerns, depending on the size of the congregation.

In addition to the heads of these units, church officers may also include
a clerk, treasurer, financial secretary, moderator (who may be the
pastor or a lay person), historian, and Sunday School superintendent. In some churches, these officers collectively constitute an
advisory council or board; alternatively, the Board of Deacons
serves this function. However, the church itself, that is, the congregation, is the supreme governing body. In some churches certain
responsibilities may be delegated to various boards and committees.
And as suggested, considerable power is wielded by the pastor and by
the chairman of the Deacon Board. But traditionally, all matters of

substance, whether concerning finances, program activities, spiritual affairs, or social concerns are to be considered in regularly convened church meetings of the entire membership.

Baptist Autonomy in Modern Urban Society

Because Baptist "denominations" are so loosely knit and local churches largely autonomous, an examination of the denominations alone is misleading insofar as a survey of Baptist activity is concerned It is true that the president of the convention can exercise a certain degree of control over individual pastors through the patronage system of prestigious appointments to various boards and committees. But at the same time, individual pastors have the option of not participating in that arena. The pastors of very large churches, in particular, are able to build substantial power bases in their own right and thereby effect significant change in their local communities, as well as nationally. Because Baptist ministers are essentially free of accountability to a denominational hierarchy, they have often been less vulnerable to civil and economic suppression, a factor of significance in their traditional involvement in political activity and community advocacy. For example, no event of recent times highlighted this circumstance more than the civil rights movement. Although Martin Luther King, Jr., was himself in disfavor with the head of the convention to which he belonged, for example, the mass movement he led was populated disproportionately by pastors and members of local Baptist churches.

As we will point out in our chapters on black churches in politics and economics, the principle of autonomy has made black Baptist churches quite successful in adapting to the conditions of modern urban society in the twentieth century. Although this autonomy has been reflected largely among black Baptist preachers in political careers or in carrying out large-scale economic projects, it is by no means limited to them alone. Lay black Baptist women like Nannie Burroughs played important political roles prior to the civil rights movement, while Fannie Lou Hamer, Ella Baker, Diane Nash, Marian Wright Edelman, and Bernice Reagon Johnson, among many others, were key leaders during the struggles of the 1960s. The whole area of the relationship between religious principles and values among black congregations and the kind of socialization that is produced has been inadequately studied, so no firm conclusions can be drawn at this time. However, field observations and some of the data collected on politics and economics tend to support the view that black

Baptist churches have been more successful in adapting to modern urban society.

Status of Women

Ostensibly in defense of the authority and autonomy of local churches, none of the national conventions has taken a formal stand either for or against ordination of women. Neither NBCA nor NBC, Inc., has officially reported any known instances of women pastoring churches affiliated with their conventions. However, the three known cases of black Baptist women pastors have usually occurred when wives replaced their pastor husbands who died unexpectedly.[24] PNBC has a few women clergy; how many of these were ordained in other denominations before coming to PNBC is not known. Attitudes toward ordination of women vary from church to church and association to association. The Baptist Ministers Conference of Baltimore, for example, has admitted a number of women pastors to its membership since 1979. The neighboring conference of Washington, D.C., on the other hand, severed its relationship with the Baltimore Conference in protest of this action. Thus, while the principle of congregational autonomy has helped black Baptist churches success-fully adapt to the urban scene, it also has had a negative side in the failure to produce resolute collective action to improve the situation for women clergy. The issue of black women clergy is explored in more detail in chapter 10 [of *The Black Church in the African American Experience*].

Women may presumably serve in any lay office in the local church; in practice, only a very few are trustees, and fewer still serve as deacons. In NBCA women generally hold no offices, either locally or nationally, in any but the traditional women's organizations. Women officers at the national level of NBC, Inc., are restricted to the usher's auxiliary and the women's convention movement, except that a woman serves as executive director of the Sunday School Publishing Board. In PNBC a woman heads the Congress of Christian Education, and the constitution specifically states that women, clergy or lay, may hold any office of the convention.

The International Dimension of Foreign Missions

As early as 1815 the African Baptist Missionary Society of Richmond was organized by two black ministers, Collin Teague and Lott Carey, with the aid of a white deacon, William Crane.[25] In 1821 Lott Carey became the first black Baptist missionary to Africa. Like the black Methodist Daniel Coker, he was sent to Liberia under the auspices of the American

Colonization Society on the second ACS expedition to West Africa. However, Carey also voiced the sentiments of some free African Americans regarding the lack of justice and equality in the United States, and their desire to emigrate. He said, "I am an African and in this country, however meritorious my conduct and respectable my character, I cannot receive the credit due either. I wish to go to a country where I shall be estimated by my merits not by my complexion."[26] Carey also laid the foundation for a theology of missions in Africa for the Baptists. However, much of the black Baptist missionary endeavors were limited to Liberia and the West Coast of Africa during the nineteenth century. In 1889 the Baptist Foreign Mission Convention published a magazine called *The African Missions.*[27] During the twentieth century missionary efforts were extended to Central and South African countries.

The missionary ventures of the African American Baptists in the Caribbean basin were carried out by one of the organizers of the earliest black Baptist churches in the Savannah River region, Rev. George Liele. As early as 1784 Liele had established the First Baptist Church of Kingston, Jamaica.[28] Since then the missionary efforts of the black Baptists have spread extensively throughout the Caribbean island nations.

While the black Baptists founded the earliest churches and still have the largest numbers of black Christians, the Methodist movement among African Americans organized the first black denominations, which were their first national organizations. We turn now to a consideration of the black Methodists and their organizing efforts in the late eighteenth and early nineteenth centuries.

Notes

[The following notes are unchanged from original publication except that where incomplete bibliographical information was provided in chapter notes it has been completed insofar as information was available, and in note 24 information referred to in another chapter of the book has been included for the reader's convenience. Ed.]

1. Miles Mark Fisher, "What Is a Negro Baptist?" *The Home Mission College Review* 1 (May 1927), no. 1.

2. James M. Washington, *Frustrated Fellowship: The Black Baptist Quest for Social Power* (Macon, Ga.: Mercer University Press, 1986), chapters 5, 6.

3. James S. Tinney, "Selected Directory of Afro-American Religious Organizations, Schools and Periodicals," in Dionne J. Jones and William H. Matthews, editors, *The Black Church: A Community Resource* (Washington, D.C., Howard University Institute for Urban Affairs and Research, 1977), pp. 168-74. Accurate statistics on black Baptists are particularly difficult to obtain due to the simultaneous affiliations of churches, associations, and state conventions with more than one national

convention, resulting in double counting. More recent estimates for the Southern Baptist Convention and American Baptists Churches Convention place black membership at 250,000 and 400,000 respectively, much of which would reflect dual affiliations. See Leroy Fitts, *A History of Black Baptists* (Nashville: Broadman Press, 1985), pp. 302, 308. Conversely, many small churches are not affiliated with any convention at all, and so are not included in any reported membership figures.

4. Jacobus Arminius, a Dutch Protestant theologian, modified the harshness of the Calvinistic doctrine of predestination by asserting that human beings have a certain amount of free will in regard to their actions.

5. For the best dating records on early black Baptist churches, see Mechal Sobel, *Trabelin' On: The Slave Journey to an Afro-Baptist Faith* (Westport, Conn.: Greenwood, 1979), pp. 250ff.

6. Scholars like Carter G. Woodson and Mechal Sobel tend to accept the latter dates between 1773 and 1775. However, a field trip to the Silver Bluff Baptist Church by Lincoln and Mamiya found that the cornerstone of the church claims a founding date of 1750. The cornerstone reads "Silver Bluff Baptist Church, Organized 1750, Rev. J. A. Goflin Pastor, Remodeled 1920, Rev. A. W. Vincent Pastor." The discrepancy has not yet been cleared up.

7. Emmett T. Martin and Nellie C. Waring, *History Book of the Springfield Baptist Church, Augusta, Georgia, 1781-1979* (Augusta, Ga.: Springfield Baptist Church, 1979).

8. Fisher, "What Is a Negro Baptist?"

9. Ibid.

10. Accounts differ as to when the convention first proposed incorporating and whether the proposal was made in response to the withdrawal of the Publishing Board, or whether it was in response to the threatened withdrawal, or if it helped precipitate the conflict leading to the withdrawal. Leroy Fitts suggests that the convention merely revised its constitution in 1916 and did not technically incorporate until the 1930s. See Fitts, *A History of Black Baptists*, p. 94.

11. The 1989 estimates cited above were obtained from interviews with officials of NBC, U.S.A., Inc.

12. Washington, *Frustrated Fellowship*, pp. 195-96.

13. The names and dates were obtained from officials of NBCA.

14. The 1989 estimates were derived from interviews with officials from NBCA. Figures for the number of churches were arrived at by prorating statistics provided by state conventions and associations reporting in 1982 and cited in the convention's *Official Journal* of 1983. The number of clergy was provided by NBCA officials.

15. See the account given by Charles Hamilton, *The Black Preacher in America* (New York: William Morrow, 1972), pp. 159-63. Also see Fitts, *A History of Black Baptists*, pp. 98-105.

16. Fitts, *A History of Black Baptists*, pp. 98-105.

17. Hamilton, *The Black Preacher in America*, p. 125.

18. Charles Butler, "PNBC: A Fellowship of Partners," *The Crisis* 89, no. 9 (November 1982), pp. 44-45. Also see James S. Tinney, "Progressive Baptists," *Christianity Today* (October 9, 1970), pp. 42-43.

19. The 1989 figures cited were estimates derived from interviews with PNBC officials and raise certain questions. For example, such large churches normally would have staffs of several ministers. Apparently only senior pastors are included in this census.

20. The data cited above were obtained from PNBC officials.

21. Distinctions may be made between "Regular" or "District" associations, which belong to state conventions, and through them to the National Convention, and "general" associations, which belong to the National Convention only, having status comparable to a state convention, but more than a regular district association. A further point of confusion is that a given state may have as many as three or four separate state conventions.

22. "Yearbook of the East Cedar Grove Missionary Baptist Association," held at the Siloam Baptist Church Eighty-Ninth Annual Session, Rougemont, North Carolina, July 4-5, 1984, p. 22.

23. John Snyder, "The Baptists," *The Crisis* (May 1920), p. 12. The reference to the role of trustees more aptly describes deacons. Particularly in rural areas, where three or four churches were served by one pastor, the power and authority of the head deacon was unquestioned.

24. For the names of the women see Dr. T. J. Jemison's quote in chapter 10, pp. 296-97. [That quote is as follows: "It's not widely known that the National Baptist Convention, USA, Inc., has had three women pastors within the past twenty-five years. One of those pastors was Rev. Trudy Trim of Chicago, who assumed that role following the death of her husband. She too recently passed. Also when Rev. Plummer of Cleveland, Ohio, became ill, his wife carried on in his absence. Many of our churches today have women assistants. The secretary of our convention, Dr. Richardson, is pastor of the Grace Church in Mount Vernon, New York. His assistant pastor is a woman, Rev. Flora Bridges. The editor of our convention's newspaper is Rev. Roscoe Cooper of Richmond, Virginia. The assistant in his church is also female. . . . I welcome women and have nothing against them. Of course, most Baptists will come to accept this very slowly. My father was adamantly against this trend and so are most of my colleagues." From an interview with Dr. Jemison reported in Anqunett Fusilier, editor, "National Baptist Convention U.S.A., Inc. Socio-Economic Programs Sweep the Nation Under the Leadership of Dr. T. J. Jemison," *The Cornerstone*, p. 22.

25. Sandy Dwayne Martin, "Black Baptists, Foreign Missions, and African Colonization, 1814-1882," in Sylvia M. Jacobs, editor, *Black Americans and the Missionary Movement in Africa* (Westport, Conn.: Greenwood, 1982), p. 64. Also see Leroy Fitts, *Lott Carey, First Black Missionary to Africa* (Valley Forge, Pa.: Judson Press, 1978).

26. Quoted in St. Clair Drake, *The Redemption of Africa and Black Religion* (Chicago: Third World, 1970), p. 51.

27. Joseph H. Jackson, *A Story of Christian Activism: The History of the National Baptist Convention, U.S.A., Inc.* (Nashville: Townsend, 1980), p. 41.

28. Ibid., pp. 5-10.

The Southern Baptist Convention, 1979–93: What Happened and Why?

Stan Hastey

This assessment of the controversy in the Southern Baptist Convention will focus on three overarching sets of issues: theological disputes, internal control, and national politics. Although other approaches might have been chosen, this basic outline provides a comprehensive framework for reviewing the most significant events and primary issues at stake in the controversy.

Theological Disputes

As has been the case in many of the controversies in the history of the Southern Baptist Convention, the dispute that surfaced in 1979 centered first in institutions of theological education.[1] According to those who organized the takeover of the SBC, Baptist schools generally had been infected by theological liberalism. Judge Paul Pressler, for example, has said that "(Liberalism) always begins in theological institutions."[2] The primary culprits, Pressler and others have maintained, were the historical-critical method of biblical study and neo-orthodoxy.[3]

Looming large behind these allegations is a long history of debate in Southern Baptist life over the need for—indeed the desirability of—theological education itself. Although anti-intellectualism is a clearly identifiable feature in American history,[4] hostility toward formal theological

Stan Hastey is the executive director of the Alliance of Baptists. Prior to that, he was director of information for the Baptist Joint Committee on Public Affairs. This paper has been presented as a lecture on several occasions and was printed in *Baptist History and Heritage*, xxviii (October 1993), 18-28, and is reprinted with permission by the Southern Baptist Historical Society. This issue of *Baptist History and Heritage* included articles and responses by the fundamentalist and moderate representatives on the subject of the controversy in the Southern Baptist Convention during the period of 1979–1993.

training in particular has been a prominent theme in American religious history.[5]

Skepticism, if not outright opposition, has characterized Southern Baptist views of theological education, especially in the Sandy Creek tradition.[6] It is not surprising, therefore, that the dispute that surfaced in 1979 centered in the SBC seminaries.

The more immediate backdrop for the controversy was a period of nearly two decades beginning in the early 1960s and the battle over Midwestern Baptist Theological Seminary professor Ralph Elliott's commentary, *The Message of Genesis,* published by Broadman Press. Although messengers to the 1962 SBC in San Francisco refused to order the withdrawal of the book, they did adopt resolutions indirectly critical of Elliott, appointed a special committee to revise and update "The Baptist Faith and Message," and elected new and more conservative trustees to Midwestern's board.

In the ensuing year, a majority of trustees succeeded in ridding the Kansas City, Missouri, school of Elliott because of his insistence on seeking another publisher for his work, following a decision by the Sunday School Board not to reprint it. In his assessment of the results of the Elliott controversy, Walter B. Shurden noted that in addition to Elliott's dismissal and the 1963 adoption of the revised and updated confession of faith, a "third and less obvious result . . . was an intensification and popularization of the suspicion of theological education and publications."[7]

Less than a decade would elapse before convention conservatives would win another round in the ongoing battle over the Bible. This time the target of criticism was volume 1 of *The Broadman Commentary* series, specifically the commentary on the Book of Genesis by British Baptist scholar G. Benton Davies. Following months of public battle in the pages of Baptist newspapers, conservatives succeeded in having the 1970 convention in Denver request the Sunday School Board to withdraw volume 1 and rewrite it "with due consideration of the conservative viewpoint." Within two months, the Sunday School Board complied.[8]

While "infallibility" was the rallying cry for conservatives in the earlier disputes, "inerrancy" became the battle cry of those who in 1979 launched a concerted effort to seize control of the SBC, an effort that culminated in 1990 when the moderate resistance gave up its countermove to regain control of the convention. From its beginnings the inerrancy party was led publicly by Paul Pressler and Paige Patterson, two Texans who had engaged in protracted battles with both the SBC and Texas Baptist establishments.[9]

Pressler and Patterson—along with other key leaders such as Adrian Rogers and W. A. Criswell—have professed that the struggle was to save the SBC from what they have called the decline of other Protestant bodies in the United States, a decline they attribute to the failure to resist encroaching theological liberalism.[10]

This rationale is particularly offensive to those Southern Baptists who long have been critical of the SBC's tendency toward triumphalism as reflected in dubious slogans and grandiose objectives, behind which lay the conviction that the SBC alone was sufficiently pure to be used of God in the evangelization of the world. Perhaps no one has put forward this view more forcefully than did Adrian Rogers in an interview with the *Indiana Baptist:*

> This is going to sound almost like megalomania, but I believe that the hope of the world lies in the West. I believe the hope of the West lies in America. I believe the hope of America is in Judeo-Christian ethics. I believe that the backbone of that Judeo-Christian ethic is evangelical Christianity. I believe that the bellwether of evangelical Christianity is the Southern Baptist Convention. So I believe in a sense, that as the Southern Baptist Convention goes, so goes the world.[11]

Indeed, the legitimacy of inerrancy as invoked by the movement's leaders as a proper and sufficient rationale to justify their successful campaign is questionable on other grounds as well. For one, inerrancy itself is variously defined and adhered to within evangelical and fundamentalist circles. As was properly and repeatedly stated by noted evangelical and fundamentalist scholars at the 1987 Ridgecrest Conference on Biblical Inerrancy, the definition advanced by the inerrancy party in the SBC has been of the most extreme form.[12]

Furthermore, commitment to inerrancy has proven to be an insufficient qualification for office to some Southern Baptists who profess it—but who nevertheless do not have the blessing of the movement's leaders. Examples abound, among them Alvin C. Shackleford, the fired director of Baptist Press news service, and Nelson Price, the Georgia pastor who defied the leaders of the new inerrancy establishment by running for SBC president in 1992 without their blessing.

Perhaps even worse, from an ethical standpoint, has been the insistence on the part of movement leaders to label moderates who for reasons of conscience do not subscribe to inerrancy—and particularly the SBC inerrantists' version—as infidels who do not believe the Bible. Even though these have a high view of Holy Scripture as measured by any reasonable set of criteria, they have been written off as liberals who do not believe the Bible. More than any other matter dividing Southern Baptists into fundamentalist and moderate camps, it is this demonizing of the opposition that has made rapprochement unlikely, if not impossible.

Despite all claims to the contrary, "Fundamentalists have demonstrated clearly that they are not interested simply in the nature and authority of the Bible but in imposing their *interpretation* of the Bible on others."[13] In the convention context, this fact has been demonstrated repeatedly since fundamentalists consolidated their power in the agencies and institutions by the application of theological litmus tests. Perhaps the most noteworthy evidence has been the questioning of prospective employees on the four examples of interpretation cited by a narrow majority of the SBC Peace Committee as determinative of orthodoxy by "most Southern Baptists.[14]

Moreover, issues in the national political arena have been defined by particular interpretations of biblical texts, interpretations then used as the basis for discharging offending employees or denying employment to potential employees. From the moderate perspective, then, the issue of biblical inerrancy as defined in its most extreme form by the inerrancy party has been, at least in part, a smoke screen hiding a larger political agenda, a theme to be addressed in another section of this paper.

Although fundamentalists have insisted that biblical inerrancy is the only theological matter at issue in the controversy, moderates have disagreed strongly. Indeed, the prevailing fundamentalists have succeeded in the systematic tearing down of what arguably are Baptists' three most distinctive theological contributions—the priesthood of all believers, autonomy of the local church, and separation of church and state. Space permits only a few examples.

Concerning the priesthood of all believers—a doctrine derived from what is unquestionably Baptists' primary theological distinctive, soul freedom—the 1988 Committee on Resolutions rejected a resolution presented by a messenger affirming the historic Baptist position, recommending in its place a statement actually denigrating its importance and extolling pastoral authority.[15]

By their discomfort with the radical, individualist principles of soul liberty and the priesthood of all believers, fundamentalists expose their own theological Achilles heel, namely, the low place given the Holy Spirit. The rank and file of ordinary Baptist people, fundamentalist leaders suggest, simply cannot be trusted—alone with their Bible and their God—to receive and appropriate divine truth. Instead, their faith must be formed and informed by "godly men" who claim to possess a higher and deeper knowledge of God than ordinary believers are capable of having. This "godly men" syndrome is perhaps the single most objectionable theological dimension of the particular strain of fundamentalism that has infected the SBC.

On local church autonomy, the SBC Committee on Resolutions in 1984 proposed and the convention adopted a statement opposing the ordination of women to the gospel ministry.[16] This resolution subsequently was seized upon by a newly constituted fundamentalist majority of directors of the Home Mission Board as the basis for denying Church Pastoral Aid to women pastors.[17]

With reference to Baptists' most distinctive contribution to the social order, separation of church and state, the convention in 1982 adopted a resolution favoring an amendment to the Constitution of the United States that would have empowered state legislatures and local school boards to write and require the recitation of prayers in public schools.[18]

In conclusion, the struggle by fundamentalists to wrest control of the SBC away from an entrenched moderate establishment was, first and foremost, a theological battle. Yet the theological issues at stake went far beyond biblical inerrancy. They included Baptist doctrines of first importance and concerted fundamentalist attacks upon them. In short, the fundamentalist party in the SBC stood on its head the old Baptist adage, as expressed by the foremost living Baptist authority on creeds and confessions of faith, William L. Lumpkin, that "(t)he Baptist Movement has traditionally been non-creedal in the sense that it has not erected authoritative confessions of faith as official bases of organization and tests of orthodoxy."[19]

Thus, moderate leaders who concluded that the struggle for control of the SBC was nontheological were not only wrong; they actually hurt the moderate cause by denying the full import of what was happening.

Internal Control

Despite the contention of a majority of the Peace Committee that "(t)he primary source of the controversy in the Southern Baptist Convention is the Bible,"[20] the clearly stated and primary objective of the inerrancy party was to gain control of the boards of trustees of the various seminaries, boards, and commissions of the SBC. Achieving this goal would enable the new fundamentalist establishment not only to enforce new policies in the nineteen convention agencies and institutions, but also to replace sitting agency heads and support staffs with people of their own choosing.[21]

That this end has been achieved is an indisputable fact. The first agency to pass from moderate to fundamentalist control was the Home Mission Board in 1986. That same year, the new majority succeeded in dismissing a presidential search committee and reconstituting the panel to reflect the new numbers. That panel then proceeded to nominate Larry Lewis, president of Hannibal-LaGrange College in Missouri, as the new president. Lewis's election marked the first major convention post to be filled by a fundamentalist.[22]

While the transition at the Home Mission Board was made quite easy by the move of Lewis's predecessor, William G. Tanner, to become executive director of the Baptist General Convention of Oklahoma, turning things around at the Foreign Mission Board would take much longer. Another factor had to do with the larger size of the board of directors of the FMB, a factor that delayed the arrival of a fundamentalist majority of overseers.

Once the working majority was achieved, however, the pressure on President R. Keith Parks and other administrators became more and more intense. Finally, in May 1992 and following repeated threats to his continued tenure, Parks announced his retirement, effective October 31, 1992, citing irreconcilable philosophical differences with his directors.

By 1987 Southeastern Baptist Theological Seminary had been captured, with the new fundamentalist majority on the board of trustees forcing the resignations of President W. Randall Lolley, Dean Morris Ashcraft, and other administrators.[23] Subsequently, Lewis Drummond, professor of evangelism at Southern Seminary, was elected to succeed Lolley. After a troubled four-year tenure, Drummond was forced to leave in favor of Paige Patterson, who reportedly had been dismissed—and then reinstated—by his own trustees at Criswell College in Dallas.

Only two other seminaries of the six owned and operated by the convention received anything other than a clean bill of health by the Peace Committee. One of these, Midwestern, was relieved of its one "problem" faculty member in 1992 when G. Temp Sparkman took early retirement for personal reasons.

The other, Southern Seminary in Louisville, Kentucky, selfconsciously has sought to avoid what its top administrators consider the mistakes of their counterparts at Southeastern by accommodating themselves repeatedly to the demands of fundamentalist trustees. Although Southern, by virtue of the large size of its board of trustees, enjoyed the advantage of being the last convention entity to be taken over, in later years it had to endure constant parries by the new fundamentalist majority. In October 1992, incumbent President Roy L. Honeycutt announced his retirement, effective at the end of 1993. His privately expressed hope was that by so doing he might better the chances that his successor be a more charitable—as over against confrontational—fundamentalist.

At the Sunday School Board, the world's largest publisher of religious materials, former president Lloyd Elder was forced to resign following a series of confrontations with hostile directors over a variety of issues. Not the least of these was Elder's outspoken support of the Baptist Joint Committee on Public Affairs. More than once Elder used the prestige of his office to hold off efforts to remove SBC funding for the Washington religious liberty agency. Beyond that, however, Elder incurred the wrath of many directors for opposing the writing and marketing of *The New American Commentary* series, to be written from the perspective of inerrancy, as well as for his defense of writers and editors of Sunday school materials and of his communications staff. After being censured in 1989, Elder finally was forced out in January 1991.

Yet none of the forced retirements or resignations at other agencies and institutions provoked the firestorm that followed the July 1991 Executive Committee firings of Baptist Press director Alvin C. Shackleford and news editor Dan Martin. Pressler himself was the person most responsible for the dismissals.

Following a series of confrontations, led in each instance by Pressler, Shackleford and Martin were dismissed on July 17, 1990, by the Executive Committee, which met in closed session with armed, off-duty Nashville police officers guarding the doors to the meeting room in the SBC building. Shackleford and Martin never were informed formally of the charges against them.[24]

Just as many moderates have distorted the true nature of the controversy in the SBC by insisting it had nothing to do with theology, so many fundamentalists have made the false claim that theology alone was the issue. Shackleford, an inerrantist of long standing, nevertheless lost his position. His dismissal—and Martin's—had to do, quite simply, with control.

In announcing their plan in 1979 to gain control of the boards of directors and trustees of SBC agencies and institutions through appointments to the Committee on Committees by a succession of SBC presidents, the architects of the takeover insisted their ultimate objective was to gain "parity" on the administrative staffs and faculties. Subsequent events have proven that claim as well to be false. Now that control is virtually absolute, nothing less than the purging of all "liberals" and the placement of "conservatives" in their places will suffice. Paige Patterson has set forth the revised objective thus:

> Some have expressed the feeling that since votes at the Southern Baptist Convention in recent years averaged a 55-45 percent differential that faculty and agency employment ought somehow to reflect that same split. While conservatives would be encouraged if the present employment picture actually reflected this idea, democracies do not function quite that way. For example, the American people have a right to vote for a president. The 45 to 48 percent who support the defeated candidate do not expect half or, for that matter, any of the seats on the president's cabinet. They anticipate no appointments from their political party to any posts.[25]

This "spoils of victory" approach now dominates the employment picture at SBC agencies and institutions.

Regardless of the damage perpetrated on faithful convention workers and teachers, not even the most partisan moderate can deny the efficiency of the fundamentalist drive to control SBC affairs. Largely because of the efforts of Pressler, who tirelessly crisscrossed the country rallying pastors and laypeople to the takeover effort, the plan worked. It succeeded as well because of its simplicity and the ability of Pressler and the other major players to remain focused on its achievement.

Finally, the success of the takeover plan can be attributed to Pressler and his colleagues' ability to mobilize large numbers of previously disengaged Southern Baptists. These were people in towns and hamlets previously largely ignored by the old SBC establishment, people who theretofore had played no role in convention affairs. Pressler in particular was able to convince these neglected constituents that Southern Baptist life was in clear and imminent danger because of theological liberalism and that they could turn the convention in a new direction. In this sense, the takeover of the SBC may be seen as a classic example of a successful populist uprising.

National Politics

Beyond purging Southern Baptist agencies and institutions of theological "liberalism," the new fundamentalist establishment was active from the beginning in a concerted effort to make of the SBC a reliable source of support for an ultraconservative national political agenda. By 1986 Paige Patterson went public with this supplemental—but hardly incidental—agenda by warning that future employment in the SBC would be conditioned on support of fundamentalist positions on such issues as abortion, euthanasia, and school prayer. This national political agenda, he said, would "go over nearly as well as the inerrancy thing."[26]

Indeed, it is more than coincidental that the rise of the fundamentalist party to power in the SBC paralleled the domination of the national political scene by Presidents Ronald Reagan and George Bush, each of whom was indebted to the New Christian Right for his election. This movement, like the SBC inerrancy party, began its rise to power in the late 1970s with the birth of Jerry Falwell's Moral Majority and the subsequent appearance of other similar groups, such as the Religious Roundtable. This latter organization was founded by Southern Baptist layman E. E. (Ed) McAteer, a member of Bellevue Baptist Church in Memphis. Several of the SBC presidents elected between 1979 and 1993 have served as directors of and advisers to these and other New Christian Right groups.

As George Marsden, one of the nation's foremost historians of fundamentalism, wrote in 1988, "It is clear that an important revolution has taken place in the inerrancy camp over the past decade, so that now it is wed to a national political program."[27]

Besides the involvement of several recent SBC presidents in partisan political activities—including current Sunday School Board president James T. Draper's campaign activities on behalf of M. G. (Pat) Robertson, an unsuccessful contender for the 1988 Republican presidential nomination—principal fundamentalist architects Pressler and Patterson have belonged to the Council for National Policy, a highly secretive, ultraconservative think tank. During at least 1989-90, Pressler was president of the group.[28] It was during a 1987 interview with Bill Moyers of Public Affairs Television, Inc., that Pressler became so agitated when questioned about his involvement in right-wing politics, including the Council for National Policy, that he abruptly terminated the interview.[29]

Within SBC institutional life, the national political agenda of the new fundamentalist leadership was most evident in the effort first to discredit, then to withdraw funding from, the Baptist Joint Committee on Public Affairs. Early in the takeover effort, the Washington agency came under severe criticism for its consistent opposition to state-written prayers in public school classrooms and to various governmental schemes to provide public funding for sectarian schools. For example, immediately before the 1982 convention in New Orleans, Paige Patterson was quoted as favoring the withdrawal of funding from the Baptist Joint Committee on Public Affairs. Of the group's executive director, James M. Dunn, Patterson said, "I think there will be something done to silence him."[30]

As a result of a 1986-87 Executive Committee probe, one of three such investigations, the SBC's representation on the BJCPA was enlarged from 15 to 18, and several heads of SBC agencies were ousted from previously ex-officio slots. This meant that the SBC Committee on Nominations was freed to nominate a larger number of at-large representatives to the BJCPA or, more properly, to the Public Affairs Committee—the name given the SBC delegation. At the same time, the investigative committee recommended and the convention approved separate and independent status for the PAC.

At the earliest opportunity, the Committee on Nominations presented and the convention elected several well-known, right-wing activists as PAC members. For the next four years, these new directors proceeded to conduct a type of guerilla warfare against the BJCPA staff and sought, without success, to have the full BJCPA reverse its historic position on several high-profile church-state issues. Among its most egregious actions was the unprecedented formal endorsement of Judge Robert Bork's nomination by President Reagan to the U.S. Supreme Court.[31]

In the end Pressler succeeded in leading the Executive Committee to recommend the withdrawal of funds from the BJCPA, which occurred in three stages.[32] In 1992 the convention formally disaffiliated itself from the BJCPA.[33]

In addition to breaking ties, the convention took a series of actions investing in the Christian Life Commission the religious liberty agenda previously assigned to the BJCPA, culminating in the 1990 revocation of the BJCPA's Program Statement and the enlargement of that of the Christian Life Commission.[34]

Although dislodging Dunn as the primary spokesman for Southern Baptists on the highly visible issues of church and state was one of the motives in the all-out war on the BJCPA, the underlying reason was to alter the SBC church-state agenda itself. Gone were the days of Southern Baptists' contending for a strict separation of church and state. In the new day, the SBC—through the Christian Life Commission—would go so far as to seek public tax monies for Baptist institutions, even churches, a proposition long considered anathema to Baptists generally.

Conclusion

In their brilliant accounts of the SBC controversy, both Nancy Ammerman and Bill Leonard have described the successful fundamentalist effort as a "hostile takeover."[35]

At the same time, Ammerman and Leonard have concluded that the demise of the old SBC establishment probably was inevitable, given the confluence of historical and sociological trends at work in the South and in American religious denominations. For more than half a century, they have noted, the old establishment successfully managed controversy and thereby avoided schism.[36]

In the end, what Leonard calls the "Grand Compromise," that is, the old establishment's earlier ability to accommodate leading fundamentalists without allowing them to take control, turned out to be a fatal weakness.[37] This entrenched elitism, developed gradually over a period of several decades, turned the SBC into an elaborate piece of ecclesiastical machinery in which vast power was vested in a relative handful of denominational bureaucrats. Long before the takeover effort was announced, the SBC had ceased to be a convention of ordinary Baptists, a virtual invitation to the kind of populist upheaval that overtook it.

As to the future of the new SBC and the old establishment now on the outside looking in, nothing but sheer speculation can be offered. Yet based on what has happened thus far, the following prospects appear at least plausible.

1. The working assumption of Pressler, Patterson, and others, that the SBC largely would hold together regardless of the predictable stresses on the convention's superstructure, appears to have been vindicated. At most, small splinters—not a major split—are likely. This, in fact, is the most attractive outcome possible for the new establishment.

2. The new establishment has demonstrated conclusively that it is skilled far beyond the ability to win elections. It has proven as well that it is fully capable of governing the complex structure of the SBC. With a few notable exceptions, the transition from old moderates to new fundamentalists has been remarkably smooth.

3. A small number of congregations, perhaps in the range of 50 to 100, will cease affiliation with the SBC and seek denominational homes elsewhere, principally in the American Baptist Churches. Nothing would please the new fundamentalist leaders more.

4. Contrary to the assumption of many, the Cooperative Baptist Fellowship is not likely to become a rival body to the SBC anytime soon. This likelihood was enhanced by the strongly stated views of R. Keith Parks, the Atlanta-based group's first missions coordinator, that the CBF should keep its missions program "under the broad umbrella of identity as Southern Baptists."[38] This assessment might change radically, however,

should the SBC move to disfellowship those congregations that choose the CBF as its disbursing agent for mission funds.

5. More and more congregations—fundamentalist and moderate alike—will deemphasize their connection with the SBC, choosing instead to carve out particular niches for themselves in their own communities. They will be more interested in portraying themselves as conservative or progressive than in flying the Baptist banner. This trend toward localism, already well underway before the controversy, merely has accelerated as a result of the bad public relations suffered by all Southern Baptists during the takeover period.

6. The SBC is likely to welcome large numbers of previously unaligned, self-described "independent/fundamentalist" congregations as a result of President Edwin Young's special task force investigating that prospect.

7. Because of this and other possible developments, it is at least conceivable that during the early twenty-first century a new, loosely knit confederation of progressive Baptists. may emerge across racial and regional lines that first divided Baptists—North and South, European American and African American—a century and a half ago. The Alliance of Baptists will continue to be a key player in discussions leading to such an outcome.

8. Regardless of future configurations of Baptists, however, what is clear is that the day of big-time denominationalism as best embodied by the old Southern Baptist Convention has come to an end, the self-described megalomaniacal views of Adrian Rogers notwithstanding.[39] The true heresy of this period of Baptist history was that committed by a group of people who convinced themselves they were, in Bill Leonard's inspired phrase, "God's last and only hope."

Notes

1. Walter B. Shurden, "The Southern Baptists' Educational Holy War: A Review Essay," *Planning for Higher Education* 19 (Winter 1990-91), 34-36.

2. Paul Pressler, "Firestorm Chats," tape recording of an interview conducted by Gary North (Fort Worth: Dominion Tapes, 1988).

3. See, e.g., Paige Patterson, "Stalemate," *The Theological Educator* (Special Issue: "The Controversy in the Southern Baptist Convention," 1985), 4-6.

4. See Richard Hofstadter, *Anti-Intellectualism in American Life* (New York: Knopf, 1963); Penrose St. Amant, "An Outline of the History of Religion in the United States" (unpublished), 12-14.

5. See Gilbert Tennent, "The Danger of an Unconverted Ministry," and John Hancock, "The Danger of an Unqualified Ministry," *Religious Issues in American History,* ed. Edwin Scott Gaustad (New York: Harper & Row, 1968), 28-45.

6. H. Leon McBeth, *The Baptist Heritage: Four Centuries of Baptist Witness* (Nashville: Broadman, 1987), 230-31.

7. Walter B. Shurden, *Not a Silent People: Controversies That Have Shaped Southern Baptists* (Nashville: Broadman, 1972), 110.

8. Ibid., 111-17.

9. Considerable research and writing remain to be done concerning the fact that most of the major principals in the struggle came from Texas. Much of the discontent of Paul Pressler and Paige Patterson, for example, centers on what they have claimed is liberalism at Baylor University and the Texas Baptist Christian Life Commission.

10. Patterson, "Stalemate," 6-7; Paul Pressler, "An Interview with Judge Paul Pressler," *The Theological Educator* (Special Issue, 1985), 15-17.

11. Adrian Rogers, "Adrian Rogers Analyzes Convention Issues from Conservative Perspective," *Indiana Baptist,* June 2, 1992, 21.

12. *Proceedings of the Conference on Biblical Inerrancy 1987* (Nashville: Broadman, 1987); Gordon James, *Inerrancy and the Southern Baptist Convention* (Dallas: Southern Baptist Heritage Press, 1986), 23-30; Clayton Sullivan, *Toward a Mature Faith: Does Biblical Inerrancy Make Sense?* (Decatur, Ga.: SBC Today, 1990); Rob James, ed., *The Takeover in the Southern Baptist Convention* (Decatur, Ga.: SBC Today, 1989), 18-21.

13. Shurden, "Educational Holy War," 34.

14. 1987 SBC Annual, 237.

15. 1988 SBC Annual, 68-69.

16. 1984 SBC Annual, 65.

17. 1988 SBC Annual, 165; Nancy Tatom Ammerman, *Baptist Battles: Social Change and Religious Conflict in the Southern Baptist Convention* (New Brunswick: Rutgers University Press, 1990), 223-24; Carolyn Weatherford, "Shaping of Leadership Among Southern Baptist Women," *Baptist History and Heritage* 22, July 1987, 18; Carolyn DeArmond Blevins, "Patterns of Ministry Among Southern Baptist Women," *Baptist History and Heritage* 22, July 1987, 47; Anne Thomas Neil and Virginia Garrett Neely, eds., *The New Has Come: Emerging Roles Among Southern Baptist Women* (Washington: Southern Baptist Alliance, 1989), 22; Richard E. Groves, "The Freedom of the Local Church," *Being Baptist Means Freedom,* ed. Alan Neely (Charlotte: Southern Baptist Alliance, 1988), 25-36.

18. 1982 SBC Annual, 58.

19. William L. Lumpkin, *Baptist Confessions of Faith* (Valley Forge, Pa.: Judson Press, 1959), 16.

20. 1987 SBC Annual, 233.

21. A detailed account of this strategy was set forth by Pressler in his "Firestorm Chats" interview with North.

22. Ammerman, *Baptist Battles,* 223-30.

23. James, *Takeover,* 30-32.

24. For an account of events precipitating the firings, see Stan Hastey, "The History of Associated Baptist Press," unpublished manuscript of address delivered at Mercer University, Macon, Georgia, Oct. 9, 1992, 1-13.

25. Paige Patterson, "My Vision of the Twenty-First Century SBC," *Review and Expositor* 88, Winter 1991, 41.

26. Shurden, "Educational Holy War," 34; Bill J. Leonard, "Southern Baptists and a New Religious Establishment," *The Christian Century,* Sept. 10-17, 1986, 775-76.

27. George Marsden, "The New Paganism," *The Reformed Journal,* Jan. 1988, 3-4.

28. Nancy Pressler, family Christmas letter, 1989.

29. Dan Martin, "Moyers Challenges Committee Action," Baptist Press, Feb. 24, 1989, 9.

30. Jim Asker, "Baptists Will Tackle 'Inerrancy' Question," *The Houston Post,* June 12, 1982, 6AA.

31. Ammerman, *Baptist Battles,* 241.

32. See 1988 SBC Annual, 33; 1990 SBC Annual, 62; 1991 SBC Annual, 32.

33. 1992 SBC Annual, 40.

34. 1990 SBC Annual, 47-55.

35. Ammerman, *Baptist Battles,* 253; Bill J. Leonard, *God's Last and Only Hope: The Fragmentation of the Southern Baptist Convention* (Grand Rapids: Eerdmans, 1990), 183.

36. Leonard, *God's Last and Only Hope,* 1-24.

37. Ibid., 58-64.

38. Greg Warner, "Parks Says He's Interested in Post If Fellowship Stays Southern Baptist," Associated Baptist Press, Nov. 24, 1992, 1; Warner, "Parks Accepts Offer to Lead Fellowship's Missions Program," Associated Baptist Press, Nov. 30, 1992, 1.

39. See n. 11.

Introduction to Part II.
The Search for Authority:
Baptist Use and
Interpretation of Scriptures

The sacred Scripture has been at the heart of both private and public faith development for most Christians since the Reformation. Among those who have relied most heavily—if not exclusively—on the specific, exact, and authoritative meaning of Scriptures in general and specific texts in particular, Baptists have been notable. "Bible believing"—in both the best and worst sense—is a phrase that comes immediately to mind when the name "Baptist" is mentioned. Of course, Baptists have frequently disagreed about the specific nature of the beliefs the Bible contains. Baptists, more than many others, have also debated which translation of the Bible is trustworthy.

Because Baptists have many traditions and do not rely on creeds, the authoritative use of Scripture is a particularly troublesome challenge. No Baptist would deny that Scripture is authoritative, yet nearly every Baptist has a different perspective regarding which interpretation is authoritative, and all Baptists claim the authority of Scripture to validate private faith and corporate church and community practice. The Baptist use and interpretation of Scripture, therefore, is at the heart of the tension between freedom and responsibility in both personal and community life and faith.

The following articles focus intensely on this issue from three uniquely distinct perspectives, each presented by an able Baptist biblical scholar:

Molly T. Marshall reviews some of the traditions of post-Reformation Christian use of the Scriptures. She focuses on several Baptist examples as evidence that the task of interpretation rests at the heart of the tradition of liberty of conscience. Her essay reminds us of the inevitability of subjectivity in the task of interpretation. She suggests that we have much to learn by discovering *why* others have heard the Scriptures speak to them as they do. In sharing their experience we may broaden our faith.

Joel B. Green approaches the challenge of biblical interpretation as a problem of hermeneutics and makes the case that our hermeneutical perspective is profoundly shaped by the "community of discourse" in which we develop our life and faith. He offers possibilities for expanding our interpretive skill, conditioned by a recognition of our own particular place in the broad community of faith.

David M. Scholer brings his focus to the problem of boundaries between individuals and communities of faith. Granted that freedom of interpretation is a cherished Baptist principle, are there not inviolable faith-community boundaries regarding interpretations of Scripture? As he addresses that issue, our dilemma in balancing freedom and responsibility becomes clear.

Each article—separately and together—reminds us of how sacred the Bible's materials really are to Baptists and why it is important that we take seriously the task of biblical interpretation.

Exercising Liberty of Conscience: Freedom in Private Interpretation

Molly T. Marshall

Discourse about methods for interpreting the Bible is much more constructive than fussing about theories concerning the nature of Scripture itself—something in which certain Baptists from the South have had far too much experience in recent years![1] It is important to remember, in the words of Rob James, that "Baptists have most often been united around the Scriptures, rather than around this or that doctrine or theory *about* the Scriptures."[2] Thus, in the context of responsible freedom, let us consider how Scripture *actually functions* in the life of the individual and the Baptist community of faith within the larger matrix of Christian history.

As heirs of the Reformation, *sola scriptura* remains paramount to Baptist identity. Yet, to call us a "people of the Book" (as has often been done in the overheated discussions of the twentieth century) is technically incorrect. "People of the Book" is a quotation from the Qur'an, which urges: "Do not dispute with the People of the Book: say, we believe in what has been sent down to us and what has been sent down to you" (Sura 29.45). Thus, it is really much more problematic to call Christians the "people of the Book" than to call Muslims or even certain Jews so—with the exception of Christian fundamentalists. It is fundamentalism, according to John Barton, "that comes closest to adopting in Christianity a theory of Scripture like the majority Islamic view of the Qur'an—as supernaturally inspired in origin, inerrant in content, and oracular in function."[3] Such a view leaves no room for a history of interpretation, the social location and personal experience of the interpreter, the context of the community, or new insights prompted by the midwifery of the Holy Spirit. It certainly

---

Molly T. Marshall is professor of theology and spiritual formation at Central Baptist Seminary, Kansas City, Kansas, and was previously a member of the faculty at Southern Baptist Seminary, Louisville, Kentucky. This paper was presented at "Called to Responsible Freedom: A Conference on Baptist Distinctives," at Green Lake, Wisconsin, August 1996.

precludes a significant tradition within Baptist life, the dissenting tradition born of liberty of conscience.

Alongside the emphasis on the centrality of the Bible, Baptists have made their own the other two Reformation watchwords: *sola fidei* and *sola Christi*. A place of stability has been constructed upon these three affirmations. Treating any of these alone—that is, abstracting Scripture, faith, or Christ from an interdependent relationship—creates as great a problem as trying to construct a Christology without attention to pneumatology or trying to speak of God as Creator without attention to God as Redeemer. Hence we interpret Scripture through faith according to the measure of Christ, for he is the Incarnate Word and the Bible is the written word; one expresses and one refers, as John Macquarrie puts it.[4]

The Dissenting Heritage of Baptists

The focus of this essay is the "freedom of private interpretation" as a Baptist principle of biblical interpretation. I approach this with a measure of caution because I do not believe that *purely* private interpretation can ever be completely satisfactory. To quote John Wesley: "No one can be a Christian alone." To be a Christian is to live with accountability to the gathered community, of which we are a part. Thus, when we speak of Baptist distinctives, such as the "liberty of conscience" or the "priesthood of all believers," we are not simply exalting individualism; rather, we are acknowledging the profound capacity and responsibility each human being has in relation to the Holy One who addresses us one by one, who abides within each Christian, and who gifts and calls us for distinctive contributions to the *missio dei*.

A hallmark of Baptist identity is the affirmation that each individual is competent to interpret Scripture according to the dictates of conscience and the guidance of the Holy Spirit.[5] Baptist identity was initially forged by direct appeal to the authority of Scriptures as our forebears contended for believers' baptism, voluntary faith, and the freedom of the gathered community over against the established church regulated by the state. Thus, the necessarily individual aspects of Christian discipleship were buttressed by the vital Baptist freedom of the right of private interpretation. Indeed, simply taking another's word for something was seen as an abdication of a believer's fundamental right and responsibility. In 1652 Roger Williams warned: "It is the command of Christ Jesus to his scholars [Rogers called all Christians "scholars"] to try all things: and the liberty of trying what a friend, or even what an enemy presents hath ever proved an especial means of attaining to the truth of Christ."[6] The dissenting tradition of Baptists has been shaped by the freedom to study the Scriptures, believing that God hath "yet more truth and light to break forth from God's Word."[7] More recent Baptists have affirmed the continuation of the historic Baptist principle of freedom in individual interpretation.[8] It is a natural concomitant of voluntarism. William H. Brackney summarizes this stress on individuals:

> Partly a reaction to collectivism, and partly a component of the *via moderna of* western thought, voluntarism emphasizes the capacity and capability of believers. Created in God's image "for good works" and redeemed by Christ, individuals can make a difference and are responsible to participate in the life of the church and as agents of transformation, spiritually and morally, in their societies.[9]

We have noted the elements of Reformed tradition issuing out of the sixteenth-century Reformation. Our concern about biblical interpretation can be assisted further if we will consider our Anabaptist heritage as well. Rather than beginning with revelation as "a way of securing epistemological foundations" as the scholastics of the Reformed tradition do, the Anabaptists began not with a theory of inspiration, "but with a sense of participation in the Story, of being addressed by a living Word."[10]

Focusing on epistemological foundations leads inevitably to the acrimonious and arid debates that have ravaged the Baptist family during the twentieth century. These developments have resulted from a neglect of the Anabaptist insights about the personal dimension of biblical interpretation.[11]

Perhaps more than any other contemporary Baptist, James McClendon has recovered "the baptist vision" that reads Scripture with a "hermeneutic of participation." He recognizes that this vision "allows a variety of Bible readings, a variety of applications, depending on time and place and, of course, on the *individuality* of the readers of Scripture in each time and place."[12] This approach affirms the authority of the entire canon but begins with and is centered in the Jesus story. He writes: "The Bible is a book whose explanation centers in the one upon whom it centers—Jesus, and the God whose gospel Jesus preached. . . . If we have come to that center, we read the Bible aright."[13] His forebears in this include the Mennonite tradition and the London Confession's support for scriptural authority with *Christ as norm*. This idea has remained central in Baptist confessions although it has been lost in the scholastic arguments about the Bible. Through our baptism, we are drawn into the life, death, and resurrection of Jesus; his story becomes our story, and we complete his story through our individual and communal participation. It is an "incarnational discipleship." Under the guidance of the Spirit all Christians can read and interpret the Bible. Though the linguistic conventions for speaking about humanity have changed, we should agree with the intent of the British Baptists' statement of 1948: "We firmly hold that each man must search the Scriptures for himself and seek the illumination of the Holy Spirit to interpret them."[14]

When the Anabaptist stress on the covenant community is neglected,[15] Baptists can and have taken "liberty of conscience," "soul competency," and the "priesthood of the believer" (accent on *the believer)* to mean that one can believe what one chooses and has the "right of personal judgment" in matters of faith and doctrine.[16] Contemporary Baptist ethicist Michael Westmoreland-White reminds us that "such an individualism has no place for church discipline (whether formative or corrective) since no one has the authority to interfere with anyone else's 'private' religion. Genuine Baptist liberty is twisted into normlessness"[17] when the freedom of private interpretation is devoid of ecclesial context.

Likewise, the neglect of their Anabaptist roots can and has led Baptists to forget liberty of conscience altogether (which can foster a "ministry of dissent") and reduced the priesthood of believers to no more than an assertion of the nonnecessity of a human mediator in prayer. Excessive individualism, devoid of communal dimensions, cannot lead to mature Christian discipleship.

Many contemporary Baptists believe that recent years have shown our ecclesial tradition to be more vulnerable to authoritarianism than individualism—hence we need its fresh expression to bring new life to the people of God. One Baptist theologian to realize the dangers of demagogic authoritarianism and hyperindividualism—both overacting postures—is Elizabeth B. Barnes. In her monograph *An Affront to the Gospel?* Barnes convincingly argues that historic Baptist focus on the individual conscience alone before God, even in leading Baptist "divines" such as Francis Wayland and E. Y. Mullins, led to the divorce of salvation from actions for social justice—the latter being considered incidental to faith.[18] Baptist acceptance of slavery, segregation, huge disparities in wealth, the oppression of women, and many other injustices can be traced to this hyperindividualism. Barnes goes on to work for a more adequate Baptist ecclesiology using insights from the early work of Karl Barth and strongly affirms a *proper* focus on the individual in the face of current forms of Baptist authoritarianism and ethical negligence.[19] The balance she seeks allows the preservation of individual freedom within the community of faith. It is difficult to hold these two loci of authority together.

In a recent work on biblical interpretation, Sharon Ringe and Frederick Tiffany note the tension between an authoritative reading of the church's Scripture and the contemporary current of individualism:

> Such an orientation tends to privatize religion into the spiritual task or quest of each believer. The popularized notion of the "priesthood of all believers" is invoked to claim that each individual can read the Bible for himself or herself. The awkward juxtaposition of these two tendencies of privatization and universalism within the church would seem to create a particular tension in the arena of biblical interpretation.[20]

Their point is well taken, for tension will ensue, but the interpretive task of each believer cannot be forsaken.

The Role of Private Interpretation

After all these demurrers, what is the rightful place for freedom in private interpretation? What does the spiritual practice of private interpretation offer the life of the believer that he or she can gain in no other way? What does it offer the community?

Translating the Bible into the vernacular and placing it in the hands of the laity (against the protestations of the clergy) was a signal reform of the sixteenth century.[21] Later, commenting on this populist movement, Thomas Hobbes expressed his horror at the prospect of an "everyman [*sic*] theology":

> After the Bible was translated . . . everyman, nay every boy and wench that could read English thought they spoke with God Almighty, and understood what he said when by a certain number of chapters a day they had read the Scriptures once or twice over.[22]

Such criticisms notwithstanding, this revolution beckoned a new responsibility in discerning the Word of God. This hard-won privilege (and responsibility) has not always been sufficiently prized—as recent internecine skirmishes have demonstrated.

Recently, speaking at the National Bible Conference (Green Lake, Wisconsin), Manfred Brauch, president of Eastern Baptist Theological Seminary, distinguished between two ways of reading the Bible: (1) to read for *information,* to know more—in this reading, we are the subject and the Bible is the object; and (2) to read it in terms of *formation,* which is not to read the book, but to "let the book read me." This approach allows the Bible to address and interrogate the reader. This moves toward *transformation* as the Bible accomplishes its purpose in the interpreter's life. Too often Sunday school methods have left us reading for information, objectifying the Bible so that we might become champions of that dubious game "Bible Trivia." Many of our Baptist quarrels have debated the facticity of Eve's "priority in the Edenic fall," a sun standing still, an axhead floating, a sojourn in the belly of a big fish, a late-night stroll on the Sea of Galilee, ad nauseum. Surely that is an immature way to engage the church's measure of God's ways with humanity. Besides, it has lost the natural way that Baptists have approached the Bible, that sense of participating in the story, "making the story of the Bible their story," as Lindbeck puts it.[23]

Kathleen Norris, in *The Cloister Walk,* tells of her experience of praying the liturgy of the hours with the Benedictines at St. John's Abbey.[24] As you may know, the Psalter is the staple of that cycle of prayer. Her experience of being brought to new faith through this discipline led her to believe that as the words of Scripture plowed their way into the soil of her heart, she was being transformed by the guidance they provided. She was finding "answers" to life's deepest questions and balm for life's deepest hurts. Surely this was happening in a communal context, yet her experience was uniquely her own as the Bible exegeted her life. Information was a secondary concern at best.

In a significant article, "The Primacy of Consent and the Uses of Suspicion," Ben Meyer instructs the biblical interpreter about a proper subjectivity when approaching the text. It is imperative that the biblical interpreter cultivate a "disposition of openness to the horizon, message, and tone of the text." This is not an impersonal curiosity, but an "orientation to consent," which I believe is formed in community. This manner of being attuned to the text then can allow the individual's analytic suspicion to function freely.

Giving attention and sympathy to the text makes the interpreter ready to pursue the secondary matter of suspicion. Suspicion "belongs to critique; that is, it belongs to the effort to say, not what the text means (that is the task of interpretation), but how adequately and authentically it means what it means."[25] It is the person who loves the Scriptures and regards them as holy who can best exercise this dimension of critical realism.

Perhaps the Bible is most deeply personal to the reader when she or he is practicing that ancient spiritual discipline *Lectio Divina.* In solitude with the impress of the Spirit we can voice our perplexed longings and unknowing. Elizabeth O'Connor offers good direction for this form of "meditative reading":

> Let the readings be a stepping-off place for your meditation that will give you your own questions and answers and guide. Practice in meditative reading is not only to hear what an author is saying, but to give our own thoughts and feelings an opportunity to be fully heard. This means we expose ourselves to the possibility of change; whenever we listen to ourselves or to another we take this risk.[26]

In this painstaking weaving of the Scripture with the tattered threads of our lives, new fabrics of understanding are created. In a recent article in the spirituality journal *Weavings,* Wendy Wright speaks of the varied ways "that scripture texts weave themselves into our lived composition":

> We proclaim the word in community, we preach it, we study it on our own. We consult it as ethical and religious guide. We memorize it and reenact its stories on feast days and recreate them in melody in our hymns. But it is the more subterranean ways that we internalize scripture that truly form us.[27]

Freedom in private interpretation means that we interrogate the text with the most difficult and painful questions we bear. The female seminary student writing an exegesis paper in her Hebrew Scripture class suddenly is thrown headlong into rending questions by the "text of terror" about the rape and dismembering of the Levite's concubine in Judges 19. Horror washes over her as she realizes that the man who allows this to happen to his common-law wife (in order to protect himself) is revered in the Scriptures as a faithful member of the Israelite community. There is no censure of his action. What is she to make of this text? Is this woman counted of so little value because of her uncertain marital status? Does the male invariably have prerogative to dispose of "his woman" as he pleases? Why does God not rescue the young woman from her abusers? (She remembered that God had spared Isaac; she also remembered that a similar story had happened in Sodom as Lot offered his virgin daughters to protect the men in his hospitality from gang rape. Is this an "approved" biblical pattern?) And what claim does the God rendered in this text have on her own young female life? Is she of more worth than her sister in faith of earlier time?

How can she bring the questions she has forged in private into the community? If they remain unspoken, quite probably they will remain unredeemed, or at least without the perspective other faithful readers can offer. It is the challenge of the larger hermeneutical circle to hear the terror and prophetic fire that careful private engagement of the Bible can elicit. It is the challenge of the worshiping community to allow the troubling, neglected texts of Scripture to provide interpretive leaven for those less disturbing texts. It is the unavoidable responsibility of the church to wrestle with "the strange world of the Bible" in order to understand their own world more clearly. The church is comprised of individuals whose freedom of private interpretation can challenge comfortable complacency.

Perceiving truth may put the interpreter into conflict with others, especially if it points away from closely held tradition. Truth not only puts our former way of life at risk, it can be quite threatening to those who presume to have an unequivocal grasp of the ways of God. Fred Craddock describes how persons often resist new truth:

> History demonstrates that anger is generated not alone by hearing one who is wrong but one who is right. Hearing the truth we painfully recognize puts us at war with ourselves, and when at war with ourselves we tend to make casualties of others, especially those who create the discomfort.[28]

Like grace, truth is not cheap. It has a compelling reality that reorients one's whole life. As Ringe and Tiffany remind us, "An important step in responsible interpretation is learning to be attentive to readings from many distinct persons and communities.[29] Listening to the interpretive insights of individuals is a Baptist distinctive worth preserving. The female voices in the Baptist tradition have been silenced for too long.

Further, white Baptist communities have not listened sufficiently to the readings of Scripture by African American Baptists. I well remember when one of my students in a seminar on the theology of the Synoptics asked if he might treat in his term paper the Cyrene who was conscripted to carry the cross of Jesus. I asked why; there really was not much textual evidence about that particular pericope. He responded by telling me of the significance that Simon had in his black church tradition; Simon was a biblical figure with whom others who had been pressed into service could identify. He bore the cross willingly because he saw a purpose his oppressors missed. This student's reading of Scripture opened up a new vista of understanding as he explored a perspective that I (and other white members of the seminar) simply did not know. Womanist scholars have taught me about Hagar, one who had little say in the disposition of her body because of her mistress and master's behest. As a "sister in the wilderness" she represented the story of countless black women whose survival depended on functioning in ways dependent and demeaning.

How much we have missed by suppressing private interpretation or being inattentive to a reading that comes out of a different social location! Provincialism can occur when the particularity of freedom is ignored. Rather than being a threat to the life of the community that calls the Bible its guide, private interpretation can give new perspective and bring powerful insight to a community in need of the fresh illumination through the Spirit of God.

Notes

1. For some of the contours of the discussion in Southern Baptist life, see the collection of essays edited by Robison B. James and David S. Dockery, *Beyond the Impasse? Scripture, Interpretation, and Theology in Baptist Life* (Nashville: Broadman, 1992).

2. Robison James, ed., *The Takeover in the Southern Baptist Convention: A Brief History* (Decatur, Ga.: SBC Today, 1989), 6.

3. John Barton, *People of the Book? The Authority of the Bible in Christianity,* rev. ed. (London: SPCK, 1993), 1.

4. John Macquarrie, *Principles of Christian Theology,* rev. ed. (London: SCM Press, 1977), 318-19.

5. British Baptist H. Wheeler Robinson, *The Life and Faith of the Baptists,* rev. ed. (London: Kingsgate, 1946), gave sustained attention to the perils that can accompany this simple and direct use of Scripture by individuals. He writes, "The strength of Baptists lies in their Scriptural individualism, their weakness chiefly in the defects of their quality" (140). Further, the "individual believer is encouraged to interpret it for himself, but he often lacks the most elementary training for this" (141).

6. Cited in E. Y. Mullins, *The Axioms of Religion* (Philadelphia: Judson Press, 1908), 56.

7. This phrase is attributed to John Robinson, a leading exponent of English Separatism and pastor of the Pilgrims.

8. In the latter part of the nineteenth century, the Baptist Union of Great Britain and Ireland affirmed their faith in "the Divine Inspiration and Authority of the Holy Scriptures as the supreme and sufficient rule of our faith and practice: *and the right and duty of individual judgment in the interpretation of it.* " As cited in G. Keith Parker, *Baptists in Europe: History and Confessions of Faith* (Nashville: Broadman, 1982), 280. (Italics added for emphasis.)

9. William H. Brackney, "Voluntarism in Baptist Tradition," *Defining Baptist Convictions: Guidelines for the Twenty-First Century,* ed. Charles W. Deweese (Franklin, Tenn.: Providence House, 1996), 92.

10. Michael L. Westmoreland-White, "Implications for the Current Debate Over Baptist Identity: A Response to Glen Stassen, 'Finding the Evidence for Christ-Centered Discipleship in Baptist Origins by Opening Menno Simons' Foundation-Book,'" unpublished paper delivered to the joint meeting of the National Association of Baptist Professors of Religion and the College Theological Society, University of Dayton, Dayton, Ohio, May 30, 1996, 13ff.

11. See George Hunston Williams, *The Radical Reformation* (Philadelphia: Westminster Press, 1962), 816-32.

12. James Wm. McClendon Jr., *Systematic Theology: Doctrine* (Nashville: Abingdon Press, 1994), 46, emphasis mine.

13. Ibid., 38.

14. "The Baptist Doctrine of the Church," in Roger Hayden, ed., *Baptist Union Documents,* 1948-1977 (London: Baptist Historical Society, 1980), 7.

15. Two articles argue cogently for the Anabaptist influence on both General and

Particular Baptists. Cf. Lonnie D. Kliever, "General Baptist Origins: The Question of Anabaptist Influence," *The Mennonite Quarterly Review* 36, no. 4 (Oct. 1962), and, in the same journal issue, Glen H. Stassen, "Anabaptist Influence in the Origin of the Particular Baptists."

16. Timothy George, *Theology of the Reformers* (Nashville: Broadman, 1988), 96ff., offers a balanced treatment of the priesthood of all believers as it is found in the theology of Martin Luther.

17. Westmoreland-White, "Implications for the Current Debate Over Baptist Identity," 17.

18. Thus, Wayland could write in *Elements of Moral Science* (Boston: Gould and Lincoln, 1852), 200-201: "Every human being is, by his constitution, a separate, and distinct, and complete system, adapted to all the purposes of self-government, and responsible, separately, to God, for the manner in which his powers are employed. . . . He need assign no other reason for his conduct than his own free choice. Within this limit, he is still responsible to God; but . . . he is not responsible to man, nor is man responsible for him."

19. Elizabeth B. Barnes, *An Affront to the Gospel? The Radical Barth and the Southern Baptist Convention* (Atlanta: Scholars Press, 1987), 1-8.

20. Frederick C. Tiffany and Sharon H. Ringe, *Biblical Interpretation: A Roadmap* (Nashville: Abingdon, 1996), 207.

21. George, *Theology of the Reformers,* 79-80, notes this remarkable shift: "The invention of the printing press together with Luther's German Bible did in a sense 'unchain' the Scriptures by making them available not only to scholars and monks but also to ploughboys in the fields and milkmaids at their pails. We cannot appreciate the role of Scripture in Reformation theology without being aware of the enormous revolution in sensibilities which accompanied the widespread distribution of the Bible in Europe."

22. Thomas Hobbes, *Works*, William Molesworth, ed. (London: n.p., 1839-1845), 6:190, cited in George, *Theology of the Reformers*, 80.

23. George Lindbeck, *The Nature of Doctrine* (Philadelphia: Westminster Press, 1984), 118.

24. Kathleen Norris, *The Cloister Walk* (New York: Riverhead Books, 1996).

25. Ben F. Meyer, "The Primacy of Consent and the Uses of Suspicion," *Ex Auditu* 11 (1986): 31-32.

26. Elizabeth O'Connor, *Our Many Selves* (New York: Harper & Row, 1971), xviii.

27. Wendy M. Wright, "Seasons of Glad Songs: Entries from a Notebook on Scripture and Prayer," *Weavings: A Journal of the Christian Spiritual Life* 11, 4 (July/Aug. 1996): 9.

28. Fred B. Craddock, *John,* Knox Preaching Guides, ed. John H. Hayes (Atlanta: John Knox, 1982), 68.

29. Tiffany and Ringe, *Biblical Interpretation*, 14.

Biblical Authority
and Communities of Discourse

Joel B. Green

Introduction

Although one hears only rarely today of "the battle for the Bible,"[1] voices concerned with the contemporary crisis in biblical authority are plentiful.[2] This shift in language is not without consequence. In earlier decades the battle lines were drawn with reference to the relative appropriateness of a series of dogmatic formulations about the intrinsic character of the Bible—its inerrancy (detailed? partial? irenic?) and/or infallibility, for example.[3] More recently, pressing questions of a different sort have surfaced with the result that affirmations concerning the Bible's character are not as prominent as are questions concerned with how to measure fidelity to its message. The contours of the "crisis" we face are formed, too, by some circles of the church where the contemporary relevance of Scripture can no longer be taken for granted or is even flatly denied.

How do we account for this state of affairs? What can be done to address it? These are the two primary questions I will address in this essay. First, we will explore in a necessarily cursory way three promising landmarks on the landscape of contemporary discussion about biblical authority. Following this, I want to suggest what is at stake in discourse about biblical authority and interpretation. Setting the stage in these two ways serves to accord privilege to the question to which we will turn in the final, major section of this essay—namely, How can we speak today of the practical authority of the Bible? Or, to put the question in a slightly different way, How does the Bible function authoritatively in practice? As I hope to

Joel B. Green is Associate Professor of New Testament at the American Baptist Seminary of the West and Graduate Theological Union, Berkeley, California. This paper was presented at "Called to Responsible Freedom: A Conference on Baptist Distinctives," at Green Lake, Wisconsin, August 1996.

indicate, because our questions about the authority and relevance of Scripture arise to a large extent from the practices of persons and communities professing to be Christian (and intra-ecclesiastical controversy concerning those practices), an examination of the authority of the Bible *in practice* is a fruitful way to engage this discussion. More importantly, an examination of biblical authority from this vantage point is oriented toward the formation of Christian character and identity, along with behaviors marked by Christian faithfulness, that are always the best confirmation of the validity of one's beliefs about and practices with regard to the Old and New Testaments.[4]

Biblical Authority Today: Setting the Stage

Exposing and exploring some of the grounds of the problem of biblical authority will help us to discern more precisely the nature of the issues facing us. It is also true, of course, that how we identify this dilemma will help to determine the compass points we will use in our exploration of ways to address it. By way of setting the stage, I will highlight three theses concerning the character of biblical authority and interpretation that together crisscross both American culture as many of us experience it and the culture of biblical studies at the turn of the twenty-first century.

First, the problem of the authority of the Bible is first a problem of authority. The possibility of generalizing about "American culture" has been problematized in recent decades by recognition of an inherent glossolalia that refuses to be silenced in favor of the one voice of what many have assumed to be the great American story. However, even this problem can be taken as evidence of my first observation—namely, that, as a people, we have acquired and we now propagate an impassioned distrust of any authority external to ourselves and/or to our communities of reference. We will not have others speaking for us or telling us what to do, and we have learned to be wary of attempting to speak for others.

Speaking of what they label as the American middle-class—an identification implicated in its own shortcomings for being too white and too urban, for example—Robert Bellah and his team have nevertheless put their collective finger on one of the chief cultural menaces whose tentacles find their way into crevices of all kinds. This is our fierce individualism—a pattern of dispositions and practices that defines life's ultimate goals in terms of personal choice, freedom in terms of being left alone by others to believe and act as one wishes, and justice as a matter of equal opportunity for individuals to pursue happiness as each person has defined it for her- or himself.[5]

If the problem of the authority of Scripture is grounded in part in what Bellah refers to as "ontological individualism," then it is exacerbated even more in American Baptist circles by the conjunction of twentieth-century American individualism with a seventeenth-century emphasis on individual conscience. One might concede the wisdom of the development of the notion of "soul freedom" in the context of repressive communitarian existence. It is quite another thing, however, to witness the wholesale baptism of tendencies toward autonomous individualism by the dogma of soul freedom. (And this is not even to mention the more problematic doctrine of "soul competence"!)

Whether knowingly or not, those from whatever community weaned on a distrust of power have their intellectual champion (or patron saint) in the French theorist Michel Foucault. For Foucault and his followers, and they are a flourishing breed, discourse is imbued with dimensions of domination; discourse itself is a mode of power by which inequality is enacted, promulgated, and legitimated. "Truth" is a social construct, and whoever has power can and does determine its content.[6]

This radical critique of authority and its legitimation has, for some, cast long shadows of doubt on biblical authority as well. To one who has supped at the table of Foucault, it may be only natural (1) to allege that the Bible's authority is undermined by the reality that all or most of the biblical texts were generated by persons in power (males, heterosexists, and the like); (2) to relativize, minimize, or even disavow the potential reach of the Bible's authority since, it is alleged, the biblical canon itself was constructed by "conquerors" in early Christianity; and (3) to repudiate the wisdom of our Christian forebears since biblical interpretation has largely resided in the hands of those (again, males, heterosexists, and the like) born on the winning side of history.

The Foucauldian notion that discourse is wholly determined by, and is solely in the service of, power thus incriminates authority of all kinds, including biblical authority. Taken to such extremes, though, this way of thinking provides us with much too blunt an instrument for understanding the communicative function of discourse of all kinds, including discourse with and about the Bible. Power is a pervasive relational and social phenomenon, to be sure, but power is not *everything*.[7] Recognition of these books as canonical and not others, for example, arose from consensual as well as conflictive processes. As John Goldingay observes, "Power was a factor in the canonical process, but not the sole factor, and awareness of it as an aspect of the process should not lead to a reductionist approach to that process."[8] Moreover, our uneasiness, embarrassment, or fear of power, and our tendencies to think of power always as coercive or inhibiting, overlook Foucault's own awareness late in life that power has "as much a creative, positive aspect as it does an exclusionary, silencing one."[9] It is also worth reflecting on the difference between indicting discourse as necessarily and invariably in the service of power and recognizing that, even if all discourse originates from within particular social forms and practices, it does not necessarily mirror or support those cultural norms. Cultural products are capable of absorbing social values and expressions of institutional authority in order to undermine them, too.[10] Consider the treatment of the Roman Empire in that discursive instrument we know as the Book of Revelation![11]

Second, the problem of the authority of the Bible is a product of a loss of the voice of the Bible. The loss of biblical voice can be traced along two parallel tracks—the loss of "the songs of Zion" in wider American discourse and the diminished role of the Bible as a resource in theology, ethics, and the pulpit.

One need not delve far into the annals of American life to see the profound influence of biblical language and metaphor, the biblical story and vision of liberation. Recognition of inspiration from Scripture is axiomatic in the study of literature and art, but public life has been similarly influenced. While seeking to uncover the impetus for "acts of compassion" in American life, Robert Wuthnow discovered a positive correlation between charitable behavior and familiarity with the story of the good Samaritan. People who profess no connection with the church and who prove incapable of reciting the story in recognizable form, nevertheless speak of "the good Samaritan effect." Wuthnow notes that this parable has become "one of those ancient myths that embodies the deepest meanings in our culture. In learning it and reshaping it we define what it means to be compassionate."[12] Although Wuthnow has put his finger on the sort of influence about which we are concerned, he is more optimistic about the capacity of the story of the good Samaritan to inspire acts of compassion than we may be. His study provides examples of people's attempts to retell the story—examples that are distressing in their tendency to discard the challenge of the story, at least in its first-century sociohistorical context, and especially in its Lukan cotext (Luke 10:25-37). The Lukan parable confronts its audience not with the general need to show compassion, but more pointedly with compassion for "people not like us," "the outsider," "the enemy." We may take solace in the apparent reality that people are being motivated to compassionate acts at all, but the story Wuthnow constructs at least invites us to reflect on the consequences of the loss of firsthand engagement with Scripture among persons in and outside of the church.

Similar reflections might be encouraged by a reference to "climbing Jacob's ladder" or to that "sweet chariot," about to "swing low," "coming for to carry me home." Here we find remarkable illustrations of the use of "biblical language," in the form of hymnic doublespeak, to give significance to a historic vision of liberation. Today, though, images of liberation derived from the biblical tradition have been replaced with the codependent-and-recovery language of popular psychology,[13] and not many of us are aware of the metaphorical reach of "Jacob's ladder" as a reference to the Underground Railroad.

One might think, and justifiably so, that a diminished role for Scripture in the public arena could never be replicated in systematic theology, ethics, and preaching. In fact, it is now a familiar complaint that academic biblical scholarship fails to provide the help the Christian community needs in interpreting its own Scriptures. The gap between biblical scholarship and Christian preaching has often been emphasized, but one need not look far in the twentieth century to see the move of theologians and ethicists away from biblical studies and to other disciplines in search of authoritative infrastructures for their constructive work: philosophy, sociology, and the natural sciences in particular.[14] The reasons for this transformation in theological method and ethical discourse are undoubtedly legend, but heading that list is clearly the mode of biblical study accredited by scholarly procedure and practiced in scholarly society in the past two centuries. That is, the enormous gap between academic study of the Bible and theology, ethics, and the preaching ministry of the church can largely be articulated in terms of the legacy of the historical critical paradigm in biblical studies.

According to the famous formulation of Karl Barth, systematic theology "does not ask what the apostles and prophets said but what we must say on the basis of the apostles and prophets."[15] The hegemony of the historical critical paradigm in biblical studies, however, has left theology with little access to "what the apostles and prophets said," since (1) biblical study has developed into a specialization open only to those capable of working within the security of accredited scholarly procedures; (2) issues of religious relevance or the religious use of biblical texts have consistently occupied a slot at the bottom of the list of priorities among professional interpreters of the Bible, if such issues were thought to belong on

that list at all; (3) the historical critical paradigm has engendered a
historical skepticism of such proportions, and drawn the "strange world
of the Bible" as so profoundly remote from our own, that many graduates
of our theological institutions (both liberal and evangelical) are left with
the question, Is there anything of consequence, anything "true" to proclaim? and (4) even at its best, the scientific approach embodied in the
historical critical paradigm generates little by way of resources for the
larger theological and ethical task, much less for the sermon.

To speak of the chasm between church and biblical studies regarding
the competing purposes of biblical interpretation today is to state the
obvious. According to Robert Morgan, for one kind of reader, Scripture
refers to the texts by which we contemplate the history of Israelite and
Christian religion while the other is concerned with the texts by which we
orient the meaning of our lives. He observes, "If the tensions [between
biblical scholars and religious communities] are less in evidence today
than formerly, that is not because they have been resolved, but because
fewer biblical scholars are theologians."[16]

To those outside the guild, it may be surprising to hear that the Bible
and theology need to be brought into dialogue with one another, and that
those who have begun to do so are engaged in interdisciplinarity. But this
is precisely the state of affairs in which we find ourselves today.[17]

*Third, the problem of the authority of the Bible is intertwined with the
enormous metamorphoses current in hermeneutics and biblical interpretation.* For those concerned with biblical authority in practice, the contemporary setting cannot be painted without reference to the enormous
upheavals that have shaken the foundations of biblical study in the last
third of the twentieth century.[18] Among these the most noticeable is the
fallen hegemony of the historical critical paradigm and concomitant
disillusionment among students of Scripture concerning the promise of
isolating the single "intended," correct meaning of a biblical text. Evidence abounds everywhere in biblical studies of a search for aims and
approaches that are not tethered to the historical mode of critical inquiry
that has characterized biblical scholarship in the modern period. The
meaning of biblical texts is itself more and more regarded as polyvalent,
with different methods oriented to locating textual significance (1) behind
the text, treating the text as a window into the historical events and
processes informing the text; (2) in the text, according privilege to the text
itself as a cultural product or artifact and as literature, so that validity in
interpretation is adjudicated with reference to the evidence provided by
the text itself, and not by more or less possible reconstructions of a

pre-textual history or tradition; and (3) in front of the text, accounting for the reality that different readers and reading communities, situated in distinctive cultural settings, often hear a text and construe its significance differently. Variation at this juncture has yielded a dazzling array of strategies for engaging biblical texts.[19]

Less obvious thus far in biblical study, but of far-reaching significance, is the critical turn in how the goal of hermeneutical inquiry is articulated. In the nineteenth century, the hermeneutical enterprise was generally oriented toward the discovery and accumulation of "meaning." In the twentieth century, hermeneutics came to appreciate more the communicative function of texts. That is, hermeneutics has come to be more concerned with the capacity of texts to produce certain transforming effects rather than simply to transmit certain information. What is remarkable, though, is that, even in the twentieth century, *biblical* study has proceeded on the basis of nineteenth-century concerns with an information-oriented paradigm and has embraced hermeneutical concerns with formation and transformation only very recently and only then by voices crying in the wilderness.[20]

Our current state of affairs is aptly caricatured by Kevin Vanhoozer. He refers first to "inactive reading": "Like those who only hear the tune of a Brahms symphony, these inactive readers only listen for the plot or for the proposition." Inactivity might refer equally to the unskilled reader who lacks the sensitivities necessary to explore the significance of a biblical text, and to those content with explaining a text at a distance, disengaged personally from its questions and challenges. There is, secondly, "reactive reading." Such readers, recognizing that no reading is innocent or devoid of ideology, formulate the reading experience as a battleground whereby readers seek to overturn the perspectives of both the text and the history of its reading in order to replace them with one's own. Vanhoozer notes, thirdly, the presence of "hyperactive reading," interpretation without frontiers. These readers allow that texts are susceptible to infinite meanings, so that one could never accord privilege to one as specially endowed with authoritative status. Having sketched the horizons of biblical hermeneutics in this way, Vanhoozer goes on to raise the possibility of an "ethics of reading" that acknowledges the presence not only of readerly interests but also of textual interests, and that calls for our response to the text, allowing "the meaning to move from page to practice." "If biblical interpretation excludes this performative dimension," he concludes, "we may well decide that the Bible is not being interpreted enough."[21]

The Power of Biblical Hermeneutics

It may be that the appropriate response to the challenges outlined above would be a full-blown *apologia* for the authoritative status of the Bible. This is not the route we will take, however, for three reasons. First, I take it as axiomatic that, for those of us who believe that Christian faithfulness has as its content following Jesus in discipleship, the authority of the Bible is simply a presupposition. This is both because of Scripture's normative status as witness to the gospel and because Jesus and the people of God before and after him, turned to Scripture in order to discern the purpose of God, the identity of God's people, and criteria for determining how to fulfill their vocation in new contexts. Affirmation of "biblical authority," then, does not replace belief in the God of Jesus Christ with belief in "the Bible," but does draw attention to the reality that these textual witnesses are indispensable and without peer in providing access to the significance of Jesus Christ.[22]

Second, those who are not persuaded by Scripture's witness to Jesus—who is the unifying center of Christian Scripture—are not likely to be persuaded of its authoritative status even by elaborate argumentation in support of that status.

Third, it is a stinging criticism of the people of God in every age, not least in our own, that an affirmation of the authority of Scripture has never guaranteed biblical fidelity; indeed, often enough such affirmations have been used as identity badges behind which communities can shield their own views and behaviors from the Word of God. In the mid-1970s, David Kelsey noted that the authority of Scripture relates fundamentally to what the Scriptures do as Scripture, and insisted that "part of what it means to call a text 'Christian scripture' is that *it functions to shape persons' identities so decisively as to transform them.*"[23] Rather than syllogistic reasoning for biblical authority, then, we are more interested in evidences of biblical authority, the witness of lives lived in conformity with the biblical message.

But this raises the critical issue: Who determines what this message is? How does one arrive at a reading of Scripture that might function authoritatively in Christian communities?

These are not abstract questions; indeed, they are amply attested within the Scriptures themselves, in narratives of the struggle to discern the divine aim. Such a struggle is narrated in Luke 4:1-11, Luke's account of the testing of Jesus in the wilderness by the devil. The Scriptures of Israel have an important role in the whole scene, which contains numerous echoes of Deuteronomy 6–8. Consequently, as the narrative moves from the first and second temptations to the third, we are aware that Jesus' ears are attuned to the voice of God in Scripture. The devil shares our recognition and so attempts to speak with God's own voice, using the words of Scripture (4:9-10; cf. Ps. 91:11-12). Because the devil is not a reliable character in the Gospel of Luke, we might be tempted simply to dismiss his use of the Scriptures as obviously fraudulent. But this does not address the hermeneutical quandary here. Both Jesus and the devil quote Scripture; why prefer one reading over the other?

Fundamentally, the issue here is related to Jesus' radical commitment to the one aim of God, God's eschatological agenda. The devil introduces an alternative aim, a competing agenda. He wants to recruit Jesus to participate in a test of the divine promises of Psalm 91. In doing so the devil overlooks the crucial fact that the psalm is addressed to those who are known for their fidelity to God; that is, even in the psalm faithful obedience to God is the controlling need. Jesus, then, does not deny the validity of God's promises as quoted by the devil, but rejects the suitability of their appropriation in this context. He recognizes the devil's strategy as an attempt to deflect him from his single-minded commitment to loyalty and obedience in God's service, and interprets the devil's invitation as an encouragement to question God's faithfulness. Israel had manifested its doubts by testing God, but Jesus refuses to do so (cf. Deut 6:16).[24]

As the Third Gospel continues, we follow Jesus in ongoing dialogue with scholars and Pharisees. These persons serve as interpreters of Scripture and, then, as monitors who observe Jesus' own practices in order to measure their conformity to interpreted Scripture. The focal point of the conflict between Jesus and these persons is their divergent views of God and God's purpose, divergent views that lead them to read the Scriptures in competing, even contradictory ways. In their speeches in Acts, Peter, Stephen, and Paul continue to ground their understanding of the gospel and, thus, of the communities of disciples of which they are themselves members, in their reading of Scripture. They interpret the Scriptures of Israel in order to establish a fundamental continuity between the ancient past of God's promises, the present, and the future, all by way of legitimating the gospel of Jesus Christ and the communities that take this gospel as their basis for existence, coordinating center, and missionary mandate. Clearly, many of the Jewish people had alternative readings of those same Scriptures. These lead eventually to the parting of the ways between Judaism and this messianic sect—both of whom, nonetheless, claim the Scriptures of Israel as their own. Here we have (basically) the same texts regarded as authoritative, but interpreted differently so as eventually to yield separate communities of faith.[25]

All of this is to say that Christian identity has to do with more than an affirmation of biblical authority, and that, with respect to struggles over the interpretation of authoritative texts, the stakes are high indeed. How, then, can we speak of the practical authority of the Bible?

Biblical Authority in Practice: Possible Avenues

In some ways the current moment does not commend itself to the fainthearted, so many are the questions and so few are the assured results. How does one navigate through shifting sands? This is nonetheless a creative period, one well-suited to the exploration of fresh prospects for grappling with the relationship between Scripture and the church. Before outlining a way forward, four other possibilities, all of which have contemporary proponents, need to be noted.

Return to Dogmatic Hermeneutics

The idea of a "dogmatic method" is suggested in Edgar McKnight's analysis of exegesis in the ancient and medieval church. He uses this label to draw attention to an interpretive approach in which factors or systems (theological and philosophical) beyond the biblical text were involved, even determinative for establishing the meaning of the text.[26] Although the specifics are quite different from those he discusses, incarnations of "dogmatic hermeneutics" are very much in evidence today wherever a predetermined position or an unexamined assumption is allowed to constrain the possible meaning or range of meanings available to readers of biblical texts. Within Protestantism, the "rule of faith" has generally been the doctrine of "justification by faith"—so much so that recent attempts to rethink the meaning of those biblical texts on which this doctrine has been based have been met with stiff resistance. Similarly, for many charismatics in this century, a prior commitment to the experience of a second blessing as the normal Christian autobiography has been determinative for the interpretation of many New Testament texts. In some feminist circles today, the authority and interpretation of particular biblical texts are circumscribed by a commitment to a reconstructed "community of equals." Jesus studies in recent decades have been plagued anew with the tendencies of scholars to find in their portraits of him that for which they had been looking. Indeed, one of the most popular examples of "dogmatic hermeneutics" is also one of the most alarming—namely, the attempt to settle questions of ethical comportment by asking the question, What would Jesus do? This question typically serves as an invitation to download into the discussion one's own personal view of Jesus, with the result that a reconstruction of the historical Jesus is uncritically pressed into service in one's own (or a local congregation's) agenda.

To assert the authority of the Bible, on the other hand, is to leave open at every turn that our interpretive tradition is erroneous and requires reformation. To assert the authority of the Bible is to come to it anew again and again, in humility, not only with our questions but with an openness to its questions; to leave open the possibility that this text will speak a word over against my interpretive community; to recognize Scripture's privileged position vis-à-vis the church; and thus to resist the nagging temptation to which we so easily succumb of substituting our word for God's Word.

This is not to discount the presence and appropriateness of some restraints on the significance of a biblical text. Attending to the cotextual location of a given text is itself an exercise in the control of meaning, since cotext exerts pressure on meaning.[27] Moreover, all language is embedded in culture,[28] and because biblical texts will have been generated within particular discourse situations, it behooves modern interpreters to engage as fully as possible in an exploration of the cultural presuppositions biblical writers shared with their contemporaries. The location of biblical books in their function as "canon" also reminds us that the canon itself serves as a context within which the church construes the meaning of particular biblical texts.

Embrace a New Magisterium

With what I hope is only characteristic hyperbole, Stanley Hauerwas, in his book *Unleashing the Scripture,* insists that "no task is more important than for the Church to take the Bible out of the hands of individual Christians in North America." Why does he propose such inanity? In his view American Christians as a whole lack the necessary skills for reading the Bible. The skills he has in mind, though, are not "reading skills"; they do not relate to readerly competence in the various forms of criticism that help to define academic biblical study. He argues instead that the Bible is capable of being understood only in the midst of a disciplined community among believers whose practices embody the biblical story. Until these communities are formed from persons presently "possessed by habits far too corrupt for them to be encouraged to read the Bible on their own," the meaning of the Bible must be conveyed by "spiritual masters." Inasmuch as some two-thirds of Hauerwas's study is comprised of his own "sermonic exhibits,"[29] we are left to suppose that Hauerwas himself is one of those few American Christians who possess the right to read the Bible.

Hauerwas is right, of course, to insist that our capacity to hear well the voice of Scripture is calculated by our commitments, our dispositions, our behaviors. "Presenting ourselves to God and being willing to be transformed lead us to discernment of God's will, rather than vice versa."[30] Apart from his direct assault on Baptist sensibilities, particularly on the value placed on soul freedom, what is most troubling about Hauerwas's proposal is his complete failure to indicate the nature of his own community of discernment, the communal context of his own reading of Scripture, his own accountability to Christians struggling together to discern the shape of faithful practices, and the quality of his own formation that (according to his own canons) gives him the right and obligation to read Scripture—not only for himself but for us as well. This may be the most troubling aspect of Hauerwas's proposal, but the most important problem with it lies elsewhere. Almost by definition, the magisterium he supports denies the reality that the Word of God is scandalous in its specificity. The word of God came to John in the wilderness at a certain time, in the context of a particular politico-religious framework (Luke 3:1-2). Paul wrote to the Philippians, a particular people in a particular place, at a particular time for particular reasons. Even if the gospel embraces the whole cosmos and is universal in its claims, life in light of the gospel is lived by persons living in economically deprived southeast Dallas, on farms in the central valley of California, and in the suburbs of Seattle—so the specific demands of faithful living cannot be predetermined or engineered for distribution for the masses. The relevance of Scripture for Christians seeking to live out their vocations in diverse settings must be worked out by Christians interpreting Scripture in those diverse settings. A weekly video from the home office will not do.[31]

This is not to say that each local congregation is self-legitimating when it comes to biblical interpretation. Nor is it to deny the wisdom of a teaching office at supralocal levels of church life.[32] The particularity of revelation requires engagement with Scripture at the local level, but also threatens the development among local congregations of myopic vision, ingrown and un–self-critical faith. Local congregations must be in conversation with biblical interpretation among others seeking to be faithful disciples—across time and across lines of all kinds, be they generational, urban or suburban or rural, gender-related, racial, national, political, and so on. Local congregations need the whole body of Christ, global and historical, in order to remain open to the authority of Scripture to speak in voices not usually heard in their own contexts.

Adopt the So-called Wesleyan Quadrilateral

As one who has drunk deeply from the Wesleyan well, it is alarming to me to see the so-called Wesleyan Quadrilateral imported into other Christian traditions, even among American Baptists.[33] Since its introduction into United Methodism in 1970, many United Methodists are able to cite the four components of the Quadrilateral—Scripture, reason, tradition, and experience; and many will insist that these are in some sense equal norms for the theological task and that this alliance of authorities derives from Wesley. In actuality, though, this is nothing more than "a modern Methodist myth"[34] that cannot be attributed in its usual form to Wesley. In his *Works,* Wesley repeatedly states that Scripture alone ought to determine Christian teaching, by which he means, "The more the doctrine of any Church agrees with the Scripture, the more readily ought it to be received. . . . The more the doctrine of any Church differs from Scripture, the greater cause we have to doubt it."[35] Wesley even adopted the label used to disparage him and his movement, "Bible-bigots," and sees the Bible both as source and norm for truth. What, then, can be made of the so-called Quadrilateral? First, it is worth noting that The United Methodist Church has qualified in what sense it will continue to engage its theological task with reason, experience, tradition, and Scripture serving as theological sources; at its General Conference in 1992, it revised its earlier statements to embrace clearly the primacy of Scripture over the other three. Second, if one were to be true to Wesley, one would have to recognize that his conception of authority is best summarized by the bundling of not four but five authorities—Scripture, reason, Christian antiquity, the Church of England, and experience—as a single but complex locus of authority. "Reason and antiquity are needed for proper [biblical] interpretation. The Church of England testifies to Scripture's authority in a manner binding upon its clergy. Experience proves the promises of Scripture to be true."[36]

Why has the so-called Wesleyan Quadrilateral proven so alluring? Undoubtedly, its attractiveness is grounded in modernist impulses that accord privilege to rationality and individualism. Modern persons may be drawn to the Quadrilateral since it seems to allow reason and experience the function of independent criteria capable of overruling the witness of Scripture and/or tradition. In this revisionist formulation, "experience" means "my experience in the world," not the personal witness to the truth of God's promises of which John Wesley spoke.

With reference to experience, Wesley was trying to incorporate a soteri-ological category—specifically, the notion of "conversion"—into the theological enterprise.[37]

Hence, appeals to Wesley of this sort are ill-founded, though we can learn from Wesley, who calls himself *homo unius libri* ("a person of one book"), that, in the end, Scripture is never really "alone." Hence, even if the Reformation notion of *sola scriptura* may point to the import of biblical authority, it is not a very complete description of the role of the authority of the Bible in practice.

Defend a "What It Meant/What It Means" Hermeneutic

Numerous voices today would have us turn back the clock, so to speak, and continue to engage in an approach to biblical interpretation that has three steps (observation, interpretation, and application) or two (determine what it meant, then determine what it means). This strategy, we are told, holds out the promise of a use of Scripture that provides us with an objective base from which to launch constructive theology. As one impor-tant scholar has it, "The basic principle is that the significance of the text is derived from its original meaning; the meaning determines the signifi-cance."[38] As Baptist New Testament scholar C. René Padilla insisted long ago, this scientific approach assumes the impossible by asking interpreters to shed their modern clothing in order to stand on the nonexistent ledge of neutrality and objectivity in order to delineate the "original meaning" of a biblical text.[39] Clearly, one of the most significant contributions of feminist criticism in the past two decades has been its fundamental challenge: All interpretation is influenced and conditioned by the interests and social location of the interpreter.

Liberationist hermeneutics is not the only source for this dis-ease with the historical critical paradigm, however. Philosophical hermeneutics in the twentieth century has likewise given birth, as it were, to the signifi-cance of the reader. According to earlier perspectives, readers "received" meaning from texts; now the role of the reader in the production and actualization of meaning is increasingly recognized.[40]

Given these theoretical considerations, it should come as no surprise that the "what it meant/what it means" hermeneutic has failed to isolate "the" meaning (singular) of biblical texts and, consequently, has provided little of significance for the theological task or for the worship and witness of the church. Nevertheless, the impulses behind this paradigm should not escape us, for they point to the necessity of our taking seriously the contextual framework (or discourse situation) in which the biblical texts were generated and first read.

Biblical Authority and Communities of Discourse

Having reviewed and found wanting four candidates for addressing the question, How can we speak today of the practical authority of the Bible?, we come finally to a constructive proposal. As the heading—"Biblical Authority and Communities of Discourse"—suggests, this proposal will locate the practice of biblical authority within communities of biblical interpretation that take seriously a range of conversation partners. Before outlining those levels of conversation, however, I need to make explicit my understanding of the locus of biblical authority in the Christian practices of theologizing, ethical discourse, preaching, and daily witness.

The problem of articulation

My perspective on the authority of the Bible in practice takes its starting point from the assumption that we engage in appropriation of the biblical message not simply (and sometimes not at all) by reading the content of its message into our world, but also (and sometimes only) by inquiring into how the biblical writers have themselves engaged in the task of theology and ethics.[41] This is true above all because the biblical writers were universally concerned to shape a community that discerns, embraces, and serves the divine purpose more than they were to outline in detail the precise beliefs and habits of that community. In writing the Third Gospel, for example, Luke bears witness to the divine visitation that makes redemption and redemptive community possible, and invites persons to participate as coworkers in this redemptive aim—not to render his audience dependent on him as a kind of "teacher of righteousness." Perhaps more intuitively this is true because the biblical writers address some issues that are of little direct significance in our world (where, for example, Emperor Augustus and the Jerusalem temple are no more), while neglecting to address other issues that have become pressing in some of our communities (the ordination of homosexuals and the ramifications of the Human Genome Project, for example).

In his study *Communities of Discourse,* Robert Wuthnow has drawn attention to a helpful approach to questions of this sort. Although he is concerned with the Protestant Reformation, the Enlightenment, and the rise of European socialism, his methodological considerations are equally apropos a reading of Luke's narrative. He characterizes his investigation as a study of the problem of articulation—that is, how ideas can both be shaped by their social situations and yet manage to disengage from and often challenge those very situations. In the case of the aspirations of Luke, we might ask, How can the Third Gospel be situated in and reflect a particular socio-historical environment while at the same time work to undermine that environment? How can Luke gain for his narrative a hearing among a people whose understanding of "the way the world works" is being subverted by that narrative? What strategies does he adopt? How has he engaged in theological and ethical reflection? How has he invited his audience into the reflective and constructive task of discourse on discipleship? To what authorities does he appeal? What vision of "the new world" does he present; and how does he solicit contemplation on and service in that world? In short, to learn "Lukan theology" is to grapple with more than the content of the Lukan message; it is also to explore how Luke engages in the theological task and the strategies by which he engages his audience in transformative discourse.

My point, then, is that the authority of the Bible in practice is realized, first, by our attending to the ways the biblical materials themselves engage in the theological task, shaping authentic witness in particular cultural settings; in this way the Scriptures provide a methodological framework for our own struggle to work out the implications of the Good News in our own cultural settings. In reflecting critically on Christian witness, then, we attend to Scripture again in order to evaluate the authenticity of our witness—to determine, so to speak, whether we have gotten our theologizing "right." Our understanding of the authority of the Bible in practice, then, takes seriously the role of the Bible as generative source as well as its function to demarcate the parameters of authentic witness.

Levels of conversation

Given that no interpreter comes to Scripture "clean," that all of us bring with us our own commitments and interests, what is to keep the interpretive enterprise from degenerating into self-legitimating pragmatism? How can we affirm not only the anthropological fact but also the interpretive significance of readerly interests and continue to speak of the authority of Scripture? The crucial relevance of this line of questions is evident in the history of biblical interpretation, in which the Bible has repeatedly been drafted in order to provide divine warrant for sometimes heinous practices. By correlating the affirmation of "biblical authority" with the notion of "communities of discourse," I have already pointed the way toward a pertinent consideration—namely, the importance of interpretive practices that participate in a series of dynamic conversations:

1. *Cross-cultural*—taking seriously the cultural contexts both within which the biblical text was shaped and within which contemporary interpretation takes place, in order to inhibit the wholesale cultural imperialism that surfaces when we assume all people everywhere and in all times believe and act as we do.

2. *Canonical*—taking seriously that, within the canon, one finds a diversity of voices that sometimes balance and counterbalance one another, all of which are canonical, and so which legitimate a certain range of diversity within and among the people of God.

3. *Historical*—taking seriously that we are not the first persons to read Scripture, that our own readings of Scripture are, for good or bad, at least partially formed by previous interpreters, and that our mothers and fathers in the faith may contribute to our attempt to articulate the significance of the gospel in our worlds.

4. *Communal*—taking seriously that the biblical witness is itself concerned with the formation of faithful communities of God's people, and that biblical interpretation, in order to *be biblical,* must take place in the context of faith(ful) communities.

5. *Global*—taking seriously that our communities, which keep us from developing private and idiosyncratic interpretations, are themselves subject to tunnel vision and self-legitimation, and thus need the witness of believers who are "not like us" as conversation partners.

6. *Hospitable*—taking seriously that, even as God's grace extends to all people, so we may learn from those whose lives seem not to be oriented around God at all—persons, then, who may be able to remedy our tendencies toward interpretive arrogance.

Cultural relativity: The "problem" with Scripture

Some biblical texts seem so culturally embedded in their ancient settings as to be of little or no immediate relevance to contemporary readers.[42] Not many of us practice the holy kiss, for example, in spite of clear scriptural admonition (Rom. 16:16). Nor, in spite of the clarity with which Jesus instructs his followers to do so, do we often engage in footwashing (John 13:14). And this is not even to index those texts whose message seems altogether to fall short of escaping their limited cultural horizons, such as the news that the 144,000 "redeemed of the earth" consists of "those who have not defiled themselves with women" (Rev. 14:4).[43]

With regard to this problem, we must simply acknowledge, first, a hermeneutical fact: We all choose to embrace some biblical texts as of particular relevance while not adopting others, at least in a literal way. Hence, the question facing us is not, Do we find some biblical texts so rooted in their cultural settings that they seem of little immediate relevance to us? Rather, the question is, How do we determine whether a biblical directive is so rooted in its cultural setting? Three rules of thumb may be suggested.[44]

1. Determine the relative amount of emphasis given a subject in the biblical witness. Here we presuppose that particulars close to the heart of what it means to be God's people will be repeated often.

2. Determine the degree to which the biblical witnesses are uniform and consistent on a given issue. Here we affirm the reality that the biblical materials themselves do not always speak with one voice, but must address questions in a variety of cultural settings. If, in different cultural settings and socio-historical circumstances, scriptural voices address similar concerns in different ways, the message probably is culturally rooted. One may think of the different viewpoints represented in the pages of the Bible on the question (very important in the first century!) of eating meat sacrificed to idols (cf. Acts 15; Rom. 14; 1 Cor. 8; Rev. 2–3), for example.

3. Determine the degree to which a writer's cultural situation provides only one option (or limited options) within which to work. Why, for example, did the early church choose from among two male followers of Jesus when they sought to replace Judas? Since the only criterion mentioned is that this person should be one who has "accompanied us during all the time that the Lord Jesus went in and out among us" (Acts 1:21-22), why were women (who met these qualifications— cf. Luke 8:1-3; 23:49, 55) not included in the selection process? Jesus and the early church, like those of other creative moments, faced what I have outlined above as "the problem of articulation"—that is, the necessity of working *within* the constraints of one's historical particularity while at the same time calling (some of) those constraints into question. In a male-dominated world, could the choice of a woman as leader be "heard"? What may be of more far-reaching consequence, then, is the way issues of status, including those related to gender and sex, are generally disparaged in the Third Gospel and Acts.

Reading the Bible as communication: Overcoming the subject-object dichotomy

In this historical moment it is crucial to reaffirm one of the most important gains of hermeneutics in the twentieth century. This is the capacity of biblical texts to form and transform us, not only to inform us. According to this formulation, Scripture is not an object to be manipulated, dissected, explained. It is, rather, a subject, a partner in conversation, with questions and challenges of its own. "Biblical authority in practice," viewed against this hermeneutical horizon, entails according privilege to its questions of us and seeking to have our experience conformed to that faith and practice of which Scripture speaks.[45]

Conclusion

For many of our contemporaries, the idea of an authority external to the individual person is itself problematic, so that the possibility of biblical authority is undermined before it can even be seriously engaged. Unfortunately, many of our contemporaries affirm in some sense the authority of the Bible and/or the Bible as God's Word, but do not embody its message or otherwise allow the Bible to function authoritatively. Some go to great lengths to affirm its authority but refuse to listen to its questions of them, while others disconfirm their affirmations of biblical authority by failing to undertake a close reading of its contents. Still others have been blinded or have blinded themselves to the reality that none of us has direct, individual access to Scripture, that all of us bring with us the totality of our lives, which have been historically and socially shaped in ways that open up some interpretive possibilities and close others, so that we are shielded from hearing fully the multiform and multivalent message of Scripture.

Against the backdrop of these and related realities, I have attempted in this essay both to indicate the crucial import of biblical authority for the life of God's people and to sketch a way of taking seriously the authority of the Bible in practice. Central to this view is the location of biblical interpretation within communities of the faithful, which are themselves located both within the whole people of God and within the human family. Equally central is the recognition that biblical texts and readers each have interests, even if belief in biblical authority accords privilege to the interests of the Scriptures. This is done in part by placing biblical interpretation at the intersection of numerous paths of accountability, allowing for the development of local readings that are in critical conversation with wider concerns so as to inhibit private, idiosyncratic, and/or self-legitimating uses of biblical texts. Finally, the framework I have attempted to sketch emphasizes the capacity of the biblical materials to serve as local manifestations of the divine Word in specific past times and distant places, *and* to transcend the cultural horizons within which they were generated so as to speak as God's Word to those of us concerned similarly to discern the way of God in our own local (and global) contexts. This perspective, however, recognizes that Scripture is much more than a series of propositions or timeless truths; that the Scriptures shape our views of God and the world, our dispositions and behavior; and that the Scriptures often function authoritatively by inspiring, directing, and evaluating our own theological and ethical ruminations. How we should live, then, is a question to be engaged by communities of the faithful themselves, struggling to put into practice the authority of the Bible.

Notes

1. The phrase is borrowed from Harold Lindsell, *The Battle for the Bible* (Grand Rapids: Zondervan, 1976).

2. See, e.g., Donald G. Bloesch, *Holy Scripture: Revelation, Inspiration and Interpretation* (Downers Grove, Ill.: InterVarsity Press, 1994), 30-45.

3. See the helpful survey in Robert K. Johnston, *Evangelicals at an Impasse: Biblical Authority in Practice* (Atlanta: John Knox, 1979). Johnston's own focus on issues of interpretation presaged well the issues that would become central to the discussion (cf. Robert K. Johnston, ed., *The Use of the Bible in Theology: Evangelical Options* [Atlanta: John Knox, 1985]).

4. For this emphasis, see Stephen E. Fowl and L. Gregory Jones, *Reading in Communion: Scripture and Ethics in Christian Life* (Grand Rapids: Eerdmans, 1991); Stephen E. Fowl, "The New Testament, Theology, and Ethics," in *Hearing the New Testament: Strategies for Interpretation,* ed. Joel B. Green (Grand Rapids: Eerdmans; Carlisle: Paternoster, 1995), 394-410; Joel B. Green, "The Practice of Reading the New Testament," in Green, ed., *Hearing the New Testament,* 411-27.

5. Robert N. Bellah, Richard Madsen, William M. Sullivan, Ann Swidler, and Steve M. Tipton, *Habits of the Heart: Individualism and Commitment in American Life* (Berkeley: University of California Press, 1985).

6. Cf. Michel Foucault, *The Archaeology of Knowledge,* World of Man (London/New York: Routledge, 1972). The best introduction to Foucault is Paul Rabinow, ed., *The Foucault Reader* (New York: Pantheon, 1984). I have provided an oversimplification of Foucault's thought. The logic behind theories of discourse power is more nuanced: (1) Everything is discourse; (2a) discourse is determined by those in power; (2b) as a social construct, discourse lacks objective foundation; therefore, (3a) nothing has objective foundation and (3b) truth-claims are constituted by whoever is in power.

7. For this point, as well as for a more thoroughgoing critique of discourse power theory, see Richard Freadman and Suemas Miller, *Re-thinking Theory: A Critique of Contemporary Literary Theory and an Alternative Account* (Cambridge: Cambridge University Press, 1992).

8. John Goldingay, *Models for Scripture* (Grand Rapids: Eerdmans; Carlisle: Paternoster, 1994), 107.

9. So George L. Dillon, "Discourse Theory," in *The Johns Hopkins Guide to Literary Theory and Criticism,* ed. Michael Groden and Martin Kreiswirth (Baltimore/London: Johns Hopkins University Press, 1994), 212.

10. See, e.g., Pierre Bourdieu, *Language and Symbolic Power* (Cambridge,

Massachusetts: Harvard University Press, 1991); and esp. Robert Wuthnow, *Communities of Discourse: Ideology and Social Structure in the Reformation, the Enlightenment, and European Socialism* (Cambridge: Harvard University Press, 1989).

11. This is helpfully explored by Richard Bauckham, *The Theology of the Book of Revelation,* New Testament Theology (Cambridge: Cambridge University Press, 1993).

12. Robert Wuthnow, *Acts of Compassion: Caring for Others and Helping Ourselves* (Princeton: Princeton University Press, 1991), 161. See chap. 6.

13. Cf. Robert N. Bellah, "The Recovery of Biblical Language in American Life," *Radix* 18, 4 (1988): 4-7, 29-31.

14. Not everyone has deserted the Bible in his or her search for authoritative Christian witness. Some have refused to distinguish biblical exegesis and systematic theology, as though the Word of God in our contemporary socio-historical contexts were identical to the revelatory message delivered in those earlier contexts; in this case, the task of theology, ethics, and preaching has been simply to reassert and secure the results of exegesis. Others have simply brought with them to the Bible their own practices and beliefs or the practices and beliefs of their communities, and found them authenticated.

15. Karl Barth, *Church Dogmatics,* vol. 1: *The Doctrine of the Word of God,* pt. 1 (Edinburgh: T. & T. Clark, 1975), 16.

16. Robert Morgan with John Barton, *Biblical Interpretation* (Oxford: Oxford University Press, 1988), 17 (see 1-43).

17. See Francis Watson, *Text, Church and World: Biblical Interpretation in Theological Perspective* (Grand Rapids: Eerdmans, 1994).

18. This is helpfully documented and interpreted in Anthony C. Thiselton, "New Testament Interpretation in Historical Perspective," in Green, ed., *Hearing the New Testament,* 10-36.

19. See, e.g., John Barton, *Reading the Old Testament: Method in Biblical Study* (London: Darton, Longman, and Todd, 1984); Green, ed., *Hearing the New Testament.*

20. See Anthony C. Thiselton, *New Horizons in Hermeneutics: The Theory and Practice of Transforming Biblical Reading* (London: Collins, 1992).

21. Kevin J. Vanhoozer, "Hyperactive Hermeneutics: Is the Bible Being Overinterpreted?" *Catalyst* 19, 1 (1992): 3-4.

22. John Goldingay, *Models for Interpretation of Scripture* (Grand Rapids: Eerdmans; Carlisle: Paternoster, 1995), 2-3.

23. David H. Kelsey, *The Uses of Scripture in Recent Theology* (Philadelphia: Fortress, 1975), 90-92.

24. Joel B. Green, *The Theology of the Gospel of Luke,* New Testament Theology (Cambridge: Cambridge University Press, 1995), 26-28.

25. James D. G. Dunn, *The Partings of the Ways: Between Christianity and Judaism and Their Significance for the Character of Christianity* (London: SCM; Philadelphia: Trinity, 1991), observes the tension within Second Temple Judaism and in the beginnings of Christianity between Scripture understood as normative revelation and its interpretation (esp. 251-54). His assertion that "this tension is not an aberration within the people of God, but *constitutive of the human attempt to recognize and respond to divine revelation"* (252) is undoubtedly correct, though it needs to be counterbalanced with his awareness elsewhere that both Christianity and Judaism placed limits on the range of acceptable diversity of interpretation.

26. Edgar V. McKnight, *Postmodern Use of the Bible: The Emergence of Reader-Oriented Criticism* (Nashville: Abingdon, 1988), 29-44.

27. Cf. Umberto Eco, *The Limits of Interpretation,* Advances in Semiotics (Bloomington: Indiana University Press, 1990), 21: "[S]ymbols are paradigmatically open to infinite meanings but syntagmatically, that is, textually, open only to the indefinite, but by no means infinite, interpretations allowed by the context."

28. Cf. Michael Stubbs, *Discourse Analysis: The Sociolinguistic Analysis of Natural Language* (Chicago: University of Chicago Press, 1983), 8; G. Gillian Brown and George Yule, *Discourse Analysis,* Cambridge Textbooks in Linguistics (Cambridge: Cambridge University Press, 1982), 27-31; Peter Cotterell and Max Turner, *Linguistics and Biblical Interpretation* (London: SPCK; Downers Grove, Ill.: Inter-Varsity Press, 1989), 68-72.

29. Stanley Hauerwas, *Unleashing the Scripture: Freeing the Bible from Captivity to America* (Nashville: Abingdon, 1993), 15-16.

30. Goldingay, *Models for Scripture,* 194. See further, Fowl and Jones, *Reading in Communion.*

31. One of the most significant contributions of Bourdieu's work as this relates to biblical scholarship is his insistence that practices arise at the intersection of one's dispositions and particular social contexts; in new contexts the same dispositions will become manifest in new practices (e.g., *Language and Symbolic Power*).

32. See Wolfhart Pannenberg, "The Teaching Office and the Unity of the Church," in *The Future of Theology: Essays in Honor of Jürgen Moltmann,* ed. Miroslav Volf, Carmen Krieg, and Thomas Kucharz (Grand Rapids: Eerdmans, 1996), 221-32.

33. See H. Darrell Lance, "Response to 'The Bible and Human Sexuality,'" *American Baptist Quarterly* 12 (1993), 327. Whether Lance is correct in his assessment that the *quadrivium* attributed to Wesley (wrongly, as we shall see) accurately describes *Baptist* practice cannot be considered here.

34. See Ted A. Campbell, "The 'Wesleyan Quadrilateral': The Story of a Modern Methodist Myth," *in Doctrine and Theology in The United Methodist Church,* ed. Thomas A. Langford (Nashville: Abingdon, 1991), 154-61.

35. Cited in Bloesch, *Holy Scripture,* 141.

36. Scott Jones, "John Wesley on the Authority and Interpretation of Scripture," *Catalyst* 19, 1 (1992): 2, 6.

37. Albert C. Outler, "The Wesleyan Quadrilateral—in John Wesley," in *The Wesleyan Theological Heritage: Essays of Albert C. Outler,* ed. Thomas C. Oden and Leicester R. Longden (Grand Rapids: Zondervan, 1991), 21-37 (esp. 26-28, 35).

38. I. Howard Marshall, "How Do We Interpret the Bible Today?" *Themelios* 5, 2 (1980): 9. The language "what it meant and what it means" is taken from Krister Stendahl, "Biblical Theology," in *The Interpreter's Dictionary of the Bible,* 5 vols., ed. George Arthur Buttrick (Nashville: Abingdon, 1962), 1:419-20.

39. C. René Padilla, "The Interpreted Word: Reflections on Contextual Hermeneutics," *Themelios* 7, 1 (1981): 18-23 (esp. 19).

40. See the helpful introduction in Kevin J. Vanhoozer, "The Reader in New Testament Interpretation," in Green, ed., *Hearing the New Testament,* 301-28. More broadly, see, e.g., Umberto Eco, *The Role of the Reader: Explorations in the Semiotics of Texts,* Advances in Semiotics (Bloomington: Indiana University Press, 1979); J. Severino Croatto, *Biblical Hermeneutics: Toward a Theory of Reading as the Production of Meaning* (Maryknoll, N.Y.: Orbis, 1987).

41. This section borrows heavily from Green, *Theology of the Gospel of Luke,* 132-33.

42. This section borrows heavily from Green, "Practice of Reading," 425-26.

43. Our recognition that this qualification refers pointedly to (1) an army of

fighting men who (2) have kept themselves free of the cultic defilement incurred through sexual intercourse (cf. Richard Bauckham, *The Climax of Prophecy: Studies on the Book of Revelation* [Edinburgh: T. & T. Clark, 1993], 230-31), which (3) must symbolize for John martyred men *and* women and children does not detract from the problematic assumptions of this metaphor.

44. These are adapted from David M. Scholer, "Contours of an Evangelical Feminist Hermeneutics," *Catalyst* 15 (1989) 2, 4.

45. Goldingay, *Models for Scripture,* 194.

The Authority of the Bible and Private Interpretation: A Dilemma of Baptist Freedom[1]

David M. Scholer

Introduction

It is my task to introduce historically the topic and the issues of the dynamic tension for Baptists between the solid affirmation of the authority of the Bible and the deep commitment to soul freedom and its implications for one's freedom to interpret the Bible for oneself. From their historical beginnings to the present, the commitment of many Baptists to the authority of the Bible appears often to have been undermined and vitiated by the equally strong commitment of many other Baptists to the right of individual or private interpretation of the Bible. Our Baptist commitment to the individual's freedom to interpret the Bible has also been threatened by a view of the Bible's authority that excludes the legitimate possibilities of varying understandings of the biblical text.

A commitment to biblical authority tends to imply or suggest that the Bible has a relatively clear message and that the meaning of biblical texts is relatively clear. Thus, the Bible can exercise its authority over the hearers and readers who, if obedient and faithful, submit to its authority—that is, its clear teachings. On the other hand, the history of biblical interpretation makes it overwhelmingly clear that there are, in fact, conflicting interpretations of the Bible and of specific biblical texts. Thus, private interpretation moves in the direction of creating a veritable confusion of conflicting interpretations to the degree that the very authority of the Bible appears to be undermined and vitiated.

David M. Scholer is Professor of New Testament at Fuller Theological Seminary, Pasadena, California. This paper was presented at "Called to Responsible Freedom: A Conference on Baptist Distinctives," at Green Lake, Wisconsin, August 1996.

Two simple stories from my own experiences in Baptist churches point to our dilemma. On one occasion, when I was making a presentation on principles for biblical interpretation, a man who was obviously upset by my talk said to me at the door: "Professor Scholer, you are a professor; you go ahead and interpret the Bible. I will simply accept what it says." The other incident took place in the context of a heated discussion over the issue of baptism for new church members who had been baptized as infants. One man rose to his feet with his Bible in hand and proclaimed in a loud voice, "My Bible says. . . ." Both stories add to the dilemma. Not only do private interpretations of the Bible lead to conflicting views that seem to threaten biblical authority, but further, private interpreters tend to understand their interpretation as the only valid one possible consistent with the maintenance of biblical authority.

The Baptist commitment to the authority of the Bible is rooted, of course, in the larger Protestant Reformation affirmation of *sola scriptura.* This commitment held that the locus of authority was in the Bible itself and was not to be found in the Catholic *magisterium.* The Reformers, and subsequently the Baptists, wanted the Bible to speak for itself and did not wish to have the Catholic *magisterium,* or anything else, speak for the Bible.

For Baptists, in distinction from some others of the Reformation period, this meant also that creeds should not be allowed to determine the meaning of the Bible. The Bible was to be "free" to *speak for itself,* and that freedom for the Bible was found in the commitment to allow each person, ostensibly, to determine what it was that the Bible was speaking. Thus, somewhere in the history of the Baptist movement, a defining motto arose: No creed but the Bible!

As we know, however, Baptists, virtually from the beginning, issued and adopted what were generally called "confessions" of their faith. Even if the actual line was sometimes rather thin, they considered these to be voluntary witnesses to their collective faith rather than imposed and determining creeds that defined one's faith. And yet, in actual historical practice, the confessions served as a sociological boundary defining a type of "communal private interpretation" that distinguished one kind of Baptist from another kind of Baptist, as well as defining Baptists over against other expressions of the Christian faith. Part of our dilemma, therefore, is the difficulty of determining to what degree voluntary confessions should control individual/private interpretation.

What church history has taught us, especially since the Protestant Reformation, is the reality that, perhaps regrettably, the Bible does not interpret itself. The problem is the classic hermeneutical interface between the text (what I once heard Brevard Childs call "the coercion of the text") and the reader.[2] The reality is—whether it is viewed as a grim reality or not—that the dilemma is endemic to the very nature of the Bible. "If it is not irreverent to say it, our hermeneutical dilemma is but a reflection of the eternal, transcendent God's revelatory dilemma."[3] The Bible is comprised of discrete texts, each of which was written within a concrete, particular context; in this sense all of the Bible is historically and culturally located. Whatever divine and normative authority we ascribe to the Bible has to be given to *this kind* of Bible. It is an additional reality that all hearers and readers of the Bible also exist in historical particularity. "All [biblical] interpretation is socially located, individually skewed and ecclesiastically-theologically conditioned."[4] And further, much to our chagrin, we have to come to terms with the very elusive role of the Holy Spirit. Various theological and pietistic traditions, including our own, claim, of course, that the Holy Spirit is the guide and guarantor of the correct or proper interpretation. However real the Spirit's guidance may be, our perception of it is found only within the contexts of particular interpreters. The claim of the Spirit's direction never settles any dispute.

Thus, the dynamic tension between the authority of the Bible and the freedom or right of individual or private interpretation is not simply a Baptist dilemma. Much more, it is a dilemma inherent in the very nature of the Bible and the inevitable process of its interpretation. It is a dilemma faced by all Christians, experienced and discussed in varying ways. Precisely because of the broader nature of the dilemma, I have chosen to develop the problematic of the dynamic tension by the utilization of a wide and very selective range of examples and parallels from the history of the church, some of which will stem from Baptists and many of which will come from other traditions. Further, in order to gain some kind of objectivity or distance from our current struggles with this dynamic tension and dilemma, I have chosen to use only pre-twentieth-century examples and parallels in my development of the problematic before us.

Case Studies from the Early Church

It may be helpful to look first at three illustrations from the history of the early church as a way to further illumine our understanding of our own dilemma.

The New Testament Use of the Old Testament

First, we could reflect very briefly on the hoary issue of the New Testament use of the Old Testament. Here we have within the canon itself evidence of our dilemma. Consider the different ways in which Genesis 15:6 ("And [Abraham] believed the LORD; and the LORD reckoned it to him as righteousness" [NRSV]) is used by James (2:21-24) and by Paul (Rom. 4:9; Gal. 3:6). Or reflect on Paul's interpretation of Deuteronomy 25:4 ("You shall not muzzle an ox while it is treading out the grain" [NRSV]), in which he implies that this injunction was actually intended by God from the beginning to be justification for financial remuneration for church leaders (1 Cor. 9:8-12)! It is not my intention to attempt to resolve anything now about these classic texts. Rather, I want to show that the interpretive dilemma of a text's authority and varying personal interpretations of it are problems endemic to the very texts of Scripture themselves.

Tertullian

A second illustration may be drawn from Tertullian, a church father from Carthage, North Africa, who wrote about A.D. 200. I am deeply fascinated by Tertullian's various battles with heretics over the interpretation of Scripture, right at the time that a concept of an authoritative New Testament canon was emerging.

At the conclusion of his work *Prescriptions against Heretics,* Tertullian makes this telling observation: "I think I may say without fear of contradiction that by the will of God the Scriptures themselves were so arranged as to furnish matter for the heretics. For without the Scripture there can be no heresy."[5]

Tertullian admits that Scripture yields multiple and conflicting interpretations—and is frustrated by this recognition. Earlier Tertullian says of the heretics that "they plead Scripture," but "arguments about Scripture achieve nothing but a stomach-ache or a headache. . . . False exegesis injures truth. . . . They rely on passages which they have put together in a false context or fastened on because of their ambiguity."[6] Tertullian's solution is to argue that the heretics have no "legal ownership" of Scripture; only those who embrace "the true Christian teaching and faith" will discover true interpretations.[7] We readily see here the conflict of rival claims and their respective foibles in biblical interpretation. But Tertullian may well hint at a conclusion not to be despised—private interpretations can vitiate the authority of the Bible; biblical authority may have meaning only within a community's consensus of interpretive boundaries.

A delightful illustration of Tertullian's dilemma is found in his work *On Baptism,* written against the female leader of the gnostic Cainite sect, which argued, from their reading of the Bible, that water baptism was unnecessary. Tertullian says that these Cainites argued that, according to the New Testament evidence, Jesus did not baptize people (see John 4:2), Paul had a major disclaimer about baptism (see 1 Cor. 1:17), and the apostles were never baptized.[8] As upset as Tertullian is with the heretics' claim that the apostles were never baptized (Tertullian says of them: "those thorough-going scoundrels, raisers of unnecessary questions"[9]), he is equally upset by the "right-wing" defense of the faith that argued that the apostles "underwent a substitute for baptism on that occasion when in the little ship they were aspersed with the waves."[10] For Tertullian, private interpretation from what he perceived as either the "left" or the "right" could trivialize and subvert Scripture.

Hippolytus

The third and final example from the early church comes from Hippolytus, an early third-century A.D. church father, in his work *Against Noetus*. Noetus was a modalist active about A.D. 200. Modalism was the view that it was God the Father who was incarnate and crucified. Noetus and his followers, according to Hippolytus, argued their views from the Scriptures. But Hippolytus is not pleased with their interpretations. He says that "whenever they want to get up to their tricks, they hack the Scriptures to pieces."[11] At the conclusion of his refutation of Noetus's scriptural interpretations, Hippolytus says that the truth is found in Scripture. "Not in accordance with private choice, nor private interpretation, nor by doing violence to the things that God has given—but rather . . . in the way God himself resolved to reveal [it] through the Holy Scriptures."[12] Hippolytus witnesses to the same dynamic tensions between the authority of the Bible and private, varying interpretations as does Tertullian.

Parallel Case Studies from Other than Baptist Groups in Nineteenth-Century American Church History

It is instructive as well to look at four non-Baptist Christian movements in nineteenth-century America that provide some parallels to our Baptist dilemmas of private interpretation and biblical authority.

Noyes and the Oneida Community

John Humphrey Noyes (1811-1886) is remembered primarily as the founder of the Perfectionist Oneida Community (1848-1881), one of the most successful communitarian experiments in American religious history.[13] For our purposes it is important to note that Noyes studied at

Andover Theological Seminary and then at Yale Divinity School until he was expelled for his Perfectionist beliefs, which he developed there. What is significant is that Noyes understood that what he was developing in his form of radical Perfectionism, which ultimately led to a lifestyle that transcended the usual moral codes (the sexual ones are the most remembered in Noyes's case), came directly from the Bible. His preliminary community was gathered in 1844 at Putney, Vermont, where one of the principal activities, and the only religious one Noyes approved, was intense Bible study.[14] In fact, the community there was first known as the Putney Bible School. By 1847 Noyes believed that the kingdom of God had come; by 1848 the community moved to and was established at Oneida, New York. Life at Oneida was rather controlled by Noyes. Again, for our purposes, it is worth noting that among the required community activities, every Tuesday evening was set for Noyes's lectures on "Bible communism," and every Sunday evening Noyes lectured on biblical teachings.[15] The Oneida Community attracted attention for many reasons, including its disciplined life and its economic successes, but the primary focus of attention was the completely free and open sex practiced within the community, justified by Noyes's biblical understanding that the kingdom of God had come and that the Oneida people were now living in the resurrection. Such a movement, clearly outside any of the then understood boundaries of traditional and accepted Christianity, arose from many factors, of course, but among them was a deep sense of the critical value of private interpretation of the Bible over against all other authorities who, in Noyes's case, were perceived to be misguided.

Miller and the Adventist Movement

William Miller (1782-1849), born in Massachusetts, became a member of a Baptist church by 1816. After intense personal study of the Bible, Miller concluded by 1818 that Christ would return about 1843. Miller, evidently due to some uncertainty, kept his findings to himself until 1831, when he began to speak publicly about his ideas. In 1833 his Baptist church in Vermont gave him a license to preach, and in 1836 he published a book entitled *Evidence from Scripture and History of the Second Coming of Christ, About the Year 1843.* In 1838 or 1839 Joshua V. Himes from Boston began to popularize and promote Miller's ideas, which resulted in what was called the Millerite movement, which grew in his own time to number about fifty thousand people. Miller subsequently recalculated the date of Christ's return to a day in 1844, but the failure of the predictions did little or nothing to hinder the development of what we know today as the

Adventist movement, the major legacy of which is the Seventh-day
Adventist denomination.[16] The Millerite/Adventist movement grew directly out of a form of intense, private biblical interpretation that pro-
pounded a reading of the Bible different from the beliefs held by other
Christians who were committed to the authority of the Bible.

One good example of private interpretation in connection with the
Millerite movement is that of a woman from Glastonbury, Connecticut,
Julia Evelina Smith (1792-1886). She learned Hebrew and Greek and
translated the entire Bible into English from the original languages sometime in the 1850s. She did this so that her small Bible study group of
women could determine whether the Millerite teachings were true. They
concluded that the Millerite teachings were inaccurate. In 1876 Julia
published her Bible. It remains to this day the only instance of a publication
of a complete Bible translated into English from the original languages by
an individual woman. In the preface she wrote:

> It may be thought by the public in general, that I have great confidence
> in myself, in not conferring with the learned in so great a work, but as
> there is but one book in the Hebrew tongue, and I have defined it word
> for word, I do not see how anybody can know more about it than I do.
> As for the Latin and Greek, I have no doubt many have searched deeper
> into the standard works than I have, but I think no one has given more
> time and attention to the literal meaning of the Bible text in these
> languages. . . . There may be some little inaccuracies. . . , but I think
> never has the sense of the Original Tongue been altered.

Julia's sister Abby Smith, in a letter to a newspaper, explained something of the decision she and her sister Julia made to publish the Bible:
"This work would show that a woman could do what no man had ever
done, alone, and what is considered by all the greatest of works." Such is
this example of nineteenth-century private interpretation, which also
reflects the women's rights movement at that time.[17]

Campbell and the Restoration Movement

A third and very significant case relates to Alexander Campbell (1788-
1866) and the movement he founded, known within as the Disciples of
Christ and by outsiders as the Campbellites.[18] Campbell was born in
Scotland and was influenced there by James and Robert Haldane, who
taught that the church should return to primitive Christianity as taught in
the New Testament. In 1809 Campbell settled in Pennsylvania. Here he
and his father started the Bush Run Church, which ordained Campbell in
1811. In 1813, after becoming convinced by arguments for baptism by

immersion, the Bush Run Church became part of the Redstone Baptist Association, an affiliation that continued to 1825. By 1832 Campbell's group, known as the Disciples of Christ, and a group known as Christians led by Barton W. Stone, merged to form the Christian Church (Disciples of Christ).

What is most significant about the Campbellite movement for our purposes is their radical commitment to New Testament Christianity: they wanted to restore the church to what it originally was, as depicted in the New Testament. Thus, this project is part of what is known as the Restoration Movement. The Campbellite Restorationists believed that the majority of the church was, in fact, misinterpreting the Bible. Richard T. Hughes, in his major new study of this movement, *Reviving the Ancient Faith.* . . , notes that Campbell opposed the various denominations by stressing private interpretation. In Hughes's words: "[Campbell] urged people to reject the authority and traditions of their churches and to read and interpret the Bible for themselves."[19] But, as Hughes notes: "To be sure, Campbell advocated the freedom of each individual Christian to understand Scripture for him/herself. But Campbell's rational bent led him to systematize the teachings of Scripture in a way that moved inevitably toward uniformity and orthodoxy."[20] In other words, the boundaries of the movement came into conflict with a radical application of the principle of private interpretation.

The Campbellite-Restorationist movement's attitude toward the Bible is often summarized in the motto: "Speak where the Bible speaks; be silent where the Bible is silent." Two interesting observations might be made in reference to the two sides of this slogan of private interpretation. First, it is interesting to note that the Campbellite movement, so ardently devoted to restoring primitive Christianity as found in the New Testament, has historically been strongly opposed to the practice of speaking in tongues (glossolalia), even though this was clearly part of primitive Christianity. To those outside the movement, this appears to be an interpretive and hermeneutical anomaly—*not* speaking where the Bible speaks—given the rhetoric of the place of the New Testament in and for the movement.

Second, it is quite well known that the traditional Campbellite movement forbids the use of musical instruments in Christian worship on the grounds that the New Testament is silent here, so the movement should imitate that stance. Yet some forms of the movement have broken with this position and have formed different branches or denominations of this tradition. Even among the faithful, traditional noninstrumentalists, there is discussion over whether the places where the Bible is silent should be understood as prohibition (the traditional stance) or as freedom (an impulse to break with tradition).

The Campbellite history demonstrates rather clearly the power, the impulses, the inconsistencies, and the problems of private interpretation within the context of a firmly and publicly held commitment to the clear authority of the Bible.

Nyvall and the Covenant Movement

A final and crucial case involves David Nyvall (1863-1946), born in Sweden, who emigrated to the United States in 1886 and became a leader both in the Swedish-American community and within the Covenant Church (known originally as the Swedish [Evangelical] Mission Covenant Church, after its Swedish parent, and today as the Evangelical Covenant Church).[21] The Swedish (Evangelical) Mission Covenant movement, actually originally part of a larger revival movement within the Swedish State Lutheran Church, was begun by Paul Peter Waldenström, who stressed the supremacy of the Bible over the Lutheran Church creeds. The slogan he developed was "Where is it written?" The Swedish (Evangelical) Mission Covenant movement intended to base itself only on the Bible; creeds and confessions were not to determine belief.

Nyvall, then only twenty-three, preached at the second annual meeting of the Covenant in America in 1886. His sermon was entitled "Abide in the Word." In this sermon he stressed his belief that the Bible was the people's book and that the Bible, and the Bible alone, should be the source of all Christian teaching and piety. This commitment Nyvall called an "irrevocable responsibility" and a "compulsion." In 1893 Nyvall gave a report on the Covenant movement to the World Parliament of Religions in Chicago. He stressed there the absolute commitment to the Bible, but noted, significantly, that "Where differences of theology coexist with a pure Christian life and faith in Jesus Christ, these are permitted to exist as unavoidable in our imperfect knowledge of the truth."[22]

As indicated, Nyvall was keenly aware of differences within the Covenant movement over the nature and interpretation of the Bible. Nyvall produced in 1893, with others, a denominational catechism (*Kristlig troslära,* or Teachings on Christian Faith) in an attempt to help pastors with little education and to suggest guidelines for the development of the Covenant movement. This work, however, provoked some concern, for some saw it as a threat to the individual's freedom to answer the Covenant question "Where is it written?"

Nyvall continued to argue for the commitment to the Bible's authority and in an 1898 lecture made it clear that he did not endorse either verbal inspiration or inerrancy. What he urged was the combination of understanding the Bible as a life-giving authority to be appropriated by the freedom of the believers. However, by the 1920s, Covenant leader Gustaf F. Johnson (1873-1959) began to promote the Fundamentalist agenda concerning the Bible, evolution, and millennial eschatology. This led to a major battle within the Covenant movement. During this dispute Nyvall and Nils Lund (1885-1954), an emerging New Testament scholar and theological educator within the Covenant, who in a 1920 lecture endorsed an amillennial interpretation of eschatology, were accused of heresy. It was not until the Covenant annual meeting of 1928 that Nyvall and Lund were exonerated and not until 1933 that a kind of "peace agreement" was signed that allowed both sides to coexist within the Covenant.

One interesting example of the "peace agreement" from 1935 seems not even to be known to most Covenant church historians. For the school year 1935-1936, second term, the senior young people and adult departments' Covenant graded lesson was entitled *Outline Studies of the Book of Revelation*. Two separate lesson books were published, neither of which made reference to the other. One was by Nils Lund, representing the amillennial interpretation, and the other was by Isak Höyem, representing the millennial interpretation.[23]

The struggle over the authority of the Bible, individual interpretation, and denominational boundaries is evident today in the Evangelical Covenant Church with respect to the issues surrounding baptism. The Covenant tradition not only practices both infant and adult baptism, with complete openness on the modes of baptism, but the tradition also has indicated that Covenant leaders and pastors, whatever their personal convictions might be, must be open to and willing to practice all forms of baptism with integrity and respect. Due to controversy within the denomination, the 1966 annual meeting of the Covenant adopted an official statement on the practice of baptism, which has, ironically, become the only doctrinal statement Covenant ministers must sign. In other words, in a tradition fiercely committed to the sole authority of the Bible with an accompanying rejection of all creeds and confessions and a strong endorsement of individual freedom of interpretation, the decision made in 1966 was to require a doctrinal commitment, the intention of which was to preserve and respect everyone's freedom to answer the question "Where is it written?" in one's own way. The baptism tension and dialogue continues. The Covenant's scholarly journal, *The Covenant Quarterly,* devoted an entire double issue entitled "A Study of Baptism" (November

1995–February 1996) to dialogue and discussion of the issues within the Covenant Church.[24]

Thus, the Covenant movement illustrates and illumines the same dilemma Baptists face concerning the interplay of fundamental commitments and social realities: the authority of the Bible, the freedom of individual interpretation, and the possibility and integrity of the voluntary community of a common denominational life. Various people within our Baptist life, depending on the circumstances and the issues, perceive all three of these commitments—biblical authority, the freedom of individual interpretation, and the viability of denominational life—as deeply threatened.

Three American Eighteenth- and Nineteenth-Century Illustrations of Baptist Radical Commitment to Private Interpretation

Let us now turn our attention to three examples of radical commitment to the freedom of individual or private interpretation from eighteenth- and nineteenth-century Baptists in America.

American church historian Nathan O. Hatch, in a delightful and insightful article on the issues of our dilemma, draws attention to the observations that John W. Nevin, a German Reformed theologian, made in 1848 about Christianity in America. Hatch summarizes Nevin's remarks:

> an exclusively biblical form of Christianity was the distinctive feature of American religion. . . . this emphasis stemmed from a popular demand for "private judgment," involved a wholesale dismissal of historical and systematic theology, and stripped the institutional church of all mystery and authority. Americans . . . had caricatured the meaning of *sola scriptura* . . . by interpreting it through the lenses of individualism and democracy.[25]

Hatch, in his discussion of the tensions between the authority of the Bible and private interpretation in eighteenth- and nineteenth-century American Christianity, includes three fascinating Baptist examples.

Elias Smith

Elias Smith (1769-1846),[26] who began his pastoral career in 1790, was a respected Calvinistic Baptist pastor in Woburn, Massachusetts, when he began to raise questions about his theological tradition. According to Hatch, Smith "denied that his own interpretation of Scripture should be mediated by any other authority, historical or ecclesiastical. . . . [and insisted] that the unfettered conscience must encounter for itself the *ipse dixit* of the New Testament."[27] This journey led Smith to found the Christian Connection, a radical group that held to "no creed but the New Testament."[28] Later Smith became a Universalist, and throughout the rest of his life he went back and forth between the Christian Connection and the Universalist General Convention.

Elhanan Winchester

Elhanan Winchester (1751-1797),[29] born in Massachusetts, became a Baptist in 1770 and eventually was pastor of Baptist churches in Massachusetts, of the Baptist church in Welch Neck, South Carolina, and of the First Baptist Church of Philadelphia.

Winchester, regarded as one of the best preachers in Philadelphia in his time, began to move toward a belief in what he called universal restoration. Winchester describes the process:

> I shut myself up chiefly in my chamber, read the Scriptures, and prayed to God to lead me into all truth, and not suffer me to embrace any error; and I think with an upright mind, I laid myself open to believe whatsoever the Lord had revealed. It would be too long to tell all . . . ; let it suffice . . . to say, that I became so well persuaded of the truth of Universal Restoration, that I determined never to deny it.[30]

Winchester's universalism created a great controversy within the First Baptist Church of Philadelphia. He was dismissed in 1781; several of the congregation left with him and formed the Society of Universalist Baptists.

William Smythe Babcock

William Smythe Babcock (1764-1839), a relatively unknown New England Baptist preacher, knowledge of whom comes only from his 1801-1809 personal journal, founded a Free-Will Baptist Church in Springfield, Vermont, in 1801. With that as a base, Babcock preached extensively in upper Vermont and New Hampshire; he estimates, for example, that in 1802-1803 he traveled over 1,500 miles and preached 297 sermons. Babcock had an increasing concern that he might be relying too much on others for his Christian understanding. By 1809 he and his congregation had broken contact with the monthly meeting of the Free-Will Baptists and established their own independent church. Hatch summarizes this as follows: "They agreed to defer to only one authority, the rule and guide of the Scriptures. . . . Babcock could not abide anyone having the right to suggest to him the parameters of biblical teaching."[31]

What Elias Smith, Elhanan Winchester, and William Smythe Babcock teach us may well be a matter of discussion and debate. They do seem, however, to be rather clear illustrations of the dynamic tension, even conflict, between a community's commitment to the authority of the Bible and the encouragement of the individual's freedom of private interpretation. In all three of these radical instances, the pastors left their traditional Baptist communities in order to preserve their private interpretations. Although the sociological pilgrimages of these three pastors may not be typical, their conceptual attitudes toward the Bible and its interpretation both reflected Baptist heritage and tradition and also shaped Baptist perceptions of how biblical authority actually worked. Perhaps these historical examples suggest that the bipolar tension of biblical authority and private interpretation needs to be expanded to include the third dimension of voluntary community boundaries. This, of course, makes the dilemma deeper and more complex.

An American Nineteenth-Century Illustration of the Baptist Threat to the Freedom of Biblical Interpretation

A very important, and final, illustration of a different type may be noted here—a case of a Baptist threat to the freedom of biblical interpretation. I refer to the nineteenth-century case of Crawford Howell Toy (1836-1919).[32]

Toy became a professor of the Old Testament at Southern Baptist Theological Seminary in 1869. Due to his views of Darwinian evolution and of Wellhausen pentateuchal criticism, great controversy arose, and Toy was forced to resign from Southern Seminary in 1879. He completed a distinguished career as a professor at Harvard University from 1880 to 1919.

Of considerable relevance to our concerns is Toy's inaugural address, delivered on September 1, 1869, at Southern Seminary, then located in Greenville, South Carolina, entitled "The Claims of Biblical Interpretation on Baptists. . . ."[33] Toy's address, which is rarely actually cited, is a defense of what was then called the grammatico-historical method of exegesis, what today we would generally call the historical-critical method. Toy gives a long history of exegesis, identifies Baptist contributions to the study of Scripture, and argues for the importance of solid exegesis of the Bible.

Toy stresses that "on Baptists there rests a special obligation in respect to the Scriptures." The Baptist obligation rests on two factors. First, there is the complete reliance on the Bible. As Toy writes: "We accept all that [the Bible] teaches, and nothing else. In doctrine and practice, in ordinances and polity, we look to it alone for instruction, and no wisdom or learning of men avails with us one iota, except as according with the inspired Record."[34]

Second, Toy argues that Baptists have a greater obligation toward the Bible because of their more favorable position, which involves two aspects. First "is the freedom from human control . . . which gives us a singular advantage."[35] He goes on to admit that Baptists might be prejudiced, but he notes that at least they are free from all forms of human authority, including Articles of Faith. He says, "We hold ourselves accountable to God alone, and suffer no man's individuality to be swallowed up in the impersonal mass of the body to which he belongs."[36] That is quite an affirmation of the right of private interpretation! The second aspect of the favorable position is what Toy calls "the greater purity in which we hold the truth of the Scriptures." He wants to make it clear that this is a humble, not an arrogant, claim. By this claim he understands that Baptists are, more than other Christians, "in accord with the spirit of the Inspired Word. . . . Without some such oneness of feeling, correct understanding is not possible, and he is best interpreter . . . who has most of it."[37] I find this very intriguing, for I understand it to mean that, according to Toy, correct interpretation of the Bible comes in the context of a frame of reference that agrees with the Bible, that is, some kind of confessional or theological stance, even though Toy may not have chosen to say it that way. This presents a fascinating tension with Toy's strong commitment to the freedom of individual interpretation.

Toy, after his long history of exegesis, notes that the task of interpreting the Bible is work and that Baptists should draw on the advances in the knowledge of Hebrew and Greek, archaeology, physical science, and the history and geography of the ancient Near East. He then asks what Baptists should do. His answer is that they should continue to witness to the sole authority of the Bible and that they should be concerned with the proper spirituality of the interpreter. Again, Toy emphasizes the importance of the Bible alone: "Let it be remembered . . . that commentaries are not of equal authority with the Bible. . . . As a Baptist, he violates his own principles when he elevates any human utterance into the position of infallible guide."[38]

Toy concludes by noting two errors into which Baptists, with their obligation to biblical interpretation, might be led. "First," Toy writes, "it is possible for us to pervert the doctrine of the illumination of the Holy

Spirit into a plea for fanaticism." The second error is the "neglect of learning."[39]

Clearly, Toy envisions the problems of what he would see as uncontrolled and/or uninformed private interpretations, which would, in fact, detract from the authority of the Bible within the community of responsible faith. In other words, Toy's passion for private interpretation does not embrace fanaticism or ignorance, and it is assumed, without further identification, that such aberrations would be readily known. What is ironic, of course, at least from our perspective, is that Toy, who so brilliantly and carefully laid out a responsible Baptist approach to the issues of the authority and interpretation of the Bible, became in his Baptist context the one who was judged to have the uncontrolled, and thus unacceptable, private interpretation.

Thus, C. H. Toy clearly expressed in 1869, in his way, the Baptist commitments to biblical authority and private interpretation, noting the tensions and dangers of these commitments. And in 1879 Toy became the victim of someone else's application of his own perception of danger.

Conclusion

This historical survey of examples and parallels has been intended to help our understanding of the dynamic tensions between biblical authority and the freedom of individual interpretation. Let me now give some concluding reflections about our Baptist commitments and dilemma.

As already noted, the tension between the authority of the biblical text and the interpretation of the text in any form is a problem endemic to the Bible. The Bible, simply put, requires interpretation. It is also clear that commitment to the individual freedom of interpretation among those who hold to the sole authority of the Bible engenders special tensions and problems.

Sometimes, when biblical authority is perceived to be threatened, its advocates attempt, often coercively, to control, muffle, or silence the variety of interpretations, as if this preserved the Bible's authority. It does not. A variety of interpretations are, at least in part, due to the very nature of the Bible.

On the other hand, sometimes, in an effort to preserve the freedom of interpretation, private interpretation takes the course of undermining biblical authority, or, more precisely, of undermining the often intangible boundaries of a particular believing community's understanding of biblical authority.

The history of Baptists and other groups within the Church suggest that however deeply held the commitment to the individual freedom of interpretation might be, there are, in actual practice, invariably community boundaries. These boundaries, although sometimes quite elastic, establish some beliefs that are drawn from the perceived implications of biblical authority and stand against the absolute exercise of private interpretation.

The Baptist tradition has generally defended the absolute right of individual interpretation, often for widely diverse persons or communities that may have a great theological or religious variance from its own norms. It has, nevertheless, usually set intra-community boundaries, which are often assumed and/or not explicitly articulated, but which limit de facto radical private interpretation. Traditionally for us, some of these primary community boundaries, understood to be direct implications of biblical authority, relate to baptism, church governance, religious freedom, and the like. When these boundaries are perceived to be broken, either one group excludes the other or one group voluntarily separates from the other.

Thus, it seems clear to me that the endemic nature of the problem of biblical interpretation and the history of the bipolar tension between biblical authority and private interpretation suggest that these two poles need to be related to a third element in some triangular way. I refer here to what I would call a believing community's internal confessional tradition, even if such a confession is not expressed in any objective, written statement. It seems to me that the historic Baptist commitments both to the authority of the Bible and to the freedom of individual interpretation were meant to be responsible affirmations within a communal, consensual understanding of the Christian faith for those making these commitments.

Thus, in practice, the Bible, which in fact can only be appropriated through interpretation, is to be free from determined interpretations of human authority (for example, the Catholic *magisterium* or creeds), but also free and open to individual interpretation. That is, all persons should have access to the Bible on *its* own terms but not on *their* own terms. Interpretations were always understood to be subject to the whole counsel of the Bible and the guidance of the Holy Spirit, which in practice were known only in those often elusive community boundaries.

Therefore, the principle I would propose is the freedom of the individual to interpret the Bible within the responsible boundaries of the faith community to which she or he voluntarily belongs. I am painfully aware that this declaration hardly solves our most pressing problems. The dilemma remains, and probably will always remain, one of indefinable tension: one between the perceived understandings of the Bible's authority and the limits which the particular Baptist church, association, alliance, group, or denomination can tolerate of individual or private interpretation.

To put this in another way, I would cite a maxim I coined in the context of the gospel's horizontal dimensions against any view that limits the gospel to an individualistic vertical dimension: "The Christian faith is personal but not private." Applied to our concern here, this would mean that everyone has a *personal* responsibility to access the Bible, but no one has *private* control of it. Just as there is no private canon, there is no private interpretation that disrespects the wisdom, counsel, and tradition of the church at large and certainly none that can disrespect the understanding of one's faith community.

I am also helped by Bruce J. Malina's model of the three aspects of freedom: freedom of choice, freedom from obstruction, and freedom for the attainment of a goal or value.[40] My application of this model to our dilemma would understand that all persons have the freedom whether or not to choose the principle of *sola scriptura* in its truly Baptist sense; that all persons can and should access the Scripture free from the obstructions of imposed dogma, creeds, and the like; and that all persons should interpret the Scripture, however, not with a privatizing or individualizing freedom, which I think is a perversion of the Baptist tradition, but with a freedom to move toward the goal or value of a responsible interpretation shared in one's community of faith.

We defend the freedom of persons to engage in interpretations that break community boundaries, even in ones that destroy communities of faith or ones we think are uninformed, irresponsible, or even weird. But the freedom of interpretation that is in dynamic tension with any meaningful concept of biblical authority must be carried out within the triangular interaction of biblical authority, interpretative freedom, and the faith community's boundaries. To be sure, those boundaries are often unclear, may themselves be items for debate, may shift or change with time or circumstance, but are nevertheless part of the interpretive dilemma (or trilemma?) of responsible freedom.

Notes

1. This essay draws to some degree on my unpublished paper "Biblical Authority in the Baptist Tradition," given on June 2, 1990, at the second meeting of the Baptist-Mennonite Dialogue sponsored by the Baptist World Alliance and the Mennonite World Conference and held at the Associated Mennonite Biblical Seminaries, Elkhart, Indiana, June 1-4, 1990.

2. I am quite aware of these issues. I list here, in chronological order, six articles I have written that deal with hermeneutical issues: "Unseasonable Thoughts of the

State of Biblical Hermeneutics: Reflections of a New Testament Exegete," *American Baptist Quarterly* 2 (1983): 134-41; "Feminist Hermeneutics and Evangelical Biblical Interpretation," *Journal of the Evangelical Theological Society* 30 (1987): 407-20 (reprinted in *Evangelical Review of Theology* 15 [1991]: 305-20; abridged as "How Can Divine Revelation Be So Human? A Look at Feminist Biblical Hermeneutics," *Daughters of Sarah* 15, no. 3 [May/June 1989]: 11-15); "Issues in Biblical Interpretation," *Evangelical Quarterly* 60 (1988): 5-22; "Contours of an Evangelical Feminist Hermeneutics," *Catalyst* 15, no. 4 (April 1989): 2, 4; "The Nature of Biblical Authority: A Moderate Perspective" in *Conservative, Moderate, Liberal: The Biblical Authority Debate,* ed. C. R. Blaisdell (St. Louis: CBP Press, 1990), 57-68; and "The Importance of Teachers in the Church," *Theology, News and Notes* 42 no. 3 (Oct. 1995): 15-16.

3. "Issues in Biblical Interpretation," 21.

4. "Unseasonable Thoughts," 140; repeated in "Issues in Biblical Interpretation," 11.

5. *Prescr.* 39; the translation of all Tertullian *Prescription* texts is from S. L. Greenslade, *Early Latin Theology: Selections from Tertullian, Cyprian, Ambrose and Jerome,* Library of Christian Classics 5 (Philadelphia: Westminster Press, 1956). This quotation is from Greenslade, *Early Latin Theology,* 60.

6. *Prescr.* 15-17 (Greenslade, *Early Latin Theology,* 41-42).

7. *Prescr.* 19 (Greenslade, *Early Latin Theology,* 43).

8. *On Baptism* 11-14.

9. *On Baptism* 13; the translation here is by E. Evans, *Tertullian's Homily on Baptism . . .* (London: SPCK, 1964), 31.

10. *On Baptism,* 12 (Evans, *Tertullian's Homily,* 29).

11. *Against Noetus* 4.2; the translations here are by R. Butterworth, *Hippolytus of Rome, Contra Noetum* (Heythrop Monographs 2 [London: Heythrop Monographs, 1977], 50).

12. *Against Noetus* 9.3 (Butterworth, *Hippolytus of Rome,* 66).

13. I am dependent here on D. E. Pitzer, "Noyes, John Humphrey," *Dictionary of Christianity in America,* ed. D. G. Reid (Downers Grove, Ill.: InterVarsity Press, 1990), 831-32; and S. Klaw, *Without Sin: The Life and Death of the Oneida Community* (New York: Penguin, 1993).

14. Klaw, *Without Sin,* 23-51, esp. 49.

15. Ibid., 76.

16. I am dependent here primarily on G. Land, "Miller, William," *Dictionary of Christianity in America,* 740-41; and T. P. Weber, "Miller, William," *Dictionary of Baptists in America,* ed. B. J. Leonard (Downers Grove, Ill.: InterVarsity Press, 1994), 189-90.

17. Julia's Bible is *The Holy Bible: Containing the Old and New Testaments; Translated Literally from the Original Tongues* (Hartford: American Publishing Co., 1876). The letter cited is found in Julia's book, *Abby Smith and Her Cows, With a Report of the Law Case Decided Contrary to Law* (Hartford: American Publishing Co., 1877; reprinted in the American Women: Images and Realities series, New York: Arno, 1972). For a full-length study of Julia's life, see Susan J. Shaw, *A Religious History of Julia Evelina Smith's 1876 Translation of the Holy Bible: Doing More Than Any Man Has Ever Done* (San Francisco: Mellen Research University Press, 1993).

18. I am dependent here on T. L. Miethe, "Campbell, Alexander," *Dictionary of Christianity in America,* 214-15; R. T. Hughes, *Reviving the Ancient Faith: The Story*

of the Churches of Christ in America (Grand Rapids and Cambridge, Eng.: William B. Eerdmans, 1996), a major and significant study; and on my own experience over many years with students and professional colleagues from this movement.

19. Hughes, *Reviving the Ancient Faith*, 26.

20. Ibid., 99.

21. I am dependent here on S. E. Erickson, *David Nyvall and the Shape of an Immigrant Church: Ethnic, Denominational, and Educational Priorities among Swedes in America* (Acta Universitatis Upsaliensis, Studia Historico-Ecclesiastica Upsaliensia 38; Uppsala 1996), esp. chap. 7, "Let Us Take Our New Testament Seriously," 204-22; and on my own extensive experience within the Evangelical Covenant Church.

22. Erickson, *David Nyvall*, 207, quoting the *World Parliament of Religions* (1893), 1517.

23. These two booklets were published in 1935 in Chicago by the Covenant Book Concern. This information is not found in Erickson's book. I learned it from some Covenant "old-timers," one of whom had a copy of each, which she (Viola Theorell) graciously gave to me.

24. This double issue is vol. 53, no. 4, and vol. 54, no. 1. The editor is Wayne C. Weld, a professor at North Park Theological Seminary. *The Covenant Quarterly* copyright is held by Covenant Publications in Chicago.

25. N. O. Hatch, "Sola Scriptura and Novus Ordo Seclorum," in *The Bible in America: Essays in Cultural History,* ed. N. O. Hatch and M. A. Noll (New York/Oxford: Oxford University Press, 1982), 59-78; this quotation is from p. 60. Hatch draws Nevin's views from his "Antichrist and the Sect System," reprinted in *The Mercersburg Theology*, ed. J. H. Nichols (New York, 1966), 93-119.

26. See also G. T. Miller, "Smith, Elias," in *The Dictionary of Baptists in America,* 250.

27. Hatch, "Sola Scriptura and Novus Ordo Seclorum," 67.

28. Miller, "Smith, Elias," 250.

29. See also G. T. Miller, "Winchester, Elhanan," in *The Dictionary of Baptists in America,* 291.

30. Hatch, "Sola Scriptura and Novus Ordo Seclorum," 68, quoting from E. Winchester, *The Universal Restoration . . .* (London: printed for the author and sold by T. Scollick, J. Marsom, and the printer, 1788), pp. xvii-xviii. The Harvard University Press catalog lists numerous reprints of this work both in England and in the United States to as late as 1843.

31. Hatch, "Sola Scriptura and Novus Ordo Seclorum," 69.

32. Here I am dependent on W. R. Estep, "Toy, Crawford Howell," *The Dictionary of Christianity in America,* 1182; W. R. Estep, "Toy, Crawford Howell," *Dictionary of Baptists in America,* 268-69; and W. A. Mueller, *A History of Southern Baptist Theological Seminary* (Nashville: Broadman, 1959), esp. chap. 6, "Crawford Howell Toy," 135-42.

33. This was published in 1869 in New York by Lange & Hillman; it is 61 pages in length. Of course, as will be clear in all the citations from this address, Toy wrote before our sensitivity to inclusive language.

34. The quotations in this paragraph are from Crawford Howell Toy, "The Claims of Biblical Interpretation on Baptists. . . ," inaugural address delivered Sept. 1, 1869, Southern Seminary, Greenville, S.C., 5.

35. Ibid.

36. Ibid., 6.

37. The quotations in this paragraph, ibid.

38. Ibid., 54-55.

39. Ibid., 55.

40. B. J. Malina, "Freedom: A Theological Inquiry into the Dimensions of a Symbol," *Biblical Theology Bulletin* 8 (1978): 62-73.

Introduction to Part III.
Defining the Boundaries of
Baptist Community: Who Are We?

Baptist diversity comes from many sources: Racial, ethnic, theological, political, social, and experiential differences have helped to define Baptists. As we have seen, the strong tradition of independence has guaranteed that nearly every unique Baptist formation has given birth to a new direction or a new practice under the Baptist umbrella. And, without the unifying discipline of a creed or the strong tradition of authoritative institutions, these differences seem at times to be exaggerated. Thus, one of the major questions Baptists have to confront is the most basic one: Who are we?

The articles in this section approach this problem of definition from a variety of perspectives.

Eldon Ernst, for example, provides us with forty years of American Baptist development through the eyes of his own spiritual journey and from the perspective of his own formation of identity as a Baptist. Many readers will find places along his journey where memories will unite his experience with their own; others will gain an insider's perspective regarding recent Baptist self-consciousness.

James Dunn merges the impassioned spirit of faith and commitment to the deep principle of soul freedom and independence in his essay. One easily makes contact with the powerful spiritual forces that have given vitality to Baptist life and activity as they emerge in his words, and the privilege of freedom takes full flight against any who would provide a more orderly definition of Baptist life than it can tolerate.

Bill J. Leonard, chronicler of the events of Southern Baptist life over the last fifteen years, provides a remarkably clear understanding of the many identities that have fought for recognition and dominance, specifically in Southern Baptist affairs, but more broadly in the Baptist family as well. Even as some forces seek to provide greater theological definition among Baptists, Leonard demonstrates that the result may be greater diffusion and plurality.

In his offering, Malcolm Shotwell proposes that Baptist identity could be both clarified and strengthened if Baptists could return to the association as a center of activity and decision making. Making his case that one source of "diffusion" in Baptist life is a lack of specific communities in which churches can participate, he provides an interesting call to reclaim an old Baptist principle: associationalism based on geographical local or regional boundaries.

Finally, Nancy Ammerman helps us to view our character and our identity as Baptists from a sociological perspective. Not surprisingly, her work enables us to understand that some of the diffusion and confusion of Baptist life may be the result of social forces beyond our control, and that Baptists and Baptist churches are self-consciously exhibiting many strains also experienced by other organizations.

These articles will enable the reader to view Baptists in broad perspective and to search for the common themes that ultimately may enable us to provide more certain answers to the question of identity—or perhaps at least to be convinced that a continuing "crisis of identity" is part of the character of Baptist life.

American Baptists:
An Autobiographical Quest for Identity

Eldon G. Ernst

Introduction

Now and then Baptist Christians feel responsible to express their minds as freely and objectively as possible within the subjective context of their life experiences. After all, tracing and analyzing one's spiritual pilgrimage as a testimony of faith is at the core of Baptist tradition. Discovering American Baptist identity has been part of my pilgrimage.

1939–1961

To the best of my knowledge, I have been an American Baptist all of my life. Technically, of course, I was not a Baptist of any kind until baptized into church membership in 1950 at age eleven at the Queen Anne Baptist Church in Seattle, Washington, which allowed me to take Communion (though this was not a strictly closed Communion congregation) and vote on admission of new members.[1] Since that time, like many American Baptists, I have had one foot solidly planted within the tradition and one foot wandering around outside.

My Baptist identity questions began early on. I recall being puzzled, for example, that we really were American Baptists, even though we were called the Northern Baptist Convention. It seemed odd, too, that my church was a rather conservative congregation happily identified with the Convention, yet a Conservative Baptist Association recently had been formed by churches that had left the Convention because of its supposed liberalism. Most confusing, the very year of my baptism (1950) we were renamed the American Baptist Convention, though in fact we really were Northern

Eldon G. Ernst is the academic dean of the American Baptist Seminary of the West in Berkeley, California. This paper was presented at "Called to Responsible Freedom: A Conference on Baptist Distinctives," at Green Lake, Wisconsin, August 1996.

Baptists (as opposed to Southern Baptists). Northern, Southern, Conservative, liberal, American—who were we, anyway?

Religion and politics added complexity. It seemed that all Baptists believed in religious freedom and church-state separation, but they disagreed about how the church should be involved in public issues, if at all. Clichés, caricatures, and popular reputations made denominational identities less than clear-cut. American (or Northern) Baptists, as part of the nation's Protestant mainline, for example, had the reputation of advocating liberal-leaning positions within the arena of civil politics as a social mission expression of their constitutional religious freedom. Southern Baptists, however, avowedly outside of the Protestant mainline, reputedly emphasized personal evangelism more than social mission and assumed the harmony of their conservative religion and civil politics. But I wondered about President Harry Truman, a Southern Baptist liberal Democrat, who did not impress my Northern Baptist Republican parents. Then there was the matter of Billy Graham, the Southern Baptist conservative evangelist whose mid-1950s Seattle campaign affected me deeply spiritually. By then his popularity had garnered somewhat reluctant support from the local Council of Churches (American Baptists included), and he clearly was mixing conservative politics and religion by serving informally and unofficially as the White House "chaplain" to President Dwight Eisenhower (whom my parents strongly supported).[2] For me the waters were further muddied a few years later when I had a Damascus-Road-like conversion experience to the Democratic Party and political philosophy while a student at Linfield College in McMinnville, Oregon, where Mark Hatfield, a Conservative Baptist (not to be confused with American or Southern Baptist) was a popular liberal Republican governor whom I also admired.

Who were the American Baptists? How had they reconciled their commitments to religious freedom and church-state separation to their involvements in civil political power? Being an American Baptist, these questions naturally would help energize my identity pilgrimage in the years of religious and political upheaval ahead.

My questions about American Baptists expanded and intensified during my Linfield College years (1957-1961) over issues of Bible, theology, and ethics. I took wonderful courses in the Old and New Testaments that followed moderately critical approaches. Knowledgeable professors engaged students in the Bible with spiritual passion for its complex riches that affected some of us deeply. Yet we also knew about long-standing charges from self-styled fundamentalist Oregon Baptist churches that Linfield classrooms dangerously qualified biblical authority by wavering from a literal reading of the texts. It had not helped Linfield's reputation among these churches that courses in philosophy, history, and sociology introduced students to so-called neo-orthodox and liberal theologians, including even proponents of the famous (or infamous) social gospel. But for decades Linfield's academic openness and excellence had enriched the American Baptist Christian influence within a broadening range of persons both within and outside of the churches in the Pacific Northwest and beyond. Indeed, I was growing both intellectually and spiritually in the faith from the freedom of thought and expression that came within Linfield's American Baptist atmosphere, even though it involved real tension and conflict with many (perhaps the majority) of regional churches.[3]

Excursus 1: A Regional Identity

Among Oregonians live a special breed of American Baptists. The denominational tradition would not be complete, nor could it be fully understood, without them. They demonstrate as well as any that the Baptist tradition is first and foremost a history of persons, activities, organizations, and events related to free churches. Oregon, as a new frontier of church life at a most critical time in American and Baptist history, presents insights into a major element of the distinctive heritage of what today we know as the American Baptist Churches in the USA.

American Baptist church history west of the Rocky Mountains began on May 25, 1844, at West Union, Oregon. On that day five pioneer settlers extended the hand of fellowship to one another, thereby recognizing themselves as a congregation of Christian believers voluntarily bound together by the following remarkable covenant, which poignantly expresses their convictions and contextualizes their experience:

> Whereas, in the Providence of God, a few names of us, the professed followers of Christ; who hold to one faith, one Lord, and one Baptism, have been thrown together in these Wilds of the West, and being Members of Churches in the United States, desirous of keeping the worship of God in our neighborhood, and in our Families—Agree: that we hereby Constitute and come into Union—first giving ourselves to the Lord, and then to each other and Covenant, that we will meet together to Worship God, and keep the Commandments and Ordinances of God's house, and are hereby constituted into a Church.[4]

Who were these persons who believed that they had been "thrown together" in the "Providence of God" on the Oregon frontier in 1844, giving them the holy audacity to declare themselves a church "without benefit of minister, deacon, or recognition council"? Who else, but Baptists? They were Baptists from Missouri, that border frontier state where the Oregon Trail began and in which northern and southern influences met, sometimes clashed, and otherwise coexisted. In 1844 they were American Baptists, more or less northern- or southern-oriented (the West Union group were northern-oriented). Had they remained in Missouri a year or two longer, they would have had to make a more drastic choice to identify with the new Southern Baptist Convention or remain within the structures of the northern-centered American Baptist Missionary Convention, the American Baptist Home Mission Society, and the American Baptist Publication Society.[5]

The Civil War broke the nation and the churches, as historian Clarence Goen has documented, and the churches in Oregon Territory likewise suffered division. But most Oregon Baptist churches finally supported the Union, even though a majority of Oregon pioneers had southern midwestern roots.[6] Consequently, whereas the Civil War regional divisions made lasting impact on Oregon Baptist churches and associations, northern Baptist identity predominated among them during the next half century through their association with American Baptist mission society networks that after the turn of the century joined to form the Northern Baptist Convention (1907). By then the Oregon Territory, and American Baptist church life within it, had become divided into the Pacific Northwest States of Oregon (1859), Washington (1889), and Idaho (1890). The Baptist Convention of Oregon was distinct from, though cordially related to, the Northwest Baptist Convention.[7]

Sorting out American Baptist identity was a struggle for Oregonians from the beginning. First, they had to distinguish themselves from the sectarian churchly Landmark movement on the one hand, and from the antimission hyper-Calvinist Baptists on the other hand. This involved willingness to allow some flexibility in congregational and associational life over such issues as open versus closed membership and Communion, alien immersion, even the possibility of fellowshiping with paedobaptists! As new Baptist settlers arrived, denominational unity was pressured by diversity in theology and practice of churches in various rural areas (which tended to be more strict) and more urban areas (which tended to be more flexible). Occasionally congregations "excluded" members temporarily over matters of discipline (even David Lenox, in whose home the West Union Church was founded, was excluded for a time), and the West Union Church itself was threatened with expulsion from the Willamette

Association (formed at the West Union Church in 1848), over the alien immersion issue.[8]

After the formation of the more centralized and eastern-based Northern Baptist Convention in 1907, with its mainline ecumenical Protestant tendencies, Oregon American Baptist identity became increasingly stressed. Oregonians always have been an independent people overall, uneasy with mainline anything, whether government, business, or religion, especially if it were eastern-based, or California-based, or even Seattle-based (such as in Seattle's innovative First Baptist Church, once known as the "mother church" of the Pacific Northwest with connections into British Columbia and Alaska). Moreover, though never fully conforming to nationwide definitions, Oregonians have been rather more conservative than liberal in orientation, including religion, and especially including Baptists. It is small wonder, then, that the twentieth-century conservative schisms from the Northern Baptist Convention in 1933 and 1947 over issues of Bible and theology, social mission and ecumenism, hit Oregon American Baptists even harder than they did the denomination nationwide. In most centers of American Baptist life, such as Chicago (where the Northern Baptist Theological Seminary was formed in 1913 to counter the University of Chicago Divinity School), the modernist-fundamentalist controversy became largely institutionalized into coexistence within the denomination. But in Oregon the conservatives predominated, both thwarting American Baptist growth by schism and rendering its more liberal constituency a relatively small minority.[9]

When in 1957 I enrolled in Linfield College and became an associate member of the closely related McMinnville First Baptist Church, I stepped into a moderately liberal atmosphere within a largely conservative Baptist church population. American Baptists in Oregon were only half as numerous as were Conservative Baptists. But they had weathered their storms with a determination to persevere stubbornly as a strong minority church network representing the distinctive qualities and commitments of the American Baptist denominational traditions.[10]

1961–1967

My Baptist identity quest within the Oregon environment became further clarified when a dynamic American Baptist denominational leader of evangelism named Jitsuo Morikawa spoke on campus as part of the Baptist Jubilee Advance (1959-1964). The Baptist Jubilee Advance was to culminate in the 1964 celebration of the 150th anniversary of the

formation of the American Baptist Triennial Convention in Philadelphia
(1814).[11] Morikawa inspired young persons like me to commit themselves
to Christian ministry. His exciting social mission advocacy cast as "an
evangelistic lifestyle" was undergirded by a stimulating theological orientation that proclaimed personal and social salvation. How disconcerting
it was, then, to learn how harshly Morikawa was attacked by his theological critics in powerful denominational positions. Here was a man, son of
Buddhist Japanese immigrants to Canada, who had been reborn into
Christian discipleship and then educated at both the fundamentalist Bible
Institute of Los Angeles, and Southern Baptist Seminary in Louisville, as
well as UCLA. Here was a now well-educated American Baptist clergyman who went on to youth ministries in mission churches of the Los
Angeles City Mission Society, then to ministry among fellow Japanese
Americans in the Poston Relocation Center in Arizona during World War
II, and finally to lead the First Baptist Church on Chicago's south side to
new life. Here was a man, it seemed to me, who had a more thorough
understanding of the Christian mission imperative within the principalities
and powers surrounding and permeating diverse human lives than did his
most ardent detractors who wanted to see him expelled from denominational leadership. Morikawa's sense of the denomination as "a family
where differences were present but held together by family ties and
loyalty" seemed convincing to me.[12] The American Baptist tradition was
more complex than I had realized. Fortunately, it remained broad enough
to include Jitsuo Morikawa, this prophetic Baptist voice within traditional
and bureaucratic "mainline" American Protestantism, at a critical point in
its modern history.

So I went on to prepare for Christian ministry at an American Baptist
seminary. I chose Colgate Rochester Divinity School both because its
reputation promised openness to Morikawa-like Baptists, and because I
wanted to experience life in a different region of the country. I was not
disappointed on either count. Western New York presented a different kind
of American Baptist culture, no better or worse than Oregon's, but different. The seminary's halls reeked proudly of Walter Rauschenbusch's great
social gospel legacy, a legacy that some American Baptists have detested.
Rochester's Lake Avenue Baptist Church, where I did my field education,
carried on the dynamic tradition of Helen Barrett Montgomery—author,
educator, preacher, world mission and ecumenical leader, women's rights
advocate, president of the Northern Baptist Convention in 1920—and
most of all a pillar of the local congregation. The Baptist Missionary
Training School, recently moved to Rochester from its longtime Chicago

location, kept the vital tradition of women's leadership in American Baptist life alive in the seminary also, though this, too, was not valued in some denominational and church circles.[13]

Meanwhile, in the Colgate Rochester Divinity School classrooms biblical studies were seriously and stimulatingly critical. Theology classes ranged wider than I had before imagined. Church history courses broadened my vision of what Professor Winthrop Hudson called the "great tradition of the American churches," and extended to various Christian traditions in other times and places. I learned from professor John Skoglund how to preach and lead public worship in the broad free church tradition.[14] Throughout all of this I continued to grow in the faith.

My growing awareness of the broad scope of the American Baptist expressions of that free church tradition challenged and at times complicated my Christian identity consciousness during my seminary years (1961-1964), both further solidifying my one foot in the tradition and stimulating my other foot to wander into hitherto unexplored Christian territories. Baptists truly differed from Lutherans, from Anglicans, surely from Roman Catholics and Eastern Orthodox. I embraced American Baptist freedom distinctives (which by now I could rattle off like a creed), though I also learned of the rich manifestations of the larger body of Christ in other traditions as well. I was excited, therefore, to witness American Baptist involvement in ecumenical discussions when international representatives of the World Council of Churches met at the seminary in Rochester. By then I knew enough about the larger Baptist tradition, however, not to be surprised at some of my wife's California Swedish Baptist relatives' strong negative feelings about the WCC or any mainline Protestant ecumenical entanglements, for that matter.[15]

In the fall of 1963 I attended the seminary seniors' conference at Green Lake, Wisconsin. Here I came face-to-face with American Baptist seminarians whose identity quests were leading in rather diverse directions, some far more conservative than mine, some more liberal. Though not everyone got along well, we generally left with a feeling that the denominational family benefited from including us all.

In May of 1964 I was ordained by the Lake Avenue Baptist Church in Rochester, following my presentation and a spirited discussion of my ordination paper among representatives of the Monroe Association churches. My one difficulty was insisting on using the word *sacrament* for baptism and the Lord's Supper (a preference I still have over the more legalistic word *ordinance*) even though I knew this was near sacrilege for Baptists. They approved my ordination anyway, feeling that my rather odd point of dissent would not threaten anyone's faith or the ecclesiological foundation of the denomination. (In 1968 at Green Lake the denomination would debate the validity of ordination itself at a theological conference, with little consensus on many points.)[16]

Meanwhile, the larger cultural dimensions within the American Baptist fellowship increasingly had broadened my Christian identity quest through close association with African American Baptists from the South who had come to Colgate Rochester Divinity School for seminary education, for essentially the same reasons I attended. By the time I left Rochester for New Haven for further study at Yale, I had become powerfully committed to the civil rights movement, whose nourishment came primarily from black churches and the great social-theological, preaching, and organizational leadership of Martin Luther King Jr. Naively, however, I underestimated the degree to which many American Baptists in 1964 opposed King and the movement he led. Some would have disfellowshiped him from the denomination had they possessed the power to do so. Fortunately, the American Baptist tradition proved broad enough to include this saintly public political social activist, even though he had but one foot planted in the denomination.

Connecticut, it turned out, was like neither western New York nor Oregon with regard to American Baptist culture. There two early Baptist traditions met and eventually forged a working relationship. In the wake of the eighteenth-century spiritual and evangelical Great Awakening and in the ethos of American revolutionary struggles for independence and constitutional guarantees (including religious freedom), fiercely independent New England Baptist dissenters from the established church came into coalition with the long-standing Philadelphia associational and confessional tradition—a sort of common-law covenantal marriage of various mission-oriented societies that would only be legally and bureaucratically formalized in 1907 with the formation of the Northern Baptist Convention. From its New York–based center of mainline Protestant power near the Rockefeller-funded Riverside Church and the ecumenically conceived Interchurch Center, the denomination thus brought increased centralization to its institutional life, which extended westward to Pacific shores and beyond—to mission centers throughout the world.[17]

Religiously, therefore, I felt at home in Yale's graduate department of religious studies, where few cared one way or the other if you were this or that kind of a Baptist, or whatever. Such Baptist freedom—freedom of the "disinterest" of those around you—is not the situation most conducive to growth in the tradition, however, without much intentionality and effort.

My effort to pursue Baptist identity included a twofold academic agenda. First, I studied the history of Christianity with Yale's Baptist legendary world mission historian, Kenneth Scott Latourette. In a class on the expansion of Christianity, I examined American Baptist mission history, and there not only encountered Adoniram and Ann Judson and others, but again bumped into Jitsuo Morikawa. To my surprise (and seemingly ignored by most of his most ardent supporters and opponents), his evangelistic theology turned out to be essentially a Barthian, neo-orthodox version of the Calvinist tradition that had permeated much of American Baptist history. Second, I looked for Baptists within the historic maze of American religious history, and they turned out to be almost everywhere. In my doctoral dissertation research I found Baptists fully represented in the Protestant mainline at the time of what seemed to me to be its "moment of truth" experience, or what Robert T. Handy has called the "second disestablishment" following World War I.[18]

Excursus 2: A National Identity

American Baptist mainline Protestant identity had developed over a century and a half, though not without internal strife and occasions of dissent from ecumenical decisions. During the 1830s Baptists dissented from the interdenominational American Bible Society over the proper translation of the word *baptizo,* for example, thereby organizing their own American and Foreign Bible Society.[19] But overall they flourished cooperatively and competitively within the multidenominational evangelical empire that unfolded in the westward-expanding Protestant-defined nation, resulting by the end of the nineteenth century in a hegemonic, quasi-religious establishment.

Within this emerging mainline tradition, American Baptist identity found distinctive expression in an 1876 volume entitled *The Baptists and the National Centenary.* "Our denomination smells of the soil, as the smell of a field which the Lord hath blessed."[20] Such was the tone of the book. American Baptists identified with the nation's growth and prosperity; having recovered from the Civil War's brokenness, the nation now would fulfill its manifest destiny in the modern age of science and invention, industrialism, and social-economic progress.

But who were American Baptists? David Benedict had given an answer in his influential *A General History of the Baptist Denomination in America and Other Parts of the World* (1848). American Baptists were all Baptist churches in the nation, including those in associations and those "unassociated." Baptists had so flourished within the American laissez-faire free enterprise system so well provided for in the First Amendment to the Constitution that they almost could speak of a triumphant American Baptist Christendom in-the-making. Even other movements and denominations were becoming "Baptists *de facto*," in Benedict's words, by moving toward Baptist principles of religious freedom and the purity and simplicity of the church. By the end of the century it even was possible to conclude that "the nineteenth century was pre-eminently a Baptist century" because the Baptists' advocacy of religious freedom had governed the growth of the American Republic.[21]

The 1876 centennial volume celebrated American Baptist achievements in home and foreign missions, in higher education, and in literary productivity by theologians, historians, and biblical scholars. Though by no means did all American Baptists feel comfortable or identify with the religious power sectors of American life (many Oregonians did not, for example), the denomination as a whole was represented at the energizing heart of the northeastern-centered mainline Protestant establishment. Indeed, it seemed, the mainline itself was being baptized by immersion.

Benedict's work concluded with the observation that American Baptists were "passing into a new and maturer [*sic*] stage of denominational life," requiring more efficient and centralized organization of programs and resources to meet the challenges of the second century.[22] [Ed. note: See the chronology of the denomination's history, p. 216.] This new stage came in 1907 when the Northern Baptist Convention was formed and immediately became a member not only of the newly organized Baptist World Alliance (formed in 1905 in London) but also of the newly formed Federal Council of Churches of Christ in America (1908). Little did anyone then imagine that within two decades these Northern (later American) Baptists would find themselves in the throes of an American mainline religious depression that would last until the post–World War II religious resurgence of the late 1940s through early 1960s, after which the mainline denominational decline would resume.

Meanwhile, in 1950 and again in 1972, the denomination reorganized in attempts both to clarify its national identity and mission and to make its polity facilitate local congregation-centered ecclesiology with greater centralized yet institutionally democratic efficiency. During the disruptive years of American military involvement in Vietnam, on the eve of the national Bicentennial, the Study Commission on Denominational Structure (SCODS) was appointed (1968), resulting four years later (1972) in the more churchly "American Baptist Churches in the U.S.A."[23] However, in light of the mounting skeptical attitude of American citizens toward centralized government of any kind following the Vietnam War and Watergate debacle, but also consistent with traditional regional and other expressions of American Baptist diversity, it is not surprising that the churches' responses to this denominational restructuring have varied measurably.

1967–1996

During my student years in Connecticut, signs of the waning of the postwar religious resurgence were appearing, but they were hard to detect as such. Although I felt at ease as a Baptist at Yale, I did not always feel as comfortable in some Connecticut churches that did not fully appreciate the larger parameters of the evolving American Baptist tradition. I served as interim pastor in one such congregation that was not enamored of the powerful Interchurch Center tradition (a hostility not allayed by the denominational center's subsequent move to the Valley Forge "holy dough-nut"). Some in the congregation hated Martin Luther King Jr., while others loved him—a source of profound conflict. Yet I grew immeasurably in that American Baptist community of faith. Within its tension-filled diversity, God's grace in Christ broke through barriers even as they remained standing. The key to this mystery, it seemed, was maintaining diversity within the fellowship. Baptists had not thrived from being like-minded so much as by engaging their differences while praying together within the beloved community.

My encounter with Baptist diversity, however, had just touched the tip of the iceberg. From Connecticut my Baptist Christian pilgrimage returned me westward to Pacific shores, and not just any Pacific shores, but California's, and not just anywhere in California, but Berkeley across the bay from San Francisco. I began teaching at the Berkeley Baptist Divinity School (now the American Baptist Seminary of the West) in the explosive year 1967.[24] Here, to say the least, was yet another distinctive cultural—or should I say countercultural—expression of the historic American Baptist tradition.

Newcomers to California have experienced culture shock since Osgood Church Wheeler, a young New Jersey pastor, arrived in 1848 on the eve of the gold rush. He came under the auspices of the American Baptist Home Mission Society to begin evangelizing and planting churches in a land that seemed as distant as China. His early impressions of San Francisco were of a place not remotely resembling the Christian culture of the mid-Atlantic states. Spanish Mexican Roman Catholicism, plus a Russian Greek Orthodox presence, rather than British Puritanism, defined the colonial heritage. "Mohammed and Buddha and Confucius each has a system of his own [in California]," he noted, "and each openly and avowedly stands opposed to Christianity." Varieties of Roman Catholics, Jews, and Protestants soon joined the onrush of humanity to California—a phenomenon that has continued ever since.[25]

American Baptists in California shared the Christian civilizing mission mentality common to nineteenth-century mainline Protestants, but they never quite succeeded in this endeavor. Because there never developed a Protestant hegemonic establishment in California, there was no early twentieth-century experience of disestablishment. Rather, the California Protestant experience always has been of a plurality of religious traditions on relatively equal footing, each with a great variety of expressions within an environment that is also unusually secular.[26]

In such a place Baptists have thrived in every imaginable variety. Altogether they are the largest religious body next to the Roman Catholic Church. Southern Baptists are by far the most numerous, followed by American Baptists, followed by several predominantly black denominations.[27] American Baptist diversity is fully displayed. I have been personally in contact with only a few of the many ethnic Baptist congregations—Anglo, African, German, Italian, Swedish, Chinese, Japanese, Burmese, Indonesian, Lao, Mexican, and Native American.

Over the years, moreover, I learned firsthand about Baptist fundamentalists and dispensationalists, Pentecostalists and charismatics, new and neo and conservative evangelicals, neo-liberals and neo-orthodox, Chicago "process modes of thought" modernists, and varieties of sometimes competing liberationists. As a member of the Baptist Peace Fellowship of North America, I discovered how pacifists and social realists could live together in constructive dialogue.[28]

In the mid-1970s, following the period of Vietnam War upheavals when the United States celebrated its bicentennial, I spoke as an American religious historian and wrote frequently on the struggle of the mainline churches to reorient themselves from being acculturated custodians of national values to being prophetic critics of the nation's seeming contradiction of those values. In this context American Baptists, like other mainline Protestants, had begun their modern decline with the accompanying identity crisis that we know today. Now freed from national bondage, the question became "What brings new life?"[29]

Meanwhile, now fully immersed in the pluralistic interfaith life of the

Graduate Theological Union (GTU), without losing my Baptist footing, I extended my ecumenical foot into hitherto little-explored territory. For six years I taught at the Franciscan School of Theology, where I was named a "Baptiscan." I discovered that in some respects Franciscans have been rather ornery mavericks within the Roman Catholic world much like Baptists have been in the Protestant world—both with their own brand of free evangelical qualities, neither too much at home with power and wealth nor unacquainted with them. Was I still an American Baptist? Of course! More surely than ever I lived within the broad tradition with more "soul freedom" than I ever had known before. There my family and I have been active members of a fine, century-old, vibrant American Baptist congregation, the First Baptist Church of Berkeley—a deeply spiritual, theologically biblical, personally evangelistic, and socially activist faith community with world mission vision that embraces a wide diversity of persons in its fellowship and ministry.[30] What could be more American Baptist?

In April of 1988 an old question resurfaced. I presented a paper on the topic "Religious Commitment and Political Power" to the Pacific Coast Theological Society meeting in Berkeley. The occasion was the upcoming national presidential election in which Baptist preachers on opposite partisan sides aspired to be candidates. Neither Pat Robertson nor Jesse Jackson were American Baptists, but to most "outsiders" that fact was not obviously significant. Baptists were Baptists, after all, and how could they square their historic dissent from church-state entanglements with such meddling in civil politics? Even the renowned historian Henry Steele Commager, criticizing President Reagan's endorsement of independent Baptist Jerry Falwell's "moral majority" agenda, recently had written an article for the *New York Times* entitled "Keeping the Pulpit Out of Politics."[31] As the token Baptist at that ecumenical gathering, my task was to analyze the aggressive pulpit politics phenomenon of recent years. The mayor of Berkeley also had been invited to speak on the "religion and politics" theme. Lively discussion followed. I had lamented Reagan's "moral majority" endorsement on political and moral grounds but had defended the Baptist preachers' constitutional right to advocate their religious values in the political arena. Speaking from experience, Mayor Loni Hancock offered guidelines for bringing religious values into civic politics. I was heard not as a sectarian Baptist, but as an ecumenically oriented American Baptist speaking from within the historic mainline interdenominational tradition of American Protestantism, which for at least a century and a half had projected religious values powerfully within the political civil order. For over twenty years, after all, I had hobnobbed with Presbyterians, Congregationalists, Lutherans, Methodists, Episcopalians, Unitarian-Universalists, three kinds of Roman Catholics, Eastern Orthodox Christians, Jews, and Buddhists. Thus far my American Baptist identity had not only remained intact, it had broadened and strengthened. It did not waver that afternoon at the venerable Pacific Coast Theological Society.

After eight years as a Baptist with one foot somewhat in dispersion, in 1990 I returned to the American Baptist Seminary of the West (ABSW) as academic dean. Would I fit in? One wonderful experience at the annual meeting of the Los Angeles Baptist City Mission Society gave me an affirmative answer. The multicultural life of this vast fellowship, calling for social justice ministries combined with "praise celebrations" in several languages, made me feel at home (even though my musical taste preferred Bach and Mozart!). Over the past six years I have rejoiced at the rich diversity of persons who have graduated from ABSW: Anglo-European, African, Hispanic, Asian Pacific, and Native American racial ethnicities; men and women of wide-ranging ages; a broad spectrum of theological and cultural orientations.

My half-century-long quest for American Baptist identity thus has explored the mainline as well as various side roads and some detours into off-road terrain. Has my Christian freedom pilgrimage kept me responsibly within denominational boundaries? I believe that it has, for this is the denomination that in the 1976 national bicentennial volume entitled *Baptists and the American Experience* celebrated its distinctive tradition as rooted in *E Pluribus Unum* (out of many, one).[32]

Conclusion

1. In his notable sermon at the 1912 Northern Baptist Convention in Des Moines, Iowa, Henry L. Morehouse declared that "the primary unit in our denominational organization is the local church." The "churches constitute the denomination," he explained. "No local Association, no State Convention, no general missionary organization, not even the Northern Baptist Convention, is the denomination."[33] Following this ecclesiological principle, in the subsequent decades American Baptists on the national level consistently refused pressures to draw confessional boundary lines that would exclude certain of their increasingly diverse churches. Those unwilling to live within this diversity left the denomination voluntarily, while others became American Baptists for the unusual freedom the

denomination offered. Is this an ecclesiological principle of the denomination's moving into the twenty-first century? Does the wholeness of the denomination depend on including all of its diverse congregations, whether associated or not within their regions, whether they embrace or dissent from certain denominational policy statements and resolutions? If so, how can the denomination facilitate these precious freedoms and the soul liberty of its members without destroying the underlying unity of its life?

2. Keeping unity and diversity in creative tension has been an essential quality of American Baptists' sense of responsible freedom, and this is a key to the denomination's continuing raison d'etre. In 1984 the denomination's general secretary, Robert C. Campbell, called pluralistic American Baptists to reaffirm their unity in the words "evangelical, ecumenical, interracial, and international." But within these categories, large plurality and wide diversity remain distinguishing marks of the denomination that must be seen as gracious and challenging gifts of God to American life. American Baptists have been part of the mainline as well as dissenters from it. They have both embraced and dissented from ecumenism. They have activated social ministries and dissented from them. They have taken denominational stands on public issues while acknowledging dissenting positions from within. They have facilitated cultural pluralism as well as the most radically liberal and conservative theologies within the community of faith. The beauty and risks of this plurality of diverse American Baptists interacting freely was starkly displayed at a remarkable denominational theological conference held in Berkeley on the ABSW campus in 1986 entitled "Patterns of Faith: Woven Together in Life and Mission."[34] Is it possible for a faith tradition of such diversity to persevere? If so, a passion for unity must permeate the tensions of freedom.

3. But is there an underlying unity? In the mid-1980s a Commission on Denominational Identity reported that in their diversity American Baptists continue to share "the fundamental Christian beliefs" that provide an "overarching unity." American Baptists have been radical Protestants, carrying the doctrines of justification by grace through faith and the priesthood of all believers to extremes with a passion for Christian freedom.

Theologically they have not used creeds and confessions to secure their orthodoxy but have used them instead as working, contextual theological documents. Confessionally they have relied on the people struggling theologically out of their life experiences through study and unfettered discussion of the Scriptures within the community of faith, guided, they have believed, by the working of the Holy Spirit in their midst.[35] In this way they have thrived freely as a rather conservatively orthodox tradition, holding to a trinitarian faith based on a high Christology, though even here not squelching dissent. My own sense is that for most American Baptists, God not incarnate in Jesus Christ would be an irrelevant abstraction; and without the Holy Spirit, God would be but an abstract idea. Cannot American Baptists still describe themselves as a wide variety of persons who believe, profess, and experience God's saving grace in Jesus Christ through the working of the Holy Spirit and seek to follow a life of Christian discipleship freely within worshiping, ministering communities of faith and mission? If so, it is not inclusion of diversity but a temptation to exclude dissenting minorities from the denominational fellowship that threatens a distinctively American Baptist identity.

4. American Baptist identity is primarily a distinctive history of variously associated churches—an ecclesiological tradition within the body of Christ, the church universal. But even this history, the tradition itself, carries little authority. There is precedent for nearly everything in Baptist history, for Baptists have been quick to depart from precedents when convinced of the Holy Spirit's leading, thereby often making new precedents out of departures from old ones. American Baptists are a non–tradition-oriented tradition. Will this tradition, energized by a passion for Christian freedom, continue into the next century? We must believe that it will. A wise company of former denominational leaders recently reminded us "that we have much to remember about who we are and even more to learn about where God is leading us in the years that move toward the next millennium." Daniel E. Weiss, general secretary of the American Baptist Churches in the U.S.A, assures us that "the future is bright if we actualize the community God offers us."[36] I agree with him. And if enough others likewise agree, then we can say that the American Baptist churches' pilgrimage continues.

Notes

1. *History of Queen Anne Baptist Church 1886-1996* (printed by Queen Anne Baptist Church, 1996). By allowing alien immersions, the church was not strictly closed Communion; but the church required baptism by immersion upon profession of faith for both church membership and participation in the Lord's Supper. See Norman H. Maring and Winthrop S. Hudson, *A Baptist Manual of Polity and Practice* (Valley Forge, Pa.: Judson Press, 1991), 85-92, 170.

2. The Graham-Eisenhower relationship is described in John Pollock, *Billy Graham* (London: Hodder and Stoughton, 1966).

3. Kenneth L. Holmes, ed., *Linfield's Hundred Years: A Centennial History of Linfield College,* McMinnville, Ore. (Portland: Binfords & Mort, 1956). For

conservative opposition to Linfield, see Albert W. Wardin, *Baptists in Oregon* (Portland: Judson Baptist College, 1969), 407-15, 421-23.

4. Clifford R. Miller, *Baptists and the Oregon Frontier* (Ashland: Southern Oregon College, 1967), 25.

5. On the Missouri Baptist tradition, see J. Gordon Kingsley, *Frontiers: The Story of Missouri Baptists* (Jefferson City, Mo.: Missouri Baptist Historical Commission, 1983). The quotation is from Miller, *Baptists and the Oregon Frontier,* 25.

6. Clarence C. Goen, *Broken Churches—Broken Nation* (Macon, Ga.: Mercer University Press, 1985); and Wardin, *Baptists in Oregon,* 71-76.

7. J. C. Baker, *Baptist History of the North Pacific Coast* (Philadelphia: American Baptist Publication Society, 1912), 3-4.

8. Wardin, *Baptists in Oregon,* 41, 111-22. Baptism was the primary issue during the nineteenth century. Alien immersion meant baptism by other than a Baptist congregation. Paedobaptism meant infant baptism. Most Oregon congregations practiced closed (versus open) membership and Communion, thereby requiring believer's baptism within a Baptist congregation (see n. 1). The essence of Baptist ecclesiology was felt to be at stake. See, e.g., G. W. Purify, *Paedobaptist Immersions* (Forestville, N.C.: North Carolina Baptist Bible and Publication Society, 1854), and J. M. Frost, *Paedobaptism: Is It from Heaven or of Man?* (Philadelphia: American Baptist Publication Society, 1875).

9. Ray Bloomberg, *Our First Baptist Heritage 1869-1984* (Seattle: Seattle First Baptist Church, 1985), esp. chap. 6, "Mother Church"; and Perry J. Stackhouse, *Chicago and the Baptists* (Chicago: University of Chicago Press, 1933), chap. 9, "The Dangerous Years: 1913-23."

10. Wardin, *Baptists in Oregon,* 571. Despite their decline, Wardin concludes that "American Baptists nevertheless remain an important religious body and exert an influence on Oregon religious affairs far out of proportion to their numbers," 532.

11. Eldon G. Ernst, "The Baptist Jubilee Advance in Historical Context," *Foundations* 9 (Jan.-Mar. 1966): 5-36.

12. Hazel Takii Morikawa, *Footprints—One Man's Pilgrimage: A Biography of Jitsuo Morikawa* (Berkeley: Jennings Associates, 1990), 90. See also articles on Morikawa plus some of his sermons and lectures in *American Baptist Quarterly* 12 (June 1993).

13. O. D. Judd, *An Historical Sketch of Colgate Rochester Divinity School* (1963); and Helen Barrett Montgomery, *Helen Barrett Montgomery: From Campus to World Citizen* (London: Revell, 1940).

14. Winthrop S. Hudson, *The Great Tradition of the American Churches* (New York: Harper & Row, 1953); and John E. Skoglund, *Worship in the Free Churches* (Valley Forge, Pa.: Judson Press, 1965).

15. John E. Skoglund, "American Baptists and the Ecumenical Movement after Fifty Years," *Foundations* 4 (April 1961): 112-19. On the complex relationships among Swedish and American Baptists in the United States, see articles in *American Baptist Quarterly* 6 (Sept. 1987).

16. On the use of the words *sacrament* and *ordinance* see Maring and Hudson, *A Baptist Manual of Polity and Practice,* 145-47. On the theological conference see *Foundations* 12 (April-June 1969).

17. William G. McLoughlin, *Soul Liberty: The Baptists' Struggle in New England, 1630-1833* (Hanover: University Press of New England, 1991); Francis W. Sacks, *The Philadelphia Baptist Tradition of Church and Church Authority, 1707-1811* (Lewiston, N.Y.: Mellen, 1989); and Albert F. Schenkel, *The Rich Man and the*

Kingdom: John D. Rockefeller, Jr., and the Protestant Establishment (Minneapolis: Fortress Press, 1995).

18. Robert T. Handy, *A Christian America: Protestant Hopes and Historical Realities* (New York: Oxford University Press, 1984), 159-84; and Eldon G. Ernst, *Moment of Truth for Protestant America: Interchurch Campaigns Following World War One* (Missoula, Mont.: American Academy of Religion and Scholars' Press, 1974).

19. Robert G. Torbet, *A History of the Baptists* (Valley Forge, Pa.: Judson Press, 1980), 278-79.

20. Lemuel Moss, *The Baptists and the National Centenary: A Record of Christian Work, 1776-1876* (Philadelphia: American Baptist Publication Society, 1876), 291.

21. J. B. Gambreil, "Baptists and the Twentieth Century," in A. H. Newman, ed., *A Century of Baptist Achievement* (Philadelphia: American Baptist Publication Society, 1901), 448; David Benedict, *A General History of the Baptist Denomination in America and Other Parts of the World* (New York: Lewis Colby and Co., 1848), viii, 906-24.

22. Moss, *Baptists and the National Centenary,* 295.

23. Robert T. Handy, "American Baptist Polity: What's Happening and Why," *Baptist History and Heritage,* July 1979, 12-21, 51.

24. Sanford Fleming, *For the Making of Ministers: A History of Berkeley Baptist Divinity School, 1871-1961* (Valley Forge, Pa.: Judson Press, 1963). In 1968 California Baptist Theological Seminary merged with Berkeley Baptist Divinity School and was renamed American Baptist Seminary of the West.

25. O. C. Wheeler, *The Story of Early Baptist History in California* (Sacramento: California Baptist Historical Society, 1889), 16-17. See also Sanford Fleming, *God's Gold: The Story of Baptist Beginnings in California, 1849-1860* (Philadelphia: Judson Press, 1949), 52-63; and Norman H. Maring, *Baptists in New Jersey* (Valley Forge, Pa.: Judson Press, 1964), 141-202.

26. Eldon G. Ernst and Douglass Firth Anderson, *Pilgrim Progression: The Protestant Experience in California* (Santa Barbara, Calif.: Fithian Press, 1993).

27. Albert W. Wardin, ed., *Baptists around the World* (Nashville: Broadman & Holman, 1995), 469-70.

28. Paul R. Dekar, *For the Healing of the Nations: Baptist Peacemakers* (Macon, Ga.: Smyth & Helwys, 1993), 255-70.

29. Eldon G. Ernst, *The American Bicentennial and the Church: A Celebration in Tension* (San Francisco: Glide Publications, 1975); Wade Clark Roof and William McKinney, *American Mainline Religion: Its Changing Shape and Future* (New Brunswick: Rutgers University Press, 1988); and William R. Hutchison, ed., *Between the Times: The Travail of the Protestant Establishment in America—1900-1960* (New York: Cambridge University Press, 1989), 303-9.

30. Charles M. Jones, "Berkeley Baptists," *The Pacific Baptist,* May 15, 1915, 10-12; and Eldon G. Ernst, "A Century of Community Ministry, 1889-1989, First Baptist Church of Berkeley," unpublished paper prepared for the church's centennial celebration.

31. Henry Steele Commager, "Keeping the Pulpit Out of Politics," reprinted from the *New York Times* in the *Oakland Tribune,* Sept. 23, 1984, C-4, and quoted in Eldon G. Ernst, "Historical Observations and Religious Commitment and Political Power," *Pacific Theological Review* 23 (Spring 1989): 30. For American Baptist discussion on these issues during the late 1980s, see articles in "Baptists and Church-State Issues" in *American Baptist Quarterly* 6 (Dec. 1987).

32. James E. Wood, Jr., ed., *Baptists and the American Experience* (Valley Forge, Pa.: Judson Press, 1976), esp. "Baptists of the North," by Robert G. Torbet, 267-78, and "Baptist Pluralism and Unity," by Penrose St. Amant, 347-60.

33. Henry L. Morehouse, *The Making and Mission of a Denomination* (Philadelphia: American Baptist Publication Society, 1912), quoted in William H. Brackney, gen. ed., *Baptist Life and Thought: 1600-1980* (Valley Forge, Pa.: Judson Press, 1983), 293.

34. Papers from the "Patterns of Faith" conference are published in *American Baptist Quarterly* 5 (Dec. 1986). Robert Campbell's remarks were printed in *Capital Baptist,* Feb. 16, 1984, 1, 8, and quoted in H. Leon McBeth, *The Baptist Heritage* (Nashville: Broadman, 1987), 607-8.

35. W. J. McGlothlin, *Baptist Confessions of Faith* (Philadelphia: American Baptist Publication Society, 1911), xi-xii; and William Lumpkin, *Baptist Confessions of Faith* (Philadelphia: Judson Press, 1952), 16-17. On the movement of American Baptists away from use of confessions of faith during the past century and a half, see Gilbert R. Englerth, "American Baptists: A Confessional People?" *American Baptist Quarterly* 4 (June 1985): 131-45. For the Commission on Denominational Identity report and related discussion, see "American Baptists: A Unifying Vision," *American Baptist Quarterly* 6 (June 1987). This conference on Baptist distinctives continues the denomination's tradition that began in 1954 at Green Lake of gathering periodically for what might be called free confessional discourse. Out of the 1954 conference developed the journal of history and theology, *Foundations,* which ran from 1958 through 1981 and was succeeded in 1982 by *American Baptist Quarterly.* See George D. Younger's first editorial in *Foundations* 1 (Jan. 1958): 3-6.

36. Daniel Weiss, "ABC 2000: Meeting the Conditions for a Baptist Future," unpublished Drexler Lecture delivered at American Baptist Seminary of the West, Feb. 21, 1996, 8; and "An Open Letter to American Baptist Congregations and Pastors from Some Former Leaders of ABC/USA, *American Baptist Mission,* March/April 1996, 13-16.

American Baptists—Twentieth-Century Denominational Chronology

1900   Northern Baptist Denominational Societies meeting in Detroit
        appoint a Commission on Coordination

1905   American Baptists attend first meeting of Baptist World Alliance
        in London

1907   Northern Baptist Convention established in Washington, D.C.

1908   NBC a charter member of the Federal Council of Churches

1911   General Conference of Free Baptists join NBC
        Ministers and Missionaries Benefit Board formed

1912   NBC Department of Social Service established

1915   World-Wide Guild for women created by Northern Baptists

1917   Children's World Crusade organized

1919   NBC begins New World Movement (1919-1924), joins Interchurch
        World Movement

1920   NBC Board of Promotion formed to oversee unified budget
        Fundamental (later Conservative) NBC Fellowship organized
        The Baptist begins publication

1921   Helen Barrett Montgomery elected first woman NBC president

1922   The American Baptist Publication Society begins using the name
        "The Judson Press"
        NBC at Indianapolis rejects a uniform confession of faith

1926   *New Baptist Hymnal* is published; Year of Evangelism focus

1928   Association of Baptists for World Evangelism formed

1930-32 Laymen's Foreign Mission Inquiry—*Rethinking Missions*

1933   Schism forms General Association of Regular Baptist Churches

1934   The Council on World Evangelism established

1936   Baptist Joint Committee on Public Affairs organized
        Forward Movement Fund expands NBC missions

1938   *The Chronicle* founded by American Baptist Historical Society

1939   *Baptist Leader* and *The Secret Place* introduced

1940   Baptist Pacifist Fellowship organized (NBC)

1941   Baptist Youth Fellowship (BYF) organized

1942   New Development Program launched for college
        and seminary endowments

1944   Northern Baptist Assembly opens at Green Lake, Wisconsin

World Missions Conference held at Green Lake

1945 World Mission Crusade inaugurated by NBC (completed 1947)

The Crusader (tabloid newspaper) begins publication

1947 Schism forms Conservative Baptist Association of America

Crusade for Christ five-year program begins

1948 NBC a charter member of World Council of Churches

1950 NBC changes name to American Baptist Convention ABC, a charter member of the National Council of Churches

First World Fellowship Offering received

1951 National Council of American Baptist Women organized

First America for Christ offering received

1953 Churches for New Frontiers campaign launched

1954 ABC theological conferences at Green Lake begin

1955 ABC women's mission societies integrate with ABHMS and ABFMS

The Year of Baptist Achievement—focus on Christian education

Commission on the Ministry established

1956 The Danish-Norwegian Baptist Conference of America joins ABC

1958 *Foundations* succeeds *The Chronicle*

1959 Baptist Jubilee Advance begins 1959-64 (150th anniversary of Triennial Convention founding)

1960 Baptist Peace Fellowship replaces Baptist Pacifist Fellowship

1961 Convocation on the mission of the church

1962 New ABC Headquarters at Valley Forge, Pennsylvania

The Puerto Rican Baptist Convention joins ABC

1966 ABC creates Office of Ecumenical Relations

1968 Denominational conference on ordination at Green Lake

ABC Black Caucus organized

1969 ABC Statement of Denominational Purpose adopted

1970 ABC and Progressive National Baptist Convention (founded 1961) enter into an "associated relationship"

Mission and *Crusader* magazines become *The American Baptist*

American Baptist Indians and Hispanics form caucuses

1971 American Baptist Charismatic Fellowship organized

1972 ABC restructured and renamed American Baptist Churches in the U.S.A.

First national youth gathering at Green Lake

Asian American Baptists form a caucus

Fund of Renewal to assist minority groups (ABC and PNBC)

1973	ABC and Church of the Brethren enter "associated relationship"

1973 ABC and Church of the Brethren enter "associated relationship"

Key '73 three-year evangelistic life style emphasis begins

1975 Youth Ministry '77 launched

Feminism and the Church Today program begins

1978 First Mission in America conference at Green Lake

1979 Study Commission on Relationships (SCOR) creates new denominational by-laws

1980 First American Baptist Indian Conference meets in Oklahoma

American Baptist Women in Ministry denominational conference

1981 National Convocation on Evangelism in Los Angeles

1982 *American Baptist Quarterly* succeeds *Foundations*

1983 ABC General Board adopts "Autonomy and Interdependence within the American Baptist Denomination: A Declaration"

1984 Baptist Peace Fellowship of North America founded

1986 Commission on Life and Theology conference in Berkeley ("Patterns of Faith: Woven Together in Life and Mission")

1987 ABC,USA Sanctuary Convocation in Pittsburgh

1988 "The People Called American Baptists" statement of identity

The Judson Bible Series, all-Baptist curriculum, introduced

American Baptist Consultation on AIDS in New Jersey

1989 ABC becomes official observer in National Association of Evangelicals

Faith Faces Issues conference in Boston

1990 First Black Church Education conference held in Ohio

1992 Association of Welcoming and Affirming Baptists organized

American Baptist Evangelicals founded

National Hispanic Christian Education Conference

National Evangelism Convocation in Washington, D.C.

American Baptists in Mission replaces *The American Baptist*

1994 Social Ministries conference in Detroit ("Living the Whole Gospel")

Denominational emphasis on ABC 2000 launched in San Jose

1996 "Called to Responsible Freedom: A Conference on Baptist Distinctives" held at Green Lake

Being Baptist

James M. Dunn

I'm a Texas-bred, Spirit-led, Bible-teaching, revival-preaching, recovering Southern Baptist. That's neither a boast nor a whimper, just an explanation of "where I'm coming from," as the kids say.

This is not about to be an old man's reverie. I wouldn't dare waste this precious platform with self-indulgent display. Rather, the notion that "to whom much is given . . . of him much is required" haunts me.

I am semiscared but gratefully eager to talk turkey with you. For fifteen years American Baptist churches have been family to my wife, Marilyn, and me. We owe you big: You rescued the perishing; you accepted the "designated hittee" and you took in the banishee.

So hear what I say, please, as an expression of genuine gratitude, tender testimony, and also as an urgent warning. It's sort of a review of pitfalls to avoid as seen from the pit.

For any born Texan the spirit of the Republic undergirds the only Baptist creed, unwritten but universal: "Ain't nobody gonna tell me what to believe." Texas Baptists are an ornery sort.

Historian Leon McBeth calls us "jalapeño Baptists." In the tossed salad family of Baptists (we *do* resemble a tossed salad more than some stew or burgoo; no melting-pot mentality marks our togetherness!), we, like a jalapeno, can add spice and excitement to the dish, but getting too many together at once can bring tears to your eyes.

A few years ago Martin Marty wrote about what he called the "baptistification of America." Whether one laments that development or likes it, baptistification has, indeed, taken place in America's churches. Consider that:

If soul freedom is important,

If the priesthood of all believers is more than a slogan,

James M. Dunn is executive director of the Baptist Joint Committee on Public Affairs. This address was given to the General Board of the ABC/USA meeting in Valley Forge, Pennsylvania, December 1995.

If you insist on interpreting the Bible for yourself,

If you defend the right of each person to come to the Bible and believe you are led by the Holy Spirit to seek its truth,

If you believe that you must accept Jesus Christ personally, freely or not really,

If you assume the church should function as a democracy,

If you believe that in the fellowship of churches each one is autonomous, and,

If you accept no pope, presbyter, president, or pastor to rule over you,

If you are convinced that religious liberty is the password to public witness and that the separation of church and state is its essential corollary,

If you believe that no mortal has the power to suppress, curtail, rule, or reign over the will of the congregation, then

You have probably been *baptistified.*

These consistent freedom factors form an orderly pattern. Being Baptist also means maintaining respect, affirmation, and honest honoring of differences. After all, if people are free, they may not agree with us. They have a right to be wrong.

The absence of a creed does not mean the lack of coherent content to one's belief. One can identify Baptist principles that logically stick together. In fact, if we have anything to offer the larger family of faith, it is precisely these implications of freedom. Soul competency is the greatest contribution of Baptists. It is beyond, prior to, and deeper than the Reformation doctrine of "priesthood of all believers."

We say no to creedalism, no to connectionalism, no to hierarchy, and no to theocracy because all are violations of the biblical manifesto in Galatians 5:1: *"It is precisely for freedom that Christ has set you free."*

For instance, we have no ruling pastors. The expression "ruling pastor" is an oxymoron, and the pastor who thinks he or she is one is an ordinary moron.

George W. Truett, in his 1920 religious liberty speech, cast the concept in rhetoric that was politically correct in the Victorian era but it rings true today: "The right to private judgment is the crown jewel of humanity and for any person or institution to dare to come between God and the soul is a blasphemous impertinence and a defamation of the Crown rights of the Son of God."

It was exactly a fundamentalist attempt to escape from freedom back into structured certainty that set Paul off against the Galatians. And did it get him in an uproar! Galatians 3:1 reports that he called them "stupid," "foolish," "idiots" (various translations), and in Galatians 5:12, he uttered his harshest words—this apostle of 1 Corinthians 13! He wished *castration* for those who preferred legalism over faith, meritocracy over Christ, and nit-picky, performance religion over soul freedom. In other words, he reserved his toughest treatment for people who fear freedom.

But before we are too hard on those Judaizers, let's tell the truth, for in truth we all agree with Brunner in our innards when he warned of the "awful burden of freedom." Pluralism, pietism, and polarism plague us all.

We all have trouble living with pluralism, a dominant characteristic of our times. As Russell Dilday said at the M & M [Ministers and Missionaries Benefit Board] luncheon this June [1995], "the aimless uncertainty of our post-modern culture worries us. The bland absence of conviction nudges us to adopt creeds."[1] Martin Marty describes the motifs of this culture as "disorientation, marginality, fluidity and a hodge podge pluralism." The result of the freedom that we call pluralism is not without burdens, among them Brunner's "awful burden of freedom." Princeton professor Clifford Geertz says that "thanks to the deprovincialization of the world, we're going to be in each other's faces more. That's part of our problem. We are face to face with folks and facts we have never faced before."[2]

Edwin Gaustad points out that we are already experiencing that syndrome in the tide of multiculturalism that "has raised the consciousness of the academic community, even as it has also raised the contentiousness within that community."[3] Baptists are not alone in contending with a new pluralism. But we must be faithful to freedom if we are to be Baptists.

The danger of ethical relativism is frequently linked to pluralism. In fact, the word *pluralism* is used pejoratively by many evangelicals, often as a code word for the absence of absolutes. For most of us Baptists, the absence of absolutes is absolutely unthinkable.

The anthropologist Geertz says it well:

Understanding what people think doesn't mean you have to think the same thing. You don't just say "whatever you do is fine." Just saying "it's their culture" doesn't legitimize everything. . . . I hold democratic values, but I have to recognize that a lot of other people don't hold them. So it doesn't help much to say "This is the truth." That doesn't mean I don't believe anything.[4]

Geertz argues that the task is to find a way to keep one's values and identity while living alongside folks who have other values—values you can neither destroy nor approve. The biblical response to pluralism is to be faithful rather than creedal.

Look at this snapshot of the political pluralism among Baptists. Of the eight politicians at the top of the elective pecking order in American life, seven are Baptists: Clinton, Gore, Gephardt, Gingrich, Byrd, Lott, and Thurmond. By that count we have a lot to answer for!

Some fearful Christians respond to the frightening specter of pluralism even among Baptists with a moral creed. We may be unwilling to impose a theology, but we have always been quick to come up with a nice moral measure for all believers. Every generation and geography has had one. When I was a teenager in Texas it was:

> I don't drink,
> I don't chew,
> I don't go with
> Girls who do.

I was interviewed last year for the *700 Club* and was shocked when the reporter put a political creed to me. He asked, "Do you believe, Dr. Dunn, that anyone can be a Christian and a Democrat?" That's a pretty tight litmus test. But moral creeds do have a way of becoming political and making the pluralism, which is a fact of life, a call to arms, a crusade.

Ken Chafin argues that the political religionists lose steam without their politico-religious creed.

> Much of the heat goes out of the Christian Right when it moves too far beyond its feelings about abortion and homosexuality. These biblical literalists forget that their Bible never discusses abortion as society is dealing with it today. They are correct that both the Old Testament and the New Testament appear to treat homosexual conduct as sin, but they completely ignore the fact that the same Bible supports war, never questions slavery, assumes that women are the property of their fathers or husbands, allows parents to execute children who disobey, and even pictures God as ordering the slaughter of innocent children."[5]

A moral creed is no better than a theological one. It's probably worse because it is culture bound.

Chafin continues, "The Bible is set in a specific time and culture, not a book to be put in the hands of some Forrest Gump–like preacher who applies it literally to the complex problems of our society."

The complexities of our pluralistic society demand a greater dependence on the Bible, a deeper reliance on faith, and more fervent prayer than simpler times may have called for. We need to be more Christian than ever and not triumphally or proudly, more Baptist also.

A second challenge to our Baptistness is pietism. We must also confront clinging pietism. I speak of the dictionary definition sort, not that of the genuinely pious soul. Webster's dictionary says of pietism: "The principles and practices of one who seeks to substitute the devotional for the intellectual ideal in Christian experience; also affectation of devotion." The American Heritage definition is "affected or exaggerated piety."

We cannot afford merely to talk about the Bible. Rather, we who take the Bible seriously must take it so seriously that we understand the language, the historical context, the sociological setting. We should tolerate no light-fingered lifting of proof texts to back our preconceived notions.

I speak to you out of sad experience. The largest non–Roman Catholic religious body in this nation has been destroyed. Superficial sloganizing about the inerrancy of the Scriptures was used in a political power struggle. Baptists believe the Bible. Unfortunately, when we fall into contests about who believes it the most, everyone loses.

Many recent struggles in Baptist life are tarred with the assumption that the only alternatives are (1) to quote a few passages as if what they say ends debate, or (2) to not care what the Bible really says about the matter. But there is another interpretative ground: to figure out the real point of biblical passages understood in context. The mentality that says, "The Bible says it, I believe it, that settles it," is a cheap cop-out and unworthy. It is for the lazy who are not ready to work at serious interpretation and for the fearful who are afraid of the results of rigorous study.

We reject the pre-Galatian dominion theology of Rousas J. Rushdoony and his reconstructionists. In his *Institutes of Biblical Law,* he pushes the legalism that appeals to the propositionally inclined. He says, "If the law is denied as the means of sanctification, then, logically, the only alternative for believers is Pentecostalism, with its antinomian and unbiblical doctrine of the Spirit." No! No! But we are not so much "people of the book" that we are bibliolatrous bookworms. We are also people of the Spirit. Marty calls Baptists the "most experiential" of all the major faith groups.

Of course, we also reject the level of subjectivism that leaves us a navel-gazing bunch of "touchy feelies." C. S. Lewis laments those Christians who relied on "tickle around the gizzard." We are not merely animated Christian computers, rightly relating rules and regulations. No amount of correct doctrine can substitute for a regenerate life in Christ.

On the other hand, an ancient heresy is sometimes tagged "a gift of the Spirit." When one claims to "know the mind of Christ," he revives a hoary heresy. The 1644 London Confession had it right: "We confess that we know but in part and that we are ignorant in many things which we desire to seek and know." With humanity should come humility.

Dealing with pietism leads us to face the fact of a polarism that plagues our entire culture, the third obstacle to being Baptists that I want to say a bit about. Polarism, or dualism, is the tyranny of false and limited choices. We suffer a Manichean dualism whether we have thought about it or not. Most folks in American Baptist life are ready to choose sides on any divisive question. Americans believe "it's gotta be this or that." It's hard for us to live with ambiguity. Baptist Harry Truman said he hated those "two-handed fellers who are always saying, "on the one hand. . . . But on the other hand." We may be often in error but never in doubt.

All Americans tend to suffer this deadly dualism. In this we are more often captives of the culture than Baptists of the Bible. We have allowed the prevailing "this or that" tendency to lock us in little boxes.

Jesus didn't do that. He said "neither," "both," and "you're all wet" (a loose translation) when small-minded people tried to trap him: "Ye hath heard it said, but I say unto you," was a familiar response. In response to a particularly well-known question, he responded: "Render unto Caesar and unto God." You know the pattern.

Kudzu recently said to the preacher Will B. Dunn, "I'm questioning my ambivalence." Brother Dunn replied, "We're all ambivalent." Kudzu came back, "But I'm ambivalent about my ambivalence." We've all been there.

We live with competing values, principles that must be held paradoxically, goods that complement rather than contradict. You may think of God's providential foreordination and the concept of free moral agency. The dynamic dyads abound. They hit us every day, and not just in seminaries.

We tend to think we are capable of ultimate answers rather than proximate solutions, usually the best we can do. This is not an idle word game. The very issues that trouble American Baptists today can be seen in the light of ideas that must be held in creative tension. For instance, it's not either *sola fidei* (faith alone) or *sola scriptura* (Scripture only). It's both. The conservative American Baptist Bernard Ramm did us all a favor with *The Pattern of Authority*.[6]

We cannot force a choice between autonomy or interdependence unless our goal is to destroy the denomination, our mission outreach, and all the positive things we do together. Denominational headquarters for Baptists is always the local church. Each church is sovereign in its own affairs, yet we choose to work together, and God will gravely hold accountable those who destroy the fellowship.

Some would insist that the autonomy-interdependence debate is mere polity—there's no such thing. Polity is not the red-headed stepchild of doctrine. Polity is theology incarnate, doctrine with flesh on the bones, two sides of the same coin.

Maybe much of our tension could be made constructive rather than destructive if we would simply read Everett Goodwin's *New Hiscox Guide for Baptist Churches.* He makes the philosophical practical. The classic quality of the book "endures because Hiscox stays true to basic Baptist principles."[7] No Baptist body has any right to divide, exclude, or upset the apple cart until every participant has read *Hiscox,* taken a test on it . . . and passed the test. It's the poll tax for using the label "Baptist."

The seemingly insurmountable differences we face can be met only in a church that is a divine-human institution. Glenn Hinson reminds us that "God has created human beings with a faculty other human beings cannot control, the 'I' at the center of our being, which even the Almighty God will not trample." Yes, there is a divine dimension to our fellowship, but it is toted in the brown paper bag of our humanity.

So we pursue a sanctified ambivalence—knowing that again and again we all have to decide, not too sure that we're right. Oliver Cromwell, for example, begged the certain Scots "by the bowels of Christ" to consider that they might be mistaken.

We must choose over and over between the individual and the institution. We daily decide between the instant approach and the incremental. I frequently pray, "Lord, I have need of patience and I want it right now." Serious problems arise when we try to achieve here on earth what has been promised to us only in heaven. If you need a text, perhaps you remember the parable of the wheat and tares growing together.

We are often torn between the idealistic, perfectly noble biblical ideas and the incarnational reality. After working with laws, historical forces, messages through prophetic mouthpieces, drama, and fireworks, God chose to send a human being, even a little baby. We keep having moral and ethical challenges because of God's habit of working through people.

Freedom and responsibility are always inextricably linked. Every freedom carries responsibility piggyback. Every responsibility implies certain freedoms. For faith to be authentic, it must be free.

So any intrusion between you and your spiritual capacity, you and your God, you and your growth to the full-fledged person you might become if no one intervenes—any such intrusion is about the worst evil I know.

Dan Weiss said it well:

[Freedom is] the gracious act of granting a fellow believer the right to be wrong, or at least to have convictions other than our own. If history teaches us anything it is that Baptists, while always being confessional people, ultimately hold to the Scriptures as the final authority, and not the commentaries or someone else's interpretation. We have learned that to allow someone to tell us how we must interpret the Bible ultimately leads to unwanted ecclesiastical authority and spiritual oppression. Our ancestors and our fellow Baptists in many parts of the world today are paying and have paid too high a price for that liberty for us to casually reject it in the heat of a specific controversy.[8]

I love the hymnist's glimpse of God's grace. I count on it. I couldn't live without it. Sometimes I even remember to extend it to others:

There's a wideness in God's mercy
Like the wideness of the sea;
There's a kindness in His justice
Which is more than liberty.

But we make His love too narrow
By false limits of our own;
And we magnify His strictness
With a zeal He will not own.

Last week, Browning Ware announced his retirement from the First Baptist Church of Austin, Texas. For several years he has written a column for the local paper. Here's a recent one in which he suddenly felt the need to confess. Some of us might identify with him:

When [I was] younger, I thought there was an answer to every
    problem. And for a time, I knew many of the answers.
I knew about parenting until I had children.
I knew about divorce until I got one.
I knew about suicide until three of my closest friends took their lives
    in the same year.
I knew about the death of a child until my child died.
I'm not as impressed with answers as I once was. Answers seem too
    pallid, sucked dry of blood and void of life.

Knowing answers seduces us into making pronouncements. I still have a few friends or acquaintances who are 100 percent sure of most anything and are ready to make pronouncements on homosexuality, AIDS, marriage problems, teenage pregnancies, abortion, sex education, or whatever is currently coming down the pike. But when we get shoved into our valley of the shadow, a pronouncement is the last thing we need.

A friend wrote recently, "I, too, get Maalox moments from all who know." I'm discovering that wisdom and adversity replace cocksure ignorance with thoughtful uncertainty.

More important and satisfying than answers is The Answer. "Thou art with me"—that's what we crave. There may or may not be answers, but the Eternal One would like very much to be our companion.

Enough said.

Too much, maybe.

Notes

1. Russell Dilday, formerly president of the Southwestern Baptist Theological Seminary in Ft. Worth, Texas, was removed from office for failing to maintain theological orthodoxy to the satisfaction of fundamentalist trustees. He was the speaker at the Ministers and Missionaries Benefit Board luncheon at the 1995 Biennial of the ABC/USA in Syracuse, New York.

2. David Berreby, "Clifford Geertz," *The New York Times Magazine*, April 9, 1995, p. 46.

3. Edwin S. Gaustad, "Barbarians and Memory," *The Journal of Church and State,* Vol. 37, No. 1, Winter 1995, p. 9.

4. Berreby, p. 47.

5. Kenneth Chafin, "Is the Christian Right More Right than Christian?" *Report from the Capital*, October 4, 1994. Ken Chafin was the director of training schools for the Billy Graham Evangelistic Association.

6. Bernard Ramm, *The Pattern of Authority* (Grand Rapids: Eerdmans, 1957).

7. Everett C. Goodwin, *The New Hiscox Guide for Baptist Churches* (Valley Forge, Pa.: Judson Press, 1995). See esp. 14-17, 31-38, 49-62, 87-103, 178-85.

8. Daniel E. Weiss, Report of the General Secretary to the General Board of the American Baptist Churches, USA, June 16, 1995, p. 3.

One Denomination, Many Centers: The Southern Baptist Situation

Bill J. Leonard

The Cooperative Baptist Fellowship, the Alliance of Baptists, Baptists Committed, the Conservative Baptist Fellowship, Baptist Theological Seminary—Richmond, George W. Truett Theological Seminary, Mid-America Baptist Theological Seminary, Gardner-Webb School of Theology, Beeson Divinity School, Baptist Center for Ethics, Smyth & Helwys Publishers, Associated Baptist Press, *Baptists Today*. That list, far from exhaustive, is but a brief sample of the ever-expanding network of organizations related in some way to something called the Southern Baptist Convention, the largest Protestant denomination in America. Most, though not all, of these groups were established by persons linked to the so-called moderate contingent of the SBC, individuals and churches who lost in a fifteen-year political and theological struggle to control the national denomination. While that convention-wide conflict has created significant fragmentation, as yet no formal schism has occurred. In fact, these new organizations are supported by congregations and individuals who continue to retain some type of Southern Baptist identity and affiliation.

From its beginning in 1845 the SBC established a powerful sense of denominational loyalty among its adherents, utilizing programmatical, cultural, and theological forces to unite varying regional, local, and ideological subgroups. The connectionalism created by the Convention held within it the seeds of both unity and disunity. On one hand, the denomination formed an identifiable religious and organizational center, uniting a surprisingly diverse constituency in common education, publication,

---

Bill J. Leonard is a Baptist church historian who has written extensively on the subject of Baptist history and institutions. He was previously on the faculty of Southern Baptist Theological Seminary in Louisville, Kentucky, and is now the dean of the newly forming Divinity School of Wake Forest University. This paper is from *The Changing Shape of Protestantism in the South,* Marion D. Aldridge and Kevin Lewis, eds. (Macon, Ga.: Mercer University Press, 1996), and is reprinted with permission.

missionary, and other benevolent endeavors. As inevitable cultural and denominational transitions occurred, however, the constituency, hopelessly divided over theology and polity, established numerous centers of ecclesiastical life, each in varying ways continuing to claim or cling to fragments of the Southern Baptist mantle.

The Loss of the Center

The structure of the national denomination, now solidly under fundamentalist control, continues to maintain traditional agencies and institutions, appealing for support to customary allegiances among its members. While many remain supportive of such denominational enterprises, others across the theological spectrum seem less invested in promoting and underwriting "the program." Although they dominate the national bureaucracy, fundamentalist leaders seem unable either to recreate a new denominational center that will unite the fundamentalist majority or to articulate a strategy for dealing with the recalcitrant moderate minority. As they lose the financial and programmatic support of moderates, fundamentalists also face declining denominational loyalty on the part of their own constituents.

While SBC moderates are increasingly hesitant to sustain traditional programs and funding mechanisms, many are also unwilling to break completely with the mother denomination. And while persons and churches across the theological spectrum continue to claim the name Southern Baptist, their Baptist identity is nurtured less by participation in the national denomination than through a variety of subgroups inside and outside the Convention. The Southern Baptist Convention, therefore, remains a huge denominational bureaucracy but with new centers of energy and organization evident at almost every level of the traditional Southern Baptist system. Historic loyalties remain so deep and powerful, however, that even those many opposed to present fundamentalist agendas still maintain a stubborn reluctance to relinquish either the name Southern Baptist or official membership in the denomination itself.

Fifteen years have passed since SBC fundamentalists first elected Adrian Rogers, pastor of Bellevue Baptist Church, Memphis, as president of the convention. Since that time, Rogers and a succession of like-minded presidents have overseen the appointment of fundamentalist trustees to all convention-owned agencies and institutions. In short, fundamentalists now control those national entities, including six seminaries, the huge Sunday School Board publishing house, the Home and Foreign Missions boards, the Christian Life Commission, Annuity Board, Educational and Historical Commissions, and the Executive Committee, that assembly charged with the day-to-day administration of the Convention.

These agencies reflect the connectionalism of the convention system established with the founding of the denomination in 1845. That system created a more intricate relationship between churches and denominational organizations than had the older society structure that characterized earlier Baptist cooperative endeavors. The convention plan united multiple agencies and ministries around a single center—the Southern Baptist Convention. The society, on the other hand, was an autonomous confederation of individuals, churches, and regional associations focused on an exclusive benevolent task related to missions, publication, education, or evangelism.

As the SBC controversy and certain transitions in American denominational life have impacted the system, however, Southern Baptists seem to be returning to particular forms of the society method. Indeed, a certain implicit societization is evident throughout SBC life, creating innumerable centers of ideology and action. That new reality may be illustrated through a survey of various organizational, educational, regional, and local transitions in SBC life.

Before we turn to those changes, it is important to offer one more clarification. The movement away from the denominational center is not limited to moderates. It characterizes Southern Baptists across the theological and political spectrum. While recent history has given evidence of new organizations founded by those of the moderate faction, the fundamentalist bloc was among the first denominational subgroups to found new educational institutions, to develop alternative funding mechanisms, and to look beyond the SBC for teaching materials and missionary opportunities.

As the controversy evolved, fundamentalists and moderates reversed roles. Early on, fundamentalists were unapologetically critical of the denominational system, while moderates upheld the tradition. Fundamentalists now call for unyielding denominational loyalty, while moderates are generating their own specialized societies. How long these groups can remain part of the Southern Baptist family is impossible to estimate.

Organizational Centers

The move away from the denomination as center is evident in the growth of new organizational structures among Southern Baptists. This phenomenon first became apparent in the actions of SBC fundamentalists during the 1970s and 1980s. Frustrated because of their limited voice in shaping Convention policies and actions, fundamentalists often "designated" funds toward or away from specific convention agencies. Some fundamentalist congregations reduced their support of the Cooperative Program, the denomination's corporate funding mechanism. They also supported a variety of new programs and institutions that were outside official SBC structures but were aimed at Southern Baptist constituents.

When the six Southern Baptist seminaries seemed too liberal or insensitive to fundamentalist concerns, two new schools were established. These included Mid-America Baptist Theological Seminary, Memphis, founded in 1971, and Luther Rice Seminary, originally in Florida, now in Atlanta, founded in 1979. Although neither receives SBC funds directly, both claim Southern Baptist identity. Both are staffed by Southern Baptist professors and educate persons for ministry among Southern Baptists.

When fundamentalists felt that their views were not presented in the state Baptist periodicals, they formed their own publications, the *Southern Baptist Journal* and the *Southern Baptist Advocate*. These newspapers contained fundamentalist critiques of the denominational system, exposed liberalism in denominationally funded institutions, and made direct attacks on convention employees, particularly seminary and university professors. These actions directed energy and identity away from the denominational center. Try as they might, the leadership of the SBC during those turbulent years could not refocus denominational unity on common missionary or evangelical endeavors.

As fundamentalists gained increasing control of the national denomination, SBC moderates also initiated new organizations and networks. One of the earliest such entities was the Southern Baptist Alliance (now the Alliance of Baptists) begun in 1986. It originated as a specific reaction to increasing fundamentalist dominance in convention life. The statement of purpose declared: "The Southern Baptist Alliance is an alliance of individuals and churches dedicated to the preservation of historic Baptist principles, freedoms, and traditions and the continuance of our ministry and mission within the Southern Baptist Convention."[1]

Princeton Seminary professor Alan Neely writes that the last phrase regarding the SBC "was a calculated addition," not acceptable to all involved in the new group. Yet, he continues, "it was accepted as a practical necessity in order to avoid being regarded as a splinter group bent on leading people and congregations out of the SBC."[2] By 1991 that phrase was "quietly dropped" from the statement of purpose, and in 1992 the Southern Baptist Alliance became the Alliance of Baptists.

This change of name identifies a group of individuals and churches that cooperate together in mission and reach out to Baptists of various stripes. Most "Alliance churches" continue to maintain some affiliation with the SBC, however. With offices and the executive director based in Washington, D.C., the Alliance represents the most progressive (some would say liberal) organization in the moderate wing of the SBC. It funds various projects, including mission activities, occasional publications, and various education projects.

The Cooperative Baptist Fellowship (CBF) is perhaps the best-known new organization of moderates. Founded in 1990–91, its earliest formal statements declared that these moderates were not leaving the SBC but simply redirecting their energies toward more positive endeavors. One document noted that "a denomination is a missions delivery system; it is not meant to be an idol. When we make more of the SBC than we ought, we risk falling into idolatry. Twelve years is too long to engage in political activity. We are called to higher purposes."[3] These articles detailed the purpose of the CBF in terms of missions, funding, and giving "energies to the advancement of the Kingdom of God rather than in divisive, destructive politics."[4] All this did not require that these Baptists "sever ties with the old Southern Baptist Convention." Rather, they suggested, "it does give us another mission delivery system, one more like our understanding of what it means to be Baptist and what it means to do gospel. Therefore, we create a new instrument to further the Kingdom and enlarge the Body of Christ."[5]

The CBF has developed rapidly with substantial budget increases over the last three years. It receives over $14 million annually from Southern Baptist individuals and churches. With offices in Atlanta, the CBF now funds its own missionaries, contributes to the support of several new seminaries, provides scholarships for Baptist ministerial students, and offers a variety of services for Southern Baptist congregations.

An increasing number of Southern Baptist churches now permit members to designate their offerings for traditional SBC programs or the CBF. While this approach is evident only among a minority of the 35,000 SBC churches, fundamentalists have shown tremendous concern about such defections. At the SBC annual meeting in 1994, the Convention voted to reject all monies that came directly from the CBF. Until then, the CBF offered several funding plans, one of which allowed traditional support for SBC agencies. Contributions were sent through the CBF offices in Atlanta rather than denominational headquarters in Nashville, however. The Convention's rejection of those funds led to the end of that option from the CBF. CBF supporters have also formed state organizations that foster various regional programs, further expanding the decentralization of SBC-related churches.

One question remains unanswered. How long can the Cooperative Baptist Fellowship maintain its shadow relationship with the Southern Baptist Convention? Many fundamentalists insist that the CBF has all the characteristics of a denomination and should declare itself as such, offering Baptists a choice between one denominational organization or the other. Many inside and outside the CBF wonder if and when the movement should become a denomination. At this time, leaders seem willing to wait before making any definitive declaration or burning bridges irrevocably with the SBC. The CBF leaders recognize that few of their constituents are willing, even now, to break all ties with the SBC. For the present they seem content to remain officially in the SBC, offering options for those nonfundamentalists who prefer the traditional mechanisms of the denomination and those who do not.

The CBF is not the only new movement under development, however. A variety of special-service organizations have also appeared among SBC moderates. One of the most successful is the Smyth & Helwys Publishing Company based in Macon, Georgia. Established in 1990, the company markets books and teaching materials primarily for a Southern Baptist audience. The initial statement of purpose reads:

> The purpose of Smyth & Helwys is to offer supplemental and alternative materials for Baptists who have become increasingly concerned about the future direction of the Convention Press and Broadman [SBC publishing houses]. . . . Those involved in the formation of Smyth & Helwys feel it is time for a press committed to freedom of inquiry and reverent biblical scholarship, but which is at the same time autonomous and therefore free from denominational controversy.[6]

The publishers soon established a new Bible study curriculum known as "Formations" for use in Baptist churches. They recently projected publication of a commentary series for moderate Southern Baptists and other evangelicals. In only four years the corporation has expanded rapidly, recently completing construction of a new office building in Macon. Smyth & Helwys is a completely autonomous organization with no direct ties to CBF or any other Baptist body. Clearly, its constituency parallels that of the CBF. It represents another (voluntary) society-type association alongside the SBC.

The Smyth & Helwys "Formations" Sunday school material is only one curriculum now used by churches associated with the SBC. During the last decade Southern Baptist churches have expanded their use of Sunday school curriculum beyond the denomination's Sunday School Board. Sales at that agency have declined as churches have looked to other sources from the conservative publisher David C. Cook to Smyth & Helwys's "Formations" to American Baptist and other mainline denominational publishing houses.

Educational Institutions

The establishment of Baptist organizations is also evident in the rapid expansion of new educational institutions for ministerial students aimed primarily at a Baptist constituency. Indeed, the proliferation of Baptist seminaries and divinity schools has been so extensive that Daniel Aleshire, vice president of the Association of Theological Schools (ATS) recently noted that, since World War II, Baptists have founded more seminaries than any other denomination.

The Southern Baptist Convention currently funds six theological seminaries spread across the country from Wake Forest, North Carolina, to San Francisco. While these schools have been at the center of numerous denominational controversies throughout the convention's history, they also have facilitated an extensive network of denominational education and placement.

As already noted, fundamentalist dissatisfaction with the SBC seminaries led to the founding of additional Baptist seminaries. These included Mid-America Baptist Theological Seminary and Luther Rice Seminary. The latter school developed an extensive curriculum by correspondence, offering its own—marginally accredited—master's and doctorate degrees. Criswell College, founded by W. A. Criswell, longtime fundamentalist pastor of First Baptist Church, Dallas, Texas, offers Bible School degrees to Baptist ministers. These institutions continue to train Southern Baptist ministers and missionaries. They have created their own networks of SBC fundamentalists.

As the six SBC seminaries came under the control of fundamentalists, SBC moderates moved to establish new educational institutions for ministerial training. The first of these was Baptist Theological Seminary, Richmond, Virginia, founded in 1991. That school receives no SBC funds but does obtain money from both the Alliance of Baptists and the Cooperative Baptist Fellowship, as well as from a variety of SBC-affiliated congregations and individuals.

By 1994 numerous theological institutions were founded; others are scheduled to begin operation by the year 2000. Those already under way include Gardner-Webb School of Theology, Gardner-Webb University, Boiling Springs, North Carolina; George W. Truett Theological Seminary, Baylor University, Waco, Texas; Hardin-Simmons School of Theology, Hardin-Simmons University, Abilene, Texas; and Beeson Divinity School, Samford University, Birmingham, Alabama. Although the latter school was not founded specifically in response to the SBC controversy, and donor bequest mandates a more ecumenical faculty and student body, its primary constituency comes from Southern Baptists. Mercer University, Macon, Georgia, and Wake Forest University, Winston-Salem, North Carolina, have indicated plans to establish new divinity schools but only when appropriate funding can be secured. In response to fundamentalists' dismissal of Russell Dilday as president of Southwestern Baptist Theological Seminary, Fort Worth, a group of Texas Baptists are studying the feasibility for a consortium of theological centers across the state. Baptist seminaries, like spring, are "bustin' out all over."

At the same time, an increasing number of Southern Baptist students are discovering the broader world of theological education outside Southern Baptist institutions. Both Duke University Divinity School and Candler School of Theology, Emory University, have established Baptist Houses that offer specific courses and identity to Baptist students at those institutions. Other seminaries and divinity schools are discovering that the Southern Baptist market is fertile ground. Many offer scholarships that make them competitive with the six SBC seminaries.

Transitions in the nature of theological education for Southern Baptist ministers have significant implications for ministerial identity and Baptist denominational consciousness. In the past, the vast majority of SBC ministers were educated in the massive seminary system. These schools not only inculcated a powerful denominational identity into their students, but their alumni support system linked graduates with the larger denominational network promoting SBC programs, publications, missions methods, and ministerial placement. Seminaries helped maneuver ministers into the corporate system of the SBC. Now the pipelines to the six seminaries are drying up or being redirected. Newer schools are more regionally oriented or exist outside the denomination entirely. Clearly, the next generation of Southern Baptist ministers will have a different identity from that of their predecessors, whatever their choice of a seminary or divinity school. Churches must learn to ask new questions and explore new resources for securing ministers, all of which has major implications for denominational organization and identity.

Regional Transitions

Equally important to denominational life are the changes now taking place regionally throughout the SBC system. This is particularly evident in the changing relationships between the national SBC and the individual state conventions.

Concerning the connection between the national convention and state Baptist conventions, the SBC constitution reads, "While independent and sovereign in its own sphere, the Convention does not claim and will never attempt to exercise any authority over any other Baptist body, whether church, auxiliary organizations, association or convention."[7]

In the Southern Baptist system, state conventions are autonomous bodies that originally provided special programs, agencies, and institutions for Baptists in those southern states that formed the convention. By the 1950s, as Southern Baptists expanded throughout the nation, additional state conventions were established. These conventions hold their own annual meetings, usually in the fall, to elect officers who appoint nominating committees for trustee boards controlled by the state denomination. Historically these state-funded agencies included Baptist hospitals, children's homes, mission programs, and state Baptist colleges and universities. In the denominational system, seminaries were owned and operated by the national denomination, while colleges were controlled by the states. With the establishment of the Cooperative Program of collective denominational funding in 1925, Southern Baptist churches in each state forwarded their denominational monies to the state conventions, which then sent a portion of those funds to the national body, retaining the rest for state-run operations. While states were autonomous, they were closely linked to national SBC programs, funds, and identity. Those relationships are now being renegotiated, particularly from the perspective of the states.

Marse Grant, moderate editor emeritus of *The Biblical Recorder*, Baptist paper in North Carolina, wrote recently that

> Baptist state conventions finally are exercising their autonomy so effectively that Nashville and its obedient entities understand what's happening. States are taking seriously the protection given them by Article IV [in the SBC constitution]. . . . No longer do states believe that it's "traditional" for them to send their money to the [SBC] executive committee with few or no questions asked.[8]

As the controversy extends throughout denominational life, state conventions are reexamining their connections to the national denomination. For example, the Baptist General Convention of Texas, the SBC's largest state organization, recently approved a redefinition of Cooperative Program funding for member churches. In the new plan, congregations will be considered "cooperating churches" (participants in the Cooperative Program) if they contribute to the traditional Cooperative Program system; if they give money only to Texas Baptist programs; or if they choose to designate funds to other mission efforts such as the Baptist World Alliance, the Baptist Joint Committee on Public Affairs, or the Cooperative Baptist Fellowship. This plan represents a new definition of what it means to be a Southern Baptist church, expanding connections and identity toward multiple Baptist entities, related or unrelated to the national denomination. In response to these actions, Morris Chapman, fundamentalist president of the SBC Executive Committee, declared that the plan is "a departure from the partnership which has long existed between the state convention and the SBC."[9] The Texas plan could essentially turn the state convention into its own regional denomination linked financially to varying Baptist entities inside and outside the old SBC. In response, Texas fundamentalists moved to establish their own fellowship of conservatives to provide direct funding to the national denomination, further evidence of factionalization.

Texas is not alone in redefining its SBC connections. North Carolina Baptists can now select alternative funding procedures that permit reallocation of money to and away from fundamentalist or moderate programs. Virginia churches may choose one of three plans that allow traditional SBC contributions, funding Cooperative Baptist Fellowship alone, and a combination of the two. All this suggests that states are asserting their autonomy and providing constituents with multiple choices in order not to alienate large numbers of persons or congregations in their particular region. Virginia fundamentalists have founded their own organization, Southern Baptist Conservatives of Virginia, channeling funds directly to it and away from the state Baptist convention.

At the same time, traditionally state-operated institutions, such as hospitals and universities, are renegotiating their relationship with their respective conventions. Hospitals were among the first to distance themselves from the parent Baptist bodies. Often this involved a mutual agreement born of the state convention's fear of ascending liability for malpractice or other cases against Baptist hospitals. More public and poignant, perhaps, has been the decision of numerous colleges and universities to redefine relationships with the Baptist conventions that owned and operated them.

There are more than sixty Southern Baptist colleges and universities across the United States, most related directly to the Baptist conventions in their particular states. Many were founded in the nineteenth century, originally with self-perpetuating boards of trustees. Over time these colleges were united with state conventions, which provided substantial funding and appointed trustees. During the last two decades, however, some of the best-known Southern Baptist institutions of higher education have claimed greater autonomy, redefining their ties with the states. Schools such as the University of Richmond (Virginia) and Wake Forest University (North Carolina) were among the first universities to change their status. As their endowments increased and student bodies diversified, these schools concluded that the control by the Baptist state convention was no longer to their advantage. These concerns were exacerbated as the controversy between moderates and fundamentalists extended throughout the SBC, made particularly poignant in the turmoil that beset trustee boards in several of the seminaries. Since 1990 a number of Baptist-affiliated institutions have modified charters and bylaws to allow boards of trustees to become self-perpetuating. These include Furman University, Greenville, South Carolina; Baylor University, Waco, Texas; Stetson University, DeLand, Florida; and most recently, Samford University, Birmingham, Alabama; and Mississippi College, Clinton, Mississippi. In another arrangement, the North Carolina Baptist Convention approved a plan whereby Baptist colleges and universities in that state may appoint their own trustees in direct proportion to the amount of money they receive from the convention.

Recent trustee actions at Samford University illustrate the transition under way in many schools. Founded as Howard College in 1841, Samford's original trustee board was self-perpetuating. In 1845 the board amended its charter to permit trustees to be selected by the Alabama Baptist Convention, organized that same year. In 1994 trustees, by a 30-2 vote, returned appointment powers to the board itself. The board released the following rationale for the revisions:

> It appears that political factors increasingly impact the Southern Baptist Convention, with obvious potential to disrupt the Alabama Convention. These factors, along with proposals concerning denominational trustees here in Alabama, have raised the possibility that great harm could come to Samford. If the election of Samford trustees—who have ultimate responsibility for Samford University—is placed in doubt every year, and the threat of "stacking" the Board of Trustees with persons of particular political loyalties is ever-present, and Samford is regularly harassed with minor charges only to be exploited for what appear to be political objectives, then the University's current operations and future progress are jeopardized.[10]

Trustees will continue to be chosen only from Alabama Baptist churches. The university will maintain its Christian orientation within a Baptist perspective. The action, trustees noted, was "intended to protect Samford from the future ebb and flow of denominational politics."[11] In short, the trustees simply returned their selection process to that of a private institution, or society, with fraternal, though not appointive, relationship with the Alabama Baptist Convention.

Barely a week after the Samford action, the trustees of yet another Baptist institution, Mississippi College, took a similar action. Trustees of that school released a statement noting that the action was taken "to ensure that Mississippi College can remain true to its Baptist heritage and tradition of serving all Mississippi Baptists and their churches by distancing the College from denominational politics."[12]

These two Baptist institutions are simply the latest in a growing number of Baptist-related colleges and universities that are redefining their relationship to their respective state conventions. While issues of politics, finances, and institutional stability are evident in each case, the changes also have the effect of creating new, autonomous centers of Baptist educational and ecclesial identity.

Local Issues

The movement away from the denominational center is nowhere more evident than in transitions taking place at the local level. From the beginning of the Baptist tradition, the local church has formed the basis of Baptist ecclesiology. Congregational polity was based on the belief that Christ was head of the church and his authority mediated through the local communion. Early Baptists mistrusted organizational entanglements that might undermine the authority and centrality of the specific congregation. One of the great achievements of the SBC denomination builders was their ability to create a strong sense of loyalty in such a fiercely independent people. Such identity was not easily achieved and not without controversies over missions, Sunday schools, cooperative giving, and other expressions of collaborative endeavor.

Yet by the 1950s, and probably well before, Southern Baptist churches understood themselves in and through the national and state conventions. They utilized educational materials produced by the Sunday School Board, sent messengers to the annual meetings, contributed to the Cooperative Program, called ministers educated at Baptist colleges and seminaries, and understood their primary religious identity as cooperating Southern Baptists. All that is changing.

As with other mainline denominations, intermarriage and enlistment programs have brought persons to SBC churches who have neither the familial nor cultural experience of Southern Baptistness. The denominational controversy has impacted numerous local congregations, contributing to schism and ministerial termination. Some estimates suggest that some 120 Southern Baptist ministers have been terminated by SBC churches. A growing number of congregations permit members to designate funds to causes inside or outside the SBC. As already noted, churches across the theological and political spectrum now utilize a variety of educational and resource materials, many of which are not published by the SBC. Fundamentalists and moderates alike acknowledge that the old denominational loyalties are stronger among persons over fifty while the younger generation seems less likely to follow the traditional denominational line, whatever their theological orientation.

This is particularly evident among those influenced by the so-called megachurch movement, now rapidly affecting Southern Baptist life. Megachurch methods are setting agendas for congregations across the SBC. A megachurch may be defined as a congregation of several thousand members, dispensing specialized services targeting specific subgroups, usually led by a charismatic authority-figure pastor, and organized around distinct marketing techniques. Megachurches are essentially mini-denominations, offering in one congregation many activities previously administered through the larger denominational system. Many of these churches minimize their denominational affiliation, publish their own educational materials, fund their own missions programs, and send a smaller percentage of their funds to the denominational enterprise. Younger ministers, both fundamentalist and moderate, influenced by megachurch trends, are less likely to expend their energy on denominational battles. Indeed, many speak of the death of denominations and the rise of new megachurch paradigms for ministry in the twenty-first century. Clearly, megachurches create new ecclesiastical centers that redirect energies toward local-church-based ministry and away from traditional convention programs and policies. Their impact on Southern Baptists deserves extensive study and analysis.

Conclusion: Intentionality and Identity

Localism has also contributed to a growing sense of intentionality among SBC-affiliated churches. With the decline of denominational consciousness and the fragmentation of denominational programs, many churches are confronting questions of identity. For example, what does it mean to be Baptist? What elements of the Baptist heritage should be retained and passed on to another generation?

In earlier, more denominationally conscious times, strategies for missions, evangelism, social ministry, and Baptist identity were articulated by the denomination. Churches simply ordered literature, adopted prescribed programs, and wrote checks for missions funding. As those old connections are changed or eliminated, churches must be more intentional as to their identity and purpose within the Baptist heritage. Many are reasserting the idea of the local church as the center of mission, learning, worship, and ministry, and are utilizing their resources to support ministry inside and outside traditional denominational programs.

At least in the short term, these transitions point to a return to something like the society method that characterized Baptists' first attempts at denominational cooperation. The society method was a way in which Baptists who did not trust "hierarchies" beyond the local church joined together in missionary and benevolence they could not accomplish on their own. Each society was itself autonomous, established to provide particular ministries in home or foreign missions, education, publication, or benevolence. Membership was extended to individuals, churches, and other Baptist associations. These organizations were clearinghouses for ministry, bringing together persons of varying regions and theological persuasions in common action. Churches and individuals "shopped around" for those programs that particularly captured their energy and interest. Funding came from direct appeals to the constituency, not from a centralized denominational finance system. In fact, when the SBC was first created, "delegates" to its annual meetings included representatives of churches and associations as well as solitary individuals, all of whom had made the necessary contributions to the work of the fledgling denomination.

At the present time Southern Baptists function on several levels of denominational identity and support. While the old system remains, engendering continued loyalty from large numbers of persons, new forms of cooperation, organization, and action are evident throughout SBC life. Theological disputes and political machinations have created a tremendous spirit of mistrust among and within the various regional and ideological subgroups that compose the convention. While a powerful sense of denominational identity lingers, particularly among those over the age of fifty, a growing number of Southern Baptists do not think of their primary religious identity in terms of an exclusively denominational identity. Not only are regional and local associations reasserting their autonomy, but new Baptist-supported agencies also are being established.

A de facto society method is returning to the denomination. At every level of denominational life, questions arise as to what it means to be Baptist and how to pass on a Baptist identity to a new generation raised in the midst of controversy and transition. Those leaders—national, regional, and local—who refuse to confront these powerful realities will find the future most unmanageable. For Southern Baptist moderates and fundamentalists alike, the twenty-first century may be a most difficult period for establishing a new denomination or maintaining an old one.

Notes

1. Alan Neely, "The History of the Alliance of Baptists," in Walter B. Shurden, ed., *The Struggle for the Soul of the SBC* (Macon: Mercer University Press, 1993), 109.

2. Ibid.

3. Daniel Vestal, "The History of the Cooperative Baptist Fellowship," in Shurden, *Struggle,* 267.

4. Ibid.

5. Ibid.

6. Cecil Staton, "The History of Smyth & Helwys Publishing," in Shurden, *Struggle,* 229.

7. *SBC Constitution,* cited in Marse Grant, "States Rights: A New Assertion by Baptist State Conventions?" *Baptists Today,* Sept. 9, 1994, 8.

8. Ibid.

9. Toby Druin, "Committee Wants Texans to Count Fellowship Part of Cooperative Program," *Baptists Today,* Sept. 9, 1994, 5.

10. "A Report to Alabama Baptists," Sept. 13, 1994, typescript.

11. Ibid.

12. "Mississippi College Announces Change in Board Selection Method," press release, Sept. 22, 1994, typescript.

Reclaiming the Baptist Principle of Associations

Malcolm G. Shotwell

Introduction

In recent years the associational principle among Baptists has been ignored in many places and by many people. With the firm belief that associations need to be seriously reevaluated and implemented, I was motivated to address the theological and historical beginnings of the associations in England and within the United States. Based on this research, and having observed the functions of modern associations both in England and here in America, I want to sound the call for reclaiming the Baptist principle of associations—not only the principle, but a contemporary model that enables us to reclaim the biblical, theological, historical, and sociological dimensions of interdependence.

When American Baptists sought to address reorganization in recent years, I believe there was a lack of attention to the association and its relevance for the twentieth and twenty-first centuries. It is my conviction that associations allow for grassroots participation among churches, enabling a "perking up" rather than a "trickling down" concept of ministry and mission.

I love a good cup of coffee. Instant coffee is another drink and is acceptable only as a last resort. Drip coffee is palatable, but a "real" cup of coffee, with a firm, full-bodied flavor, is perked! Likewise, the best theology of the church and the most effective ministry and mission occurs

Malcolm G. Shotwell was the executive minister for the American Baptist Churches of the Great Rivers Region until his retirement in December 1996. This paper was presented at "Called to Responsible Freedom: A Conference on Baptist Distinctives," at Green Lake, Wisconsin, August 1996. It is a condensation of a dissertation submitted in partial fulfillment for the D.Min. degree at Eastern Baptist Theological Seminary. An authorized facsimile of the entire work is available from UMI Dissertation Information Service, Ann Arbor, Michigan (1-800-521-0600).

not by "instant" programs or proclamations trickling (dripping) down from some denominational hierarchy.

The thesis of this presentation is that the most authentic ministry and the most effective mission happens when the grass roots struggle with needs and "perk up" through interdependence. With interest and enthusiasm arising from struggle and ownership among the cooperating churches, the larger components of the denominational family can more purposefully be called upon for assistance.

Denominational and interdenominational bodies become more effective when they encourage the "perking" among the churches-in-association and refrain from "instant" or "trickle down" pronouncements and programs that lack "full-bodied flavor"!

Sociological, Biblical, Theological, and Linguistic Foundations

In every culture there can be found sociological evidence of interrelatedness. *Networking* is a modern term, yet its meaning and purpose can be documented in any grouping that is seeking to be a family, a community, a tribe, a clan, a nation, or an association.

Amphictyony was the name given in Greek, Old Latin, and Etruscan city-states for groups who centered around a common temple for religious performances. In the *Encyclopedia of Religion and Ethics,* Leonard Whibley writes extensively on this religiopolitical model, suggesting that "the simplest form of union which can be traced in the earliest times is the union of people of kindred race within a continuous area around a common temple."[1]

Plato proposed "an ideal organization for a state or amphictyonic confederacy."[2] The best-known of these confederacies was the Delphi amphictyony, consisting of a league of twelve distinct groups of people who met twice a year, in spring and autumn, and were protected by a holy truce. It is believed by some who have studied this form of interdependence that the Greek Olympics trace their origin to the athletic contests that were a part of these amphictyonic meetings.

Some scholars have suggested that "the sacred society of the Israelite tribes was in fact an ancient Israelite amphictyony."[3] From the reading on the pros and cons of the Greek amphictyony and the Israelite confederation, it seems clear to me that interdependence among people is a sociological process. David O. Moberg, author of *The Church as a Social Institution,* observed:

Early in history it became apparent that people could accomplish much more by working together than by acting independently. Out of mutual aid, common defense, and struggles with the enemies for scarce goods and values grew the sense of togetherness or solidarity which is at the core of institutional unity. . . . Cooperative attitudes and behavior became so entwined with each other and so habitual for members that they operated unconsciously as if they were external forces and not personal acts.[4]

In the search for a biblical base for the associational principle, we can begin by looking at how the early Christians manifested interdependence. In the "core writings" of Paul[5] we can find five primary examples. In Romans 15 there are two. First there is reference to spiritual blessings received. Romans 15:26-27 reads:

For the churches in Macedonia and Achaia have freely decided to give an offering to help the poor among God's people in Jerusalem. That decision was their own; but, as a matter of fact, they have an obligation to help them. Since the Jews shared their *spiritual blessings* with the Gentiles, the Gentiles ought to use their *material blessings* to help the Jews. (TEV, emphasis added)

This contribution for the poor, which Paul took to Jerusalem on behalf of a grateful people in Macedonia and Achaia, was in response to a primary reason for Christian interdependence—namely, the *sharing of spiritual blessings*. The decision to move beyond the Jewish community and to make Christianity worldwide is a first indication that religion is more than an individual's relationship with a divine being. One person and his or her god can have a religion, but it takes at least two people and God, as revealed in Jesus Christ, to constitute Christianity.

Romans 12 reveals that the sharing of these spiritual blessings has prompted the *sharing of material blessings* in the form of contributions for the poor in Jerusalem—a second evidence of interdependence.

In 1 and 2 Corinthians, as well as in Romans, there is a third evidence: the *sharing of messengers and helpers*. In Romans 16:1-2 we find: "I commend to you our sister Phoebe, a deacon of the church at Cenchreae, so that you may welcome her in the Lord as is fitting for the saints, and help her in whatever she may require from you, for she has been a benefactor of many and of myself as well" (NRSV). Here "helping" is a two-way street, and the ingredients of interdependence call for *mutual sharing of messengers and helpers*. The one who is sent (partner, fellow worker, messenger, deacon) to help is also one who needs to receive help—the principle of interdependence at its best!

In the core writings of Paul there is evidence of a fourth ingredient of interdependence—namely, the *sharing of significant relationships*. All of Paul's letters include mention of individuals by name (e.g., see Rom. 16:3-16, where twenty-five individuals are named). Paul placed much importance on friendships, both individual and corporate. There was no room for "Lone Ranger Christianity."

A fifth example of interdependence is the *sharing of love and comfort*. A hallmark text in the early church is Galatians 6:2. *The Cotton Patch Version of Paul's Epistles* says it graphically: "For the essence of the Christian life is to shoulder the loads of one another."

The earliest available manuscript on the biblical/theological rationale for the Baptist association is found in the *Abingdon Association Records* in England dated October 1652. At a meeting of "chosen numbers of the churches, viz. Henly, Reading, and Abingdon" three purposes/functions of the association were recorded—namely, (1) to have firm communion with each other, (2) to give and receive in case of want and poverty, and (3) in consulting and consenting to the carrying on of the work of God.[6]

At a second meeting the next month the number of churches in association had grown from three to five.[7] By the third meeting in as many months, the overarching purpose of these "particular churches of Christ" was *"to hold firm communion each with other,"* and the threefold function was expressed as follows:

> 1. In point of advice in matters and controversies remaining doubtful to any particular church, Acts 15:1-2, 24-28; 16:1-2.
>
> 2. In giving and receiving, in case of the want and povertie of any particular church, 1 Cor. 16:3.
>
> 3. In consulting and consenting (as need shall require and as shall be most for the glorie of God) to the joynt carrying on of the work of the Lord that is common to the churches, as choosing such messengers as we find in 2 Cor. 8.19. And in all other things wherein particular churches ought to be serviceable and to manifest their love each to other.[8]

Walter Shurden, professor at Mercer University, in his study of associationalism in America, suggests "four definite conclusions" from a study of the theological foundation for associations:

> 1. Baptist theology prohibited Baptist churches from living in total isolation from each other. Because a local church was not the whole church, Baptists emphasized the interdependence of churches, as well as their independence.
>
> 2. Baptist theology facilitated associational development . . . theory

made practice much easier. Of course, Baptist theology did not demand an organization called "association," but Baptist theology did demand association.

3. Baptist ideas about the universal and local churches combined to form a theological structure for associations.

4. An association, often considered a larger church, acted in the name of Jesus Christ and without fear of impairing democratic processes of local congregations.[9]

Research on the etymology of *association* reveals that it was first in use as a verb. It can be traced back in religious usage to 1398. The first recorded use of the word was in this sentence by Trevisa Barth: "Angels ben . . . *assocyat* and couplyd togyders in the joyefull companye of god."[10] By 1535 *association* was in use as a noun.

Russell Bennett, in a socio-theological study of Baptist associations, chose to use the following definition, introduced by G. R. Ford in his Th.D. dissertation on *The Baptist District Association of Virginia:* "Association refers to the organization through which the Baptist churches of the same general geographical area voluntarily cooperate in matters of mutual interests."[11]

The word *association* among Baptists has come to refer to an organized effort on the part of cooperating churches to be in ministry together, and it has also been used together with the word *principle* to denote a primary, basic doctrine of interdependence.

A quote from Morris West, former principal of Bristol Baptist College in England, will serve as the conclusion to this overview of the sociological, biblical, theological, and linguistic foundations for this call for a renewal of the Baptist principle of association:

> The Bible says "can two walk together unless they be agreed" and I think the association was saying things together. When you've said something together then conversation becomes a potential journey. I think there was therefore growth from the talking to the walking. On the whole, that is the way it [the association] grew—some walked more closely than others.[12]

A Historical Quest

For the Baptists the seventeenth century was a time of beginnings. Their first churches emerged during this time, and they forged their distinctive denominational structures. *From the first, Baptist churches were committed to the concept of interchurch cooperation. The Baptist association and the general assembly gave both local and national structure to their church life.* Through a series of confessions Baptists defined their faith, and by testimony and suffering, they hammered out their concept of religious freedom for all.[13] (Emphasis added.)

Most Baptist historians would seem to agree with these observations expressed in 1987 by H. Leon McBeth, then Southwestern Baptist Seminary professor. Precedent was earlier expressed by W. T. Whitley, the British Baptist historian who wrote in 1932: "From the beginning Baptists were not 'Independent'; they always sought for fellowship between the different churches, and they were very successful in arranging for permanent organization."[14]

In 1607 or 1608, to escape persecution, John Smyth and Thomas Helwys and a group of followers left England and went to Holland. In 1609 Smyth, exiled in Amsterdam, baptized himself and others to form the first English Baptist congregation. In 1611 or 1612 Helwys and a small band of followers returned to England and established the first Baptist church on English soil. By 1624 five Baptist churches in London were associating together. In 1644 seven congregations joined together in the signing of a confession of faith. Article XLVII reads:

> And although the particular Congregations be distinct and severall Bodies, everyone as a compact and knit Citie in it felfe; yet are they all to walk by one and the same Rule, and by all meanes convenient to have the counsell and help one of another in all needful affaires; of the Church, as members of one body in the common faith under Christ their onely head.[14]

According to available documents, the first general meeting of what later would be called an "association" was held on November 6-7, 1650, at Ilston in South Wales.[15]

There seemed to be five major functions of the early associations: First, *to stand on a biblical base.* Ian Sellers, professor at Northern Baptist College in Manchester, England, believes "that the association idea among Baptists arose, probably, because of their feeling that they ought to follow scripture principles which they saw reflected in the New Testament, particularly in the Acts of the Apostles. That would be a powerful theological stimulus for them."[16] Similarly, Walter Shurden sees this same origin/purpose emerging among Baptists in America from 1707 to 1814: "When Baptists began to explain and justify associationalism, they did it in three ways. One, the associational idea was consistent with biblical teachings. Two, associations were consistent with Baptist theology. Three, associations were needed for effective co-operative ministries."[17]

A second function of the early associations was *to affirm their beliefs and actions.* In 1624 representatives from five General Baptist churches met in London and took joint action "to repudiate the characteristic Mennonite views rejecting oath taking, service in the magistracy and military service."[18]

Robert Torbet, American Baptist historian, in *A History of the Baptists,* summarizes the numerous and varied use of Baptist confessions of faith, all supporting this second major function of the early associations. Torbet suggests five primary roles of the confessions, which would serve as five reasons for the ongoing purpose of associations:

1. To maintain purity of doctrine;
2. To clarify and validate the Baptist position;
3. To serve as a guide to the General Assembly or local association in counselling churches;
4. To serve as a basis for fellowship within local churches, associations, or a General Assembly;
5. To discipline churches and members.[19]

A third function of associations was *to seek counsel and support.* The Confession of Faith of 1644, which has already been mentioned, illustrates the fact that the gathering of ministers and churches was for mutual counsel and the offer of help when needed.

A reading of available association minutes of the second half of the seventeenth century points to the need for counsel and support. In the earliest minutes of the West Country (later the Western Association), we find that in 1653 and 1654 the minutes contain queries from the churches for counsel, advice, and direction from their brethren in the faith. For example: "whether that imposition of hands on all baptized believers be an ordinance of Christ under the Gospel?" and "whether a woman may speak in the church at all, and if at all, in what cases?"[20]

A fourth function was *to affirm and strengthen ministry.* As we saw from the earliest known association minutes (South Wales, November 6-7, 1650), there was a desire to maintain a constant ministry. This led to financial support, the need for training of ministers, and fraternals.

The fifth function was *to reach out and start new churches.* John Nicholson, a Baptist Union area superintendent, believes that the associational principle originated "in a more natural way through new churches being planted and wanting to keep in touch with the Mother Church, and as ministers went out and started new churches, so they kept in touch with the minister of their home church."[21]

Isolationism and rugged individualism, fear of centralization and control were obstacles to associational life that constantly challenged those who

saw the need for interdependence and championed the desire for cooperation. Strict Independents on the one hand and central "state church" control
on the other caused those who came to be known as Baptists to find a
middle ground, where neither separate identity nor uncompromising
central control would be the choice. Out of these two extremes the
associational principle was emerging and finding a place and purpose for
Baptists in England.

The Philadelphia Baptist Association has often been referred to as the
first association of Baptists in colonial America. However, at least thirty-
seven years before the beginning of the more familiar Philadelphia Association, four General Baptist congregations in Rhode Island were
gathering for annual meetings. In 1670 elders and messengers from
General Six Principle Baptist churches assembled in association for
"setting in order the things that were wanting" and for addressing "any
difficulties that might arise."[22]

On September 8, 1767, representatives from eleven churches met at
Warren, Rhode Island, to consider the formation of a new association.
Three representatives from the Philadelphia Association, now sixty years
in existence, attended and shared a letter, drafted in Philadelphia during
their annual association meeting on October 14–16, 1766. In part the letter
read:

> A long course of experience and observation has taught us to have the
> highest sense of the advantages which accrue from associations; nor
> indeed does the nature of things speak any other language. For, as
> particular members are collected together and united in one body, which
> we call a *particular church,* to answer those ends and purposes which
> could not be accomplished by any single member, so a *collection and
> union of churches into one associational body* may easily be conceived
> capable of answering those still greater purposes which any particular
> church could not be equal to. And by the same reason, a *union of
> associations* will still increase the body in weight and strength, and
> make it good that a *three-fold cord* is not easily broken.[23] (Emphasis
> added.)

Robert Torbet observed:

> The significance of the Association cannot be overemphasized, for
> without violating Baptist church autonomy it provided a source of
> guidance and unity at a critical period of organization in the denomina-
> tion. In addition, it afforded a pattern of democratic polity which was
> destined to be well received in the liberty-loving colonies.[24]

Three factors contributing to the weakening of the associational principle in America were: first, the single-purpose societies; second, Landmarkism; and third, the nineteenth-century revivals. Stressing a personal response to a conversion experience, rigid individualism weakened early connectionalism, which had bound Baptists together in associations during the seventeenth and eighteenth centuries. Interdependence among the churches was being ignored in favor of a limited, local church view.

Norman DePuy, when he was editor of *The American Baptist Magazine*, wrote in 1971: "SCODS [the Study Commission on Denominational Structure] is a stewardship thing: it's an attempt to get the fat out of our administration, inertia out of our mission, muscle into our money, and people into our polity."[25]

From a national and regional perspective, SCODS was an attempt to address the fat and the inertia as well as the muscle and the people. But the study and the recommendations stopped without addressing the associational principle at the grass roots.

Harvey Everett, associate general secretary for field operations for American Baptists during the time of SCODS, admits:

> We took the heart out of the association with the structural changes. We had no place for it but never said it. We wanted its functions to be done, we knew they were important, but they were as varied in their achievements and in their acceptance as there were associations. . . . We have become too heavily dominated by the national organization.[26]

American Baptist historians like Winthrop Hudson, William McNutt, Norman Maring, and Robert Torbet were sounding a cry for more attention to the associational principle in the reorganization of the denomination, but it seemed to have been ignored. In April 1958 Hudson sought to call his denomination back to the associational principle in a provocative article in *Foundations* entitled "Stumbling into Disorder." Beginning with the observation that the denominational structure of the Baptists was confused and in disorder, Hudson sought to dispel the belief held by some that the present Baptist structure was derived from the New Testament or from historic Baptist principles. Rather, said Hudson: "Our denominational structure has not been the product of biblical, theological or even rational considerations. It was derived from an ad hoc basis as an efficient money-raising technique and to serve certain sectional and partisan concerns."[27] Hudson concluded with the observation that the local association, which he claimed was "the most important unit in the whole denominational structure," was being bypassed. He saw this as a serious consequence of the organizational disorder among Baptists in the North. He believes that they continue to "stumble into disorder by ignoring this historic and theological basic ingredient in Baptist polity." Hudson observed that "all significant functions of the Associations have been taken away, and they are left to eke out a bootless existence."[28]

William McNutt, former professor of church history at Crozer Theological Seminary, joined Hudson in bemoaning the fact that associations in the American Baptist Convention family were declining in influence and power. Having labeled the association as the "keystone in the arch," he felt the center of influence and control was moving too far from home base. He saw as much danger in overcentralization as in too great a decentralization but felt at that time in Baptist history that "the present ailment of the Association is symptomatic of the former."

In 1958 Paul Harrison, a professor of religious studies at Pennsylvania State University, authored a social case study of the American Baptist Convention. Entitled *Authority and Power in the Free Church Tradition,* Harrison's study took issue with the discrepancies that existed between Baptist polity and the Baptist doctrine of the church. He made a case for *freedom* and *authority* being complementary terms and called for the strengthening of the associations. "If local churches are to be free from domination by a secular power or from the authority of an ecclesiastical oligarchy," wrote Harrison, "they must associate with one another, each recognizing the authority of the other, none claiming absolute autonomy or authority, and all recognizing the temporal but preeminent authority of the association of churches so long as they wish to derive the advantages of associational membership."[29]

Harrison, like the Baptist historians I have quoted, was sounding a cry for reclaiming and renewing the Baptist principle of associations. Again, it seems his voice was ignored.[30] He predicted:

If the congregations were united in associations, the mind of Christ would be sought by the common gathering of the churches, and the association would legitimately proclaim the Word as discerned by the united churches. Perhaps if the leaders of the American Baptist Convention could hear the voices of the several associations, rather than the infinite clamor of a multiplicity of independent churches, they could act for the churches and be respected as a legitimate ecclesiastical power.[31]

Harrison went on to predict that the trend to have local churches identify with and express themselves "through nothing smaller than the state or national convention" would not overcome the problems introduced by "impersonalization, distance, and a lack of technical knowledge."

William McNutt probably said it best when he warned that the association is "pivotal in Baptist polity." In 1959 he called for a "five-year moratorium on centralization in favor of the association." He suggested before SCODS that "current denominational weakness is proportionate to associational decadence."[32]

The national reorganization of American Baptists strengthened relationships at the state, regional, and national levels to some degree, but it did not go far enough. It failed to address the associational principle at the grass roots. That principle still remains to be addressed.

The Future of Associations

The Association is not an organization to be set over against the churches or to be added as an extra to the churches. It is just the life of the churches together. As the life of a family derives from the attitudes, actions, spirit of each member of the family, so the Association is strong or weak, enriched or diminished by the manner in which each church shares the common life. The churches are members together in the Body of Christ and the Association is one mode of expressing and experiencing this togetherness. This is our need. This is our obligation. It is as vital today as in the past.[33]

These words of L. G. Champion, former principal and tutor in church history at Bristol Baptist College, need to be heard loud and clear if we are to reclaim the Baptist principle of association for the closing years of this century and into the next.

My study of the associations in Great Britain yielded a fourfold function of associations there: (1) fellowship, (2) communication, (3) mission and evangelism, and (4) expression of public opinion. Here in America the Baptist association has been called "the keystone in the arch,"[34] "one strand in a threefold cord,"[35] and "a vital link in our chain of being."[36] However, in some regions and in the experience of some leaders, associations have become crumbled stones, weak strands, missing links, or "a bootless existence."[37]

F. Russell Bennett has diagrammed the "wrong" and the "right" ways to view the relationships of churches-in-association (see diagram, p. 254).

I believe it was the "wrong" approach that helped cause the General Baptists in England to almost disappear! Insisting that churches skip over the local association and refer major questions and decisions to the national governing body in London was as much a factor, I believe, in the weakening of General Baptists as was the theological move toward Unitarian or universal theology. General Baptists, like Particular Baptists, were strongest when their associational life was strong.

The same seemed true in the American context. When the Philadelphia Baptist Association operated with the "right" relationships, ministries and mission were alive and growing. When efforts were set forth to move the association into a more hierarchal governing body, churches began to rebel and to create new associations. In recent years SCODS and SCOR (Study Commission on Regions) attempted to move American Baptists into a design similar, I fear, to the "wrong" diagram.

Bennett, a Southern Baptist research writer, in commenting on these two approaches, observed:

> The association is not a society to serve the churches but a fellowship through which the churches, in the spirit of Christ, serve one another. The fellowship of mutual concern among neighboring congregations of like faith and order is an essential expression, not as cause but as consequence of the intention of Jesus.[38]

John Naisbitt, in *Megatrends,* used the term *networking,* which may be a good word for the associational principle today. He wrote:

> The failure of hierarchies to solve society's problems forced people to talk to one another, and that was the beginning of networks. . . . Simply stated, networks are people talking to each other, sharing ideas, information and resources. The point is often made that networking is a verb, not a noun. The important part is not the network, the finished product, but the process of getting there—the communication that creates the linkage between people and clusters of people.[39]

Technically speaking, Naisbitt should have said that networking is a participle, which is a verbal noun. This calls to mind our etymology of the

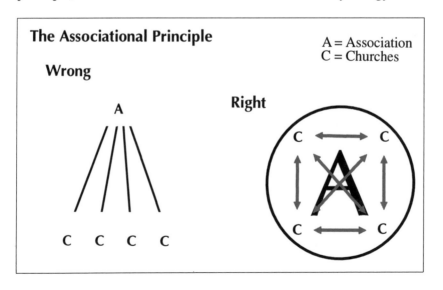

The Associational Principle

A = Association
C = Churches

Wrong

Right

A

C   C   C   C

C   C
C   C

word *association,* which was first in use as a verb: "to associate." Associating and networking call for action/participation; so the end result is an active noun, when people listen to each other, share, and work together. Naisbitt continued:

Networks exist to foster self-help, to exchange information, to change society, to improve productivity and work life, and to share resources. They are structured to transmit information in a way that is quicker, more high touch, and more energy-efficient than any other process we know.[40]

Could this be a modern-day definition for *associations?* As Baptists, we have fought and taught against "hierarchies," but we have not done the best job of "networking."

Baptist historian William Brackney, now at McMaster University in Canada, in a provocative article entitled "What Ever Happened to the Association?" said that "we need to learn again how to wrestle in love with difficult issues and to celebrate one another's successes and bear one another's burdens."[41]

In recent months American Baptists have been reminded that the local church is the primary unit of mission, and some are saying that this is a new paradigm. I say it is an old paradigm revisited and that it is long overdue. But I fear that this renewed emphasis on the local church will still be inadequate until and unless we see that churches-in-association are the vital units of mission. No one church alone can do it.

In the late 1960s and early 1970s, with the emphasis on SCODS and SCOR, we got a new ABC logo. The old one had consisted of a cross superimposed in front of the globe, with a church in the lower left corner. When the new logo was introduced, the symbol for the church was missing. I objected but felt that I was a "voice in the wilderness." In retrospect, we have experienced years with little or no emphasis on the local church as the primary unit of mission, and we certainly have ignored the cluster or association or network of churches at the grassroots level as being an essential unit.

I rejoice that we are again looking at the role and function of the local church, but I sound a cry! Returning to an emphasis on the solo church without attention to interrelatedness can be as damaging as ignoring it altogether. Even the Lone Ranger had Tonto!

Norman Maring and Winthrop Hudson, in their most recent revision of *A Baptist Manual of Polity and Practice,* added a significant section entitled "The Revival of the Associational Principle." They said:

It has long been debated whether associations can be, or should be, revived. In theory it seems plausible that the association could again have an important place in denominational life, forming a bridge between local churches and the regional and national organizations. Comprising a number of churches, each association makes available a combination of strength and wisdom that can supplement the resources of the local church. Through consultation and cooperation, each association might be strengthened and mutual tasks undertaken more efficiently. . . . A stronger associational life might well contribute to the kind of solidarity of the denomination which many feel is needed.[42]

Conclusion

In the south aisle of St. Paul's Cathedral in London is a statue of John Donne, dean of the cathedral during the time of the black plague, when thousands of people in Europe and in Britain were dying. When a body was buried in London, the bell in St. Paul's would toll.

One day, as Donne sat at his study desk, he heard the bell toll, signifying yet another burial. He wrote some words, which I believe illustrate the associational principle.

No man is an isle entire of itself;
Every man is a piece of the continent,
A part of the main.

If a clod is washed away by the sea,
Everyone is the less,
As well as if the promontory were,
As well as if a manor of thy friends,
As if thine own were.

Every man's death diminishes me,
Because I am involved in mankind;
And therefore never send to know
For whom the bell tolls;
It tolls for thee.[43]

One day, while visiting St. Paul's, I reflected on these words as I stood by Donne's statue. Turning to my right, I noticed W. Holman Hunt's famous painting entitled *The Light of the World*. As I continued to ponder Donne's words, I began to recall some words of Jesus, artistically portrayed by Hunt's painting of Jesus standing at the door: "Listen! I am standing at the door, knocking; if you hear my voice and open the door, I will come in to you and eat with you, and you with me" (Rev. 3:20 NRSV).

These words were first addressed to a church! Jesus wants to come and live not only in us individually, but in our churches. No church is an island entire of itself! Relationships are essential.

As I was meditating, the intercom came on, and the priest at St. Paul's welcomed the many tourists present. He reminded us that this was not a museum, but a church in which to worship and serve the living Lord. He invited us to join in praying the Lord's Prayer. When we got to the words, "Thy kingdom come, thy will be done, on earth. . . ," I paused and thought: *That's it! That's what the association is all about! Together, with the living Lord within and among us, we are called as churches to work together so that God's kingdom may come, God's will may be done, on earth as it is in heaven!*

The term *Independent Baptist* is a contradiction. We are dependent people. First, we are dependent on God, our maker, our redeemer, our director. Second, we are dependent on others. No one of us is an island entire of itself! That's true for individuals and for churches! Christianity is *not* a solo sport; it is team work!

In several associations and among the American Baptist Churches of the Great Rivers Region, a fourfold purpose of the association is emerging—namely, (1) communication, (2) creativity, (3) cooperation, and (4) community. In a covenant we have captured these four Cs:

We will gather periodically for

I. Communication
to open and keep open relationships among the churches within our association; SO THAT

II. Creativity
can emerge, as we learn from each other and together discover new and/or improved ways of enabling effective ministries within our churches, associations, areas and region; ALLOWING FOR

III. Cooperation
as we discover ways of working together to best accomplish goals and objectives of the various components of our denomination and among other denominations and groupings; TO THE END THAT

IV. Community
will become a reality within and among the churches of the associations as we seek to be vital witnesses for our Lord and Savior, Jesus Christ, who calls us into Christian service.

Notes

1. Leonard Whibley, "Amphictyony," in *Encyclopedia of Religion and Ethics* (New York: Scribners, 1926), 1:394.

2. Allen H. Jones, "The Philistines and the Hearth: Their Journey to the Levant," *Journal of Near Eastern Studies* 31, no. 4 (1972): 345.

3. Martin Noth, *The History of Israel* (New York: Harper & Row, 1960), 88, 95-96.

4. David O. Moberg, *The Church as a Social Institution* (Grand Rapids: Baker, 1984), 241.

5. Core writings are distinguished from secondary Pauline writings (referred to as "authentic groupings") and Deutero-Pauline material.

6. B. R. White, ed., *Association Records of the Particular Baptists of England, Wales, and Ireland to 1660* (London: Baptist Historical Society, 1974), 3:126. (Hereafter cited as *White Records.*)

7. Ibid., 3:127.

8. Ibid., 3:127-28.

9. Walter B. Shurden, *Associationalism Among Baptists in America* (New York: Arno Press, 1980), 75.

10. James Murral, *New English Dictionary* (Oxford: Clarendon, 1888).

11. F. Russell Bennett Jr., *The Fellowship of Kindred Minds* (Atlanta: Home Mission Board, 1974), 150-151.

12. Personal interview with Morris West, Sept. 15, 1988, Bristol Baptist College, Bristol, England.

13. H. Leon McBeth, *The Baptist Heritage* (Nashville: Broadman, 1987), 20.

14. W. T. Whitley, *A History of British Baptists* (London: Kingsgate, 1932), 53.

15. *White Records,* 1:3.

16. Personal interview with Ian Sellers, Oct. 7, 1988, in his home, Wellington, England.

17. Shurden, *Associationalism,* 103.

18. Robert G. Torbet, *A History of the Baptists* (Valley Forge, Pa.: Judson Press, 1982), 43.

19. Ibid., 46.

20. *White Records,* pt. 2.

21. Personal interview with John Nicholson, Oct. 5, 1988, at his home, Leeds, England.

22. Winthrop S. Hudson, *Baptists in Transition* (Valley Forge, Pa.: Judson Press, 1979), 38.

23. David Spencer, *The Early Baptists of Philadelphia* (Philadelphia: William Syckelmoore, 1877), 95.

24. Torbet, *History of the Baptists,* 214.

25. Norman R. DePuy, *The American Baptist Magazine,* April 1971.

26. Personal interview with Harvey Everett, Feb. 15, 1989, Country Meadows, Reading, Pennsylvania.

27. Hudson, *Baptists in Transition,* 83.

28. Ibid., 110.

29. Paul M. Harrison, *Authority and Power in the Free Church Tradition* (Princeton: Princeton University Press, 1959), 220.

30. Personal communication with William Brackney, Dec. 1989, in which he observed that American Baptist leaders were fearful of Harrison and would not be interviewed for a follow-up study.

31. Harrison, *Authority and Power*, 224.

32. William McNutt, *Polity and Practice in Baptist Churches* (Chicago, Philadelphia, Los Angeles: Judson Press, 1959), 150.

33. Minutes taken by L. G. Champion contained in *Bristol and District Association of Baptist Churches, 1823-1973,* 40-41.

34. McNutt, *Polity and Practice in Baptist Churches,* 145.

35. Spencer, *Early Baptists of Philadelphia,* 95.

36. William Brackney, "What Ever Happened to the Association?" *The American Baptist,* May/June 1987, 59.

37. Hudson, *Baptists in Transition,* 110.

38. Bennett, *Fellowship of Kindred Minds,* 138.

39. John Naisbitt, *Megatrends* (New York: Warner Books, 1982), 213, 215.

40. Ibid., 215.

41. Brackney, "What Ever Happened to the Association?" 59.

42. Norman Maring and Winthrop Hudson, *A Baptist Manual of Polity and Practice* (Valley Forge, Pa.: Judson Press, 1991), 189.

43. John Donne, "Devotions," 1b, xvii, 1623, as quoted in *Bartlett's Familiar Quotations,* 4th ed. (Boston: Little Brown and Co., 1968), 508.

Congregation and Association: Rethinking Baptist Distinctives for a New Century

Nancy T. Ammerman

Baptists, we are told, celebrate the freedom of individual persons and the autonomy of local congregations while also calling those persons into responsible church membership and those congregations into voluntary cooperation. It sounds so simple—a balance between freedom and responsibility, between autonomy and interdependence. But our recent experience tells us that it is not so simple. A variety of crises has brought us to this point where we are rethinking how that balancing act works. Sociologically it seems useful to put our current dilemmas into the cultural context of our longer history, our recent past, and our future. The tensions we now face have a long modern history, but they are dilemmas that are taking on new meaning as many of the assumptions of modernity break down. I begin with a brief excursus on this tradition-to-modern-to-postmodern transition, then follow it with some thoughts on the relationships our new world makes necessary and possible.

Our Cultural Moment

First, the big picture—just where are we in history? The modern world alongside which Baptists were born is one that has been characterized by its reliance on science and reason, by its ever-increasing specialization of labor, and by its pluralism of cultures. Religion in this modern situation has responded with a remarkable degree of accommodation. It has accommodated to Enlightenment rationalism by creating an explainable faith,

Nancy T. Ammerman is professor of sociology of religion at the Center for Social and Religious Research, Hartford Seminary. She has written extensively on Baptist life and especially on the character and role of Baptist churches and institutions. This paper was presented at "Called to Responsible Freedom: A Conference on Baptist Distinctives," at Green Lake, Wisconsin, August 1996.

one increasingly independent of mystery and miracle. It has accommodated to the specialization of labor by accepting its place in the private sphere, leaving politics and work to other specialists. And it has accommodated to pluralism by adopting an attitude of tolerance and civility, by giving up missions and evangelism in favor of dialogue. At heart, religion has become an individual preference, a leisure pursuit kept carefully out of the arenas in which it just might cause trouble.[1]

Lest you think that what I have just described is an accommodation that applies only to "liberals," let me remind you of some of our own Baptist accommodations. Along the way, especially in the latter part of this century, we have sometimes erred in the very modern direction of excess freedom. We have been a people who proclaimed, for instance, that each believer is a priest, able to come to Scripture without a mediator. Yet that idea has often been distorted into a pernicious modern individualism. We have spoken of the priesthood of the believer and made it equivalent to "me and my Bible." The by-product was a very modern, privatized faith. Similarly, we nonfundamentalists have often responded to the challenges of pluralism with an anemic "civility" that is neither a genuine acceptance nor honest disagreement. We have acted as if the only two options for responding to a pluralistic world were either an intolerant fundamentalism that claimed a truth so narrow as to be useless or a wishy-washy liberalism that claimed a truth so broad as to be meaningless. We have thought that we had to choose between practicing a narrow sectarian independence and maintaining a smiling, back-slapping refusal to talk about anything that matters. Our associations—person to church and church to denomination—have often ceased to be meaningful because they deny the real differences among us, lest those differences tear us apart.

The modern problem of pluralism has brought us to this point. At an earlier point in Baptist history, especially for Baptists in the South, unity of culture was sufficient to bind associations together. Even when people disagreed, they assumed a common "brotherhood" that held them together. Later, in the more modern and diverse situation of this century, brotherhood became an ideal toward which to work, rather than an assumed reality in which one lived. But today, neither of those situations prevails. Traditional uniformity has disappeared, and modern liberal solutions to the problem of difference are increasingly suspect. We simply no longer believe that we will somehow find a universal common ground on which everyone can stand. The ideal of the melting pot is increasingly less attractive. But is there a viable alternative as we look toward a postmodern future? Without universal brotherhood, can we keep from descending into warring tribalisms and "identity politics"?

On Being Bilingual

I have been helped in thinking about this dilemma by the work of Old Testament scholar Walter Brueggemann.[2] In a provocative article with a difficult title, "On the Legitimacy of a Sectarian Hermeneutic," he recounts the story of one of Israel's encounters with the Assyrians. They are surrounded, and the enemy commanders meet Israel's commanders on the wall of the city. They begin to speak to the Israelites in Hebrew, demanding surrender and setting out the terms. The Israelites, however, refuse to carry on the negotiations in Hebrew, insisting that their language be reserved for their own particular uses. They also insist that they be allowed to retreat behind the wall for a community consultation. There, behind the wall, they speak Hebrew, the language in which the story of God's actions in the world can be told. There they spend time coming to terms with what has happened to them and with how it fits into God's story. Only then do they return to negotiate, in the language of the empire, having clarified, in their own language, what their position must be.

Brueggemann uses this story to argue for the need to be bilingual. We need both the language behind the wall and the language on the wall, both our own particular language in which God's name is spoken and the language of the realm, in which deals are negotiated. The modern world told us to forget the language behind the wall. If everyone just learned the language of the realm, we would be fine. But what we have learned is the extent to which we need those special, local, particular places, those people whose accent we recognize, those stories that remind us of who we are. We need the places where the rituals are familiar, where we can sing the music and can teach our children the songs, dances, recipes, and mating rituals of the home town. In the quest to be intelligible to everyone, we discovered we had nothing to say.

We need to be bilingual—speaking our own native language while also speaking a common language shared with people alien to us. We know we have to develop ways to talk to each other; the dangers of tribalism are too great. But at the same time, to live only in that global village is not to have a home. To speak only the universal language is to miss the stories from home that form us.

The dangers of sectarianism are lessened and the potential for public discourse enhanced by our memberships in multiple communities, our knowledge of multiple languages. Few of us have only one place called home, and those multiple identities often give us cross-cutting interests and values. We share some things with one group and other things with the next. Such plural sensibilities help to prevent complete polarization and to further the conversations we need to have among ourselves.

Even conversation may be, however, too modern a metaphor. Often our most basic experience of shared activity is not words, but gesture and ritual and physical contact. We sing and eat and kneel and exchange kisses of peace. And in so doing, we recognize connections—and differences—we will only later be able to put into words.

Nevertheless, it is the basic principle of bilingualism that ought to inform our reclaiming of associational responsibility for a postmodern era. We can no longer form associations on the assumption that we share so much cultural and theological baggage in common that we need not be explicit about the basis for our cooperation. Nor can we afford to form associations in which we cannot talk about our differences, associations that impose a false universalism. Difference is what potentially divides us, but it is also what can provide the lively energy that makes our associations truly more than the sum of their parts. That principle, of course, is as old as the New Testament. There we find Paul reminding the Corinthians that their differences are necessary, that only when they celebrate those differences can they function as the "body of Christ." The modern either/or choice of tribalism versus universalism must be transformed into a postmodern both/and.

Forming Committed Voluntary Communities

It is, therefore, critical that Baptist associations begin with Baptist congregations that truly know who they are, that are "sectarian" in Brueggemann's sense. These are congregations that call individuals into a responsible commitment that can shape them in significant ways. We need congregations that claim the distinctiveness of their particular traditions, with all their regional, and ethnic, and class variations, congregations that teach the language and stories, the songs and dances, the ways of cooking and courting, the deep moral truths and ways of talking with God that make them who they are. But we need those congregations to take up that task with the keen awareness that they are not representatives of an insular culture, that they are not God's last and only hope, that some of those folkways may be colored by a sin for which their sister Baptists in other places may call them to repentance.

The seriousness with which we need to take the task of the local church is not a new problem for Baptists. Indeed, the very formation of voluntary communities is something that we can claim from our Baptist forebears, and it is something that stood in stark contrast to the world in which they lived. The normal way of doing things then was anything but voluntary and mutual. Religious matters were not unlike every other area of life. Certain people had rights and duties, while others had none. Everyone simply accepted a system that placed the vast majority of the population in a powerless position and asked a tiny privileged minority to take care of them. Baptists, however, said that the congregation itself—the masses, not the elites—should make decisions, do the work of the church, and respond to God as they felt led. Even among the other reformers breaking away from the Catholic Church, few were so radically egalitarian as the Baptists. They wedded freedom and responsibility into democratic, voluntary communities where the Bible was read and reinterpreted, where the gospel was preached and sacraments shared, where backsliding and violations of discipline were dealt with, where questions were asked and debated, and where believers rallied to care for each other in times of adversity. We have always somehow known that communities were necessary. The early Baptist insistence on the priesthood of all believers was not an individualistic polemic, but a communitarian statement of their equality before God.

The irony, of course, is that community and individuality are not opposites. This is another of the modern either/or choices that is now being seen as a false dichotomy. It is in communities that we truly discover who we, as individuals, are. In unabashedly choosing to commit ourselves to a community of sisters and brothers, we enter into the essential covenants of faith. We learn the language of our heritage, practice the customs that give meaning to our lives, and hear the stories that tell us of God's presence in the world. While God may sometimes speak to solitary individuals alone on the road, even Paul did not really know what had happened to him until he made his way to Damascus and spent days and weeks with Ananias and the company of Christians there. Without a supporting community of faith, we will soon forget just who we really are.

And the postmodern world is one in which such distinctive local communities may be both possible and necessary. They are different from earlier traditional communities in that they are chosen, not ascribed. We can choose the places to which we commit ourselves. The sociologist Stephen Warner calls this "elective parochialism."[3] It is a recognition that the world that is emerging is neither the traditional world of "parochialism" nor the modern world of presumably unfettered free choice. Once we make choices, they have consequences. They form our character, our habits of mind and practice. We need Baptist congregations that are not afraid to do just that. To be part of a Baptist congregation is to make an individual, voluntary choice. That is clear. But individual choice need not mean that the congregation then assumes it must keep hands off the person's "personal" beliefs. Congregations are not super-markets of goods and services to be chosen by random individuals at will. To be a congregation of priests is to take responsibility for each other, to form a community in which there is a distinct language to be learned—to return to Brueggemann's analogy.

Finding New Forms of Interdependence

Rediscovering that we need communities of faith, not just faithful individuals, is part of what it will mean for us to rediscover a priesthood of all believers. It will also mean that we redefine what we mean by local autonomy. It will mean neither the independently owned local franchise of the Southern Baptist Convention nor the radically independent tub floating alone on its own bottom.

For most of this "modern" century, Southern Baptists have talked local autonomy while practicing a tightly organized hierarchical system in which people at the top had visions of what a church ought to look like and eventually implemented those plans in the programs of local congre-gations. The "antimodern" fundamentalists, on the other hand, refused to cooperate with anyone, insisting that only the independent local church was sanctioned in the Bible. What is needed in this new era is neither of those alternatives, but churches and religious institutions that are both autonomous and cooperative, that know how to find their own sense of mission, their own niche, but that also know how to create networks of cooperation. Many Baptists today are reaffirming the need for each church and agency to develop its own internal culture, its own ability to shape the character of its members and the direction of its mission. But we are also discovering that we cannot do that utterly alone. We need each other.

How then do we think about new relationships among churches? How do we use our heritage of voluntary association to inform new ways of being mutually responsible? Here we move into the territory we have called "denomination," but that is a word that is increasingly hard to define. Let me suggest that there are at least two different forms of association that constitute what we mean by that word.[4] The first form has to do with the way we get things done. Denominations are formed in large measure as aids in our efforts to do what we feel called to do.

They both provide goods and services in support of the activities of local churches and serve as an association through which collaborative activities can be undertaken that extend the reach of the local congregation. Second, denominations are distinct theological traditions with religious authority standing behind those traditions.

Let's take a look at the functional, mission-oriented forms of association first. Just as our culture is moving from modern to postmodern in its basic assumptions, those shifts also affect the way we think about organizations. The quintessentially modern form of organization has been the bureaucracy, with its predictable departments and rules, its hierarchy and rationalized, credentialed forms of authority. Baptists learned in this century to cooperate with each other through regular systematic giving to a centralized budget that gave us well-developed programs and a constant flow of numbers to prove their success.

There is an irony in recent history, of course. Fundamentalists have never been enamored of bureaucracy, and in the SBC revolt, they attacked the agencies they perceived as too ready to compromise, too insistent on professional and educational credentials to recognize spiritual authority when they saw it, too out of tune with the people who were supposed to be paying their salaries. Now they are in charge of those same bureaucracies. And it is worth noting that bureaucracies have an internal power of their own. Fundamentalists may find themselves drawn ever so firmly into the rationalized, rule-oriented, professionalized logic of those organizations.

But the main point I want to make is that the fundamentalist triumph in the SBC must be seen as part of a crisis of confidence in the form of organization that had dominated Baptist life since the 1920s. Whether the theological debates created the crisis, and the organizational fallout only followed—or whether the organizational crisis precipitated the theological debates—is less important than recognizing that the crisis has thrown organizational questions into high relief.

Likewise, the crisis in the SBC is happening alongside a general crisis of confidence in American Protestant denominations. Having suffered decades of numerical decline, the upheavals of mergers and moves, serious financial crises and staff cutbacks, and internal strife over everything from the role of women to homosexuality, American denominations are not exactly standing tall. One Presbyterian executive, speaking about how disorganized denominational life feels at the moment, said, "I do not believe that we are a disorganized Church. Rather I believe many of us, most of us, maybe all of us are obsolete at the moment. To the obsolete all seems disorganized. . . . One of the things that it feels like has happened is that we have lost control." Indeed, many "mainline" groups have suffered serious organizational losses and feel as if they have lost control. It is simply no longer clear what regional and national denominations ought to be doing or how they should be doing it.

Both the crisis in the SBC and the crisis in American denominations, then, signal a period of restructuring, a period in which existing systems of power may be transformed, a move from modern to postmodern. What that might mean may best be illustrated by a series of contrasts drawn by sociologist Stewart Clegg.[5] He is careful to note that these are tendencies, not determinisms. Nevertheless, they keep appearing in so many contexts that we need to take them seriously.

First, let us consider the issues of scale and diversity. Where modernist organization was premised on mass forms, postmodernist organization is premised on niches. Part of what brought the modern era into being was a vast expansion in communication and transportation that made it possible to advertise and distribute goods over huge territories. At the same time, mass production technologies took advantage of the economies of scale to make and distribute identical items across those vast territories—the proverbial black Model-T Ford—or, in our case, the standard Sunday school quarterly.

But just as we no longer assume that one car is enough to satisfy every taste, we can also no longer assume that one set of programs can define a denomination. Those who wish to serve the needs of local congregations will be many. There will be multiple organizations serving ever more specialized demands. Rather than one publisher, there may be many, each tuned to a different niche in the religious world. Rather than a few mass-production seminaries, there may be twenty or thirty schools to which differing groups of Baptist churches turn for help. Rather than trying to produce one or two programs to meet everyone's needs, there will be multiple creators and multiple creations for multiple missions.

New forms of association, then, will need to develop highly specialized and flexible services in response to a diverse constituency, rather than mass-producing programs for consumption by every affiliated congregation. We will need to develop a kind of do-it-yourself style of collecting money and providing services, making it hard for any way of doing things to become "written in stone" or mandatory for every affiliated congregation. And by implication, these postmodernist organizations will assume diversity rather than being threatened by it. Because there is no assumption that everyone must buy the same products, there is room for pluralism.

Second, consider the impact of technology. Where modernist organization was premised on technological determinism, postmodernist organization is premised on technological choices made possible by computers. In a modernist organization, once one had tooled up to produce a certain product, it was extremely costly to retool. Today computers make it more and more possible to make modifications with a mere click of the mouse button.

To serve the needs of churches today, desktop publishing, electronic communication, data bases for mailing lists, and all sorts of other very flexible forms of technology allow easy, targeted start-up and constant, flexible responsiveness. Postmodern forms of denominational association will take full advantage of computer technology both for production of materials and for managing information. We will learn to use computer data bases to match the specialized needs of constituents with specialized services and resources.

Third, let us review the impact of democratizing and flattening the organization charts. Where modernist organizations and jobs were highly specialized and deskilled, postmodernist organizations and jobs are highly generalized and multiskilled. We used to think it was efficient to divide jobs up into smaller and smaller units so that each worker did only a very small piece of the whole (and consequently needed very little in the way of skill and needed to be directed by someone from above who had a bigger picture of what was going on). New forms of organization allow for much more flexibility and creativity, empowering workers to make decisions about how best to cooperate to get the job done, but requiring that workers have a wider range of skills.

A corollary is that decision making becomes, in fact, more democratic and localized. Each component is trusted with its own decision making and is expected to contribute to the decisions that affect the whole. By abolishing the steep hierarchy and expecting skilled participation, responsibility and authority are spread much more broadly. Individuals, churches, and board members are valued and empowered as partners in designing the programs to be carried out. Top-down hierarchy that sees people who ask questions as an impediment would be discarded. In its place would be a participatory democracy that solicits involvement and expects the end result of any discussion to be something more than what any one person could have created—a very Baptist way of doing things.

When we think about what this means for denominations, we can imagine transformations both in national structures and in configurations of local churches. At the national level it means a move away from ever more specialized experts. But beyond that it means the possibility of networks and consortiums of churches and resource groups that serve each other, pooling their practical wisdom rather than calling in experts from above.

And finally, consider the decentralizing tendency. Where modernist organizations were premised on being big and centralized, postmodernist organizations are premised on decentralized, smaller, and more flexible forms, such as subcontracting and networks. Where organizations used to think that the only way to do something new was to create a new department within their centralized structure, postmodern organizations look for ways to accomplish new tasks by forming alliances, even across national lines.

As national denominations "downsize" they will simply no longer be able to provide all the services they have previously provided—at least not directly from headquarters. What they can do is to forge links with multiple organizations that supply the specialized services they cannot. If they can no longer afford a publishing house, they may be able to ask one or more independent publishers to produce materials tailored to their denominational market. If they cannot afford a full-scale mission program, they may be able to link with other mission agencies to do the work their churches would still like to see done. This is not a matter of "taking over" these independent publishers or agencies—that's the old organizational form. Those agencies continue to do the full range of things they have been doing but ally themselves with other organizations to serve specific needs. Denominations would do their work through these coalitions and networks as much as under their own auspices. Rather than bringing every possible collateral organization under their umbrella of control, organizations would be free to find their own niche. National denominations could provide funding, join with various organizations on specific projects, and provide information about other organizations to its members.

To sum up all of this, postmodern organizations are smaller, less centralized, less prone to overspecialization within, but more specialized in their relationships with their environment, less oriented to mass production, and more flexible. If all that is true, the days when denominations drew all the functions of serving churches together under one organizational roof, dividing up those functions into ever more finely tuned specialties, producing services intended to serve everyone in roughly the same fashion are over. New forms of Baptist association can be perfectly at home in this postmodern organizational world. Baptist principles tell us about balancing freedom and responsibility. New forms of denominational association offer us new ways of putting those principles into practice.

Re-forming a Baptist Identity

But what about that other meaning for denomination—the theological one, rather than the functional one? I would argue that for most of this century, much Baptist theologizing has been done by the same structures that did our other functional tasks for us. We have depended on study course books and Sunday school lessons and (sometimes) seminary professors and traveling evangelists to do our theology for us, to tell us what it means to be Baptist. Because those denominational structures are no longer strong, we feel as if we are losing our sense of theological identity, as well as our ability to do what we need to do. Strong denominational identities have been eroded by individual mobility and choice, as well as by the weakness of national structures. People are much more likely today to be denominationally mobile—switching to whatever local congregation best suits their needs and commitments, whatever its denominational label (or lack thereof).[6] And those local churches are increasingly asserting their own autonomy—buying Sunday school materials and hymnals from whomever they please, supporting whatever mission causes they choose, and sending less money up the line to denominational headquarters. Denominational distinctives have not totally disappeared, but they are under serious siege.

It seems to me, however, that one of the salutary effects of the demise of the old institutions may be a new freedom for theology to happen in a truly Baptist way. I think we may find our identity reemerging out of all the places where people are asking about and living out what it means to be Baptist. Some of those places will be theological centers, but most will be local churches, and some will be new organizations and agencies. If we no longer have a dependable staff of paid theological experts, we may have to go back to finding our theology among the ordinary "priests" who freely choose to commit themselves to being a part of the Baptist way.

Our emerging postmodern world needs people committed to this sort of investment. As we learn to transcend modern individualism, embracing chosen commitments to particular local communities of believers, those communities can enter into the messy work of constructing local theologies. All their work, taken together and in all its incoherence, will begin to form again our sense of Baptist identity. As we take everyday actions that we label Baptist and as we make theological claims for that tradition, we will collectively redefine it. As we learn to transcend universalism, learning to be bilingual, we can work toward theologies that embrace both our unity and our diversity. We will learn to talk to each other about the ways we find God, about how the Bible speaks to us, about how life should be lived. We will disagree, sometimes passionately. We will not be bound together by common culture, so we will have to work hard at whatever common conversation we are able to have. We will have to learn the disciplines of love and trust that come because we acknowledge that Jesus is Lord and that God has good uses for our differences. The associations we form in the future will be no less free and voluntary than those we formed in the past—indeed much more so. If we are ready, we can seize this "Baptist" moment, coming together with all the paradoxical combination of freedom and commitment, autonomy and interdependence, that has characterized our heritage from the beginning.

Notes

1. This argument largely follows that made by Peter Berger in *The Sacred Canopy* (New York: Anchor Doubleday, 1969).

2. Walter Brueggemann, "The Legitimacy of a Sectarian Hermeneutic: 2 Kings 18-19," in *Education for Citizenship and Discipleship,* ed. Mary C. Boys (New York: Pilgrim, 1989), 3-34.

3. R. Stephen Warner, *New Wine in Old Wineskins* (Berkeley: University of California Press, 1988).

4. In this section I am drawing on arguments made in more detail in Nancy T. Ammerman, "Denominations: Who and What Are We Studying?" in *Re-Imagining Denominationalism,* ed. R. Bruce Mullin and Russell E. Richey (New York: Oxford University Press, 1994), and in 1993 in "SBC Moderates and the Making of a Post-Modern Denomination," *Christian Century* 110 (26): 896-99.

5. Stewart Clegg, *Modern Organizations: Organizational Studies in the Postmodern World* (London: Sage, 1990), 181, 203.

6. See Robert Wuthnow, *The Restructuring of American Religion* (Princeton: Princeton University Press, 1988).

Introduction to Part IV.
The Boundary of Freedom:
Baptists and Church/State Tensions

Perhaps the most public contribution Baptists have made to the character of religious life in America has been their consistent commitment to the principle of separation of church and state. It is a principle that the earliest Baptists in the seventeenth and eighteenth centuries first struggled to define and then to achieve. It has often been purchased at great price and requires constant vigilance to maintain. Because Baptists have so passionately required freedom for themselves, they have been at times militant in defending it for others—sometimes for others with whom they have profound disagreement or even distaste. Frequently generosity and sympathy are detected in their dedication, and occasionally agreement. But Baptist dedication to maintaining this boundary is always a matter first of self-preservation.

Baptist commitment to maintaining the elusive boundary between church and state has produced among Baptists some of the finest scholars and practitioners of church-state issues. Several of them are represented here.

The eminent Baptist historian, Edwin S. Gaustad, returns us again to the early years of Baptists in America to help us understand the specific issues that enabled Baptists to identify and build watchtowers to protect this freedom.

For almost two decades James Dunn has been the preeminent Baptist spokesperson for the principle of religious liberty, and in his article, he provides for us an understanding of the specific roles played by the founders of our nation and our Constitution's Bill of Rights. It is a primer in civic as well as religious responsibility that only one with profound Baptist instincts could provide.

Two bright lights among Baptist legal scholars and practitioners, Oliver Thomas and Melissa Rogers, both provide articles that deal with the contemporary issues and pressures that confront Baptists and others today. They move from the development of historic principles and constitutional frameworks to present challenges. They deal with the boundaries that we need to assure all people the rights and opportunities of their faith, and they confront also the barriers that must be broken lest religious expression become choked by exclusion from human activity.

Together these presentations remind us that "balance" is never static or fully achieved; it is always in process, and the process is one of creative tension.

Responsible Freedom: Baptists in Early America

Edwin S. Gaustad

Responsibility and freedom are sometimes regarded as polar opposites, especially when those shouting loudly about freedom are seen as social or political or religious undesirables. But it is lovely to contemplate the possibility that responsibility and freedom can be productive partners rather than embittered enemies. "Responsible freedom"—it makes a great phrase, and it can make for even greater history.

In the seventeenth century, when the European world was still being turned upside down in the name of religion, England plunged into civil war, and religious sectarianism rose to unparalleled heights. So many cried out for freedom; so many fled from responsibility. It was enough to give freedom a bad name, with the result that when the monarchy was restored to England in 1660, repression was restored at the same time. In the realm of religion the Church of England held all the power; the dissenters and nonconformists held none. For about twenty years freedom had been tried; the sober and the wise concluded solemnly that it did not work.

In America, or at least in Massachusetts, the sober and the wise had reached that same conclusion a generation earlier. In the mid-1630s one fanatical voice kept calling for more freedom: more freedom from the Church of England; more freedom from the civil magistrates; more freedom for Native Americans; more freedom from the Old Testament models of ancient Israel; and above all, more freedom from the burdens of a history of religious warfare, persecution, and blood. This noisy radical, Roger Williams by name, seemed intoxicated with freedom but devoid of all responsibility. And so Massachusetts took the only possible,

Edwin S. Gaustad is emeritus professor of history at University of California, Riverside, and is a widely published distinguished historian of American history and religion. This paper was presented at "Called to Responsible Freedom: A Conference on Baptist Distinctives," at Green Lake, Wisconsin, August 1996.

the only logical, step: they exiled him in October 1635. They did not say, but surely they must have thought, "Depart from us, you unclean thing."

So the following January, to prevent being deported to England where neither King Charles I nor Archbishop William Laud felt warmly toward radicals or toward freedom, Williams left his home in Salem on foot, walking through the winter snows and a "howling wilderness." For fourteen weeks he went without bed and bread. Even in such adversity, perhaps especially in such adversity, spiritual lessons could be learned. In simple poetic form, Roger Williams wrote:

God makes a Path, provides a Guide,
And feeds in Wildernesse!
His glorious Name while breath remaines, O that I may confesse.
Lost many a time, I have had no Guide, No House, but Hollow Tree!
In stormy Winter night no Fire, No Food, no Company:
In him I have found a House, a Bed,

A Table, Company:
No Cup so bitter, but's made sweet, When God shall Sweet'ning be.[1]

And so at last Williams made his way to the headwaters of the Narragansett Bay, where he negotiated with the Indians for some land, and where he named his primitive settlement Providence, "in a sense of God's merciful providence to me in my distress." Now he had freedom: acres and acres of boundless, fearsome freedom. Could he also demonstrate responsibility—responsibility for a growing family, for a growing colony, and for an insight of terrifying proportion: liberty of conscience, or soul freedom?

Williams could hardly know the answer to those questions in 1636, and perhaps not for many years later. But he knew that burdens rested on him, and he would not shirk them. Even though Massachusetts governor John Winthrop had voted with the rest of the General Court to exile Williams, the two men maintained cordial personal relationships. In the summer of 1636 Williams wrote to Winthrop inquiring, in effect: "How does one run a colony anyway?" No joint stock company supported Williams in his wilderness wandering. No English charter sanctioned his claim to the land. No magistrate had been appointed or elected. "So what, exactly, does one do to govern?" Williams asked. Meanwhile, freedom's radical reported, "The masters of Families have ordinarily met once a fortnight and consulted about our common peace, watch, and planting."

With Rhode Island on its way to a democratic form of government, Roger Williams could turn his attention to defending, as responsibly as possible, the cause of religious liberty in the Western world. Massachusetts, convinced that Williams, along with all those Baptists with whom he consorted, could never be responsible, passed a law against Baptists in 1644. A portion of it pointed out that Baptists (and Anabaptists) had throughout their history "been the incendiaries of commonwealths & the infectors of persons in main matters of religion and the troublers of churches in all places where they have been" and that people who opposed infant baptism "have usually held other errors and heresies together therewith." In view of all that and more, the only *responsible* action for Massachusetts to take was to make it illegal and dangerous to be a Baptist in the Bay Colony.[2]

In Rhode Island, Roger Williams had no interest in passing a law making it illegal to be a Puritan or a Presbyterian or a member of any other religious communion. He did have an interest, indeed a passion, to make the case for freedom in religion as powerfully as he could. So in the same year of the 1644 law against Baptists, Williams in London published *The Bloudy Tenent of Persecution, for Cause of Conscience.* Written in haste and sometimes in rage, the book wins no honor for style or literary grace. It does deserve every honor, however, for its substance: a cry of the heart against the rape of the soul. England, Williams wrote, did not embrace Christianity, but embraced that horrid and polluted mixture of politics and religion known as Christendom. Christianity Williams loved; Christendom he despised. And Christianity was too precious to be traded for a vote, an office, or even a crown. And the individual soul was too tender, too sacred, to be violated by a civil sword. But should persecution come once more, the true Christian must stand fast. "Having bought truth dear," Williams wrote, "we must not sell it cheap, not the least grain of it for the whole world." Does that sound sufficiently responsible?[3]

In London for two years, 1643-1644, Williams managed to get two books and one long pamphlet published; he also attended to some family business and even took time to cut wood to help London's poor get through a hard winter. But his main task in London, his main responsibility, if you will, was to secure a charter for his much despised colony, whose lands were eyed hungrily by neighboring Massachusetts and Connecticut. In the best of circumstances, securing a charter was not easy. Williams arrived in London in the worst of circumstances: a civil war between the parliamentary forces (Roundheads) under Oliver Cromwell and the royal forces (Cavaliers) under Charles I. Nonetheless, with a patience and tact rarely evident, Williams secured the "Free Charter of Civil Incorporation"—with two votes to spare—from the relevant eighteen-person committee of

Parliament. Armed with the charter and carrying a few copies of *The Bloudy Tenent* with him (authorities in London burned most of the other copies), Williams set sail for Boston, where he was guaranteed safe passage to Providence, so long as he moved as directly and as speedily as possible out of the Bay Colony's sacred soil. Burned in London and banned in Boston, Williams, were he not careful, might end up a folk hero.

That, however, would not be his fate. When he became president of the colony in 1655, he found his authority questioned, his integrity challenged, and his motives cast in the darkest terms. "I have been charged with Folly," Williams noted, "for that Freedom and Liberty which I have always stood for. . . . It hath been told me that I have labored for a licentious and Contentious people." Many who came to Rhode Island for religious freedom thought they should be free from all civil authority as well. "Tyranny" was the automatic response to any governmental action in Rhode Island, where irresponsibility had been elevated into a noble principle. Roger Williams knew better and had written better, but few heeded his measured words.[4]

So in one more effort, Williams wrote a letter to the town fathers of Providence to make clear, if possible, just what responsible freedom was all about. "There goes many a Ship to Sea," Williams began, and the ship was like a commonwealth or a colony. And the passengers on that ship may include "Papists and Protestants, Jews and Turks" all together on a single vessel. Now listen carefully: "I do affirm that all the Liberty of Conscience that I have ever pleaded for, turns upon these two Hinges: (first), that none of the Protestants, Papists, Jews or Turks be forced to come to the Ship's Prayers or Worship; nor, secondly, compelled from their own particular Prayers or Worship, if they practice any." Thus far, liberty; what of responsibility?

"Notwithstanding this Liberty," Williams added, "the Commander of the Ship ought to command the Ship's course; yea and also to command that Justice, Peace, and Sobriety, be kept and practiced, both among the Seaman and all the Passengers." If passengers disobeyed the captain's orders, or refused to pay their fare, or threatened mutiny, of course the captain had every right to "punish such Transgressors, according to their Deserts and Merits." Does a lawfully elected governor or president have legitimate authority? Of course. Does a Rhode Island citizen have clear responsibilities? Of course. Liberty was not the equivalent of anarchy. Soul freedom was not a synonym for irresponsibility. For what did

Williams stand and plead with all of his heart and mind? Responsible freedom.[5]

In his own day, he was too readily dismissed as "a meer weather-cock, constant only in his inconstancy." Massachusetts historians of the seventeenth century typed him as of "very self-conceited, unquiet, turbulent, uncharitable spirit." Another chronicler compared Williams to "a vessel that carries too high a sail" and is therefore "apt to overset in the stream, and ruin those that are embarked with him." And nearly two centuries later, President John Quincy Adams denounced him as "a polemical porcupine . . . an extreme puritan, quilled with all the quarrelsome metaphysical divinity of the age."[6]

Massachusetts never gave up (though in 1936 that state's legislature did repeal the sentence of exile pronounced against Williams over three hundred years before). Appraisals of Williams continue to pour in, widely varying in their judgment. In my own judgment, I believe that he can be rightly regarded as an early apostle of responsible freedom.

Now we shift the scene to the eighteenth century and, initially, to Philadelphia. The creation of the Philadelphia Association in 1707 represented another step in the direction of collective responsibility. Though at that time, Pennsylvania had only five Baptist churches, New Jersey only six, and New York none, this association, the earliest and for over a half century the only such entity among America's Baptists, achieved much. It drew up a confession of faith, ordained ministers, sent out missionaries, and in 1764 even managed to assist New Englanders in the creation of the College of Rhode Island (later, in 1804, Brown University). And the Philadelphia Association did all this without compromising the freedom of the individual Baptist congregations. It only assisted those congregations in making their freedom more responsible.

The founding of Brown followed an event, or a series of events, of major magnitude that radically reshaped the configuration and the destiny of Baptists in America. The Great Awakening, not a single revival but successive waves of revivalism in the 1740s and well beyond, spread throughout the thirteen colonies and gave Baptists their first real taste of a rapid and evangelical surge. Prior to the Awakening, Baptists gave more thought to how to survive than how to grow. Withdrawn and largely Arminian in theology, the Baptist churches—only about twenty in all the colonies in 1700—concentrated on holding their tiny congregations together and resisting the ever-present threats of schism. In the latter regard, success was minimal. In Rhode Island, for example, separate congregations of Six Principle Baptists (emphasizing the laying on of hands for all members) and Seventh Day Baptists (emphasizing the Old Testament command to "Remember the Sabbath day," that is, Saturday) divided small Baptist communities into even smaller ones.

The Great Awakening, with its Calvinist theology and fervent evangelism, changed all that. It did so, initially, by creating prorevivalist and antirevivalist factions among the Congregationalists in New England and the Presbyterians in the Middle Colonies. Especially in New England, many New Lights (that is, prorevivalists) separated from the more formal and established parish churches. These Separatist Congregationalists proved to be a fertile field for Baptists to exploit and soon to harvest. One New Light turned Baptist, Isaac Backus, proved of immeasurable value in organizing Baptists, rallying them to the cause of religious liberty, and giving the nascent denomination both an identity and a powerful evangelical thrust. One quick measure of the Awakening's broader effect on the Baptists may be seen in the growth in the number of their churches. In 1750 Baptists had 132 churches in eleven colonies. A single century later, Baptists had over 9,000 churches in thirty-one states. The spirit of revivalism and personal piety cannot account for all of this phenomenal growth, but it can certainly lay claim to a very large proportion of it.[7]

The emphasis on freedom also accounts for much of that growth, an emphasis that helps explain why America's blacks, both slave and free, turned in such overwhelming numbers to the Baptists. In the decade of the much-despised Stamp Act (1760s), the rhetoric of liberty heated up—civil and ecclesiastical liberty. When Brown was founded in 1764, its charter specified that "into this liberal and catholic institution shall never be admitted any religious tests; but, on the contrary, all the members hereof shall forever enjoy full, free, absolute, and uninterrupted liberty of conscience." All this before the U.S. Constitution had been adopted, to say nothing of the Bill of Rights! And all this a century before Oxford and Cambridge universities managed to come up with their own pale imitation of this full, free, and absolute liberty of conscience!

In 1773 members of the Baptist church in Ashfield, Massachusetts, under the guidance of their pastor, Ebenezer Smith, officially denounced the institution of slavery. They did so not on the "all men are created equal" principle of the Declaration of Independence, for that Declaration had not yet been written. Rather, loyalty to the gospel required the condemnation of slavery. "We complain of bondage," the church noted; "shall we at the same time keep our fellow man in bondage?" Jesus had set all of mankind on one level, the church added, and God "hath made of one Blood all nations for to dwell on all the Earth." Citing many scriptural references, the Ashfield congregation declared that it was "high time for the watchman to sound an alarm against this practice." In writing to Isaac Backus, Pastor Smith even dared hope that the denomination as a whole, or at least the Warren Association organized six years before, might take a stand against slavery, but this hope faltered and faded away.

Massachusetts pastor and historian Isaac Backus was more successful in organizing a broadly based protest ("massive civil disobedience," William McLoughlin called it) against the Massachusetts requirement that all dissenters apply to the authorities for a certificate that would excuse them from paying taxes to support the official Congregational church. Since 1729 Baptists in Connecticut and Massachusetts could be relieved of these ecclesiastical taxes if they gained certification (usually negotiating with a most unsympathetic town clerk) that they were indeed tithing members of a dissenting congregation. By 1773 Backus concluded that such a process violated religious liberty, for it tacitly recognized the right of the state to inquire into one's private religious views and affiliations. He therefore urged his fellow Baptists to stop applying for certificates, to refuse to pay the church taxes, and to make their witness by going to jail if it came to that. These man-made laws were bad laws; God guided his children by a higher law.

In December of 1774 Backus, in the midst of a growing revolutionary fervor, made a personal appeal before the Massachusetts legislature to take the cries for freedom more seriously. All freedom, civil and ecclesiastical, was on the line. "All America is alarmed at the tax on tea," he reminded the legislators in a region where a "Boston tea party" had been recently held. But a tax of the very same amount had been levied on the Baptists in his parish and throughout the colony. "Americans can avoid the tea tax by simply not buying tea, but we Baptists," Backus noted, "have no such liberty. We must pay your little tax now, or you threaten us with a heavier tax later. But these lines are to let you know," Backus thundered, "that we are determined not to pay either of them; not only upon your principle of not being taxed where we are not represented, but also because we dare not render that homage to any earthly power, which I and many of my brethren are fully convinced belongs only to God. Give us our freedom, and we will be responsible. Deny us this freedom, and we can only say in the words of Scripture, 'With what measure you mete, it shall be measured to you again.'"[8]

When the Revolution broke out, many questioned whether Baptists would put their shoulder to that heavy wheel. Anglicans in the South and Congregationalists in the Northeast, having been unfair to Baptists for generations, had reason to question their loyalty to the patriot cause. Confounding their enemies, however, Baptists in overwhelming numbers supported the American cause against the British. They did so, bolstered by the conviction that the War of Independence, if it were successful, really did mean a greater liberty, religious as well as civil. And in most of the colonies this proved true, as Anglicanism in particular suffered swift disestablishment in Virginia and elsewhere. In New England, however, to the deep disappointment of Backus and his fellows, the Congregational establishment held on in Connecticut until 1818 and in Massachusetts until 1833. For legal guarantees of freedom in religion, Baptists might need to look more to the national than to the local governments.

But first they looked to, and were active in, Virginia, the largest of the colonies. As soon as the Revolution began, Thomas Jefferson, along with James Madison and others, took legislative steps to separate the Anglican Church from the newly created state. Two years before that, a twenty-two-year-old Madison found himself deeply offended by the jailing of some Baptist preachers for merely proclaiming their religious opinions. Anglicans, he noted in a letter to a college chum, still engaged in that "diabolical, hell-conceived principle of persecution." "Pity me," Madison wrote, "and pray for liberty of conscience to all." When Virginia drew up a new state constitution, Jefferson, convinced that religious liberty must be built into the fundamental legal structure, proposed this language: "All persons shall have full and free liberty of religious opinion; nor shall any be compelled to frequent or maintain any religious institution." Freedom for religion; freedom from religion. Jefferson's language was not adopted at this point, though several steps in the direction of disestablishment were taken.[9]

No one seriously questioned that the privileged position of the Church of England could not be, should not be, maintained. In the midst of fighting a war for independence against England, it made little sense to continue to subsidize the church of that country. But was full, free, and absolute liberty of conscience the only, or even the best, alternative? Patrick Henry and others thought that they might strike a happy compromise between Anglican establishment on the one hand, and total separation between church and state on the other. Basically, the compromise proposed was to establish Christianity as the official religion of the state of Virginia. "All denominations of Christians," in the words of Henry's bill, "demeaning themselves peaceably and faithfully shall enjoy equal privileges."

When Henry's bill was first put to a vote at the end of 1784, after the Revolution had been waged and won, it passed by a margin of two votes. But by the rules of the Virginia Assembly, a second reading and a second vote were required. Madison succeeded in getting that second vote postponed for a year, thus allowing enough time to solicit and perhaps marshal public opinion—especially from the Virginia backcountry where Baptists and Presbyterians were strong. With Thomas Jefferson off in Paris as the new nation's minister to France, the task of defeating Henry's proposal for a multiple establishment fell on the young shoulders of James Madison. Marshaling arguments from history, logic, and revolutionary ideology, Madison composed his now-famous Memorial and Remonstrance in order to defeat the sweet reasonableness of the Patrick Henry compromise.[10]

Henry's bill had some twelve hundred signatures in support of the general assessment for the support of Christianity. Madison's Memorial carried the signatures of some ten thousand. Baptists, having on their own often sent to the Assembly petitions for legislators to remove themselves completely from the religion business, signed the Memorial in large numbers. Methodists, having just recently created their own independent denomination, also joined in support of the Madisonian sentiment. Presbyterians, especially the laity, likewise provided many signatures, as did smaller groups such as Quakers and Mennonites. When Madison presented the Memorial with such impressive backing, the Henry bill never came to another vote; it met its fate in a quiet legislative burial.

Madison's arguments proved persuasive in 1785, as they still do over two hundred years later. Sounding very much like Roger Williams, Madison spoke of the "torrents of blood" spilled in the European world "by vain attempts of the secular arm, to extinguish Religious discord." Americans have already found a better way: moderation and forbearance. Americans, Madison wrote,

> have proudly seen their nation as a refuge to the persecuted; now, they must consider a bill that can itself become an engine of persecution. For who does not see that "the same authority which can establish Christianity, in exclusion of all other Religions, may establish with the same ease any particular sect of Christians, in exclusion of all other Sects?" And should that happen, we are right back where we started from before a Revolution was fought—and at great cost—finally won.

Like Isaac Backus, Madison did not think that earthly authorities had any business, and certainly no competence, to make judgments in spiritual matters. Only one legislator can properly rule in these affairs—namely, the Supreme Lawgiver of the universe. The Christian religion does not need, does not want, the support of the state. For fifteen hundred years of official sanction have produced only "pride and indolence in the Clergy, ignorance and servility in the laity, in both, superstition, bigotry, and persecution." Or, as the itinerant Baptist John Leland said: "Persecution rips the saints to pieces, but leaves Christianity pure. State establishment of religion hugs the saints, and corrupts Christianity."[11]

Madison's Memorial cleared the legislative decks for the Assembly, at long last, to consider Jefferson's Bill for Establishing Religious Freedom. First written in 1777, nearly ten years before, Jefferson's bill was ignored, tabled, shunted aside. Now the Assembly could procrastinate no longer. After some amendments, softening some of Jefferson's unrestrained confidence in reason, the Assembly in January of 1786 passed what now became the Statute of Virginia for Religious Freedom, one of the two compositions for which Jefferson wished to be remembered on his tombstone. When Madison communicated to Jefferson, still in Paris, the great news that his statute had become law, Jefferson rejoiced. He saw that the law received wide circulation, was translated into Italian and French, and quickly became an appendix to Jefferson's own *Notes on the State of Virginia*. When Jefferson responded to Madison, he proudly proclaimed that "it is honorable for us to have produced the first legislature who has had the courage to declare that the reason of man may be trusted with the formation of his own opinions."[12]

Jefferson's statute passed in 1786. In 1787 some fifty delegates, more or less, gathered in Philadelphia to draw up a Constitution of the United States. Religion did not figure prominently in that document, for the intent was to create a civil state, not a theocracy, not even an avowedly Christian nation. Only one substantial reference to religion may be found: In Article Six we read that no religious test will be required for any office or trust under the federal government. When the time came for the people of each state to vote on whether or not to ratify the Constitution, some objected to the "no religious test" provision on the grounds that even a papist, a Turk, or a Jew might someday be elected president of the nation. Many more objected, however, that the Constitution carried no explicit guarantee of religious freedom or of other fundamental liberties.

Indeed, Rhode Islanders, including the many Baptists residing there, refused to ratify the Constitution until a Bill or Rights had been added. (Rhode Island was the first to vote for a Declaration of Independence, the last to vote for the Constitution—well after George Washington had taken office as the nation's first president.) In Virginia, Madison discovered that sentiment for ratification was so closely divided that the vote would fail unless he personally assured his friends and neighbors that the first order of business of the First Congress would be the drafting of a Bill of Rights.

In 1789, with a minimum of nine states having ratified it, the Constitution took effect. True to his word, Madison proceeded immediately to call for a consideration of amendments. Baptist interest focused directly on the wording ultimately agreed to for the initial section of the First Amendment: "Congress shall make no law respecting an establishment of religion or prohibiting the free exercise thereof." And a group of Baptists in Connecticut received Jefferson's letter in 1802 that offered his understanding of that amendment—namely, that it built a wall of separation between church and state.

Early Baptists played no unique role in the writing of the Constitution or of the Bill of Rights. Their signal contribution lay in taking the guarantees of religious liberty and running with them—from the Atlantic to the Pacific, and beyond. How responsibly they exercised these new-found freedoms was determined by the generations of those who followed them.

Notes

1. Quoted in Edwin S. Gaustad, *Liberty of Conscience: Roger Williams in America* (Grand Rapids, Mich.: Eerdmans Publishing Co., 1991), p. 46.

2. Edwin S. Gaustad, ed., *Baptist Piety: The Last Will and Testimony of Obadiah Holmes* (Valley Forge, Pa.: Judson Press, 1994), p. 16.

3. Gaustad, *Liberty of Conscience*, pp. 69-86.

4. Ibid., p. 144.

5. Ibid., pp. 145-46.

6. Ibid., pp. 211-12.

7. See, for example, Harry S. Stout, *The Divine Dramatist: George Whitefield and the Rise of Modern Evangelicalism* (Grand Rapids, Mich.: Eerdmans Publishing, 1991); Edwin S Gaustad, *The Great Awakening in New England* (New York: Harper & Bros., 1957); and the indispensable two-volume work of William G. McLoughlin, *New England Dissent, 1630-1833* (Cambridge, Mass.: Harvard University Press, 1971).

8. See William G. McLoughlin, *Isaac Backus on Church, State, and Calvinism* (Cambridge, Mass.: Harvard University Press, 1968) and Edwin S. Gaustad, "The Backus-Leland Tradition," in Winthrop S. Hudson, ed., *Baptist Concepts of the Church* (Valley Forge, Pa.: Judson Press, 1959).

9. Edwin S. Gaustad, *Neither King Nor Prelate: Religion and the New Nation* (Grand Rapids, Mich.: Eerdmans Publishing Co., 1993), p. 37.

10. Ibid., pp. 38-39.

11. Ibid., pp. 39-40.

12. Ibid., pp. 41-42.

Back to the Bill of Rights' Beginning

James M. Dunn

Bill Moyers suggests that "the symbol for our culture . . . has become the digital clock, which looks at only the present moment, with no hint of yesterday or tomorrow."[1] There is truth in what he says. So in the 200th year of the Bill of Rights it is timely to turn back to beginnings. Look back not for arcane argument about "original intent." Look back not for academic nitpicking. Rather, look back to put the origins of the Bill of Rights in context, to gain perspective, to capture the essence, so that when mixed with current conflict one will hear not simply the words but also the music.

The bicentennial of the Bill of Rights is greeted with a yawn because the magnitude of the accomplishment is not fully appreciated. The culture and personalities from which it came are utterly lost.

Word pictures, snapshots, of four key figures in the Bill of Rights' family tree hopefully will humanize the history. The roles of these chosen forebears fall along a continuum from lofty principle to lowdown politics, from abstract to concrete, from Cambridge to Culpeper. Chopping the continuum of contributions by Roger Williams, Thomas Jefferson, James Madison and John Leland into arbitrary divisions is but one design for getting back to the Bill of Rights' beginning. Special attention is here given to the first freedoms and the first words of the First Amendment, which begins the Bill of Rights. Those words are simply "Congress shall make no law respecting an establishment of religion. . . ." The words "no law," as Justice Hugo Black liked to say, mean plainly "no law," favorable or unfavorable.[2]

James M. Dunn is the executive director of the Baptist Joint Committee on Public Affairs in Washington, D.C. This article was originally printed in *Theology and Public Policy* 3, no. 2 (Fall 1991), 6-15, and is reprinted with permission of the publisher, Churches' Center for Theology and Public Policy, 4500 Massachusetts Avenue NW, Washington, D.C. 20016.

Roger Williams

Roger Williams fathered philosophically the American experiment in freedom of religion. Some of his London friends thought him "divinely mad." He shaped his colony of Rhode Island into the home of the otherwise-minded. Some detractors preferred to call it "Rogue's Island," or that sewer, or "the licentious republic."[3]

It was a far cry from socializing with royalty, as he had in London, to barren New England. He was a graduate of Pembroke College, Cambridge, a Charter house scholar from 1623 to 1629. Running interference for him had been the leading legal scholar of the day, Sir Edward Coke. Williams' famous friends and classy connections included John Milton and Oliver Cromwell. Now, it had come to this: cast out into the bitter winter, the "howling wilderness," as he wrote, "not knowing what bread or bed did mean"[4] for fourteen weeks.

It was part of the price Roger Williams paid for insisting upon freedom, and not mere toleration, as the standard for the treatment of religion. He despised toleration as the measure of the majority religion's relationship with dissenters. Toleration is a human concession. Liberty is a gift of God. Roger Williams denied government any right to enforce religious uniformity. He opposed the right of the state to collect taxes for support of the clergy. In fact, he prefigured the freedom of religion guaranteed in the First Amendment.

It is good to remember Roger Williams' warnings against thinking this land a "Christian Nation." He said, "No civil state or country can truly be called Christian, although Christians be in it."[5]

Harvard historian Perry Miller places Williams at the fount of freedom: "Now as all the world knows, this Separatist figures in history as the pioneer of religious freedom, even of democracy."[6] And, in a later work, Miller praised Williams as a "prophet of religious liberty" who has molded the American character: "For the subsequent history of what became the United States, Roger Williams possesses one indubitable importance, that he stands at the beginning of it."

Oscar S. Straus, a Jewish scholar, wrote of Williams: "He was not the first to discover the principles of religious liberty, but he was the first to proclaim them in all their plenitude, and to found and build up a political community with those principles as the basis of its organization."[7]

This practicing philosopher of freedom, Roger Williams, is nominated herewith as one of the four founders most responsible for the First Amendment. He is disproportionately important because he first challenged the old world patterns of toleration, theocracy, church-states, and state-churches. He was banished, ostracized, ridiculed, and thought to have windmills in his head. He died poor and rejected, nothing much to show for his labors—except the American experiment of religious liberty and the most vital churches in the world. As Charles Kuralt says, "Today they've put him on a pedestal. The figure atop the capitol dome is called the Independent Man. He can see the whole state [of Rhode Island] from up there, the first state to be disrespectful and disreputable and free."[8]

Thomas Jefferson

Thomas Jefferson initiated intellectually the chain of legislation that led to the First Amendment and, through agitation for it, to the Bill of Rights. He was proud of the Virginia Statute for Religious Freedom. Getting it passed was, he said, "the severest contest in which I have ever been engaged."

Patrick Henry, popular orator, had opposed the statute and pushed a contrary bill which would have established general assessments for the churches. Jefferson was in France and responded to letters from James Madison, who was leading the fight for Jefferson's proposed separation of church and state. Madison wrote, at one point, fearful that all was lost. Mr. Henry's taxation of all citizens to support the churches had passed two readings. It seemed certain to become law on passage of third reading. "What shall we do?" he asked Jefferson. Jefferson replied, "What we have to do, I think, is devotedly to pray for his [Henry's] death."[9]

As it worked out, Madison wrote the brilliant "A Memorial and Re-monstrance Against Religious Assessments"; Mr. Henry was elected governor—a post that did not have veto power; George Mason lobbied his peers; Baptists, Presbyterians and others produced petitions with thou-sands of names; the Virginia Statute for Religious Freedom passed on January 16, 1786; and Governor Patrick Henry, with no veto, signed into law on January 19, 1786 the bill he had fought. Jefferson's Statute brought into law with specificity the principled basis for the Bill of Rights:

> *Be it enacted by the General Assembly,* That no man shall be compelled to frequent or support any religious worship, place, or ministry whatsoever, nor shall be enforced, restrained, molested, or burthened in his body or goods, nor shall otherwise suffer on account of his religious opinions or belief; but that all men shall be free to profess, and by argument to maintain, their opinion in matters of religion, and that the same shall in no wise diminish, enlarge, or affect their civil capacities.[10]

The importance of this one bill cannot be overestimated. The Virginia

Statute was the "model for the guarantee of religious liberty incorporated in the U.S. Bill of Rights."[11]

What did this often forgotten law do for generations following?

It protected the right to say "no" to all religion. One does have freedom *from* religion as well as freedom *for* religion in this country, no matter what powerful presidents and popular preachers may say. Without the freedom to say "no," all one's yeses are meaningless.

It denied tax support to the churches. As Jefferson said, "to compel a man to furnish contributions of money for the propagation of opinions which he disbelieves, is sinful and tyrannical."[12]

It set out separation of church and state.

It guaranteed the free exercise of religion.

Harvard historian Bernard Bailyn called the statute "the most important document in American history, bar none."[13]

The "wall of separation between church and state" is a Jeffersonian figure of speech from a letter of his to Baptists in Danbury, Connecticut, in 1802. The present Chief Justice of the United States Supreme Court, Mr. Rehnquist, in his dissent in the *Jaffree* case, says, "The 'wall of separation between church and State' is a metaphor based on bad history, a metaphor which has proved useless as a guide to judging. It should be frankly and explicitly abandoned."[14] It is not surprising, then, with that understanding, that Mr. Rehnquist produced a novel document in the history of the United States Supreme Court in his *Jaffree* dissent. At least four times in that dissent, he states or alludes to his limited version of the scope of the First Amendment. "The evil to be aimed at," Rehnquist insists, was "the establishment of a national church, and perhaps the preference of one religious sect over another."[15] That view was, indeed, one of the views held by some of the founders. It is specifically the approach that was rejected.[16]

The revised standard version of the First Amendment holds that it simply (1) rules out favoritism among religious groups and (2) prohibits an official State church, but endorses God-in-general and supports generic religion. The Supreme Court, history, and common sense consistently contend that the establishment clause embraces much broader restraints on government than these simple prohibitions.

The record of the Senate debates over approval of the First Amendment eloquently refutes all claims that a sort of preferential establishment was all the amendment intended to prohibit. As paraphrased from Stokes and Pfeffer's *Church and State in the United States,* the debate reveals the recommended alterations to the First Amendment.

In 1789, on the first day of debate, the Senate acted:

1. A motion was made to strike out the words "religion, or prohibiting the free exercise thereof," and insert "one religious sect or society in preference to others." This motion was *DEFEATED*.

2. A second motion was made to strike out the amendment altogether. This motion was *DEFEATED*.

3. A motion was made to adopt the following instead of the words we have: "Congress shall not make any law infringing the rights of conscience, or establishing any religious sect or society." This motion was *DEFEATED*.

4. A fourth motion was made to amend the amendment to read "Congress shall make no law establishing any particular denomination of religion in preference to another, or prohibiting the free exercise thereof, nor shall the rights of conscience be infringed." This motion was *DEFEATED*.[17]

It is clear that what the founders of this Republic had in mind in this specific regard is *not* the aid-to-all-religions view of the revisionists. It was offered to them and they decisively rejected it.

Contrast Rehnquist's revisionist view with that of Justice Harry Blackmun, who shortly after the *Jaffree* case said, "We operate in the belief—almost the conviction—that in the United States there *is* a wall between religion and the State. Jefferson's influence is very strong."[18] May it ever be.

James Madison

James Madison was "the most important Founder institutionally speaking" as William Lee Miller argues and Sam Rabinove agrees.[19] In our expansive tradition of religious liberty one should not minimize Madison's philosophical and intellectual gifts. For all of Roger Williams' philosophical and practical precedents and all of Thomas Jefferson's brilliant accomplishments, yet it was little Mr. Madison who institutionalized religious liberty.

To all appearances, Madison was an unlikely candidate for greatness. He was, by his own description, sickly, frail, timid and self-conscious. He had other liabilities among the rough-hewn frontiersmen of his day. He was small, five feet four inches tall, never weighing much over 100 pounds. One contemporary called him "little and ordinary." Another said he was "no bigger than a snowflake."[20] He was wealthy. His father owned

4,000 acres of land. He was brainy and bookish. He was never a fighter. Though made a "Colonel," his only duty was on the parade ground. Nowadays on campus he would be called a "nerd," in the media the quintessential "wimp." Yet, what a man!

James Madison saw the need for a strong central government and worked to "enable the government to control the governed, and in the next place, oblige it to control itself."[21] He had learned well a sober, realistic estimate of humankind from his teacher Witherspoon at Presbyterian, pre-Princeton New Jersey College. "All men having power ought to be distrusted to a certain degree."[22] So today the checks and balances exist, given to us by the "Father of the Constitution."

Behind the scenes, he plotted and schemed, cut deals, engaged in every sort of chicanery to get General Washington to the Constitutional Convention, and then kept the only substantial record of the proceedings that brought forth the Constitution. Only after he died, when his widow, Dolly, sold his notes of the convention debates, did the nation become aware of his influence. One must agree with Fred Barbash when he says, "it is fair to say that the Constitution would not have come about without him."[23]

Many persons even today fail to appreciate Madison's role as author of the Bill of Rights. Since he had wavered in support for such a bill, some people fail to see that once he was convinced that the ratifying conventions made a bill of rights the condition for ratification, he changed his tune. Madison pledged to work for such a bill. He was true to his word. He kept his promises. As Estep says:

> Those who had staked their hopes on Madison's integrity and commitment to freedom of religion were not disappointed. On June 7, 1789, Madison, considering himself bound in honor and in duty, submitted the first version of the no-establishment clause of an amendment that after ratification became the First Amendment in the Bill of Rights.[24]

He never needed to be converted to the cause of religious freedom. In fact, he became a "patriot" at the age of 22, specifically because of his passion for religious liberty. According to Merrill Peterson, "The cause of religious freedom became Madison's passport to Revolution."[25] The Virginia squire had considered the ministry and law as career options but found his vocation in the American Revolution.

Edwin Gaustad pinpoints Madison's commitment to religious liberty:

> Madison, at the tender age of twenty-two, already found himself out of patience with neighboring Anglicans who indulged in that "diabolical, hell-conceived principle of persecution." By jailing half a dozen "well-meaning men" for merely proclaiming their religious opinions,

Madison's neighbors unwittingly launched a career committed to liberty in religion. It was his very first libertarian concern; it was to be his last. ". . . pity me, and pray for liberty of conscience to all," Madison wrote in early 1774.[26]

John Leland

Finally, John Leland symbolizes the sort of founder who provided politically for the Bill of Rights, especially the First Amendment. A Roger Williams philosophy, a Jeffersonian rationale, and a Madisonian structure would all have been useless without popular support. Bailyn says that the revivalists supplied the troops for the Bill of Rights. History supports this view. Thomas J. Curry gives credit to Leland, the least well-known of these four founders. "Until Leland," Curry writes, "no religious thinker matched the thought on Church and State of Roger Williams of the previous century."[27]

In his critical role, Leland brought together in his own life and work the converging streams that made the lively experiment of religious freedom possible. Both rationalism and pietism, according to Mead, "were but obverse sides of a single movement which gathered enough power and momentum during the eighteenth century to sweep in religious freedom and the separation of church and state over the opposition of traditional orthodoxy in the churches."[28] The merging lines of dissent made possible, rather virtually demanded, the hitherto unheard of departure from the earlier concepts of the way religion regulates society. From the Constantinian symbiosis and the sacral society that came from it until this American impertinence, all the philosophical presuppositions, structures of religion and government, and awful bloodlettings had taken place in the bedroom of the incestuous marriage of church and state, a damnable union.

The fatal attraction that had brought the two together was the appeal to have the support of the flesh for the battles of the Lord. Theodosius the Great had issued decrees for the church that finalized the union begun by Constantine. The Holy Roman Empire had with its two swords concept propped up the ill-fated marriage that brought forth the progeny of crusades and inquisition. The Protestant Reformation brought timid reformulation of the relationship but dared not consider divorce. It took the combined and collective strength of the rationalists and the radical religionists to produce in the context of the American Revolution the religious freedom guarantees of the Constitution and the First Amendment. This was a new thing on the earth. It was, as many have suggested, the only distinctive contribution of the American Revolution.

William R. Estep traces convincingly the converging lines of dissent in his *Revolution within the Revolution.*[29] He lists as champions of the uncoerced conscience, under the rubric "rationalists," such thinkers as Marsilius de Padua (1325), Castellio, (1555), John Locke, Voltaire, David Hume, Rousseau and, finally, Jefferson and Madison. Estep's honor roll of religious radicals includes Balthasar Hubmaier (1524), Menno Simons (1539), John Smyth, Thomas Helwys, Leonard Busher, Roger Williams, John Clarke, Isaac Backus and, finally, Leland. They all shared the dangerous doctrine that Christ alone is Lord.

The peculiar individualism that sprang up on this continent was the product of these two strong streams of thought. It is curious that so many scholars have somehow been able to ignore one-sidedly the partnership. On one hand, the Religious Right, as if in "hoss blinds," has seen only the evangelical contribution. The fervor of the "enthusiasts," especially in colonial Virginia, was critical to shaping America's way in church-state relations. This is especially true since they were the most politically active and numerically significant segment of the citizenry. On the other hand, admirers of the enlightened have acted as if their third grade social studies text offered adequate and sufficient explanation of the roots of civil and religious liberties by attributing them solely to the work of Jefferson and Madison. Either partial perspective is in error. Many of today's church-state conflicts might be diminished with a more complete understanding of the beginnings of church-state separation.

No one more than Leland captures the color and people power of those who demanded guarantees for religious liberty and civil rights. He was a giant of a man, on the road, among the folks. The big red-haired preacher was stumping southwestern Virginia denouncing state support for religion. On one occasion an establishment clergyman challenged him, saying "the minister should get tax support so he will not have such a hard time preparing his sermons." Leland said, "I can expound the scriptures without any special preparation." "Let's see if you can," replied the clergyman, "What . . . would you do with Numbers 22:21, 'And Balaam . . . saddled his ass'?" Leland gave the setting and proceeded, "(1) Balaam, as a false prophet, represents a state hired clergy. (2) The saddle represents the enormous tax burden of their salaries. (3) The dumb ass represents the people who bear such a tax burden."[30] Leland's humor and logic prevailed. Leland argued effectively, "Experience, the best teacher, has informed us, that the fondness of magistrates to foster Christianity has done it more harm than all the persecutions ever did."[31] The Enlightenment leaders teamed up with the frontier preachers of a liberating religion. Together they brought about the first nation on the face of the earth with real religious freedom, full religious freedom for all, even those who are not religious.

Gaustad powerfully spotlights this important contribution of the First Amendment:

> With a breathtaking economy of words, the Constitution now provided a double guarantee: first, that Congress shall do nothing to favor, promote, or endow religion; second, that Congress shall take no step that would impede, obstruct, or penalize religion. Neither hindering nor helping, government would simply leave religion alone. And religious persons, no matter how zealous or idiosyncratic their beliefs, had nothing to fear from government, nor did irreligious persons, no matter how heretical or scandalous their opinions, have aught to fear.[32]

It was Leland and hundreds like him who turned the tide for religious freedom and even for adoption of the Bill of Rights. J. Bradley Creed in his 1986 dissertation on Leland summarizes his contribution as the political engineer of the First Amendment:

> While his doctrine of the human conscience was an essential contribution to the debate over church-state issues, he did not break much new ground in terms of political theory. His genius lay in his ability to take the insights of leading political figures and make them intelligible to the common man. At party meetings and in Fourth of July speeches, he effectively mixed the basic tenets of liberal democracy with strong doses of common-sense pragmatism and pietistic fervency. John Leland and the Separate Baptists of Virginia cannot be given sole credit for the ratification of the Federal Constitution, but their role was essential. They acted as a bridge between the more landed politicians and the general populace which clamored for greater protection of individual freedoms.[33]

Warren E. Burger, former Chief Justice of the United States, is correct in his recounting of history regarding the Bill of Rights. The delegates who met in Philadelphia had decided not to have a bill of rights. "But," as Burger reminds us, "when the Constitution went to the states for ratification, there was a popular demand for additional individual liberties."[34]

The Constitution just squeaked by in three key states' ratifying conventions. In each instance it was clear that the people were demanding a bill of rights. In Massachusetts and Virginia, the provision of a bill of rights became the condition for ratification without which there would have been no constitution. The final vote in Massachusetts was 187-168 in favor of ratification; a 10-vote shift would have defeated it. Champions of a bill of rights, Samuel Stillman and Isaac Backus, led the motley mix of 25 Baptists and other separatists who agreed to vote for ratification if they were promised a bill of rights. In Virginia it was 89 to 79. The deal was clear and unmistakable. Votes to ratify depended upon pledges to support a bill of rights. The partnership of Enlightenment and evangelicalism paid off. Radical religion and Renaissance rationalism collaborated successfully.

It was the people who wanted and got the Bill of Rights. If Americans were given the opportunity to ratify the Bill of Rights now, 200 years after the fact, would it happen? There is little evidence that Americans as a people even know the content of these freedom guarantees.

Many scholars suggest that no one cares if one is not upset by the apparent direction of the present Supreme Court. The first freedoms seem to be stricken from the books by justices too tuned to the temper of the times. Justice John Paul Stevens, dissenting to a ruling in favor of harsh mandatory sentences, accused the court majority of yielding to public opinion and government arguments with "strong political appeal." A. E. Dick Howard, distinguished law professor at the University of Virginia, commented "if that is a motive at the court today, it is sad. The court is supposed to be removed from politics, to be counter-majoritarian."

Legal laypersons must work at reading the Supreme Court. Just now, many are disturbed by that reading. Justice William Rehnquist's assessment of the "wall of separation between church and state," as "a metaphor based on a bad history" that should be "frankly and explicitly abandoned," is by any measure dangerous revisionism. The Chief Justice has missed the point of the no establishment clause. Justice Antonin Scalia's glib dismissal of the need for a compelling state interest before government can regulate religion is by any thoughtful standard an outburst of judicial activism. Following Scalia's lead, the court has abandoned the free exercise of religion. The Solicitor General's eagerness to set aside the long-held tests of a secular purpose, absence of advancing or inhibiting religion, and no excessive entanglement as the measure of any church-state law is a devastating challenge to religious liberty.

The folk of the frontier in their fear of an oppressive state and corrupt church demanded protection from both. As Senator Sam J. Ervin, Jr. said, "When religion controls government, political liberty dies; and when government controls religion, religious liberty perishes."[35]

Some religionists today see the First Amendment as a one-way street designed only to protect religion from the state. These revisers hold that the Bill of Rights restricts and limits only government. While they may have the letter of the law on their side, the spirit of religious liberty and its corollary, the separation of church and state, are much broader.

Edwin M. Yoder, Jr., would agree with Madison in his theological pessimism regarding religionists. He writes:

> Ours is a world in which hot-eyed people are on the prowl, seeking to thrust their creeds into your space and mine. If they had their way, would America escape the fate of Persia, Lebanon or Ireland? Optimists obviously believe that Americans are immune to the pitfalls of spiritual pride that have ripped those societies apart. I'd as soon not run the risk.[36]

Hence we have, "Congress shall make no law respecting an establishment of religion or prohibiting the free exercise thereof. . . ."

Notes

1. "Bill Moyers' World of Ideas," transcript of Public Affairs Television telecast, May 13, 1990 (New York: Journal Graphics, Inc., 1990), p. 3.

2. Stephen Strickland, ed., *Hugo Black at the Supreme Court* (New York: Bobbs-Merrill, 1967), p. 253.

3. Charles Kuralt, *On the Road* (New York: G. P. Putnam's Sons, 1985), p. 267.

4. Oscar S. Straus, *Roger Williams: The Pioneer of Religious Liberty* (New York: The Century Co., 1894), p. 74.

5. Glenn W. LaFantasie, ed., The *Correspondence of Roger Williams* (Providence, R.I.: Brown University Press, 1988), pp. 104, 105.

6. Perry Miller, *Roger Williams* (Indianapolis: Bobbs-Merrill, 1952), p. 26.

7. Straus, p. 233.

8. Kuralt, 267.

9. Jefferson to Madison, Dec. 8, 1784, *The Federal Edition of the Works of Jefferson,* IV, P. L. Ford. ed., pp. 381-5.

10. From "An Act for Establishing Religious Freedom," *The Papers of Thomas Jefferson,* II, ed. Julian P. Boyd (Princeton: Princeton University Press, 1950), p. 546.

11. William Lee Miller, "The Bicentennial of the Virginia Statute," *The Christian Century,* Dec. 18-25, 1985, p. 1171.

12. *The Papers of Thomas Jefferson,* p. 545.

13. Quoted in Joy Hakim, "A Forgotten Fight for Religious Freedom," *Wall Street Journal,* July 26, n.yr., p. 26.

14. *Wallace v. Jaffree,* 472 U.S. 38, 107 (1985), (Rehnquist, J., dissenting).

15. Ibid. at 99.

16. See Douglas Laycock's thorough and persuasive article "'Nonpreferential' Aid to Religion: A False Claim About Original Intent," *William and Mary Law Review,* Vol. 27:875, 1986.

17. Anson Phelps Stokes and Leo Pfeffer, *Church and State in the United States* (rev. one vol. ed.; New York: Harper & Row, 1964), p. 98.

18. Harry A. Blackmun, "The First Amendment and Its Religion Clauses—Where Are We? Where Are We Going?" Remarks delivered at the National Archives, Washington, D.C., June 23, 1987.

19. William Lee Miller, *The First Liberty. Religion and the American Republic*

(New York: Alfred A. Knopf, 1986), as reviewed by Sam Rabinove in *Judaism: A Quarterly Journal of Jewish Life and Thought,* XXXV, No. 4 (Fall 1986), p. 502.

20. Fred Barbash. "A Man for 1987," *Washington Post,* March 15, 1987.

21. Ibid.

22. Ibid.

23. Ibid.

24. William R. Estep, *Revolution within the Revolution: The First Amendment in Historical Context, 1612-1789* (Grand Rapids, MI: Wm. B. Eerdmans, 1990), p. 168.

25. Merrill D. Peterson, *James Madison* (New York: Newsweek, 1974), p. 26.

26. Edwin Gaustad, "Religion, the Constitution, and the Founding Fathers," The Whitworth-Muldrow Lecture for 1987 (Rome, Georgia: Shorter College, 1987), p. 6.

27. Thomas J. Curry, *The First Freedoms: Church and State in America to the Passage of the First Amendment* (New York: Oxford University Press, 1986), p. 182.

28. Sidney E. Mead, *Lively Experiment: The Shaping of Christianity in America* (New York: Harper & Row, 1963), p. 38.

29. Estep.

30. Joseph M. Dawson, *Baptists and the American Republic* (Nashville: Broadman Press, 1956), p. 97.

31. John Leland, *The Writings of John Leland* (New York: Association Press and the *New York Times,* 1969), p. 278.

32. Gaustad, pp. 11-12.

33. J. Bradley Creed, "American Prophet of Religious Individualism." Ph.D. diss., Southwestern Baptist Theological Seminary, 1986, p. 200.

34. Warren E. Burger, "What It Means to Us," *Parade Magazine,* January 27, 1991. pp. 4-5.

35. Sam J. Ervin, Jr., "The Meaning of the First Amendment." Address in the United States Senate, April 23, 1971.

36. Edwin M. Yoder, Jr., "Court Treats Religion as Madison Intended," *News and Observer* (Raleigh, NC), July 19, 1989.

Baptists and the Establishment Clause: Our Commitment and Challenge

Melissa Rogers

The first ten words of the First Amendment to the United States Constitution are "Congress shall make no law respecting an establishment of religion." This clause, known as the Establishment Clause, prohibits the government from advancing religion, preferring one religion over another, or preferring religion over irreligion. It prevents, for example, the government from aiding any one religion or all religions, or favoring Episcopalians over Baptists or Catholics over Jews. The purpose of the Establishment Clause is to guarantee Americans' religious liberty. By putting the Establishment Clause first in the Bill of Rights, the founders demonstrated that it was of the utmost importance.

Unfortunately, the Establishment Clause often does not enjoy this kind of respect today. Indeed, many contemporary Christians react negatively to it, arguing that it places unnecessary limits on religion and even undermines religious freedom. These Christians usually look kindly on the First Amendment's other religion clause, the Free Exercise Clause, and the Religious Freedom Restoration Act (RFRA) that supports it.[1] These documents prevent the government from inhibiting religious practice. Many contemporary Christians credit the Free Exercise Clause with creating a culture in which religion has flourished and blame the Establishment Clause for everything from rising crime rates to declining SAT scores.

Rather than play favorites with the First Amendment's religion clauses, Baptists traditionally have defended both as essential to religious liberty. Both clauses guard against equally dangerous alternatives: government advancement of religion and government discouragement of religion. It is

Melissa Rogers is associate general counsel for the Baptist Joint Committee on Public Affairs in Washington, D.C. This paper was presented at "Called to Responsible Freedom: A Conference on Baptist Distinctives," at Green Lake, Wisconsin, August 1996.

only by heeding the dictates of the Establishment and Free Exercise clauses that government steers a neutral course. And, when the state is neutral toward religion, citizens are truly free to make meaningful choices about matters of faith.

Baptists, therefore, have not complained about the limits the Establishment Clause places on church-state interaction; rather, we have championed them. In this sense, we have practiced responsible freedom. We traditionally have understood, for example, that we cannot require or even allow our public schools to organize prayers for our children if we want families and churches to control this sacred act. We cannot accept tax money for religious activities if we expect to have independence from government and dependence on a higher power. We cannot legislate our way to a Christian nation.

Our forebears demanded religious freedom when they lobbied for adoption of the First Amendment, containing both the Establishment and Free Exercise clauses. Our challenge is to uphold this freedom and interpret it for a new age.

Commitment in the Past

The Constitution produced by the Constitutional Convention of 1787 contained no bill of rights. The Federalists, those supporting ratification of the Constitution, argued that such a specification of individual rights was not needed. The Constitution limited the federal government to the specific powers enumerated in the Constitution, they insisted. So, the reasoning went, any powers not specifically given to the federal government in that document (including the power to enact laws respecting an establishment of religion) were powers the government simply could not exercise.

This did not satisfy Baptists. We were a minority faith then, and as is typical of minorities, we were skeptical of reassurances from the powers that be. We knew we had better get it in writing. Baptists and other dissenters had suffered at the hands of church-state unions on these shores, a tradition carried over from England and Europe. For example, Roger Williams did not escape religious intolerance when he journeyed from his native England to the American colonies in 1631. Williams, who called for a "hedge or wall of separation between the garden of the church and the wilderness of the world," was banished from Massachusetts Bay Colony in 1635 for his heretical stand against unions of church and state.[2]

Similar forms of religious persecution and discrimination were common practice during our country's early years. For example, colonial Virginia imprisoned about fifty Baptists for "crimes" such as preaching without ordination by the established church, the Church of England. Virginia Baptists also were indicted for refusing to attend services of the Anglican church. Other offenses punishable by the state included blasphemy, sacrilege, and criticism of the doctrine of the Trinity. It also was a crime for any minister not licensed by the established church to perform marriages. Virginia citizens were required by law to tithe to support Anglican ministers and pay taxes to support the costs of building and repairing Anglican churches.[3]

Thus Baptists were keenly aware of the dangers of church-state alliances and the strong temptation for the sacred and the secular to join forces. Without an explicit barrier to such alliances, minority religions would continue to suffer persecution and discrimination for their religion.

So Baptists did what was required—they showed some political muscle. Under the guidance of a few great leaders and many dedicated followers, Baptists organized effectively, argued persuasively, and ultimately exerted a profound impact on the life of our nation.

One such leader was Isaac Backus. Backus, a Massachusetts Baptist minister and firm believer in church-state separation, was a natural political organizer. Backus used every means available at the time to communicate his message of religious freedom: tracts, petitions, letters to newspapers, public debate, and private letters. At the time of the American Revolution, Backus cannily argued that the religious taxes placed on citizens were as illegal as the British Parliament's taxation of America. He said, "All America are alarmed at the tea tax, though, if they please, they can avoid it by not buying the tea; but we have no such liberty."[4]

Another Baptist leader key to the disestablishment effort was John Leland. Like Backus, Leland was an evangelist and a native of Massachusetts, although he also ministered to citizens of Virginia in the mid-1770s. When Leland learned that the Constitution as drafted by the Constitutional Convention contained no bill of rights, he used his influence to ensure that the document ultimately would include one. Leland was particularly concerned about the damaging tendency of the state to promote religion. He warned, "Experience . . . has informed us that the fondness of magistrates to foster Christianity has done it more harm than all the persecutions ever did."[5]

Due in no small part to the work of these Baptists, Congress subsequently passed, and the states ratified, the First Amendment, which declares that "Congress shall make no law respecting an establishment of religion, or prohibiting the free exercise thereof." In later years Supreme Court Justice Hugo Black, a former Baptist Sunday school teacher, offered a good description of the meaning of this clause:

> The "establishment of religion" clause of the First Amendment means at least this: Neither a state nor the Federal Government can set up a church. Neither can pass laws which aid one religion, aid all religions, or prefer one religion over another. . . . No tax in any amount, large or small, can be levied to support any religious activities or institutions, whatever they may be called, or whatever form they may adopt to teach or practice religion. . . . In the words of Jefferson, the clause against establishment of religion by laws was intended to erect a "wall of separation between Church and State."[6]

Clarification in the Present

Given the illustrious origins of the Establishment Clause, how can we explain the fact that it is villainized by some today? Certainly there have been a few misguided court decisions that have applied the Establishment Clause in a wooden fashion, actually undermining religious liberty. But, by and large, the courts have faithfully applied the clause. Most attacks on the Establishment Clause are due not to its substance or application, but to simple misunderstanding.

One such misunderstanding surrounds the issue of political participation by people of faith. For example, you often hear that the Establishment Clause reduces religious people to second-class citizens because it does not allow them to participate fully in the political process.

But Backus and Leland certainly were no second-class citizens or political wallflowers. These Baptist leaders correctly sensed that, while government should not coerce citizens on religious matters, there was no need to separate religious fervor from political action. Indeed, their politics were fueled by their faith.

Some would argue that perhaps the Establishment Clause was properly understood in the early days of our nation, but in modern times it has been misinterpreted so as to fence religious people out of the public square. But the Establishment Clause did not bar Baptist George Truett from giving his historic address on religious liberty from the steps of our nation's capitol in 1920. It did not prohibit Pat Robertson from running for president of the United States or Jesse Jackson from speaking about his religious convictions at hearings on Capitol Hill. The Establishment Clause did not keep Louis Farrakhan from preaching to those gathered for the Million Man March on the mall in Washington, D.C. It did not even prohibit Ralph Reed from holding Christian Coalition rallies in meeting rooms at the United States House of Representatives. Properly understood, the Establishment Clause is a wall prohibiting church-state unions but an open gate to political participation by people of faith.

Another frequent misunderstanding is that only the Establishment Clause requires church-state separation and that this separation somehow threatens religion. In other words, some tie the doctrine of church-state separation to the Establishment Clause and link religious liberty with the Free Exercise Clause. Then they pit one clause against the other, associating the Establishment Clause with secularism and the Free Exercise Clause with religiosity.

This is a fundamental misunderstanding. Both clauses require the separation of church and state, which is so essential to religious freedom. The Free Exercise Clause commands church-state separation by ensuring that government takes care not to burden religion with unnecessary regulation. The Establishment Clause commands church-state separation by requiring the government to refrain from attempts to turn religion into a creature of the state. Without both elements of this separation, government and religion would find themselves in a rather cozy, unhealthy relationship. Abiding by both clauses maintains a wise distance between church and state, which helps to maintain religion's independence and integrity.

Challenges for the Future

The future of the Establishment Clause is uncertain. Misapprehensions surrounding the clause, together with a good bit of election-year political posturing, have triggered an almost unprecedented assault on the Establishment Clause in the current Congress. A wide array of legislative proposals seek government subsidization and sponsorship of religion. As that renowned constitutional scholar Yogi Berra would say, "It's déjà vu all over again." After fighting against such church-state alliances in the past, Baptists must wage the battle once again.

One of the many legislative proposals that takes aim at the Establishment Clause is the Community Renewal Act of 1996. The act is touted as a means of reviving communities by creating economic opportunity and fostering moral renewal. The problem arises in the means by which the act intends to "empower" communities. The act provides for the funneling of tax dollars to pervasively sectarian organizations that may require beneficiaries "to actively participate in religious practice, worship and instruction." Additionally, in order to qualify as one of the "renewal communities," a community must employ a voucher scheme to aid private and parochial schools.

There will be no need for relatively limited bills such as the Community Renewal Act, however, if the constitutional amendment proposed by Representative Dick Armey, a Republican from Texas, is ratified. The Armey amendment has an appealing name, the "Religious Equality" Amendment, and is couched in benign language. But it is a radical measure that would knock an enormous hole in the wall separating church and state. For example, the amendment broadly authorizes, if not requires, the government to subsidize pervasively sectarian organizations and activities of all types.

Unfortunately, many simply do not understand the dangers associated with government funding of religion as contemplated by both the Community Renewal Act and the proposed constitutional amendment. First, individuals, not their government, should choose whether to send their money to Baptist academies, Catholic secondary schools, Mormon missions, or Nation of Islam projects. Using tax money to fund religion is a violation of conscience. Taxpayers rightfully expect the state to remain neutral toward religion rather than selecting various faith groups as government-approved beneficiaries.

A second problem with government funding for religion is what we might call the "you don't get something for nothing" rule. Like most money, government money comes with strings attached. Religious organizations that receive public funds will be subject to intrusive government regulation, accounting, and monitoring.

Third, relying on government handouts will compromise religion's integrity and threaten its historic role as an independent critic of government. Religion's voice has often been heard in the halls of state precisely because it curries no favor there.

Despite the radical changes the Armey amendment proposes, its supporters cleverly insist that it would not rewrite the Establishment Clause. Instead, they argue that the amendment would restore the original meaning of the Establishment Clause, which was simply to bar the government from establishing a national church or preferring one religion over another. In other words, they insist that the Establishment Clause was not intended to prohibit government from aiding religion, as long as it aids all religions equally without preference.

Records of the debate over the Bill of Rights reveal, however, that the founders considered and rejected versions of the First Amendment that would have permitted such nonpreferential aid. For example, Congress rejected versions of the First Amendment that would have merely prohibited the establishment of a national religion or the preference of one religious sect over another.[7] Instead, Congress passed and the states ratified a broad prohibition on any laws respecting an establishment of religion.

Moreover, contrary to the suggestions of those who support the Armey amendment, it is impossible for the government to aid all religions equally without preference. The limited public purse cannot fund the myriad religious groups in our country. Thus, faith groups will compete within the government funding process. This process usually has a lot to do with political horse-trading, seniority, partisanship, and reelection and little to do with a careful consideration of the merits of various projects. All too often, only majority religions will "reap the spoils," and religion as a whole will be debased in the process.

Other defects of the Armey amendment include the fact that it opens the door to practices such as officially sanctioned school prayer and other government endorsements of religion. This, of course, endangers key Establishment Clause principles.

Hearings have been held on both the Community Renewal Act and the Armey amendment. It is unlikely that either will pass in this Congress, but they will certainly become election issues and be revived for consideration by lawmakers again in the new Congress. If the Establishment Clause and religious liberty are to continue, we must articulate for our generation the serious problems inherent in such proposals.

The Establishment Clause is not simply the law of our land. It is an outgrowth of our history in which Baptists suffered for their beliefs and led the way to religious liberty for all. It is a reflection of our theology, which prizes the freedom to choose in religious matters. For these reasons, Baptists should defend and protect the Establishment Clause.

Notes

1. In its decision in *Employment Division v. Smith,* 494 U.S. 872 (1990), the United States Supreme Court dramatically reduced the constitutional protection provided by the Free Exercise Clause. Congress responded by passing the Religious Freedom Restoration Act, a statute, to restore robust protection to the right to religious exercise.

2. Williams later established Rhode Island as a haven for full religious liberty and founded the first Baptist church in North America there.

3. Leonard Levy, *The Establishment Clause: Religion and the First Amendment* (New York, 1986), 1-4.

4. Ibid., 2.

5. Edwin Gaustad, "A Disestablished Society: Origins of the First Amendment,"

Journal of Church and State 11 (1969): 414 (quoting *The Writings of the Late Elder John Leland*).

6. *Everson v. Board of Education,* 330 U.S. 1, 15 (1947).

7. The House of Representatives rejected a version of the First Amendment that would have stated that "The civil rights of none shall be abridged on account of religious belief or worship, nor shall any national religion be established . . ." (Levy, *Establishment Clause,* 75). The Senate rejected motions that would have read, "Congress shall make no law establishing one religious sect or society in preference to others . . ." (Levy, *Establishment Clause,* 82). The Senate also rejected a draft that would have stated that "Congress shall make no law establishing any particular denomination of religion in preference to another . . ." (ibid.).

The Ebb and Flow of Free Exercise

Oliver Thomas

The year was 1776. Young "Jemy" Madison—delegate from Orange, Virginia—was concerned over a word in the proposed Virginia Declaration of Rights. The word *toleration* appeared in Article 16: "[A]ll men are equally entitled to the fullest *toleration* in the exercise of their religion, according to the dictates of conscience . . ." (emphasis added). Madison liked neither the tone (too condescending) nor the scope (too narrow) of the word. He preferred the stronger, broader term *free exercise.* By guaranteeing the free exercise of religion, Virginia could take a giant step toward putting all citizens on a level playing field with respect to religion. Short of disestablishing the Anglican Church—which he hadn't the votes to do—this was the best Madison could hope for.

But, how to do it? Being of diminutive stature and voice, Madison knew better than to offer the amendment himself. After all, the distinguished elder statesman George Mason had authored the original draft and would be on the other side. No, Madison would be smarter than that. Therefore, he chose the orator's orator to offer his amendment, the one man he could count on to outtalk Mason: Patrick Henry.

So, with Henry leading the way, the Virginia Declaration of Rights was amended to read: "All men are equally entitled to the free exercise of religion, according to the dictates of conscience. . . ." A decade later the language resurfaced in Congressman Madison's proposed amendments to the United States Constitution, and the world was changed forever.[1]

The free exercise of religion has long been an American ideal. Even before Mr. Madison amended the Constitution, numerous colonies had protected the exercise of religion. New York's Constitution of 1777 was typical:

Oliver Thomas is special counsel, National Council of Churches, and was formerly counsel to the Baptist Joint Committee on Public Affairs. This paper was presented at "Called to Responsible Freedom: A Conference on Baptist Distinctives," at Green Lake, Wisconsin, August 1996.

The free exercise and enjoyment of religious profession and worship, without discrimination or preference, shall forever be allowed to all mankind: Provided that the liberty of conscience shall not be so construed as to excuse acts of licentiousness, or justify practices inconsistent with the peace and safety of the state.

Similarly, New Hampshire protected every individual's right to freely exercise his or her religion "provided he [*sic*] doth not disturb the public peace, or disturb others in their religious worship."[2] The Continental Congress also took free exercise seriously and provided for Quakers and other conscientious objectors in the nation's first conscription law. But that is only half the story. In reality, our practice has often failed to match our preachments. Religious persecution has plagued this nation throughout much of its history—from the Salem Witch Trials of the seventeenth century to the persecution of Jews in the eighteenth century to the "Bible Wars" inflicted on Roman Catholics in the nineteenth century to the persecution of Mormons and Jehovah's Witnesses in more modern times. As late as the 1960s, Jews and Catholics were still the objects of widespread discrimination.

Then, after more than a decade of relative peace, the Supreme Court rendered a decision that again exposed the nation to the possibility of religious persecution.[3] In *Employment Division v. Smith,* the court jettisoned nearly three decades of legal precedent, reducing the Constitution's free exercise clause to little more than a guarantee of equal protection. No longer could religious groups and individuals invoke the Constitution unless their particular religious group had been discriminated against. Even laws that outlawed core religious practices (such as the use of peyote by Native Americans) could not be challenged as long as the prohibition applied evenly to all groups. Religion had been moved to the back of the constitutional bus.

Fortunately, Congress and the president can provide more rights to citizens than the Supreme Court is willing to find in the federal Constitution. The Voting Rights Act is a good example of this congressional power. The Supreme Court was unwilling to strike down literacy tests under the Equal Protection Clause, so Congress provided minority citizens with more rights by outlawing literacy tests by statute.

In 1993, after three years of legislative struggle, Congress passed and the president signed the Religious Freedom Restoration Act (RFRA), the most important legislation affecting religion since the passage of the First Amendment.[4] Supported by a broad-based coalition of more than sixty religious and civil liberties groups, RFRA guarantees citizens the right to exercise their religion free from government interference except in cases where a "compelling interest," such as health and safety, is jeopardized. Even then, the government must show that it is pursuing its interests in the manner least restrictive of religion.

Three years after RFRA's passage, free exercise rights are enjoying an unprecedented level of protection.[5] First, the Clinton Administration has established a Justice Department task force to ensure that each of the federal agencies remains in full compliance with RFRA. Each federal agency has at least one attorney assigned to safeguarding religious concerns.

Second, the Internal Revenue Service has established excellent relations with the religious community through the use of an ad hoc committee of church lawyers chaired by the Baptist Joint Committee's counsel, Brent Walker, and myself.

Third, the Equal Employment Opportunity Commission has successfully completed its first ever class-action lawsuit based on religion. At issue in the case (now settled) was Dillard's Department Store's "no excuses" Saturday/Sunday work policy.

Fourth, the Justice Department has for the first time successfully defended the right of a church to refuse to reimburse a trustee in bankruptcy for tithes and offerings received in good faith from one of its members.

Fifth, at the request of the president, the Department of Education has sent a presidential directive to every school district in America declaring that schools should not be "religion-free zones" and asking that students be allowed to exercise their faith freely in schools as long as they are not disruptive and do not harass or intimidate others.

Finally, even the federal prisons are taking extra measures to accommodate the religious needs of prisoners.

Despite all of this, some in the conservative Christian community assert that Christians are "victims" in today's society and that the public square of America has been stripped naked of religious influences. For this there can be only one response: Poppycock.

Far from naked, the public square of America is—if anything—a bit overdressed in the garb of religion. For starters, the president, vice president, and three highest-ranking members of Congress are Baptists. And eight of the nine justices of the Supreme Court are active in a church or synagogue. For as long as I can remember, the Reverend Billy Graham has prayed at our presidential inaugurations, and each day Congress and the Supreme Court begin their sessions with prayer.

On Capitol Hill, there has been a proliferation of religion in the last thirty years.[6] Groups like the Christian Coalition and the National Conference of Catholic Bishops wield tremendous influence on government. Is there a better witness than the number of Republican presidential hopefuls who lined up to seek the Coalition's blessing at its last (1996) convention?

Religious leaders of all types are frequently called upon to testify before Congress and the state legislatures on a multitude of international and domestic concerns. Even when uninvited, these religious activists are present, influencing the political process with a high degree of success on issues ranging from Dial-a-Porn to welfare reform. I speak not only as an observer, but as a frequent participant in these activities.

Finally, in the most fundamental of all public arenas—the streets—religion is alive and well. Operation Rescue is but one example of a tradition of civil disobedience that has included the abolitionist, temperance, civil rights, and peace movements.

A more accurate assessment would seem to be that religion enjoys a prominent, if not favored, role in American society. Our churches are tax exempt; gifts to our ministries are tax deductible; we don't have to file financial disclosure forms as do other nonprofit organizations, nor do we have to file for recognition as tax-exempt entities. We are protected from routine audits and investigations by the Internal Revenue Service, and our clergy's housing allowances are exempt from taxation. Religious institutions are exempt from key provisions of major civil rights legislation; we have special exemptions in both the National Labor Relations Act and Selective Service laws; we are exempt from key provisions of the Social Security tax, the Lobby Disclosure Act, and countless state and local regulations, including property and sales taxes. On top of that, our social service agencies, hospitals, universities, and other institutions can obtain millions of dollars in federal grants to assist us in providing housing, health care, food, higher education, and other worthwhile services. In fact, the nation's largest religious social welfare agency receives more than half of its budget from the federal government!

All of this is to say that the exercise of religion in the United States is free indeed. Yes, there are occasional indiscretions of a judicial or legislative body, and organizations like the Baptist Joint Committee and the National Council of Churches must continue to monitor the government to ensure that the free exercise rights of citizens are protected. But, by and large, the American people are doing a remarkable job of accommodating the needs of thousands of different religious groups—such a good job, in fact, that Jemy Madison would be proud.

Notes

1. See generally William Lee Miller, *First Liberty: Religion and the American Republic* (New York: Knopf, 1986).

2. See Michael McConnell, "The Origins and Historic Understanding of Free Exercise of Religion," 103 *Harvard Law Review* 1409 (May 1990).

3. See Douglas Laycock, "The Remnants of Free Exercise," 1990 *Supreme Court Review* 1; Michael McConnell, "Free Exercise Revisionism and the Smith Decision," 57 *University of Chicago Law Review* 1109 (1990).

4. Douglas Laycock and Oliver Thomas, "Interpreting the Religious Freedom Restoration Act," 73 *University of Texas Law Review* 209 (December 1994).

5. Two recent federal courts of appeal have upheld the constitutionality of the Religious Freedom Restoration Act. See *Flores v. City of Boerne* (5th Cir. 1996); *Sasnett v. Sullivan* (7th Cir. 1996).

6. See Allen D. Hertzke, *Representing God in Washington: The Role of Religious Lobbies in the American Polity* (Knoxville: University of Tennessee Press, 1988).

Introduction to Part V.
The Tensions of Experience and Witness in Contemporary Baptist Life

The Baptist spirit of independence encourages Baptist people to think and act both theologically and personally. As long as the Baptist spirit is alive, those who in some way define themselves within its ranks will wrestle with the personal and public issues of life as if they matter to their faith experience because they are convinced that they do. In this section a variety of Baptist leaders, laypersons, and commentators provide glimpses of what it means to them to be Baptist, to function as Baptists, and to remain faithful to Baptist principles as they understand them.

The articles in this section are not written from preeminently scholarly perspectives. They are, instead, confessional in the best Baptist sense of that word. Some are sermons, others are commentaries, and still others are personal reflections.

On January 19, 1993, Bill Moyers addressed twelve hundred Baptists at an Inaugural Prayer Service at Washington's First Baptist Church. President Bill Clinton and Vice President Al Gore, both Baptists, were among the congregation as honored guests. As a Baptist, and as a lifelong participant in public life, Moyers articulated his understanding of what it means to be faithful in the public arena and what being a Baptist has to contribute. He acknowledged the problem of balance in public and private life and offered hope that balance can be achieved.

Lawrence Sherman was raised in a Baptist home but did not affirm his faith or participation as a Baptist until well into his adult years. At his baptism he chose to participate in an ancient practice of the church—namely, testifying to his faith when he was baptized. His sermon, preached immediately after his baptism, struck a responsive chord with many. It is a powerful example of lay leadership both in experiencing and in claiming the freedom and the responsibility of the Baptist faith life.

Denton Lotz, in his role as leader of the Baptist World Alliance, perceives the delicate balance of Baptist life from a global perspective. Among the challenges he sees most clearly is the need to provide a faithful witness of inclusion and justice against the common expression of racism. His statement, first directed to a gathering of world Baptist leaders, reminds us of the balance between life in fellowship and life as members of a world community seeking the equilibrium of justice, equality, and freedom.

Shirlee Taylor Haizlip is the daughter and granddaughter of Baptist ministers. Her early life experience in the fellowship of Baptists left a powerful imprint. This article, first published in the secular press *(New York Times)*, is a strong personal statement offered in the public arena. It brings an insightful prophetic focus to the trauma of the church burnings that have become the continuing news story of the 1990s. But it also contains a touching, intimate confession as well. It reminds us that the balance of Baptist life is not achieved only within the boundaries of fellowship among Baptists, but amid the consciousness of the extremes of violence and hatred. Despite the somber events that inspired her article, it speaks with a tenderness of a Baptist heart.

A brief essay by Ralph Reavis is taken from a more lengthy unpublished paper on the development of black Baptist churches in Virginia. It articulates the formative moments of black church organization and reminds us of the tensions that were created—and still exist—between Baptists of different racial backgrounds.

Since preaching is at the heart of Baptist experience in faith and worship, we have included two sermons. The first is by Norman Johnson, who preached at the end of the Conference on Baptist Distinctives. He takes an ancient text that deals with exclusion and boundaries and examines the consequences of division. He reminds us that boundaries have a profound effect on those they contain within and on those they shut out. The second sermon was preached by Daniel Weiss, general secretary of the ABC/USA, on the occasion of his formal installation in 1989. It issues a stirring call to unity in witness, and its analysis of much that inhibits Baptists from fulfilling their mission remains true today, despite the passage of the intervening eight years.

Vincent L. Wimbush provides a perspective on scriptural interpretation which may help Baptists move beyond traditional debates regarding biblical truth. In Wimbush's view, the specific biblical record often becomes more or less significant to the degree that it connects with the experience of the reader. When the biblical story becomes *our* story, and when our story finds a focus in the biblical experience, biblical truth becomes more personally vivid and our lives are empowered by the enduring authority of the texts. This essay will reward the reader with new possibilities for approaching the Bible.

James H. Evans accepted the challenging role of summing up the broad themes of the (1996) "Called to Responsible Freedom: A Conference on Baptist Distinctives." His contribution to this work, "Living under God's Rule: Theological Reflections on Baptist Distinctives," is rooted in that nearly extemporaneous summation and is here presented with the added benefit of time for thoughtful reflection and refinement of his conference insights.

These articles serve to remind us that the challenge of maintaining balance in Baptist life—in belief, faith, witness, life, public activity, and private devotion—is an ongoing one. And it is one more likely to be recorded in personal lives than in public statements. These articles serve as an invitation to Baptists and to all persons of faith to continue to walk "in the Spirit's tether" and to strive mightily to exhibit what grace has instilled.

No Room for Bystanders

Bill Moyers

It is providential to me that Marion Hays is here this evening. Many Baptist heroes stirred my imagination when I was young, from John Bunyan and John Milton to Roger Williams and William Carey, from Adoniram Judson and Annie Armstrong to E. Y. Mullins and George Truett. But they were dead or distant heroes, admired from afar. Marion's husband Brooks was the first Baptist hero I met face-to-face.[1]

Brooks' courageous stand during the 1958 school desegregation crisis cost him his seat as Congressman from Little Rock but it won for him a place in legions of hearts. "This is Mr. Hays," said Martin Luther King when he introduced Brooks to a friend; "He has suffered with us." For Brooks, Christianity was about challenge, not comfort, and politics was a parish where one tried to serve the poor and powerless. Senator Sam Ervin said Brooks possessed an "understanding heart." It overflowed with a love that embraced even his enemies—even Orval Faubus and Richard Nixon. And he was a cheerful crusader, with humor for a lance. Like many of us he resisted the handcuffs of ideology. During his last campaign he pointed to the dog at his side and said, "Old Fergus here, who goes with me every day, is a liberal when he's sniffing through the bushes looking for a rabbit, but a conservative when he buries the bone."

I met Brooks when he was president of the Southern Baptist Convention and spoke in chapel at Southwestern Baptist Theological Seminary where I was soon to graduate. I maneuvered to be the one who drove Marion and

Bill Moyers is a theologically trained (Southern) Baptist layman and journalist. After serving President Lyndon Johnson as press secretary, he returned to broadcasting and most recently has been involved with Public Affairs Television, whose programs have had wide audiences. His programming has included a number of religious and biblical themes, as well as programs focused on religious institutional affairs. This address was delivered on January 19 at the Inauguration Eve Prayer Service cosponsored by the Baptist Joint Committee on Public Affairs and the First Baptist Church of the City of Washington, D.C. It was first printed in *Report from the Capital*, February 1993, and is reprinted by permission.

Brooks to the airport after his speech. When he learned that I had studied journalism at the University of Texas and worked for Senator Lyndon Johnson in both Austin and Washington, he put his hand on my shoulder and said: "When you finish seminary you ought to give thought to government; public service can be a calling, too." He admitted that politics could be hell sometimes, but—and he grinned that long snaggly grin of his—"after working for LBJ it should be a pleasure to wrestle with the devil."

I never forgot his hand on my shoulder, never forgot his counsel; and often through the years I have been reminded of that favorite passage of his from Isaiah, where "you who pursue deliverance, who seek the Lord," are urged to "look to the rock from which you were hewn, and to the quarry from which you were digged." Or as my own rough translation from the Hebrew says, "Remember your roots."

This is what brings us here tonight. We come not as Democrat or Republican, male or female, black or white, politician or journalist, but as members of an extended family of faith. And we are here to remember our roots. Baptists hold dear the contention of that early forbear who said that "the magistrate is not by virtue of his office to meddle with religion on matters of conscience, to force or compel anyone to this or that form of religion or doctrine, but to leave religion free to every individual con-science." That conviction is sacred to us. Yet we do not believe that separation of church and state means the hermetic exclusion of religion from politics. We believe Harvey Cox got it right when he said that in secular society "politics does what metaphysics once did; it brings unity and meaning to human life and thought." And we agree with Jim Wallis that "the relationship between politics and morality is absolutely vital to the future," that our challenge is to take the rhetoric of "values," "vision," and "new covenant" that pervaded our recent election and see if there is common ground for action.

Baptists have much to offer the conversation of democracy, beginning with candor about our own diversity and raucous history. Baptists have been to the left of the American establishment—and to the right. Jesse Jackson is a Baptist, so is Jesse Helms. Baptists defended slavery, and Baptists agitated to end it. Some black Baptist churches today are precincts of the Democratic Party, while in some white churches GOP stands for God's Own Preserve. Some Baptists read the Bible as if it were a Triple A roadmap to Armageddon; others find it a spiritual codebook to the mysteries and miracles of the Kingdom within. Millions of Baptists see American culture as the enemy. Millions of others joyfully proclaim that we are part and parcel of the show. Onlookers shake their heads at how people so disputatious could be defined by a common name; those of us who wear it shrug our shoulders at the anomalies and schisms and go on punching (usually each other).

We are Baptist for many reasons. The experience is so much a part of my story that I would be unable to explain myself to my grandson without it. Newman McLarry's ringing call to repentance took me into the waters of baptism when I was 12, and Brownlow Hasting's quiet appeals to reason took me back into those waters six years later. Between Bible drills the burly contractor who doubled as our Sunday School teacher, Bill Price, let us slug him in the stomach to prove that hard work produced a hard body. One of our sopranos sang off-key to the entire choir but no one cared because she brought the best custard pies to dinners-on-the-ground. These may seem banal recollections, but I learned about humanity in that Baptist church, learned about frailty and forgiveness and fellowship, and if the anecdotes are unremarkable, the journey wasn't.

I also learned about democracy in that church. It was the very embodiment of home rule. In deciding church affairs every believer had an equal voice. Every leader called to office—whether pastor, deacon, or teacher—was subject to a vote of the congregation; and leaders were expected to be servants, not rulers. It was the pew, and not the pulpit, that we thought should be exalted. This leveling meant we fought a lot. My father said Adam and Eve must have been the first Democrats because only Democrats could mess up Paradise, and he was certain Cain and Abel were the first Baptists because they introduced fratricide to the Bible. But faith called us to a public stand and there was no place in our politics and religion for bystanders. It never occurred to us to ask the Irishman's question, "Is this a private fight, or can *anyone* get into it?" We knew from our past that politics is where liberty is saved or lost, where issues are decided, justice mediated, and values defended. Neither church nor state is served by anemic democracy. So Baptists plunge into the thick of the fray. And we do so with an ardor for equality that springs from the hot coals of faith.

At the core of our faith is what we call soul competency—the competence of the individual before God. Created with the imprint of divinity, from the mixed clay of earth, we are endowed with the capacity to choose, to be (as my brother James Dunn puts it)[2] "response-able," a grown-up before God, making my own case, accounting for my own sins, asking my own questions, and expecting in good faith that when all is said and done I'll get a fair hearing and just verdict. At last count there are 27 varieties of Baptists in this country; the brand that appeals to many of us holds that while the Bible is our anchor, it is no icon; that revelation continues, truth is not frozen in doctrine but emerges from experience and encounter, and continuity is found in the community of faith that includes both saints and sinners. In Jesus we see the power of the Living Word over tired practice and dead belief. In his relationships with women, the sick, the outcast and the stranger—even with the tax collector—Jesus kept breaking new ground. The literal observance of the law was not to quench the spirit of justice. "The Sabbath was made for man and not man for the Sabbath."

These beliefs do not make for lawless anarchy or the religion of Lone Rangers. Nor do they mean we can float safely on the little raft of our own faith while the community flounders. Our beliefs form the ground of personhood. They aim for a community with moral integrity, the wholeness that flows from mutual obligation. Our religion is an adventure in freedom within boundaries of accountability. Governor Clinton and Senator Gore, it may be that this inbred tendency in free church life is one of the best gifts you bring to high office at this most pluralistic, fragmented, and perplexed time in our history.

There is in the tide of affairs what General George Patton called "the unforgiving minute." Decision and choice force fate. Opportunity lost is lost forever. The road not taken disappears. The unforgiving minute allows no second chances; at such a moment in our nation's life the gridlock becomes permanent, the cleavage between classes irreversible, the injustices fixed, the fiscal profligacy immutable, millions give up on the system for good, and the dream dies of forging a single American nation from our separate realities.

So this unforgiving minute—this fullness of time—begs from us—citizen and politician alike—a renewed sense of religion and politics as challenge and service. But of our leaders it makes the most severe demands. Vaclav Havel writes that while politicians are indeed a mirror of their society, the opposite is also true; society is a mirror of its politicians.[3] It is largely up to the politicians which social forces they choose to liberate and which they choose to suppress, whether they rely on the good in each citizen or on the bad. As we move toward the 21st century, Havel says, we need politicians who trust not only a scientific representation of the world but also the world itself; who live not only in sociological statistics but in real people; who trust not only the summary reports that cross their desk each morning but their own feelings; not only an adopted ideology but their own thoughts; not only an objective interpretation of reality but their own soul. The ancient Israelites had a word for this: *Hochma*—the science of the heart. Intelligence, feeling, and perception combine to create the moral imagination. *The science of the heart.*

Thirty years ago, when I was young in this town, I would not have understood this. I possessed far more energy than wisdom, and craved facts, information, and action. But time and experience, love and loss, round the rough edges of pride, zeal, and partisanship, and I see now that it is not just knowledge alone—not just facts and reasons—that will transform our lives or bring about a just society; what we also need is truth, the truth of the competent soul. It is this that enables us to respond as Gloucester does when asked by Lear: "How do you see the world?" And Gloucester, *blind* Gloucester, replies: *"I see it feelingly."*

Tomorrow at noon [the 1993 Inauguration] the real struggle begins. I can tell you that rarely is it a titanic, heroic, winner-take-all-battle. It is rather a series of daily, often small, sometimes subtle battles. Because of the persistence of what Reinhold Niebuhr called "the sinful pride and self-deception" that afflict us all (what Baptists know as "original sin"), the hardest struggle of all is the one that is waged within. The character of a government is forged every day in the soul of its leader as he chooses for power or for justice.

So I conclude where we began—with our friend Brooks Hays, and something you may have heard quoted by him over the years, something he held fast even though it cost him the office he served so well among the people he loved so much. Remember?

"It is only religion reaching the ultimate solitude of the soul that can create the unpurchaseable man, and it is only man unpurchaseable by any society that creates the sound society" (William Ernest Hocking).

Notes

1. Editor's note: Brooks Hays was an active Baptist layman and delegate to the U.S. House of Representatives from Arkansas. Following his career in the House, he served as a presidential advisor to both John F. Kennedy and Lyndon Baines Johnson, and was an advocate of several causes of justice and human concern. He was a tireless speaker and spoke to a wide variety of audiences, many of them Baptist. His speeches were invariably laced with characteristic "down home" wisdom, wit, and humor. His widow, Marion Hays, was a participant in the Inaugural Prayer Service on the occasion when this speech was delivered. Mrs. Hays died in December 1996, having achieved the age of 100.

2. Editor's note: James Dunn is executive director of the Baptist Joint Committee on Public Affairs, a cosponsor of the Inaugural Prayer Service at which this speech was delivered. Materials by James Dunn are included in this volume.

3. Editor's note: Vaclav Havel is a writer, poet, and at the time of this event, was president of the Czech Republic.

Baptist by Choice

Lawrence W. Sherman

Old Testament Text: 2 Chronicles 5:11-14.
Gospel Text: Mark 1:4-11.

Why be a Baptist? In deciding to be baptized at the age of forty, I have wrestled long and hard with that question.

I was raised in American Baptist churches. My father's family has belonged to them for over a century. My mother has been employed by them most of my life.[1] I heard enough theology at home to appreciate the doctrine of adult baptism. So when I was told as a teenager that baptism was a commitment of my whole life to following the teachings of Christ, I took it pretty seriously. I said, "That is a pretty big contract for me to sign. I'd better think about it some more."

Which I did—for a quarter of a century. If I had waited much longer, I might have had a geriatric, not a pediatric, baptism. But I didn't. At what I hope is the peak of my spiritual and intellectual powers, I chose to be a Baptist.

But why? Why belong to any church at all? Why waste a moment's thought on religion—other than to consider its political implications? And of all religions to join, why join the Baptists? They have had such lousy press for the past decade!

My generation, the baby boom, has little use for churches. I once shared that view. Sunday mornings for me were a time for much-needed solitude, a *communion* with the *New York Times,* turning off the pressure of the week and slowing down. As a young university professor, I saw Sunday

Lawrence W. Sherman is chair of the Department of Criminology at the University of Maryland. As a widely recognized expert in criminal and security issues, he teaches and consults internationally. With his wife, an attorney, he publishes *The American Security Law Newsletter,* a publication focused on the legal implications of criminal and security policies and actions. He is a member of the Board of the Baptist Fellowship of Metropolitan Washington, D.C. This sermon was preached at his baptism, April 22, 1990.

as the only time I could do serious uninterrupted writing, to publish, so that "I might not perish." For many other people, Sunday is a time to work second jobs, to make enough money to support their children.

Having children, of course, destroys any hope of a peaceful Sunday morning at home. Yet that is not enough to bring families to church. Two-career couples, in fact, find Sundays about the only time available for nurturing their families with recreation and togetherness. Going to church just splits them up again—or so it seems.

Yet all the emphasis on family time has hidden an even greater need: community time. Without the support of strong community ties, the nuclear family can collapse from its own internal pressures. For single people the need for community time is even greater.

What is community? Philip Slater, the sociologist, says a community life exists when you can go to the same place at the same time every day and see many of the people you know. By this definition, the only community most of us have is our work places.

The office is the little village where we live, the primary source of human relationships in our lives. More and more marriages, including my own, have begun with office romances. Office friendships can be a stable basis of emotional support. Yet all too often they are the *only* source of human support.

It is a capital mistake to rely on the office for nurture and sustenance of the spirit. Ambition, competition, and office politics can destroy the emotional "safety net" provided by jobs or professions. It is no accident that Washington, with so little sense of community, has the highest rate of psychiatrists per capita of any city. I suppose the only cushion many people have against a job going bad or a life coming unraveled is psychother-apy—often a medical solution to a spiritual and social problem.

Jesus and his disciples taught us, by example, the power of small groups to shape and sustain faith. Modern science has confirmed the enormous power of the groups we join. They influence who we vote for, our attitudes on racial issues, and even our physical health. Recent medical research, for example, has found that "active church members live longer lives"— although I hope no one turns that one into a bumper sticker!

Jesus never said we *must* be church members, at least not as I read the Bible. It is possible, I believe, to be a Christian without belonging to any church. Jesus even said to pray in secret, rather than playing "holier than thou" at the temple. Many modern social activists have accomplished magnificent things for justice without belonging to any institutional church.

What they have not done, I believe, is to enjoy the spiritual power of a moral fellowship set apart from our professional and occupational lives. Church may split families up into separate rooms, but it brings all its members, of all ages, together in a single community. And the purpose of that community is not making money, or making laws, or even making music. The purpose of the church community is to praise God by loving one another.

Even people who don't go to church accept the *idea* of the spiritual power of the church. Few of the unchurched would want to see this country lose all its churches. But *thinking* that churches are good for our society is one thing and *belonging* to one is quite another.

Do you remember the story of the "little red hen"? I thought of that story the other day when some economists were discussing what they call the "free rider" problem. Remember how the little red hen asked for help in *making* the loaf of bread? Nobody would help her. But when it came time for *eating* the loaf of bread, she had plenty of offers to help.

The same free riders want a society without drugs, without violence, without suicide, and without pollution. They call on the power of the church to help prevent or control these problems. But when it comes time to support the church as our fundamental moral institution, most of them cannot be found.

The reason people should join and support religious communities, then, is not just that it is good for them (which it is) and good for their families (which it is), but that it is also good for the wider society. Our world needs church communities; and churches need active members. If we want to eat the "little red hen's bread" of a "kinder, gentler nation," then we had better pitch in and help.

But why be a Baptist? Why not be something respectable, like an Episcopalian or Presbyterian?

Historically, the social status of the Baptist Church has never been very high. In my opinion it hit rock bottom when a Baptist leader announced in 1980 that "God does not hear the prayers of a Jew." The scorn this statement evoked was not caused only by its poor theology; in an era of savvy public relations, it showed that Baptists were just plain *dumb* to speak so bluntly in public. The image of Baptists was more clearly drawn as redneck, intolerant, crude, and rude. For an academic like me, with a Jewish wife, to choose to be a Baptist is at best surprising. To some of my colleagues it seems unthinkable.

I have tried other churches. During the Vietnam era I found the Quakers. At that time I committed myself to nonviolence and my vocation to the study and control of violence. I attended Quaker services sporadically for almost fifteen years. Ultimately, the lack of music and majesty in worship made it impossible for me to be a Quaker.

When we bought our current home five hundred feet from an Episcopalian church, we started attending there regularly. The majesty of worship was great. So was the sense of community. But the sermons were unbearably dull.

Then we found this Baptist church. Here was a place with great sermons, great music, and great people. After several years of associate membership, we even found a great Sunday school class.

But this is not a commercial for any particular Baptist church, for the main reason to be a Baptist lies at the core of Baptist theology: the priesthood of all believers. Any church that follows that doctrine deserves the praise I heap on the Baptists.

The Baptist faith is a *thinking person's* church. Our fellowship is founded on choice, not compliance. Each of us must seek God in our own ways and make our own decisions about what the Bible means for us. Where other churches use top-down authority, ours is founded on bottom-up commitment. First and foremost, it is founded on personal choice.

Baptists encourage responsible participation. When it comes to such tough choices as euthanasia, abortion, or capital punishment, Baptists wrestle together to define a high, biblically informed standard. At the same time, they recognize, protect, and support the freedom of responsible personal choice. So a truly Baptist church will love and stand by members who struggle with divorce or with having a child out of wedlock or with their own or another's sexual orientation. A truly Baptist church will tolerate disagreements about biblical interpretation and not, to cite a recent notorious example, fire a missionary for not believing that Jonah was swallowed by a whale.[2]

No matter how difficult each of these issues may be, Baptists are committed to allowing each member of the fellowship to reach his or her own decisions on them. What each Baptist chooses to believe is between that person and God—and no one else.

Baptists have long recognized that choice is essential to human dignity. But it has never been more important than today. For as our world becomes more technologically complex, we face more and more choices. Managing these choices is the central challenge of our information age. No theology, no style of church life, is more appropriate to this "age of choices" than the Baptist faith.

No theology, for that matter, is more appropriate for the major upheaval of our era, the opening of the Communist world. As I sat in the First Baptist Church of Budapest one recent Easter Sunday, I wondered how that once-Fascist country could adapt to freedom—how it could cope with the power to choose.

One Russian leader recently compared his own country to a frozen mastodon found in Siberia, which was taken inside and rapidly thawed. As the ice melted, the mastodon was freed. But so were the microbes from deadly diseases carried in the mastodon's fur. Ethnic and language group hatreds, anti-Semitism, and violence were the microbes he feared would soon come alive as his society unfroze.

But the Baptist church is alive in Russia and Eastern Europe. It may well be a force for love, in helping people to make their newfound choices more wisely. But it won't be easy. For the whole culture seems swamped in ancient rivalries, and few have much practice in making choices without direction. The whole culture is tied up in red tape.

We have all had our run-ins with the bureaucratic mentality. My favorite red-tape story is about a famous poet who visited a Russian museum on a subzero winter's day. He checked his hat when he went in but lost the ticket for the hatcheck counter. The hatcheck attendant refused to give it to him, saying that she had no authority to break the rules—even though it was the only hat left unclaimed, and she clearly remembered that it *was* his hat. The official tour guide intervened, but she still refused to give up the hat. The tour guide then sought out the assistant museum director, who ordered her to turn over the hat. The attendant's response was: "You are the assistant director for art, but I can only take orders from the assistant director for administration." Finally, the assistant director for administration appeared and ordered her to yield the hat, which she did.

Eastern Europe yearns to breathe free of such stifling bureaucratic orthodoxy, to find a world where people can make more choices. The end of communist dictatorship is like the death of a domineering, abusive parent. And compared to other churches, Baptists act like God is dead as a controlling parent—or that he never was one.

Instead, God gave us tools to unravel this big puzzle of our universe. He gave us the brains to get increasing control over our lives. Compared to a century ago, Americans have made enormous strides in our ability to choose the food we eat, the number of children we have, and even the room temperature we enjoy. Making moral sense of all these technically generated choices may be the main religious problem of our time.

The Baptist faith is ideal for this challenge, where no permanent dogma can hope to settle the constantly changing questions. By forcing us to think for ourselves, Baptist *theology* keeps us in mental shape for handling future shock. By stimulating our *moral imagination,* Baptist faith prepares us to recognize ethical questions about new technical and social developments.

Do you remember those crazy questions we used to get in third-grade arithmetic? Like when two trains leave two cities at different times, when do they meet? I never could figure those things out.

But I was struck by the story of a substitute teacher who once visited two special third-grade classes. One class was for the talented and gifted. The other was for troublesome children who couldn't follow orders very well. The teacher gave the same discussion problem to both classes: "How," she asked, "would you measure the weight of a big, tall giraffe?" The talented and gifted group found the problem very frustrating and complained that they hadn't yet been taught the *right* answer. But the troublesome children bubbled over with ideas. One child said, "Let's get four bathroom scales and put one under each of the giraffe's hoofs." Another said, "Let's put him on a truck, weigh the truck at a truck-weighing station, take the giraffe off, weigh the truck again, and subtract the second weight from the first."

I'm not sure I could have thought of those ideas. But I am sure that the Baptist faith is more like those troublesome kids than like the other group. When the times call for creative pathways to faith and understanding, the Baptists church wins hands down.

Baptists also lead on the grounds of *spiritual* power. For as much as it a thinking person's faith, it is also a *feeling person's* faith. Baptists need hold no illusions that rational logic can solve all problems. We know that one valid response to complexity can be a strong, simple faith that God will accept us and forgive us if we will do our best to accept God.

Some Baptists do choose pathways to faith that make me shudder. But they have that right—and I wouldn't want them not to. All the dogma in the world can't stop intolerance. But as Baptist Christians, we can work to broaden the base of understanding that will reduce intolerance, and perhaps we can forgive it.

At its best, the Baptist faith is not a crude, intolerant religion, but a richly complex and highly sophisticated belief. It is not a faith for people too dumb to think for themselves, but a forum for educated people to learn from each other's experience. It is not a faith that fears science, but an intellectual framework that accepts the challenge of making new choices.

Why be a Baptist? Walter Rauschenbusch, the prophet of the social gospel, whose picture is on a stained-glass window on the south side of our church, wrote a series of famous essays called *Why I Am a Baptist.* One reason he gave was our refusal to adopt an authoritative creed and our complete reliance on the Bible. "A creed," he said, "imposes a law and *binds* thought; the Bible imparts a spirit and *awakens* thought."

Rauschenbusch also said, "Baptists, in tying [on] to the New Testament, have hitched their chariot to a star . . . and they will have to keep moving." Like Rauschenbusch, I have come to be a Baptist by conviction. Like him, I find it impossible to be anything else. And so I chose to be baptized.

But adult baptism is more than a choice. It is a commitment to make a *million* choices, all in keeping with the Spirit of Jesus. Years ago I didn't want to make that commitment because I thought I would break it. Now I need to make that commitment because I know I will break it—and I know I need God's forgiveness all the more.

Now that I have been baptized, I won't always *do* the right thing. But in the fellowship of Baptists—the thinking person's church, the spiritual person's church—I may, with God's guidance, *choose* better what the right thing is to do.

Amen.

Notes

1. Editor's note: Professor Sherman's parents have been active participants in local, regional, and national expressions of the ABC/USA. His mother, "Peg" Sherman, was for several years the volunteer representative at the United Nations for the ABC/USA.

2. Editor's note: This is a reference to a contemporaneous event in which a Southern Baptist missionary was reportedly dismissed as a result of not ascribing to a particular biblical interpretation outlined by a fundamentalist-sponsored test for orthodoxy.

Why Are We Here?

Denton Lotz

Recent events in the life of the USA have caused the demon of racism to once again raise its ugly head. We are here to say no to racism and yes to unity.

Christians:

First of all, and very simply, we are here because we are Christians and believe that Jesus Christ has called us to be one. We are here because we believe "There is no longer Jew or Greek, there is no longer slave or free, there is no longer male and female; for all of you are one in Christ Jesus" (Gal. 3:28). We are here because the love of Christ constrains us, or as a modern translation puts it, "urges us on." Indeed, each of us from various language groups, racial groups, and socio-political backgrounds could rest at home and say it does not involve us. But the Gospel of Christ urges us on: "For the love of Christ urges us on, because we are convinced that one has died for all; therefore all have died. And he died for all, so that those who live might live no longer for themselves, but for him who died and was raised for them" (2 Cor. 5:14-15). We are here because we cannot live for ourselves, but must live for one another. This is the basis of our coming together: it is to Christ that we point, it is to Christ that we would bring this nation, it is to Christ that we would bring humanity. But how can we do that if we are not united? How can we do it when there is division among those who are followers of the Way? Indeed during this Christmas season we are made more aware than ever of the missiological dimension of Christ's call for unity as at no other time. If we do not unite, if we do not come together, we are actually denying God's love and grace to the

Denton Lotz is the general secretary of the Baptist World Alliance, a worldwide federation of Baptist denominations, associations, and unions. This statement was first given to Baptist leaders gathered for the USA Summit Against Racism in December 1995. It was first printed in the *Baptist World Alliance News*, January 1996, and is reprinted with permission of the Baptist World Alliance.

rest of humanity. In other words, we are here to tell the whole world that "Red and yellow, black and white, Jesus loves the children of the world." . . . and so do we, and if we do, then we must do something about it now as Christians and citizens of this country and this world with which we share our common humanity.

Baptists:

We are here as Baptists. In the religious persecutions of the 16th and 17th century and even today, Baptists defended religious freedom for all. It was Baptists who were martyred and proclaimed liberty for all. Whether in the gulags of the former Soviet Union, the brainwashing groups of Maoist China, or the demoralizing ghettos of many urban areas, everywhere are Baptists suffering for their faith. And thus the word Baptist overseas became a respected word. It became a word to describe individuals who were not afraid to die for what they believed, and were not afraid to live like they believed. *Baptist* became a word to describe faith, suffering, compassion, righteous living, moral behavior, and compassionate concern.

Unfortunately, in the USA, the word has often lost its sign of respect because our actions have often not lived up to our faith. The religious and secular press often have used the word despairingly, describing a fringe person not at all representative of the thousands, indeed millions of faithful men and women who live out their lives in faithful obedience to their Lord.

We are here to redeem for our people, our great history and the positive term of being Baptist. In the USA, the conventions represented number more than 30 million baptized believers. If we were to count children and friends the Baptist community in the USA would be well over 50 million believers—a considerable number of simple and deeply committed men and women who yearn for godly living and a just society. It would be irresponsible if we were not to take seriously our responsibility to our nation collectively. We are under-represented in the halls of Congress. Other religious groups are proportionately more heavily represented. Perhaps one of the reasons for our lack of political representation is the fact that historically our people have been from the poor and lower classes. The media elite do not understand us and often misrepresent us. Occasionally some of our laity become outstanding leaders and for that we are grateful. But, we are not here to support any political group or to affirm any individual. We are here as Baptist believers to condemn racism and to determine how we might together work for justice and liberty for ALL.

Leaders:

The Bible says that where there is no vision the people perish (Proverbs 29:18). The people need leaders or they will perish, and indeed are perishing. We gather here today as Baptist leaders representing millions in our constituency who do not even know who their leaders are and to whom they should look for a vision. Therefore, many look elsewhere for a hopeful sign.

We want to re-capture today the Biblical call for leadership in the name of him who spoke with authority. Our call for leadership however is not a call for authoritarianism, but is a call for servanthood.

Where outstanding leadership is lacking, often the people flounder and do not know to whom they should turn. Collectively, as Baptist leaders we are here to speak with a clear and sound voice that racism is wrong, racism is a sin, and that together as Baptist leaders we will not only condemn it, but will work together to create a structure which will elevate the good and defeat evil. We are here to find practical solutions to soul-deep problems. We are here today to affirm that as Baptist leaders we will lead because we know who our leader is, even Jesus Christ our Lord. And it is to this leader that we call our friends and neighbors, our nation and the world.

The Kingdom of God:

We are here because we believe that the rule of God will ultimately triumph over the rule of man. We are here to affirm that divine justice will one day triumph over human destruction. We are here because we believe there is a judge and a king who will one day cause "justice to roll down like waters and mercy like an ever-flowing stream."

As Christians and as Baptists, we are not so parochial to think that to us alone belongs the commandment to love and to unite. Indeed as Biblical believers we affirm that the rule of God has already begun in the life of believers and the church. Therefore, the call of Christ is a call to participate in the suffering of humanity, it is a call to prophetic action in the face of the demonic forces which would divide and defeat us.

Humanity is confronted with a choice. As the poet stated long ago, "Once to every man and nation comes the moment to decide, in the strife of truth with falsehood, for the good or evil side; Some great cause, some great decision offering each the bloom or blight. . . ."

Indeed we are here as representatives of God's rule, God's call for justice. We are here to be prophetic spokesmen not only for law and order, but for righteousness and sacrificial living and loving of all God's children, regardless of race.

We come therefore as Christian Baptist leaders praying and working for that One who taught us to pray, "Thy kingdom come, Thy will be done, on earth as it is in heaven."

We Knew What Glory Was

Shirlee Taylor Haizlip

When I was growing up in the '40s and '50s, my father would pack up
the car every August and squeeze in my mother, four children, several
dolls and a picnic lunch. It was the time before air-conditioning, and the
drive was hot, dusty and, after New York, without bathrooms.

We left long before dawn, because for a dark-skinned man driving a
large shiny sedan holding a white-looking wife, the journey from Connecticut to the South was not without peril. It was essential that each leg
of the trip be made before nightfall. We knew that safety lay within the
homes and the churches of my father's friends and colleagues, the black
ministers we would visit. They were our underground railroad.

My father was a Baptist pastor who ministered to a medium-sized black
church in a Connecticut mill town. His father was a minister who had
founded a major black Baptist church in Washington. At the beginnings
of their careers, both had led small country churches in North Carolina,
Virginia and West Virginia. Later, as popular officers of the National
Baptist Convention and known for their dramatic oratory, the two were
frequent guest preachers at rural churches throughout the South.

Traditionally, my father and his father before him preached a week of
revival services at these houses of worship. After my grandfather died, my
father continued to return to the South each year. For him, the churches
were touchstones of faith, of culture, of triumph over slavery. For him,
they were living, breathing links to the past and an indestructible foundation for the future.

There was more than a spiritual connection. When they were in college,
my four uncles, all of whom played musical instruments and had glorious
voices, would sometimes join my father and present musical programs of

Shirlee Taylor Haizlip is a communications professional and writer. She is the
author of *The Sweeter the Juice: A Family Memoir in Black and White*. This article
was first printed as an Op-Ed Section contribution in *The New York Times*, Sunday,
June 23, 1996, copyright © 1996 by The New York Times Co., and is reprinted with
permission.

spirituals and the light classics to appreciative Southern congregations, all too often deprived of other cultural experiences.

At other times, my dad, resplendent in a white suit, would offer solo recitals. When he crooned "Danny Boy" or "When I Grow Too Old to Dream" in his high tenor vibrato and with exquisite diction, the fans moved a little faster, the backs sat up a little straighter and the shouts of "Sing it, Rev!" were as heartfelt as they were for his renditions of "Amazing Grace" or "His Eye Is on the Sparrow."

I cannot hear the Three Tenors sing without thinking of my father standing in the pulpit of a spare little church, singing like a melancholy angel.

To reach many of the churches, we drove up deserted dirt roads covered by gracefully arching kudzu-fringed trees. Just when we thought we would never get there, a clearing materialized. There at its edge stood the church, often the only building for miles around, plain as a line drawing in a children's coloring book, more often than not in need of a fresh coat of paint. Never lonely looking, it seemed instead a natural part of the landscape, splendid in its simplicity.

Before the service, with admonitions of keeping our "best" clothes clean fading in our ears, my siblings and I would play with other children, running and jumping, catching fireflies, hiding and seeking in the darkening silver twilight. Each night, the revival crowd would get bigger and livelier. By the end of the week, the church was full, the room was hot and the penitents were saved.

During every service, I watched as my father, in high Baptist style, "picture painted" the stories of Moses and Job, Ruth and Esther. I listened as he moaned and hummed and sang the tales of W. E. B. Du Bois and Frederick Douglass, the Scottsboro Boys and Emmett Till. I clapped for joy as he brought the worshipers to their feet with promises of survival now and salvation later. In that place, at that time, we knew what glory was.

After the service, in the pitch blackness of a muggy summer night, we would drive back to our host's house, listening to parish gossip and ghost stories, accept offers of freshly made iced tea and every once in a while homemade ice cream. Sweetly, another church night had ended.

The best was yet to come. At the close of the week, we celebrated the homecoming, the end of the week-long revival, behind the church, where picnic benches were felicitously placed among sweet-smelling pines. We ate miles of delicious food and drank lakes of sweet punch.

Usually there was a modest graveyard somewhere near the picnic grounds. We did not play there. Our parents had taught us better than that. Mold-covered gravestones barely hinted at the life stories they marked. The bones of slaves lay side by side with the bones of their emancipated children. All of their spirits were free to be free, at last.

As I grew older, I would learn about the lives of the church members from the comfort of my mother's side. I would grow to understand that there, in that place, every single church member was *somebody.*

In God's house, if nowhere else, they were C.E.O.'s and presidents, directors and chairmen, counselors and managers. In God's house, if nowhere else, they were women of infinite grace and men of profound dignity. Forever, amen.

With traditions that began in slavery, the parishioners carried forward, bit by precious bit, the dreams of their forebears. In their roles as deacons, trustees, missionaries and choir members, those domestics, handymen, cotton and tobacco farmers and teachers sang and prayed on hard, scrabbly benches, validating and celebrating themselves and one another, warmly and well, week after week, year after year, generation after generation.

Surely their oils and essences seeped into the well-worn pews. Surely the whorls of their fingertips left lovely striations in the wood, at which their grandbabies would stare before they fell off to sleep.

Not only did they tend to the church's business, they looked after the elderly and the infirm, encouraged the young to learn, learn, learn and rallied their communities in times of economic stress, natural disaster or social crisis. It did not escape my understanding that the church encompassed all. Seldom were there outcasts.

For me as a child, those beautiful little structures were places beyond enchantment. As an adult, I understood that the churches were indeed the collective soul of black folks.

I never thought that this particular reality could end. Although I have visited the South as an adult and know that some of those churches have been abandoned, enlarged or modernized, in my mind's eye all of them remain storybook sanctuaries, testament to my own faith, the faith of my father, his father and the larger black community.

Heartsick now, my soul's light has been dimmed. Church after church in the South has been destroyed by fire, torched by arsonists. I watch the television images as long as I can. Then I hide my eyes behind my fingers, peeking at the screen as if it were a horror film, while hellish flames consume the heavenly places of my youth.

I ask my father across the void, Who will put out the flames, Dad? Where can we go now to be safe?

The Development of Black Baptists in Virginia, 1867–1882

Ralph Reavis

According to David O. Moore, an interpreter of the pre–Civil War period, by the early 1800s, most Southern states had passed laws that denied the Negro access to both general and religious education.[1] In 1819, Virginia's slave holders, having been aggravated by both the abolitionists and the Quakers, and realizing that an informed Negro represented a more powerful Negro,[2] influenced the General Assembly to enact a law forbidding

> ... all meetings or assemblages of slaves, or free Negroes, or mulattoes, mixing or assemblages of slaves, at any meeting house, or any other place or places in the night, or at any school or schools for teaching them reading and writing, either in the day or night.[3]

The Nat Turner insurrection of 1831 influenced Governor John Floyd of Virginia to make Negro uprisings the dominant concern of his 1831 statement to the Virginia legislature.[4] In that statement, Governor Floyd expressed the sentiment that the "public good requires the negro preachers to be silenced."[5]

In response to Floyd's executive message, the General Assembly enacted, on March 15, 1832, a bill forbidding any Negro, even if ordained or licensed, from holding religious or other assemblies at any time. The punishment prescribed for the offense was stripes not exceeding thirty-nine. All Negroes were forbidden to attend any religious or other assemblies if they were conducted by a Negro.[6]

In light of the oppressive legislation in the state, it is not surprising that at the time of emancipation, the majority of the half-million Negroes in Virginia[7] had no formal church affiliation. However, a majority of Negroes

Ralph Reavis is pastor of Riverview Baptist Church in Richmond, Virginia, and professor of historical studies and missions, School of Theology, Virginia Union University. This essay is derived from a more extensive unpublished manuscript of the same title. Dr. Reavis was a presenter at "Called to Responsible Freedom: A Conference on Baptist Distinctives," at Green Lake, Wisconsin, August 1996.

likely identified themselves as Baptists. Eugene D. Genovese says that most slaves preferred either the Baptist or the Methodist Church, and that the Baptists won out only because of their greater proselytizing efforts. "By the time of the antebellum period," says Genovese, "most southern blacks who professed Christianity called themselves Baptists."[8] Alrutheus Taylor says, with reference to the early years of the postbellum period, "The large body of Virginia Negroes . . . continued in the Baptist Church with which they had already connected through their master of slavery."[9]

The oppressive legislation had also prevented the vast majority of Negroes in Virginia from acquiring any formal education. However, where there had been a will—and that was often the case—there had sometimes been a way to acquire some education. W. E. B. Du Bois estimates that despite the prohibitive laws and generally unfavorable public attitude, about five percent of the nation's slaves had learned to read by 1860.[10]

Towns and cities provided a more likely setting than the country for educational opportunities for slaves. Though sentiment among whites for the education of slaves was not necessarily any more favorable in towns and cities, clandestine teaching by both literate slaves and freedmen was easier to accomplish. Even a few whites, either from stirrings of conscience or from desire for profit, ran schools for slaves despite the fact these were illegal.

When country slaves had an opportunity to learn, their teachers were not uncommonly masters or mistresses who either felt an obligation to teach them or, for practical reasons, wanted one or more literate slaves among their slave population. Perhaps even more widespread was the experience of white children disobeying their fathers and mothers and teaching their Negro playmates. Moreover, literate slaves often felt compelled secretly to impart what they could to slave brothers and sisters who wanted to learn. Historian Eugene D. Genovese says of the period immediately following the Civil War:

> The freedmen's efforts to educate themselves and their children provide one of the most moving chapters in American social history, and historians are finally giving it the attention it deserves.

Genovese goes on to say that "the roots of black enthusiasm for education lay deep in the slave past." He cites several examples: a young woman struggling to read the Bible; another woman crying because, although she could say the alphabet from a to z, she couldn't say it backward; slaves being punished with whippings for trying to learn to read. Genovese quotes George Brown Tindall's words, "Even behind the facade of slavery, a Negro leadership was developing."[12]

Virginia's Negro Baptists Strive for Autonomy

In Virginia, leadership among Negro Baptists made giant strides in a short period of time. On May 4, 1867, fifteen Negro Baptist clergymen and laymen gathered in the Zion Baptist Church in Portsmouth to organize the Virginia Baptist State Convention. The Convention was organized mainly for the purposes of spreading the gospel, evangelizing Negroes who had no memberships, and building new churches. But the group was also to become intimately involved in efforts to secure education, both religious and secular, for Virginia's Negroes. The Convention officers elected during the first annual meeting were the Reverend J. H. Gaines of Petersburg, President; the Reverend E. G. Corprew of Portsmouth, First Vice-President; the Reverend Thomas Henson of Norfolk, Second Vice-President; the Reverend Harrison Scott of Danville, Corresponding Secretary; the Reverend Henry Williams, Jr., of Petersburg, Recording Secretary; and Deacon Peter Archer of Petersburg, Treasurer.[13]

What factors led these fifteen Negro Baptist leaders to the momentous step of forming their own decision-making, leadership-providing Convention? One reason was that by the end of the war, a small number of Negro Baptist churches already existed in Virginia. Alrutheus Taylor mentions that the Harrison Street Baptist Church was established in Petersburg in 1774. He goes on to say that a church in Williamsburg had been organized in 1776, and that, by the time of the Civil War, several other Negro Baptist churches were in existence.These included several unnamed churches in Portsmouth and Lynchburg, three churches in Norfolk, and three in Richmond, two of which had been formed prior to 1856: the First African Baptist Church, pastored by James H. Holmes, and the Ebenezer Baptist Church, pastored by Richard H. Wells. Both Holmes and Wells later became active in the Virginia Baptist State Convention.[14]

These existing Negro Baptist churches, says Taylor, "formed a nucleus around which the Negroes built after the war."[15] Additionally, Negroes who had been attending white churches began to take action to form their own congregations.

Taylor insists that white churches were in favor of the exodus of their Negro memberships because they were "fearful lest Negroes might desire 'social equality.'" White Baptist churches, says Taylor, urged their Negroes to withdraw their memberships or diplomatically requested them to set up their own churches. Taylor says that in some instances Negroes were ordered to get out of the white churches.[16]

On the other hand, Harrison Daniel, while also citing examples of whites taking action to cause Negroes to leave white churches, insists that most white Baptist churches were reluctant to see their Negro members leave. His contention is supported by several examples. The Middle District Association declared that "changed relations between colored and white has [sic] not lessened our obligations to efforts at their religious instruction," and expressed the opinion that it was best for Negroes to remain in white churches. The Rappahannock Association stated that "separate organizations of the colored members of our churches should . . . neither be required nor encouraged."[17]

It is not possible to determine how many white Baptist churches sought to retain their Negro congregations and how many sought to sever relationships with them. However, those white churches which sought to keep their Negro members made the mistake of failing to recognize the changes in church rules that Negroes would require if they were to stay with white churches. The status and position of the Negro members of white Baptist churches had always been considerably lower than that of the white members, and the fact of freedom did not change that situation. Typically, only white members could vote to elect a pastor, and only white males could participate in the day-to-day regulatory affairs of the church. Negroes had to congregate in an area of the church apart from the white members; in some churches where memberships were large they were provided with a separate Sunday morning service. To these symbols of domination we must add that after the war many churches sought an exaction from their Negro members to help with church support. One may well understand why numerous Negro members of white Baptist churches, therefore, withdrew to join established or emerging Negro churches. Moreover, vast numbers of Negroes had no religious affiliations whatsoever. In view of the total situation, it was inevitable that Negro leaders would emerge and establish an organization to guide their people and promote their welfare.

W. Harrison Daniel writes that the movement among Negro Baptists toward autonomy in their ecclesiastical affairs found favor among white Baptists, and that

As the Negroes withdrew to form their own ecclesiastical organizations, they were aided and assisted in various ways by local white Baptists.[18]

Daniel goes on to describe the nature of the assistance white Baptists gave to Negroes. Officials of white churches might license a Negro member to perform certain rituals and to preach among blacks; they might even ordain a Negro member they considered worthy of the honor. White Baptists "also assisted the blacks in drafting church covenants, constitutions, and bylaws."[19] In some cases, Negroes who wanted to erect or obtain a church building of their own found that a white congregation offered its building in the interim. White assistance sometimes went so far as to grant financial assistance to help Negroes gain church buildings.

Despite significant white support for the establishment of Negro Baptist churches, it amounted to less than the Negro leadership wanted. When the Virginia Baptist State Convention met in 1869 at its second annual session, the Executive Board reported that the Convention's work would have been greater had more funds been available and had there been less opposition from whites unsympathetic to the cause of the convention:

> That there is opposition against us, cannot be disguised. Men prejudiced to our advancement, simply because of our sable hue, have held churches aloof from us, telling them that it is too expensive to join us, yet draining the churches of larger sums than we ask, or is necessary to act with us; and said sums they apply to their own selfish ends, and not to the interest of Virginia and her helpless.
>
> Let us not be discouraged, but be united; for in union there is strength. We believe that ere we meet again, a better state of feeling financially, politically, and spiritually will exist, and certainly more growth will be added unto us, and be nearer to maturity. For we propose, by the increase in wisdom and in stature. Let us trust in God.[20]

The cited quotation indicates that in the period from 1865 to 1869, some white Baptist churches had not responded favorably to Negroes who wanted to draw upon them for help. The reference to "draining the churches of larger sums than we ask" undoubtedly refers to the annual fee that some churches required of their black members despite the limited privileges of their membership.

Still, the Negro Baptists of Virginia had many reasons to rejoice when they met at their second annual session. They had begun to build their own churches, ordain their own ministers, and conduct their own Sabbath Schools. Indeed, many Negro Baptists were conducting all ecclesiastical affairs on their own. Moreover, as freemen, they were participating in the election of state legislators.

By the time of that same session, the Convention had adopted a statement of its objectives. The proceedings of the session of that year included this statement:

> Our sole object is the diffusion of the Gospel of Christ and the interest of his Kingdom, by sending missionaries, planting and training churches, and assisting feeble Baptist churches in the support of their pastors throughout the State of Virginia as far as lieth within the ability of the Convention.[21]

Relationships Between the Virginia Baptist State Convention and the Baptist General Association of Virginia

W. Harrison Daniel writes that in 1868, the year after its inception, the Convention attempted to establish friendly relationships with the white Baptist General Association of Virginia—relationships which would include the exchange of delegates at the two groups' annual meetings.[22] On the other hand, Garnett Ryland writes that it was not until 1871 that an attempt to establish correspondence with the General Association was made. He states that attempts at friendly relationships were begun when Richard Wells, then President of Virginia Baptist State Convention, delivered a letter to the General Association.[23] Perhaps the first attempt to establish correspondence with the General Association was made in 1868, and in the absence of a reply, a second attempt was made in May of 1871. In any event, since Wells cites its contents, it is apparent that a letter was delivered in May of 1871. One passage bears quoting, for it not only indicates how much Negro Baptists believed in the unity of all people under God, but also dares to allude to Negroes and whites as members as a single family:

> We are adherents to one faith, one Lord and one baptism, yea, to all vital principles of the great Baptist family; therefore, we respectfully ask correspondence with you in the laudable work of evangelizing this our State.[24]

Both Daniel and Ryland write that the Convention's letter was referred to a special committee, chaired by Dr. Jeremiah B. Jeter, a powerful leader among Virginia's white Baptists, and editor of the *Religious Herald*, the official publication of the Baptist General Association of Virginia. That committee proceeded to reject the overtures of the black Baptists. It held:

> That from considerations which we need not specify and cannot control, we deem it inexpedient to enter into an interchange of corresponding messages with the Convention.[25]

Later that same year, Jeremiah Jeter used the columns of the *Religious Herald* to elaborate upon the Baptist General Association's decision. In an essay in that paper, he made it patently clear that the General Association's view was that Negroes were different by nature from whites in undesirable ways. Jeter wrote that blacks should not be supported in endeavors that would inevitably result in social intercourse between races:

> God has made two races widely different; not only in complexion, but in their instincts and social qualities. We take it for granted that it was not the purpose of the creator that they should be blended. . . . Nature abhors the union. . . . Shall the races mingle together in churches, associations . . . or shall they act separately. . . . Religious and social intercourse are closely, if not inseparably connected. Suppose we admit colored delegates to seats in our association, we must of course, allow them to sit where they choose, in juxtaposition with our wives and daughters, and the privilege granted to them must be equally granted to their associates.[26]

The General Association's rejection was a setback to black Baptist leaders. Had their attempts to establish a more intimate association with their white brethren succeeded, the General Association might have become a source of funds for the evangelization of blacks in Virginia. Nonetheless, Virginia's Negro Baptists did not falter in their efforts to accomplish their goals. On May 9, 1872, at its fifth annual session, the Convention responded to the General Association's rejection with a vow to give up all efforts to gain supports from that group:

> Whereas, according to proffers of friendship from some of our white Baptist brethren of this state, we have attempted to open a correspondence with the General Baptist Association of Virginia, in June 1871, and whereas said association rejected our delegate, Elder Richard Wells, our offers for correspondence and interchange of messengers, and that without a just cause, to our knowledge; therefore, resolved, that we will make no further efforts for correspondence with said association, but shall proceed separate and alone of them in our work of evangelization, in the even tenor of our way—trusting in God who has no respect to every nation is accepting of Him—considering that said proffers of friendship are hypocritical, and that we have shown ourselves to be destitute of prejudice to our white brethren.[27]

One prominent white Baptist clergyman, John L. Burrows, had objected strongly to the 1871 decision of the General Association not to initiate correspondence with the Convention. He believed that an exchange of representatives would be advantageous to both groups and stated that opinion in an 1872 letter to the *Religious Herald*.

Perhaps Burrows's opinions played some part in the General Association's reversal, some eight years later, of its 1871 position. In 1879, a committee which included Jeremiah B. Jeter and Andrew Broadus, both of whom had been on the committee that prepared the 1871 statement, issued a report which included these statements:

> The colored Baptists of the State constitute an important part of our zion, and an efficient element for the spread of the gospel, the evangelization and elevation of the Colored race. . . . the committee earnestly recommends the establishment, cultivation and perpetuation of the most fraternal and cordial relations of Christian fellowship and cooperation with our brethren of the Colored churches. . . . We recommend the appointment on the part of this Association of five delegates to the Colored Baptist Convention of the State and that this Association invite such Colored Baptist Convention to send delegates to it.[28]

The report was adopted; a single white Baptist church objected; it withdrew from the Baptist General Association.

White Baptist spokesmen offered no explanation for the General Association's reversal of its position toward the Convention. In speculating on the reasons for the change of attitude, Daniel observes that at the time of the Association's rebuff of the Convention's overtures, whites in Virginia believed Negroes represented a threat to white society and to the Southern white political structure. However, by 1879, this situation had changed. The uncertainties of the Reconstruction period had ended, and Northern influences that might have affected the destiny of the Negro in ways not desired by Virginia whites appeared to have ceased.[29] Moreover, the conservatives, with their anti-Negro inclinations, had defeated the Republicans and established themselves as the party-in-power in Virginia, with the result that the Negroes of the state were "under control" to an extent that allowed whites to relax their vigilance. Alrutheus Taylor writes of the results of the 1873 elections in Virginia: "Thereafter assured of the domination of native whites, the public [i.e., the white public] ceased to direct as much attention as formerly to matters political." Taylor also points out that Virginia was undergoing an economic crisis which tended to divert attention away from the Negroes.[30]

The Virginia Baptist State Convention welcomed the new attitude of the General Association, and in ensuing years, some district associations exchanged messengers. Still, activities that reflected true cooperation were limited to white ministers holding workshops for the instruction of Negro preachers and white colporters visiting Negro church gatherings.[31]

Notes

1. David O. Moore, "The Withdrawal of Blacks from Southern Baptist Churches Following Emancipation," *Baptist History and Heritage* 16 (July 1981): 12.

2. Herbert Aptheker, *Nat Turner's Slave Rebellion* (New York: Grove Press, Inc., 1966; Evergreen Black Cat Edition, 1966), pp. 83-86. See Gerald W. Mullin, *Flight and Rebellion: Slave Resistance in Eighteenth Century Virginia* (New York: Oxford University Press, 1972). This is extremely important for an understanding of slave rebellion and other styles of resistance.

3. Joseph Tate, *Digest of the Laws of Virginia* (Richmond: Smith and Palmer, 1841), pp. 849-850.

4. John Wesley Cromwell, "The Aftermath of Nat Turner's Insurrection," *Journal of Negro History* 5 (April 1920), p. 218. For a detailed discussion on the reactions of white denominations to the slave uprisings of the 1820s and 1830s see Donald G. Matthews, *Religion in the Old South* (Chicago: University of Chicago Press, 1972), pp. 202-208.

5. Virginia General Assembly. *An Act to Amend the Act Concerning Slaves, Free Negroes and Mulattoes* (1831), 107

6. Ibid.

7. Marshal W. Fishwick, *Virginia: A New Look at the Old Dominion* (New York: Harper & Brothers, 1959), p. 144.

8. Eugene D. Genovese, *Roll, Jordan, Roll: The World the Slaves Made* (New York: Random House, 1972; Vintage Books, 1976), p. 235; Luther P. Jackson, "Religious Development of the Negro in Virginia from 1760-1860, " *Journal of Negro History* 16 (April, 1931), pp. 179-80. After the Revolution the Baptists and Methodists far outstripped the small contingent of Episcopalians in the evangelization of the Negro slaves. By 1790, eighty percent of the slaves belonged to either the Baptist or Methodist Church. For an explanation of why the Episcopal Church was unable to evangelize Negroes and Indians see Clifton Hartwell Brewer, *A History of Religious Education in the Episcopal Church to 1835* (New Haven, Conn: Yale University Press; 1924), pp. 44-53. Raboteau credits the increased growth in the Baptist and Methodist communions with the mobility of their preachers and their emphasis upon the "conversion experience," rather than religious instructions. See Albert J. Raboteau, *Slave Religion: The Invisible Institution in the Antebellum South* (New York: Oxford University Press, 1978), pp. 131-133.

9. Alrutheus A. Taylor, *The Negro in the Reconstruction of Virginia* (New York: Russell & Russell, 1969), p. 182.

10. W. E .B. Du Bois, *Black Reconstruction in America 1860-1880* (Cleveland: World, 1935: Meridian Books, 1968), p. 638; Gunnar Myrdal, *An American Dilemma*, Vol. 2: *The Negro Social Structure* (New York: Harper and Row, 1944; McGraw-Hill Paperbacks, 1964), p. 887.

11. Genovese, *Roll, Jordan, Roll: The World the Slaves Made*, p. 565.

12. Ibid., pp. 565-566; Samuel Davis records an earlier mood of the eagerness the slaves had to read and know the will of God. Samuel Davis, *The State of Religion Among the Protestant Dissenters in Virginia; In A Letter to the Rev. Mr. Joseph*

Bellamy of Bethlem, In New England (Boston: S. Kneeland, 1751), 23. This item is on microfilm in Union Theological Seminary Library, Richmond, Virginia; William Henry Foote, *Sketches of Virginia, Historical and Biographical*, first series (Richmond: John Knox Press, 1966 reprint of 1850 edition), 44.

13. Virginia Baptist State Convention, *Proceedings of Twenty-sixth Annual Session* (Richmond, Va.: Planet Electric Power Print, 1893), p. 62.

14. Alrutheus A. Taylor, *The Negro in the Reconstruction of Virginia*, pp. 186-187.

15. Ibid., p. 186.

16. Ibid., p. 183; Leon F. Litwack describes a similar black exodus from the Methodist Episcopal Church (white) to the African Methodist Episcopal Church, in Leon F. Litwack, *Been in the Storm So Long* (New York: Vintage Books, 1979), pp. 464-471.

17. W. Harrison Daniel, *Virginia Baptists, 1860-1902* (Bedford, Virginia: The Print Shop, 1987), p. 77.

18. Ibid., p. 79.

19. Ibid., p. 80. For a detailed discussion of this matter see Carlton McCarthy, ed., *The First Baptist Church of Richmond, 1780-1880* (Richmond: By the Author, 1880), p. 251.

20. Virginia Baptist State Convention, *Proceedings of Second Annual Session* (Petersburg, Virginia: Jno B. Ege's Publishing House, 1869), p. 21.

21. Ibid., p. 3.

22. Daniel, *Virginia Baptists 1860-1902*, p. 81.

23. Garnett Ryland, *The Baptists of Virginia, 1699-1926* (Richmond, Va: The Virginia Baptist Board of Missions and Education, 1955), p. 314.

24. Ibid., p. 314.

25. Virginia Baptist State Convention, *Proceedings of Fifth Annual Session* (Petersburg, Va.: Jos. Van Hold Nash Economic Job Printing Office, 1872), p. 14.

26. *Religious Herald*, 7 September 1871. See also the earlier actions of the 1867 Virginia Assembly's legislation which declared that the spiritual status of the slave did not affect his civil status, in Mary F. Goodwin, "Christianizing and Educating the Negro in Colonial Virginia,*"Historical Magazine of the Protestant Episcopal Church*, I (September, 1932), p. 144: Andrew E. Murray, *Presbyterians and the Negro: A History* (Philadelphia: Presbyterian Historical Society, 1966), p. 9. Jeremiah Jeter's anti-Negro feelings were prevalent throughout Virginia; Charles E. Wynes, *Race Relations in Virginia, 1870-1902* (Charlottesville, Va.; University of Virginia Press, 1961), pp. 122-125.

27. Virginia Baptist State Convention, *Proceedings of Fifth Annual Session*, p. 14.

28. Daniel, *Virginia Baptists 1860-1902*, p. 83.

29. Ibid., pp. 83-84. By 1879, Virginia had almost returned to the camp of the white conservatives. Only the Fourth District, the Black Belt, which later sent John M. Langston to the United States Congress, offered any hope of electing a Republican. For an analysis of the Underwood Convention, the Readjuster Party, the Conservative Party, and the suffrage question see Ralph Clipman McDanel, *The Virginia Constitutional Convention of 1901-1902*, Johns Hopkins University Studies in Historical and Political Science, No. 3 (Baltimore: Johns Hopkins University Press, 1928), pp. 1-58.

30. Taylor, *The Negro in the Reconstruction of Virginia*, pp. 264-265.

31. Daniel, *Virginia Baptists, 1860-1902*, p. 84.

They Called the Altar "Witness"

Norman S. Johnson Sr.

*The Reubenites and the Gadites called the altar Witness; "For,"
said they, "it is a witness between us that the LORD is God."
(Josh. 22:34 NRSV)*

American Baptists are a diverse lot, covering the theological, ideological, social, and economic spectrum. We also mirror a tremendous ethnic diversity. To fill the picture a bit more, we are also—forgive the redundancy—Baptists. We as Baptists are fiercely and passionately committed to "freedom." Walter Shurden, in an interesting book entitled *The Baptist Identity: Four Fragile Freedoms*, has identified four fundamental areas of freedom: (1) *Bible freedom* is the right to interpret Scripture for ourselves; (2) *soul freedom* is the right of an unencumbered relationship with God; (3) *church freedom* affirms the authority of every local congregation to order its life before God; and (4) *religious freedom* makes the classic distinction between church and state. It is this commitment to freedom that is both a blessing and burden to our collective life as American Baptists. How well we are able to negotiate diverse and sometimes conflicting claims among us may determine the future of the denomination.

The critical question is not only what separates us, but what is the center that holds us together? What can we agree on, given our theological, ideological, and ethnic differences? The question is not peculiar to American Baptists! All mainline denominations are struggling with the same question. The great national debate is whether there is a center that holds us together even as Americans. The debate over the "English only" requirement in schools is an example of this issue. We ought to be careful

Norman S. Johnson Sr. is pastor of the First New Christian Fellowship Baptist Church in Los Angeles, California. This sermon was preached at the closing worship service of "Called to Responsible Freedom: A Conference on Baptist Distinctives," on August 23, 1996, at Green Lake, Wisconsin, August 1996.

not to isolate the denominational debates from the larger sociopolitical landscape. We are contextual creatures functioning within a particular social milieu. The interplay between the personal and the social, the private and public spheres is dynamic, not static. The fault lines threatening to erupt within the denomination are present throughout our nation. In fact, every national institution is grappling with the question "Where is the center that holds us together?" How American Baptists answer this question may well provide clues to the larger collective life of the nation.

As this is a defining moment in our history, I share with you the Old Testament story of a threatened civil war among the tribes of Israel. It was a defining moment in the history of the tribal confederation. The "Moses Movement" was always on the verge of collapsing. Struggles over leadership, anxiety over scarce resources, and uncertainty about the future made the journey to freedom a precarious one. Recent scholarship is less certain of a homogeneous group making up the tribes of Israel.

The name *Israel*, according to Norman Gottwald, referred not merely to a religious community, but to a "retribalized society" concerned with issues of survival. The religion of the Yahwists was a movement specifically addressed to the life circumstances of those in revolt against the imperial and hierarchic structures of thirteenth-century Egypt. This tribal structure was, to use Walter Shurden's term, "fragile." The particular threat of the text was the outbreak of civil war. The tribes east of the Jordan, the Reubenites, Gadites, and the half-tribe of Manasseh had erected an altar in the Jordan Valley. The unilateral action of these tribes was viewed as treachery and rebellion by the rest of the Israelites. The historian implies an "us" and "them" perception of the conflict. He says:

> "When the people of Israel heard of it, the whole assembly of the Israelites gathered at Shiloh, to make war against them." (Josh. 22:12 NASB)

The stigma of "us" and "them" is generally the result of boundaries. In this case the boundary was geographical—the Jordan River. The Reubenites, Gadites, and the half-tribe of Manasseh decided to occupy the land "east of the river." The other ten tribes would occupy the land "west of Jordan." This was a troubling arrangement. The eastern tribes were Israelites who had settled in another place. They were on the "other side" of the common experience. They were the "outsiders." It was offensive to the western tribal leadership that they dared to mainstream themselves by erecting an altar in the space they occupied. The counterfeit altar was viewed as a threat to the very existence of Israel. In a telling interpretation of their action, the priest Phinehas linked the altar to several notorious episodes in the wilderness and conquest traditions. The priestly sensitivities of Phinehas are quite evident. He recounted the immorality and idolatry that occurred at Shittim (Num. 25:1-13). There Israelites married Moabite women and began worshiping their gods. The perpetrators were impaled in the sun before the Lord (see v. 4). Another Israelite man brought a Midianite woman into his family in the sight of Moses and in the sight of the whole congregation of the Israelites while they were weeping at the entrance of the tent of meeting (see v. 6). It is interesting to note the implied silence of Moses on the latter issue. Though Moses did not condemn the man (and with good reason, for he too was married to a Midianite woman, cf. Ex. 2:21-22; 18:2; Num. 12:1-2), Phinehas led the assault and killed both the man and the woman (v. 8). The second reference by Phinehas is to the "sin of Achan" (Josh. 7:1, 20-26). In stealing the "devoted things" during a military campaign, Achan was responsible for an embarrassing defeat for Israel. He too was placed under the curse and was stoned to death.

After linking the altar to a history of infamy, Phinehas implies that the land east of Jordan is "polluted" and tells the eastern tribes: "If your land is unclean, cross over into the Lord's land where the Lord's tabernacle now stands, and take for yourselves a possession among us; only do not rebel against the Lord, or rebel against us by building yourselves an altar other than the altar of the Lord our God" (v. 19). The priestly language of Phinehas strains at a few facts. It is very different from the Joshua speech (vv. 2-4; the silence of Joshua is intriguing. The voice of leadership comes from Phinehas, not Joshua.). First, though Canaan is the Promised Land, the "Lord's land," Moses had agreed with the eastern tribes, the Reubenites, Gadites, and the half-tribe of Manasseh, that they could settle in the Jordan Valley. The authorization of Moses stated de facto that they were in the "Lord's land." These tribes raised cattle, and the Jordan Valley was rich in pasturing land.

Second, the eastern tribes had acted in solidarity with the other tribes. As a condition of their settlement in the land east of Jordan, they fought alongside the other tribes in the military conquest of Canaan. They agreed to stay with the other tribes until the conquest was complete. It was only after they fulfilled their obligation to the whole that they returned to the Jordan Valley to occupy their territory. Linked only to a negative history, these tribes were an integral part of the positive history of the other tribes.

Third, in linking the erection of the altar to infamous episodes, Phinehas precluded meaningful dialogue about the matter. The issue was already decided prior to the eastern tribes having the opportunity to speak. The effective silencing of the outsiders by the insiders was accomplished by a selective reading of negative history and the proposal of the solution by those who were insiders. The altar was in fact a result of living on the other side.

To live with the minority experience is to live with the fear of being forgotten and excluded. It is the feeling of foreignness, of not belonging. Ralph Ellison refers to it as "being invisible," present but not counted, speaking but not being heard, absent in the places of power. The "whole assembly of the Israelites could gather at Shiloh" without the presence of the eastern tribes. The eastern tribes were not rebelling or acting treacherously. But they feared that the geographical boundary would eventually result in their exclusion. The tribes had no plan to establish an alternative system of ritual, no plans to usurp priestly prerogatives. They told Phinehas and the chiefs of the congregation: "No! We did it from fear that in time to come your children might say to our children, 'What have you to do with the LORD, the God of Israel? For the LORD has made a boundary between us and you. . . . you have no portion in the LORD'" (vv. 24-25). The tribes from the east, from the other side of the Jordan, built an altar of remembrance, an altar of witness, an altar that declared that despite the boundary of the Jordan, they shared in the common heritage, the common struggle, and the common faith.

The challenge of American Baptists as we feel the white heat of election-year politics and draw near to the new millennium, is to look closely and with humility at how we are drawing the boundaries. The circle is narrowing in the body politic of American society. The smaller the circle, the more the minority experience is negatively stigmatized. Like Phinehas, we can selectively interpret history, even sacred history, and demonize those who are not our enemies. The Reconstruction Movement, with its aim of a "theocratic state," makes this mistake. Those who would claim America a "Christian nation" deny this country's history of oppression and violence. It also insults those victimized by our national idolatries. Such people are robbed of their histories and the truth of their present. Phinehas was right in believing there should be a common altar. But the common altar must transcend boundaries. It must be a place for the outsiders as well as the insiders. At this altar, the full history must be embraced, not just selected portions that justify narrow, self-serving purposes. Where Phinehas was wrong was in forgetting that the altar pointed beyond itself to a God who is free.

Let us build and worship at the altar of hope and justice. It is here that we will find a God who loves this world. A God who can handle the diversity and plurality of this world. A God who is not finished with us Baptists. At this altar, the altar of hope and justice, we will discover that responsible freedom is finally freedom for God and freedom for each other. This is our center. This is what holds us together. It is the unifying aspect amid our diversity. At our altar we must join together and sing "in Christ there is no east or west"! The eastern tribes in a powerful confessional statement said of their altar: "It is a witness between us that the LORD is God" (v. 34).

The eastern tribes called the altar "Witness." In the place they occupied, on their side of the river, they shared in the common story and the common faith. In this defining moment, what will we call our altar?

Lord, We Are Ready

Daniel E. Weiss

We need to get moving. Inertia has been a plague on the people of God in almost every generation. But God only tolerates so much before calling us to get going.

This was surely the case with God's ancient people: Moses reviewed the story after forty years in the wilderness. The promise of God was always with them. They, like their successors of every generation, organized for the journey. "I took the heads of your tribes, wise and experienced men, and appointed them heads over you, leaders of thousands, and of hundreds, of fifties and of tens, and officers for your tribes" (Deut. 1:15)—like modern deacons, pastors, area ministers, executive ministers, and heads of boards. They developed a system of planning and decision making. When faced with the challenge of Kadesh-Barnea, they were commanded to take possession without fear, but when they sent out twelve planners and strategists, all but two became fearful and lost heart (Deut. 1:19-25).

The Israelites developed committees, commissions, covenants of relationships, long-range plans, bylaws, and standing rules, but in spite of God's reassurance and promise of support, they chose to stay in their tents and grumble, to tremble with fear and long for the past (Deut. 1:26-27).

"Is it because there were no graves in Egypt that you have taken us away to die in the wilderness?" they asked. "It would have been better for us to serve the Egyptians" (Ex. 14:11, 12). Once unleashed, their memories of the past were edged in gold! In Egypt "we sat by the pots of meat, . . . we ate bread to the full; . . . you have brought us out into this wilderness to kill this whole assembly with hunger" (Ex. 16:3). "We remember the fish which we used to eat free in Egypt, the cucumbers and the melons

Daniel E. Weiss has been general secretary of American Baptist Churches in the U.S.A. since September 1, 1988. This address was first delivered on the occasion of his installation as general secretary at the ABC/USA Biennial in June 1989.

and the leeks and the onions and the garlic, but now . . . there is nothing at all to look at except this manna" (Num. 11:5-6). ". . . have you brought us up from Egypt, to kill us and our children and our livestock with thirst?" (Ex. 17:3). "Why have you brought us up out of Egypt to die in the wilderness? For there is no food and no water, and we loathe this miserable food" (Num. 21:5). "'Why is the LORD bringing us into this land, to fall by the sword? Our wives and our little ones will become plunder; would it not be better for us to return to Egypt?' So they said to one another, 'Let us appoint a leader and return to Egypt'" (Num. 14:3-4).

Apparently they had forgotten that they had been in slavery, in bondage. So the Lord became angry and sent them out to wander. That grumbling generation, including Moses, would never see the land of promise. They met defeat and frustrated God's rich and exciting purposes for them. They had the people, organization, resources, and clear goals, but they lacked the will. It was more satisfying and less risky to grumble than to act.

Finally God had enough. The silence was broken. "And the LORD spoke . . . saying, 'You have circled this mountain long enough. Now turn north'" (Deut. 2:2-3). Get moving; get off dead center. Stop talking and start acting. The time for going around in circles is over!

American Baptists are at a critical, strategic, and exciting point in history as a denomination. We are called to make a difference in a radically changing, often threatening, and deeply troubled world. We are called to touch lives and transform a troubled society in ways that are consistent with God's will and vision for it.

Yet the Gallup Poll, "Unchurched America, 1988," found that 44 percent of all persons in the United States are unchurched (are not church members and have not attended church in six months). Sixty percent of those polled, churched and unchurched, said the church is too interested and preoccupied with its own organization and structure and not concerned enough with theological and spiritual issues and values.

We have been part of denominational life in this country for 175 years. Our history is rich and worthy of celebration. But could we be among those who have lost touch with the heartbeat of the people?

Newsweek recently said that the "old-line" churches have moved from "mainline" to "side line." It doesn't take much reflection or analysis to recognize that theologically, spiritually, and institutionally these are very difficult times for the groups that once dominated American religious life. Sometimes it seems that the more the moral, social, and spiritual problems of our world increase, the more our influence declines. The issue we face is not one of domination, power, or prestige. It is, at heart, one of servanthood and faithfulness. The real issue is perceiving and pursuing God's vision for us and our mission for Christ's sake in the world. What is at stake is our faithfulness to the gospel. It is, at heart, our will and capacity to be, indeed, a denomination worthy of the gospel of Jesus Christ.

The challenge we face is whether we are now able to shape a relationship to our culture based, not on our being here early in its history, or on what our culture expects from us, but on a biblically informed and enlightened vision of the church's role in the world. What is of consequence is how we discover afresh a new sense of mission and purpose that can make a powerful difference in the lives of people and society as a whole in a radically changing world.

William McKinney, who with Wade Clark Roof, wrote *American Mainline Religion: Its Changing Shape and Future,* has the ABC/USA in mind when he says:

> The old line churches have no hope of reaching out to the new populations of America—to people of color, to those drawn by the television preachers, to those who struggle to make ends meet—if they remain bound to the notion that it is possible or desirable to restore our churches to the earlier position of dominance. It is only when we accept the fact of our new off-centeredness that we will have a chance of partnership with peoples whose experience has not been at the center but rather of the margins.

Today the witness to us as to how to be a living, vital church comes to us from our sisters and brothers in the two-thirds world and on the edges of society. The store-front churches are modeling the vitality of the gospel for the cathedrals. It is the simple yet profound faith and theology of the disestablished and historically marginalized followers of Christ who are not embarrassed to act too religious or give expression to spiritual passion that once again speak the truth to the noble and mighty and sophisticated.

Whatever else Jesus Christ had in mind in the founding of his church, he clearly envisioned

- something great and of enormous cosmic significance
- something worth the trouble
- something that would make a difference
- something that could not be ignored, easily discounted, casually shoved aside, put down, limited, and restrained
- something so alive and inspired it would make waves, arouse fierce opposition, and turn the world upside down.

Jesus said, "I have come to cast fire upon the earth; and how I wish it were already kindled!" (Luke 12:49). An Anglican bishop once observed that wherever the apostle Paul went, there was a riot, but wherever he goes, they serve tea. We need to decide if God is calling us to participate in a revolution or to be guests at a tea party.

We—as a multiracial and multicultural denomination with strong evangelical traditions and commitments—can participate in and even lead a new awakening, a renewal, a revitalization in the church and the world. Our potential is tremendous. We are unique among Protestant denominations in our reflection of the new, inclusive humanity in Jesus Christ. Persons of color represent over 40 percent of our membership. We possess tremendous resources in committed and able people, educational institutions, concern for evangelism, and commitment to peace and justice.

God is calling us to see and obey a new vision, to follow the cloud by day and the pillar of fire by night. What could stop us? What could hold us back? The answer: Being content to go around in circles! Being satisfied to walk around the same old mountain when God is calling us to move on.

There is something comforting about going around in circles. There is solace in familiarity. We see the same friendly, comforting scenery over and over. There is no need to readjust to new climates, new vistas, new ideas, new ways of thinking and acting.

There is a certain comforting deception in walking around the same mountain: It gives the illusion of movement and progress. After all, the ground keeps moving under our feet. We can even rack up statistics going around in circles—miles walked, meals eaten, shoes worn out, babies born, and lives given in the effort. And going around in circles is low on the risk scale. But if familiarity doesn't breed contempt, it often breeds indifference and lethargy.

Walking in circles makes us tired. We think we must be doing something significant and important. We make plans, create and expend budgets, use resources—something must be happening. But when we finally lift our eyes, no matter how hard and diligently we have traveled, we see the same old mountain, not the Promised Land.

American Baptists, let us hear the word of the Lord: "You have circled this mountain long enough." The time has come for us to be done with those things that ensnare, entice, and entrap us into going in circles and keep us from moving on.

What are some of the attitudes and issues we need to put behind us so we can get on with what God is calling us to be and to do?

One is the institutionalism into which we have drifted at all levels of

our denominational life—a preoccupation with our structures, our mechanisms. It is a form of "temple religion." But Jesus said, "Something greater
than the temple is here" (Matt. 12:6). The church at all levels—locally,
regionally, nationally, ecumenically—must not be allowed to become just
another institution. The church, first, last, and always must be a movement,
not an institution or an establishment. Its priority must be its mission, not
its machinery. Its preoccupation must be outreach not organization. Why?
Because a movement is drawn to and motivated by factors and needs
outside of itself.

Institutions have an internal agenda for their own maintenance and
survival. Movements reach out in ministry and service to the world in all
of its needs, while institutions turn inward and are absorbed with their own
needs. Institutions don't evangelize, don't reach out, don't extend themselves. Evangelism is not part of their value system. Staying alive, however, is a major priority. Movements grow and expand and invite.
Movements upset the establishment. Movements are unpredictable.
Movements are never boring, never tedious. It's exciting to be part of a
movement, because movements are of the Spirit!

We began as a movement, coming together as local Baptist churches to
do international and home missions, education, and literature ministry. But
like many other denominations, we have become an institution, walking
around the same mountain, going in circles. We need to recapture the
movement spirit. Let us recognize that our denomination exists not as an
end in itself but as an instrument through which the gospel is advanced
and proclaimed and applied in all of its promise and wholeness.

As United Methodist bishop Edsel Ammons put it, "An establishment
(institution) talks more about our Church and less about our Christ. A
movement talks more about our Christ and less about our Church." Let
us, together then, in the power of the Spirit, be participants and leaders in
a movement. We've been circling this mountain long enough!

Another mountain inhibiting our progress is our high tolerance for
pessimism and cynicism. Let us stop believing critics, journalists, and
other gloomy naysayers and prophets of doom about the church and start
believing the promises of God. Aren't we "good news" people?

Are we victims of our current financial projections? Do past trends
irrevocably determine our future? Are we on the losing side, or do we,
indeed, participate in the triumphant power of the resurrection? Aren't
American Baptists still capable of being motivated and encouraged by
joyous opportunities for service and by our potential to make a significant
difference in the world?

Let's get out of the doldrums. Let's go beyond the mentality of survival. Let's lay aside the encumbrances of cynicism and discouragement and get on with God's work. We've been circling this mountain long enough!

Another mountain in our way is obsessive introspection. We need to stop trying to discover and define who we are and declare that we've done it. The time has come for us to be who we say we are. We are being called from circling to movement as an inviting, evangelizing, growing denomination.

- We are people who share the good news of God's reconciling grace and who invite without reticence or embarrassment persons to accept Christ and become part of a loving, worshiping, serving community of faith. When we have established five hundred new churches by 1994, let's plant five hundred more for the sake of the gospel.
- We are those who work for the defeat of injustice, the strengthening of human relationships, the dispelling of oppression, and the pursuit of world peace.
- We are people of unity—a people who celebrate and affirm our wonderful diversity but, at the same time, lift up the common elements of humanity and faith that bind together the children of God for growth and service and mission.

Yet in spite of the multicultural, multiethnic diversity within our membership, far too many of our people still feel like visitors in a white denomination. The constant struggle for partnership and mutual responsibility is still before us, but struggle we must. We've been circling this mountain long enough!

Let's also put behind us the well-worn and tedious debate as to whether God is limited to calling only persons of the male gender to ministry. We keep asking God, "Do you call women to ministry?" And God keeps saying yes and has been saying it to us for a hundred years. And the "yes" is getting louder and louder, because the "yeses" are today a total of 528 ordained American Baptist women in ministry. We've been circling this mountain long enough!

What about our place in the wider Christian community? Can we finally decide to resolve or even agree to disagree about our position as cooperating Christians? If, where two or three are gathered together in Jesus' name, he is there, shouldn't American Baptists be there too? Do we ever want to be guilty of being more exclusive than our Lord? How difficult it is to discover that God's circle of friends is larger than our own.

We are founding members of the National Council of Churches in Christ, the World Council of Churches, the Baptist World Alliance, and now we are observers at the National Association of Evangelicals. Our Lord's vision and prayer is for the wholeness of his body. One of the great tragedies and sins of the church today is our dividedness and our divisiveness. It occurs within as well as among denominations. But it's a scandal to the world, an affront to God, a weakening presence in the church, and an obstacle to evangelism. To prolong intense debase over our ecumenicity will not contribute to our moving on. Let's be responsibly involved, standing for what is important to us, making our witness, and working toward wholeness in the body of Christ. We've circled this mountain long enough!

The world sometimes sees the church's opportunity and importance more clearly than we do. Consider some of these as recognitions:

Last February it was my privilege, along with President Davis and some other American Baptists, to represent the ABC/USA in Cuba. During that visit several of us spent almost two hours with Dr. José Felipe Carneado, the Minister of Cults and Religious Affairs. We met in the offices of the Central Committee of the Cuban Communist Party. In the course of our conversation, Minister Carneado said that Cuba needs the church because it teaches morality. He noted that half the marriages in Cuba now end in divorce within one year. He indicated concern for the situation of senior citizens and the need for child care. He also noted that the youth of the nation are becoming increasingly obsessed with wanting to buy consumer goods and luxuries they see advertised on television. Here was a Marxist, philosophically committed to atheism, calling for the church to have a role in the life of his society.

I thought of our own nation and the many problems we face within it. Yet the church in this country is so divided that we hardly have the capacity to speak with one voice even when we agree. But the united moral and spiritual resources of Christians working together would be an incredibly potent force.

Some concerns are beyond controversy. Those who call themselves Christian cannot possibly be indifferent to these concerns or believe that God isn't calling the church to take a primary leadership role in relationship to their solution—for example, the cancer of drugs and the tens of thousands of our young people falling through the cracks on crack, the disgrace of homelessness in the wealthiest country in the world, the catastrophic epidemic of AIDS and the need to minister with Christian sensitivity and compassion to those living with it and to press for the allocation of resources for research that will eventually find its cure.

As American Baptists we often see ourselves as a bridge denomination—historically committed to the ecumenical movement but also evangelical with strong relationships among conservative evangelicals and charismatics.

In light of these and other overwhelming problems in our society that need immediate attention, it is time for us to put down our cudgels, put aside our theological microscopes, forget our past bickerings, and be the church of Jesus Christ.

I call for a new coalition of concerned Christian communions—mainliners, evangelicals, fundamentalists, charismatics, Southern Baptists—to unite in a battle against the insidious epidemic of drugs rotting out the core of our youth and our society; to work for decent homes and shelter for all citizens; to reach out, as Jesus did, to the lepers of our day who confront a disease that present projections indicate will in some way touch all our lives. Let us stop arguing over the nature of the Bible and begin to hear and obey it. These problems are too vast for any one segment of the church to affect. Yet together we could make a powerful difference.

Let us be catalysts at the local, regional, national, and international levels, working for unity in response to need, not to develop new organizations or structures, but to call the body of Christ together to confront these pressing needs.

Some historians have noted that the last decade of every century tends to set the tone and the agenda for the ensuing century. If that is true of a century, what about a millennium? There are some compelling questions we must face:

- Are we ready for the nineties and beyond?
- Are we ready to have a vision that transcends our corporate, organizational structure and unites us in a common mission?
- Are we ready to be a people who eagerly engage in evangelism without embarrassment and who struggle for social justice without hesitation?
- Are we truly ready to be the new humanity in Christ, sharing ownership, leadership, and responsibility with all the people of God representing the wide range of racial, ethnic, and gender diversity in this denomination?
- Are we ready to work for the renewal of the local church as the key

to our being energized afresh as a people in mission and to hold up
this emphasis as a major priority in the next decade?

- Are we ready to obey our Lord's commission to teach and disciple
  by taking seriously the need to revitalize our Christian education
  programs, particularly the Sunday school, and to bring our colleges
  and seminaries from the periphery of denominational life to the
  center, where they belong, if we are going to be a healthy and
  viable denomination with adequate leadership for our future?
- Are we ready to assume our appropriate place as a global people,
  responsive to the new realities of our world, including the shift of
  the church's "center of gravity" and influence from North America
  and Europe to the two-thirds world, and to adapt our missiology in
  response to it?
- Are we ready to join hands with concerned Christians of other
  communions to combat the evils that plague us in this world as a
  witness to the wholeness of Christ?

If we can say, "Lord, we are ready," to these questions, then we can be
on the move. We can be a renewed and revitalized denomination made up
of renewed and revitalized congregations.

The same Spirit of Pentecost is with us today, but we need to be open
to that Spirit. We need to stop circling the same old mountains. We need
to get on with God's agenda for us in the assurance of God's abiding
presence and support and to the glory and praise of Jesus Christ.

"Forgetting what lies behind and reaching forward to what lies ahead,
[let's] press on toward the goal for the prize of the upward call of God in
Christ Jesus" (Phil. 3:13-14).

Past as Present, Present as Past: Freedom to Read the Self and the World

Vincent L. Wimbush

I

A recent article in the *New York Times* ("In Search of History: When Today's Agenda Is a Prism for the Past," October 1, 1995) made the point that a type of historical inquiry that has gained greater "currency" of late is inspired by "political ends or self-validation." The sexual orientation of prominent historical figures such as Abraham Lincoln and Eleanor Roosevelt, the African identification of the rulers and glories of ancient Egypt, and the Jewish identity of Christopher Columbus are a few examples of topics pursued by such "history." This type of historical inquiry, one American historian who has written about Lincoln's sexual orientation is reported to have said, "may have less to do with the past than with the present." The horror and contempt of more "traditional" historians in every field in response to such "history" are expressed through the reported words of another Lincoln scholar: "I don't see how the whole question of Lincoln's gayness would explain anything other than making gay people feel better. . . . And I don't think the function of history is to make people feel good. Celebratory history is propaganda." These statements and the article as a whole raise quite provocative questions about both the nature and functions of history and the politics of group formation, self-definition, and affirmation.

The debates about the relationships between different groups in the United States reflects some of the same positioning and counter-positioning. For example, the longstanding relationship between black people and Jewish people raises some of the same interpretive questions and issues.

Vincent L. Wimbush is professor of New Testament and Christian Origins at Union Theological Seminary in New York City. This essay is a more developed and extended version of a presentation first given at "Called to Responsible Freedom: A Conference on Baptist Distictives," at Green Lake, Wisconsin, in August 1996.

It is a debate that has seemed in recent years in many quarters in the United States to be not only interminable, but shrill, even deafening. Politicians and pundits, establishment and street-corner preachers, philosophers, social critics, and analysts—these and others often make reference to the shared agenda between blacks and Jews during the civil rights movements of the 1950s and 1960s, suggesting thereby that the period was something approaching halcyon days, a defining moment, a golden era in the history of relations between the two peoples. However, the onset of affirmative action and debate about its definition, its politics, its general merits and effects, and the ongoing related tensions and violent incidents in major urban areas tell a different story. For different, even conflicting, reasons almost all parties and factions now seem oddly in agreement that the two peoples have in the last two decades fallen apart, perhaps into a state of irreparable conflict. There is ready consensus that the present relationship between blacks and Jews in too many places is fraught with much suspicion, resentment, bitterness, charges, and countercharges.

Another example within the large and diverse Christian camp, relevant especially in the last election year in the era of the burning of African American churches, comes to mind. It is the relationship between white evangelicals and fundamentalists and African Americans of the same or different religious persuasions. I am reminded of Ralph Reed, who very recently resigned as director of the (ironically named) Christian Coalition, who in the last year or so had spoken out on behalf of some white evangelicals about the need to repent of their past silence and even support of racism and discriminatory practices against African Americans. I am also reminded of the Southern Baptists' recent official apology for past racism and discrimination. All of these cases have to do with an emphasis upon the past—a certain reading of a past.

The arena in which tensions between any two peoples is likely to be sharpened is that of history—the interpretation and recovery of a past. Whether used as an offensive or defensive weapon, whether used to bolster some Afrocentric notions about the origins of anti-black racism in the United States or in the West generally, whether to defend the honor and integrity of the nation against all threats physical and ideological, whether to legitimize or delegitimize certain religious beliefs and communities, the retreat into historical argumentation is now much in evidence. From popular street polemical rhetoric to the emotional strains of community tabloids to the discursive twists of myriad academic conferences and books—in these and many other places, this interest in the historical has taken some bizarre twists, especially when it makes the claim "to set the record straight" regarding certain contemporary claims and their problematic relationships to the explosion of different, often competing claims.

Of course, only the most unsophisticated and un-self-critical person, whether he or she carries the title "historian" or not, is now unaware that all interests in the past are inspired, sometimes even controlled and driven (because often commissioned and funded) by, the historians' position vis-à-vis certain contemporary issues and concerns. This is the case with respect to the study of the morals of the Victorian era, nineteenth-century Russian political history, early twentieth-century German intellectual history, or the history of space research. It can hardly be less true for the study of religion in general, of the Bible in particular.

There are plenty of axes—political, economic, racial-ethnic, chauvinistic—being ground in contemporary popular and academic discussions, conferences, lectures, articles, essays, and monographs about religion and about the Bible. But that axes are being ground is not in itself the most important problem and challenge. I am in total agreement with those historians who argue not only that the questions asked about the past are now and have always been inspired by contemporary issues and concerns but also that historical methodologies must now consistently reflect such a stance. One of the urgent problems, however, is that such activity has not generally been conducive to elevation to and sure footing upon high discursive grounds, that is, to mature exchanges, learning and discovery about the other (including the other within one's own camp or denominational group). In fact, as daily news accounts around the world provide evidence, such activity has led in some places to serious rifts, even violence and death.

Historical inquiry of the sort that seeks, in its different but necessarily naive ways, merely to "establish the facts," or merely to "defend the race," or "my people," or "my religion/denomination," or "our position," simply to accuse the other as source of current problems, needs to be identified for what it is and renounced. Such "history" is problematic, not so much because it has no insights or tells no truths, but because it cannot generally even adequately, or critically, problematize the "facts" and "truths" it discovers and engages. Put another way, this type of history seems unable to address the complexities—the diversification, the shifts, the multidirectional movements, the contradictions, the layers and layerings, the overlappings—that characterize life experience past and present. More often than not, such history is viewed by all but zealous insiders as more of the unfortunate polemics to be responded to in kind. It does not take exceptional powers of discernment to recognize that in our times a truly vicious cycle of offensive and defensive polemics regarding religious life, often with the Bible playing a most prominent role, is evident. Clearly, the polemics do not involve all or even a great majority of individuals and groups, but it takes only a few particularly shrill, well-placed contenders on each side to make a phenomenon.

II

I want to suggest a different type of inquiry as part of an attempt to go beyond the current rhetorical state of things regarding the interpretation of religion and of the Bible in the United States. This suggestion is not proffered as a political or social solution or panacea but as a modest contribution toward the broadening and leavening of the discourse. I cannot be persuaded that contemporary political or social dynamics and conflicts and difficulties can be addressed without attention to the structure and dynamics of discourse between relevant parties. Such attention should have to do not only with *what* the parties say to each other, but also *how* they say what they say and think about themselves and "the other." I do not propose the abandonment of historical inquiry of religion and theology or of the Bible. What I propose is a type of historical inquiry that has affinities with the movement among some scholars and critics called "the new historicism."[1] By this I mean that I propose historical inquiry that reflects not so much the effort to establish the culturally chauvinistic or religiously sectarian "facts," but instead reflects multidisciplinary explorations that provide windows onto ongoing complex efforts in self-discovery and self-definition in the cultivation of affirming social relations and in the acquisition of social power on the part of a people.

Efforts in self-discovery and self-definition require a type of historical inquiry, a type of stretching back into the past. But, again, this stretching back into the past should not be collapsed into a type of *antiquarianism.* Insofar as the raw materials (multifaceted oral traditions and rhetorical and literary forms and genres) that are engaged are themselves traditions, legacies, and productions of generations past, they also require that attention be given to historical inquiry. The point is that the type of historical inquiry here suggested to effect positive social relations should focus less on *the true meaning* of this or that story or epic, this or that text, this or that doctrine, proscription or proposition, and so forth, than on the *dynamics of interaction between peoples.* A people's ongoing self-discoveries, self-definitions, and social relations are reflected in the ways they project, inscribe, and reinscribe their ways and fundamental character onto certain stories and texts. The forms and paradigms of certain stories and texts in turn provide forms, formats, and paradigms for the articulation and realization of communal ethos.

This history is of a different sort from what we have generally seen in recent years, particularly within either the religious polemic or scientific exegesis. It means an elaboration upon and fine-tuning of the sort of historical inquiry upon which the *New York Times* article (mentioned above) focused. In such an inquiry the past is understood as *prism* through which the self and its world are made apparent and articulated.

This essay can do no more than raise questions for more elaborate projects. It may be sufficient here to emphasize the importance of coming to terms with the functions of history in relationship to self-discovery and social relations. Since, as argued above, a working assumption for critical inquiry is that all inquiries about the past are inspired or driven by the present, the reasons for the persistence of the controversies around religious and theological/doctrinal issues and points of biblical interpretation need to be considered more carefully and seriously.[2] I should like to focus upon African Americans and white evangelicals as examples of the problems and challenges of self-discovery in relationship to biblical interpretation.

I prefer to begin the quest for self-understanding by focusing upon how a minority people has gone about defining itself, surviving, and gaining power in the context of the United States. I should like to know what forces, challenges, difficulties, and possibilities have been presented to this people. How has it tried to define itself? Within what frames of reference? Within or over against what traditions, discourses and legacies? With what myths? With what symbols? Answers to these and related questions are more likely to get us closer to a perception of the self-understandings of a still significant sector among the two communities and what it is that governs the relation of the one to others than will investigations into the argument for the black African origins of Christianity on the one hand and white evangelicalism assumed to be the contemporary legatee of Christianity on the other.

In the interest of understanding the complexity of the relations between black and white evangelicals, and in order to test the validity of the thesis about a defensible methodological route to such understanding, I think it appropriate and all the more fascinating to attempt to clarify how two peoples—given their experiences in the United States—engage a part of the same tradition. Analyzing how the same tradition is engaged by two peoples will shed light upon the *complexity of reception* of already complex traditions, their symbols and myths, within the same general social context. The focus on complexity of reception and manipulation of common tradition may in turn afford greater insight into the impetus behind the formation and maintenance of the different social worlds. In this essay only a sketch of an example of the different engagements of common tradition on the part of blacks and white evangelicals can be presented. For my purposes in writing this essay it is sufficient to offer some methodological suggestions about ways to think about the issue of communal self-definitions. I am less interested in exhausting the substantive interpretive arguments and issues.

III

The common tradition I have in mind is a mythic story that is part of a collection of traditions called "the Bible." For the great majority of blacks in what has come to be the United States the Bible is that particular collection of sacred texts—"the Scriptures"—that was transmitted first through the offices and hegemony of American evangelical Protestantism.[3] The fact that the Bible as a collection of sacred texts is held in common between the two peoples only adds to the fascinating phenomenology of the engagement of traditions and symbols.[4] Attention to black and white evangelical engagements of the multiple traditions that are contained within the Bible should highlight both the difficulty, if not impossibility, of seeking to discover in the collective mind the *one* meaning of any tradition or symbol or text. Yet the Bible affords access to more popular or broad-based cultural self-definitions, currents, and orientations than any other source. Histories of interpretations of biblical traditions, both scholarly and popular, have long provided evidence of the sometimes rather dramatic behaviors on the part of postbiblical communities that have defined themselves as guardians and tradents of biblical and other ancient traditions. Their claims notwithstanding, such communities have not simply *preserved* the ancient traditions, as much as they have in different, sometimes conflicting ways and to different degrees of intensities, *imaginatively inscribed* their own agendas of predilections and prejudices, hopes and fears, anger and joys onto the writings they have come to deem "sacred." Such inscriptions, I would argue (and this should be taken to be the major point of this essay) are also fairly clear and wide-open windows onto broad-based communal self-understandings and interests. They provide a broader yet more nuanced, more subtle, more textured view of the machinations and developments of social formations than a number of inquiries into either African origins studies or the still naive but pernicious assumptions and/or claims on the part of many whites that the Christian tradition is fundamentally European in origin, orientation, and character, with other parts of the world having been grafted on. Of course, inquiries into black and European histories *are* important, even necessary, and they often present or stumble upon important "facts" for serious consideration. But as I have already argued above, any historical inquiry that does not reflect awareness that the concerns, assumptions, even prejudices of the inquirer's present function as the catalyst for such inquiry is doomed to be parochial and unpersuasive outside a rather narrow circle; given the times, it could even be dangerous.

My call is not for artificial or superficial references to the present in every argument or on every line. It is rather a call for sophisticated self-awareness and problematizing of the self in the present as inspiration or catalyst or springboard for thinking about the past. Because it represents at least an effort to come to terms with some of the driving impulses of the present, the type of inquiry that I now call for is more likely to be persuasive beyond the narrow circle to which the "historian," both popular and establishment academic, may belong, and it just possibly may help arrest some of the damage that many historical polemical works and rhetoric have done in our times.

In an effort to be suggestive about what type of project can be taken up to effect the persuasion about which I have spoken, I want to put forward as example one story in the biblical tradition that is especially resonant still for a great number of contemporary black and white Protestants in the United States of the late twentieth century—that of the Exodus. It is widely accepted in scholarly circles and in much popular thinking that this story, created and for centuries traduced by Jews, functioned among the latter as a type of epic, a mythic cultural formation story and, more specifically, as a paradigm for hope and inspiration and revolutionary liberation.[5] There has even been discerned in the Jewish telling and retelling of the story a pattern of themes that have defined the Jewish history of struggles for peoplehood: complaints about dire straits or oppression, hope against the odds for deliverance, joining in covenant, and the building of a new order.[6]

These same themes from the Exodus story have captured the imagination of many other peoples in western history. Many non-Jews have coopted and embraced the story as their own—as though it had been created for the express purpose of calling them into being as a people, encouraging them as they experienced despair or dire straits or even oppression, strengthening their resolve, and justifying whatever directions and actions they have thought and continue to think necessary to take. From New World evangelical English Puritans to Old World ranting fascists to the highly churched Boers of South Africa, the story has been a popular part of western cultural imagination, not merely a part of a strictly religious-confessional canon. The many engagements of the Exodus story in western history are not only diverse and often conflicting and histrionic but are also ambiguous in their effects, even as they are variously described in terms of types of political, intellectual, and spiritual revolution.[7]

African Americans have also been among those peoples who have embraced the story. In fact, their relationship to the story and to much of the larger tradition of which the story is a part is in itself epic, poignant, and dramatic. I want to focus upon this people's reading of the story in order to illustrate a larger point about the dynamics and effects of interpretation of the past, here obviously using the Bible as symbol of the past. Perhaps more than most other cultural readings, African American readings of the story reflect how African Americans have understood their situations in the part of the world that has come to be known as the United States. Their situations include not only the survival of uprootedness, slavery, Jim Crow segregation, and migrations in search of socio-political and economic amelioration that failed to materialize but also their coming into being as a people.[8] Moreover, and most important for this essay, these readings betray quite a bit about the complexity of traditions and symbols, what (and *how*) traditions and symbols mean in different contexts, how they "travel" (or are represented differently in different contexts) and with what effects, and what they reveal about the complexity of social formation and the construction of self-understandings.

Given the predominant orientation of academic biblical studies, because of, or perhaps in spite of (!), my being a biblical scholar and historian of religion, I am concerned less about what *really happened* at the time of the Jewish exodus from Egypt than I am about *why* the story about the Jewish exodus from Egypt perdures, why it continues to arrest and stimulate the imagination of so many peoples in my own time and in my own world. I want to know *how* the story functions, namely, *why* it resonates with, is being embraced and manipulated by, my contemporaries. The latter often invoke it and other stories while involving themselves in world construction, world critique, world reform and world maintenance. I want to know *why* and *how* the story has come to be a part of what defines so many people in similar *and* different, even conflicting, ways. I want especially to know what are the immediate and less immediate historical, rhetorical, political, religious, socio-economic, and other influences that have shaped the ways many contemporary Jews, African Americans, white evangelical Protestants, Roman Catholics of many different ethnic backgrounds, and others now read the story.

Such interests are the impetus for my questions about the past. Just to know "the historical facts" about the Exodus is now for me neither realistic nor terribly interesting nor ultimately helpful in the effort to understand contemporary interpreting communities and my location relative to these communities. The attempt to separate the historical facts from the present that shapes and defines me as interpreter is naive.

Contemporary African Americans and white Protestants in the United States, notwithstanding the diversity in each camp, have histories of defining themselves, their worlds, and the world beyond their walls through reference to the Bible. They still define themselves in such a way, and the Exodus story has been a particularly important point of reference for both peoples. Through this story, both peoples continue to hold forth about their own radical differences—even uniqueness—from all others. Such claims are based on defining moments in their histories: their collective traumas and reversals, oppression, commitments and covenants.

But there is a rub: the shared emphasis upon and perceptions about the experiences of slavery, oppression, and liberation in the articulation of a communal self-definition does not preclude or even relativize differences and conflicts between the two communities. This may suggest many things, but among the plausible explanations, one that ought to be given due consideration is that epics, myths, and symbols have different meanings not only *between* but also within *cultures*, and this applies as well to class and gender differences.[9] It ought not be surprising that an ancient, mythic story can have a different meaning between two different peoples.

What the history of the use of the Exodus story points to as particularly important is that there can be sharp conflict among those whose rhetoric, epic texts, and (to some degree) experiences are otherwise quite similar. The Exodus story resonates with many African Americans and many white American evangelical Protestants for much the same reason: it helps both to define themselves on the basis of collective experience. For both groups, the story is a part of a language world into which they can enter for comfort and solace and perspective on the world and on themselves. It is a world from which both draw courage and resolve. For each group the story points to a never-to-be-forgotten experience. This is so not because the story is thought to contain the historical "facts" about an event long ago (although clearly there are some who confuse such a reading with their own cultural perspective) but because both groups are able to read their present ongoing experiences and self-understandings into the story!

Given some shared hermeneutical views on the part of African American and white Protestants and given their common tendency to inscribe onto the *one* story so much that dramatically and powerfully addresses pertinent human issues, it might at first seem incredible that serious conflict between the two groups could ensue. I note how common it is that interpreters ignore or underplay the complex, layered, textured character of the world of minority groups, many of which, especially on account of race, ethnicity, or religion, are considered somewhat marginal in a society. These minority groups, the "others," are still often lumped together in popular thinking and actual social relations in ways that are surprising, even shocking. One can take note, for example, of the assumptions made even today in the academy about the "others"—various racial and ethnic groups—that lead in some situations to the lumping together of nearly all non-white ethnic interests and persons into umbrella "ethnic studies" programs in college or university curricula. What is the logic, the academic and cultural presupposition, that leads to the academic and administrative grouping and supposed study of various groups in one administrative unit, under one rubric? Could one, in observing the racial and ethnic polarization (including some specific Black and Jewish polarization) around the O.J. Simpson trial, miss the point about how different peoples at the same time can have much in common and much that divides them? The polls suggested that the one "text"—the testimony and other evidence presented during the Simpson trial—was read by blacks and whites generally in totally opposite ways. There were no "facts" established such that all persons, except for the jury with the interpretive limitations pressed upon it, could agree on what should be O.J. Simpson's fate. Just as no amount of persuasive "evidence," no number of "facts" (our judicial system has never been based upon presentation of the *bruta facta*) or testimony or soaring lawyerly argumentation changed the views of the masses about Simpson in this country, so no amount of historical-critical study of the Exodus text, no amount of archaeological and scientific discovery and reconstruction of events said to pertain to the Exodus story, can determine what the story will mean to a people at any one time. The "facts" and "meaning" are, have always been, and will always be, culturally conditioned. The "facts" are in the collective culture-created, culture-focused, culture-blinking eyes of beholders.

The most critical factor in the construction of world-view and the development of meaning is not the shared text or canon, not the common rhetoric or collection of stories, but *the site of interpretation or enunciation*,[10] that is, the place within which and from which the interpreters can attempt to find voice. To ignore the difference in the site of interpretation and enunciation is to fall into serious error in an effort to understand a people. It is, after all, only the site of interpretation and enunciation that can claim to be the defining index of the interpreter(s).

Yet the site is not enough. The significance of ancient religious traditions, such as the Bible, for contemporary cultures—and thus for this essay—lies in the power that peoples invest in, project, and inscribe onto the traditions so that the peoples in turn might register, filter, or translate what for them are the things that matter most: religion, transcendence, the sacred. Texts that are set apart and called sacred, rituals, trances, possessions, and so forth, do not exist apart from their translations and mediations through cultural traditions. Sacred texts have become especially important in many cultures, most especially in American Protestant culture, as translucent prisms through which the sacred is mediated, a process that is never simply or easily carried out. The histories of African Americans and other American groups certainly provide evidence for this functioning. The complex interplay of differences and similarities in the readings of common ancient stories such as that of the Exodus among two different peoples is a reflection of the interpretive and enunciatory sites and communal readings of the larger contemporary (sociopolitical) world held in common.

Among the many challenges that will always present themselves to all Americans, but especially to African Americans and the people of whatever hue and background who call themselves Baptist, is that of diversity and pluralism. All Americans face it on account of the pluralism themes struck in the nation's founding mythic documents and on account of the demographics of the country; African Americans face it because their very origins and history—their "involuntary presence"—in what has become the United States likely will always provide the litmus test and attendant challenges for pluralism in the United States. Baptists, given their history of rhetoric about and making claims to model radical freedom and pluralism, will always be judged more harshly in light of the ideals of freedom and pluralism. Concretely, what taking up such a challenge means for all is to try to understand what it means for different groups to create and maintain their own sites for interpretation and enunciation, to inscribe and reinscribe their world-view and ethos onto texts and thereby textualize their world-views and ethos, and to respect the different sites of interpretations that define others.

No peoples can afford to be without understanding of the powers and dangers inherent in such challenges. Neither can individuals and peoples come to understand and relate to each other without understanding and respecting the social power and prerogatives in site- or culture-specific discursive formations.

IV

In the October 16, 1995, Million Man March on Washington, organizer and keynote speaker Louis Farrakhan invoked the Exodus story as he challenged hundreds of thousands of black men standing before him and those across the country. According to Farrakhan, the story challenges the men to "come out of" the bondage that so many had morally and ethically sunk into and that American existence generally had come to represent for them. That such rhetoric about the Exodus seemingly had to include comments about contemporary black-Jewish relations as well as the perfidious state of Christianity in reference to the state of African American existence is poignant. The point that neither contemporary African Americans nor contemporary Jews can be "explained" by simple reference to the ancient actors of the Exodus story should not be lost. How can a contemporary Africanist or Afrocentric reading be squared with Egyptians as villains? And how can a contemporary Jewish-settlement reading be squared with Arab-Palestinian aspirations and hopes for an "exodus" out of homelessness and liberation from despair? And how can arguments about any of our contemporary social issues such as divorce, sexuality, ordination of women, immigration, and affirmative action possibly be adjudicated by simple reference to the Bible? These questions are not about the Bible or about biblical communities; they are about the present— *our* present—challenges and problems. They cannot be addressed except by reference to the present interpretive and enunciatory sites and acts.

The Bible as we have it is not an ancient but a late modern, late twentieth-century document. And in the year 2006 it will be an early twenty-first century document. Unless we come to understand the import of this statement, we will be forever doomed to repeat again and again the hermeneutical horrors that in turn lead to horrors of different orders and effects all in the name of the Bible. No simple, unproblematic foray into the past—biblical or not—will throw much light on a situation in late modernity in which different peoples in different social locations read givens, even the same givens, totally differently—sometimes in stark conflict, sometimes in partial conflict, sometimes partly in common.

Refuge in history or in a past, refuge in an ancient text, refuge in the Bible, can provide no salvation for our late-modern dysfunctionalisms. The past can neither be the starting point nor the end point, certainly not the substitute, for the needed open-ended, honest, potentially painful discussion and debate between individuals and peoples. For we are the ones who construct and shape the structures of the past! It is the present—my present and your present—that defines the past, and it is the past as constructed by the present that in turn shapes the view of and response to the present.

This essay proposes one step toward a fruitful direction: it is an argument for careful and close reading of *cultural* (or folk) meanings of the past in texts—biblical and otherwise—as reflections of the *textualizations* of culture. Learning more about the latter represents cultivation of the art of tuning into the rhythms and orientations that constitute a people and holds the promise for deeper and richer mutual respect for cultural enunciation. Such activity is not all that must be done in order to improve the world, but it is an imperative in any effort to place relations between peoples—even between Baptists themselves—on higher discursive grounds.

Notes

1. See A. Veeser, ed., *The New Historicism* (New York: Routledge, 1988), and *The New Historicism Reader* (New York: Routledge, 1994), for introduction to and practice of the phenomenon.

2. Such reasons cannot be delineated in this essay alone, but the program flyer for this conference seems to me to dance somewhat nervously around the real issues—power and politics—that confront us, that bring us into conversation.

3. See V. L. Wimbush, "The Bible and African Americans: An Outline of an Interpretive History," in *Stony the Road We Trod: African American Biblical Interpretation*, ed. Cain H. Felder (Minneapolis: Fortress, 1991), 81-97.

4. See Wilfred Cantwell Smith, *What Is Scripture? A Comparative Approach* (Minneapolis: Fortress, 1993); *Rethinking Scripture: Essays from a Comparative Perspective,* ed. Miriam Levering (Albany, N.Y.: State University of New York Press, 1989); and *The Holy Book in Comparative Perspective*, ed. Frederick M. Denny and Rodney L.Taylor (Columbia, S.C.: University of South Carolina Press, 1985) for critical perspectives.

5. Smith, 95-96.

6. See Michael Walzer, *Exodus and Revolution* (New York: Basic Books, Inc., Publishers, 1985) for wide-ranging history of social-cultural-political interpretation of the Exodus story.

7. Walzer, especially "Conclusion: Exodus Politics," 134f.

8. See Wimbush, "The Bible . . ." for a summary historical treatment; Theophus Smith, *Conjuring Culture: Biblical Formations of Black America* (New York: Oxford University Press, 1994), for extensive, sophisticated phenomenological analysis; Albert J. Raboteau, *A Fire in the Bones: Reflections on African-American History* (Boston: Beacon Press, 1995), especially Part I.1 ("African Americans, Exodus, and

the American Israel") 17-36; and Gayraud Wilmore, *Black Religion and Black Radicalism: An Interpretation of the Religious History of Afro-American People* (2d ed. rev. and enl.; Maryknoll, N.Y.: Orbis Books, 1983), passim.

9. See Caroline Walker Bynum, "The Complexity of Symbols," in *Experience of the Sacred: Readings in the Phenomenology of Religion*, ed. Sumner B. Twiss and Walter H. Conser, Jr. (Hanover and London: Brown University Press, 1992), 266-72.

10. See Homi K. Bhabi, *Location of Culture* (New York: Routledge, 1994) 35, 36, 55, 176-8, for elaboration of issues.

Living under God's Rule: Theological Reflections on Baptist Distinctives

James H. Evans Jr.

Baptists: Pure and Simple?

Baptists are progeny of the Protestant Reformation. Like most of the other groups whose theological roots are in the reformed tradition, they were part of a spiritual protest against flawed ecclesial practices as well as the spiritual manifestation of a fresh theological understanding of the Christian faith. However, unlike some other Reformation movements, Baptists have not centered their identity in the articulation of a comprehensive theological system. This is not to say that Baptists have not written theologies, but there has been a lingering question as to whether what Baptists believe and affirm about the Christian faith is distinctive enough to support an identifiably Baptist view of life and faith.

The waning years of the twentieth century have witnessed significant changes and controversies in Baptist life in the United States. Almost all of these changes and controversies find expression in the question "What does it mean to be Baptist today?" Likewise, almost all of the difficulties in addressing this question lie in the unstated assumption that there must be some "pure and simple" understanding of Baptist life around which to center our corporate life together.

From the very beginning, Christian communities have struggled to reconcile two very different emphases within the Christian faith. On the one hand, the gospel seemed to suggest that purity and simplicity ought to mark the life of the community. Christians are called to "holiness" and

James H. Evans Jr. is president of Colgate Rochester Divinity School, Bexley Hall, Crozer Theological Seminary in Rochester, New York. This essay was first presented as a closing response to the presentations made at "Called to Responsible Freedom: A Conference on Baptist Distinctives," at Green Lake, Wisconsin, August 1996.

to embrace the Good News, which is "simple and true." On the other hand, the gospel seems to suggest that openness and acceptance ought to mark the life of the community. We are called to recognize human frailty and to embrace a gospel that "covers a multitude of sins."[1] Baptist communities, like many other Protestant communities today, are struggling with the ideals of holiness and purity. Standards of holiness and purity have become, in some instances, pretexts for inclusion and exclusion from the church.

The problem may be centered in an understanding of holiness and purity that has departed from its biblical roots. Modern individualism has defined "holiness" as a personal characteristic. We are accustomed to thinking of the holy woman or man. However, from a biblical perspective, being holy is less about living a saintly life and more about existing in a special relationship to other people. Our biblical mandate is to be "a holy people" and not just holy persons. Holiness is a social concept. We find holiness when we unconditionally affirm the presence and potential of God in every living thing. Our distant roots as a society founded on Puritanism and our modern ambivalence and fascination with the "taboo" has made it difficult to think of purity in anything but physical, especially sexual, terms. Our tendency to think of purity in light of deep-seated notions of personal defilement and taint has made it difficult to see the idea of purity in a positively biblical way. Our biblical mandate is found in the beatitude "Blessed are the pure in heart, for they shall see God." Purity of the heart is a consistent preference of God as expressed by the biblical writers. It reminds us that it is not what is on the outside of us that is important in the eyes of God, but what is on the inside.

The notion of the "purity and simplicity of the church" needs to be revised in light of the challenges Baptist communities face today. For example, the issue of the place of gay men and lesbian women in our Christian communities is, at least in part, a question of the purity and simplicity of the church. Is it possible that there is an intricate relationship between our understanding of sexual practices and deep-seated notions of purity? For example, H. Darrell Lance, a prominent American Baptist biblical scholar, has argued that scriptural references to prohibited homosexual behavior must be understood within the context of the purity codes, which focus on the clean and the unclean in ritual practices, and not the ethical codes, which distinguish right and wrong behaviors in ethical behavior in ancient Israel. It is also possible that there is an intricate relationship between our understanding of sexual identity and our bias toward a simple understanding of human development. Medical data, however, suggest that human sexual orientations and behaviors are incredibly complex. Much like the wave theory of light versus the particle theory of light, genetic versus environmental explanations of sexual orientation compete with one another, but neither fully explains the origins of sexual identity. We do not know whether sexual orientation is primarily inborn or learned.

One response to confusion regarding the ideals of purity and simplicity in Christian life is to immediately embrace the notions of diversity and complexity. Many communities and institutions have embraced these notions, but only after the fact. That is, once the diversity and complexity of humanity have become inescapable parts of our communities, we are likely to respond by embracing them as values. The problem with this response is that diversity and complexity are merely descriptive concepts but not necessarily normative values in our lives together.

To acknowledge the presence of diversity and complexity within our communities is not the same as stating the value of that diversity and complexity for our communities. I propose that the presence of diversity and complexity within our communities points to more fundamental claims regarding the richness and depth inherent within human communities. That is, diversity is not valuable for its own sake, but this diversity can point to the potential richness in varied human experiences and perspectives. Richness suggests abundance and the sharing of that abundance with every member of the community. Complexity is not valuable for its own sake, but this complexity can point to the depth dimension of community. This depth dimension suggests that communities endure over time and space and that what holds communities together is the ongoing presence of each member of the community for the other, through "thick and thin," so to speak. One of the keys to sustaining the vitality of Baptist communities today is to move from the ideas of purity and simplicity, through the facts of diversity and complexity, toward the values of richness and depth.

In what follows, therefore, I suggest a framework for understanding the challenges for Baptist communities today. This conceptual framework employs the notions of *heteronomy,* which is living under the rule of an external authority, *autonomy,* which is living under the rule of internal authority, and *theonomy,* which is living under the rule of God. This framework has found a singular expression in the theology of Paul Tillich and might be helpful as Baptists negotiate competing claims regarding our understanding of the Christian faith. I want to employ this conceptual framework to reflect briefly on three critical issues in Baptist life. They are (1) the idea of the church or Christian community, (2) a biblical interpretation in relation to authority and power, and (3) the place of religion in society. It is my hope that these reflections might contribute to future conversations on Baptist distinctives.

Heteronomy: Living by Others' Rules

Heteronomy refers to that dimension of life in which persons and communities become acutely aware of the demand to submit to external authority. This dimension has always been a part of religious life and practice. In Christianity this dimension is most clearly seen in that understanding of the faith that asserts that its salvific power comes into human existence from the outside, challenging the veracity and dependability of the authority of human experience.

Heteronomous views of community can be seen as critical to understanding those events that have taken place among Southern Baptist communities and are now taking place among American Baptist communities. The conservative takeover of the major institutions within the Southern Baptist denomination concerned the imposition of external authority. The operative assumption of this reorganization is that authentic authority is imposed from without. Among American Baptists the increasing authority exercised by some regional associations regarding some behaviors and relationships suggests that they view themselves as moral monopolies that have the ultimate word in determining who legitimately belongs in the church and who does not. A heteronomous view of community is akin to a household where certain inequities (parent/child or master/slave) exist and are seen as natural to the social order. In this view authority is normally imposed from the top down.

A heteronomous view of the Bible is one that suggests that the Scriptures provide external mandates for faith and practice. In this view the Bible is often thought of as literally inerrant and as providing a kind of litmus test for orthodoxy. Reading the Bible from this perspective focuses on the text as the place where one gets facts and information. This kind of reading allows no room for the substantive influence of the social location of the reader in the meaning of the text. It implies that the written text can and does take priority over both the social location of the text and the social location of the reader. On occasion, a distinctive role for the magisterium or teaching office of the church is claimed in order to recover the focus on the external authority of the Bible. The heteronomous view of the Bible is rooted in a particular emphasis on the Reformation principle of *sola scriptura* and is often associated with certain streams of fundamentalism. In this view, religious authority is grounded in tradition and revelation, and it is claimed to proceed from God generally unaffected by human conduits. This authority is seen as universal and applicable to everyone, believers and unbelievers alike. Authority is understood to be hegemonic and covering the totality of human experience and not just the religious dimensions of life. In this view, then, power may be legitimately used to coerce compliance to external authority.

A heteronomous view of religion in society is one of the perspectives forming the context for discussions of classic Baptist principles such as the separation of church and state and the issue of officially sanctioned prayer in schools. This view of society suggests that the "free exercise" clause of the First Amendment permits religion to function authoritatively in the public realm. It implies that religion—in this case, Christianity—is not a private affair but a legitimate set of public practices and moral affirmations that can and should have their place in political life. Thus, to prevent a Christian church from displaying a nativity scene in the lobby of City Hall violates the "free exercise" rights of each citizen. However, and perhaps more importantly, this view is based on the assumption that religion (mainly Christianity) is the basis of civil society. This is what is meant by the claim that "America is a Christian nation."

Heteronomy means living according to others' rules. It is often a part of what it means to be religious. However, the potential danger of heteronomous views of church, the Bible, and the role of religion in society is that, unless checked, the external exercise of authority can be and often is despotic.

Autonomy: Living by Our Own Rules

Autonomy refers to that dimension of life in which persons and communities become acutely aware of the presence and power of their own internal authority. Even in highly hierarchical communities this dimension has always been a part of religious life and practice. In Christianity this dimension is most clearly seen in that understanding of the faith that asserts that its salvific power is rooted in the experiential appropriation of that faith. It challenges the veracity and dependability of any authority not rooted in and verified by human experience.

Autonomous views of community are among the important keys to understanding some of the responses to the conservative takeover of the Southern Baptist Convention and to the ascendancy of conservative forces

within the life of the American Baptist Churches in the U.S.A. A new
identity is being claimed in some Southern Baptist circles as the importance of autonomous subgroups, cell groups, quasi-independent organizations, and individual congregations is rediscovered. This response is based
on the assumption that true authority in the Baptist perspective cannot be
legitimately imposed on communities from the outside, but must emerge
from within. In this sense authority is not vested in a single hierarchical
structure, but is to be found in autonomous groups and communities as
they seek to carry out their missions and mandates.

Among American Baptists the claim that regional associations have the
power to determine membership within the denomination is being coun-
tered by a renewed emphasis on the autonomy of the local congregation.
From the autonomous perspective Baptist associations are unable to
maintain control over a specific geographical region but are increasingly
forced to participate in a highly competitive environment where associations are formed more by forces within the theological marketplace than
they are by geographical proximity. An autonomous view of community
is akin to a household where roommates agree to reside together as long
as individual interests are served. There is equality in the sense that no
person exercises control over another and that this arrangement is limited
to those matters directly related to living together. While roommates may
live together, this does not mean that they have a *life* together. In this view
authority rests with the individual.

An autonomous view of the Bible is one that suggests that the Scriptures
confirm internal and experiential understanding of faith and practice. In
this view the Bible is often thought of as aesthetically beautiful and
emotionally inspirational, providing a kind of guide to understanding what
William James called "the varieties of religious experience." Reading the
Bible from this perspective focuses on the text in the quest for meaning
and the process of spiritual formation. This kind of reading gives priority
to influence of the social location of the reader in the meaning of the text.
It implies that the social location of the reader can and does take priority
over the written text. In this view the emphasis on the role of the individual
reader is an attempt to recover the internal/experiential authority of the
Bible. Here the Bible is not the property of the magisterium, but is viewed
as a public text. It can be—and perhaps can only be—rightly read in the
context of freedom from prior biblical interpretations. Rather than confirm
existing knowledge, this kind of reading can and should give rise to new
knowledge. The autonomous view of the Bible is rooted in a particular
emphasis on the Reformation principle of *sola fidei* and is often associated

with certain streams of liberalism. In this view, religious authority is grounded in human experience, reason, and culture. This authority is claimed to proceed from God through genuinely human conduits and is substantively shaped by those human conduits. This authority is seen as specifically religious authority. It is specialized authority that applies only to the adherents of the faith. In this view, then, power may not be legitimately used to coerce compliance to external authority, but to persuade according to internal authority.

An autonomous view of religion in society is the second perspective forming the context for discussions of classic Baptist principles such as the separation of church and state and the issue of officially sanctioned prayer in schools. This view of society suggests that the "establishment" clause of the First Amendment allows religion to function authoritatively only in the private realm. It implies that religion—in this case, Christianity—is not a public affair but an intimate set of deeply personal beliefs and private moral convictions that have no legitimate place in political life. Thus, to allow prayer in publicly supported schools is to thrust a private issue into the public realm in such a way as to violate the right of each citizen to freedom from any publicly sanctioned religion. However, and perhaps more importantly, this view is based on the assumption that civil society is founded on broad philosophical principles that are not essentially religious. This is what is meant by the claim that "America is a democracy."

Autonomy means living according to one's own rules. It is frequently a part of what it means to be authentically religious. However, the potential danger of autonomous views of church, the Bible, and the role of religion in society is that, unless checked, the internal exercise of authority can be and often is anarchic.

Theonomy: Living under God's Rule

Theonomy refers to that understanding of life in which persons and communities become acutely aware of the presence and power of God in us and outside of us. As noted above, heteronomous authority suggests that external authority without structure is despotic, and autonomous authority suggests that inner freedom without structure can be anarchic. Theonomy is most clearly seen in that understanding of the faith that asserts that its salvific power is rooted in the quest to live under God's rule. The notion of the kingdom of God points to the concrete expression of that quest. Living under God's rule is a journey rather than a state of being. God is found in what Howard Thurman called "the kingdom within" undergirding our inborn sense of being made in God's image. God is also found in what Jürgen Moltmann calls "the kingdom which is to come" ever calling us to a fulfillment of what we were created to be.

The major challenge facing Baptist communities today is to live under God's rule. A theonomous understanding of community is essentially what is at stake as the Southern Baptist Convention and the American Baptist Churches, U.S.A., find new forms of mission and ministry. What is clear is that Baptist communities must find a way to affirm both the autonomy of the local congregation and the associational principle in Baptist life. Theonomous perspectives may help define these affirmations.

The theonomous principle of community will affirm both the freedom and responsibility inherent in being Baptists. In the final analysis, Baptist communities will be defined by their trajectories. That is, these communities will be known not simply by what they say, or by what they do, but by their way of being and moving in the world. A theonomous community will not be held together by verbal contracts or specific collaborative projects, but by a deep-seated commitment to life together. In this sense, theonomous notions of community are at times difficult to articulate because they are more of a goal than an existing state. While there are no existing models of communities that fully capture the meaning of living under God's rule, we might compare it to a household where spouses dwell together. Here authority is collectively sought within the partnership. The authority is not found in the autonomy of the individual or in the heteronomy of communal structures. Authority, as well as power, is found in the relationship.

A theonomous view of the Bible is one that suggests that it is both a personal and a public text. Heteronomous readings of the Bible can render it a quaint relic that is the exclusive province of "specialists" and scholars. Autonomous readings of the Bible have the potential of creating idiosyncratic enclaves of interpretation that quickly lose touch with historical interpretive communities. A theonomous reading of the Bible sees it as a story whose meaning is both personal and public. To use a metaphor from the Romantic period, the Bible, in this sense, is both "a mirror and a lamp." It reflects accurately the essential structure of human experience. It lights our path as we seek to fulfill our emerging destinies. This perspective on the Bible focuses on its role in the transformation of the community, on creativity and recall, on evoking and provoking an imaginative encounter with the biblical narrative. The function of the biblical story is to unite the reader and the text in an attempt to discover the whole authority of the

Bible. A theonomous view of the Bible suggests that the acts of both writing the texts and reading the texts are socially located acts. The authority that is situated in the inspired writing of the text and the authority that emerges through the inspirational reading of the text are both important. However, in writing the biblical text and in reading the biblical text, the writer *and* the reader have a social location. They stand in the presence of God.

The theonomous view of the Bible is rooted in a particular emphasis on the Reformation principle of *sola Christi*. In the principle of *sola Christi* the authority of the text is connected with the authority of our experience of the text. A theonomous reading of the Bible experiences the Word of God as more than letters on the printed page, or the voice calling us from within. A theonomous reading of the Bible affirms that "the Word has become flesh" in Jesus Christ. A theonomous view of authority suggests that authority is grounded not in what we think or what we confess, but in how we live in relation to others. Authority is neither universally self-evident, nor privately revealed, but is grounded in our address and response to others. In this sense authority is neither hegemonic nor compartmentalized, but is comprehensive in the sense that it is centered in the relationships between people.

A theonomous paradigm suggests that we reconceptualize the traditional possibilities for the role of religion in society. The notion of the separation of church and state, as well as the notion of "a religious nation," are both important to our understanding of community. However, there is a deep cultural dissatisfaction with either of these notions as the sole basis for understanding the place of religion in society. Neither the prohibition of the establishment of religion, nor the tolerance of the free exercise of religion get to the heart of the potential of religion in society today. We need to go beyond these understandings of religion as public practice or as private sentiment, to a broader understanding of religion as *hospitality*.

Conclusion

As Baptists, we need to continue to talk about what it means to live under God's rule, that rule being first and foremost the rule of love. When we are tempted to avoid difficult conversations by appealing to some external authority, we should remember that authentic faith always seeks critical understanding. When we are tempted to gloss over legitimate theological differences by pointing to the freedom of each person to determine his or her own authority, we should remember that authentic freedom always seeks public expression and confirmation. Faith and freedom, the pillars of Baptist life, are subsumed in the rule of love. These are some of the challenges that confront Baptists today. Part of our mission should be to give voice to those who have been silenced in our midst and to bring light to those who dwell in darkness. Speech is to silence what light is to darkness. Both silence and darkness are symbols of inhumane conditions of human existence. The gospel calls us to address them in our preaching, teaching, and witness. Let us consider what it means to be the church living under God's rule. This is a *Baptist moment* in history. Let us seize it while we can!

Note

1. One might understand Augustine's debate with Donatus in light of the issue of the purity of the church. One might also understand Augustine's debate with Pelagius in light of the simplicity of the church. In both cases Augustine argued that unity, not purity or simplicity, was the essential mark of the church. Although Augustine prevailed in these debates, the notions of purity and simplicity reemerged with vigor during the Protestant Reformation.

Afterword:
Looking Backward, Living Forward

A book is a curious thing. If it is written by a single author, it tells a story or describes a situation and is either interesting or not, persuasive or not, believable or not. If it is shaped by the experiences or perspectives of many, it may be like a roomful of strangers who simply happen to pause there for a moment, or it may be more like a community. This book, I believe, became, however temporarily, a community: A collection of individuals, some known to each other and some not, have described their perception of what life as a Baptist is like, what it has meant, or how it came to be. Reflecting the dynamics of a healthy community, their contributions have enlarged the experiences of others and made for a fuller, richer understanding. In their conversation a common theme has emerged: a recognition of the tension between the seemingly opposing poles of freedom and responsibility and a hunger for balance.

As the contributors to this volume have described, the Baptist dynamic is deep, broad, and diverse. As individuals and as a movement, Baptists have carved a broad and remarkable history. Their specific legacies have marked personal faith experiences and shaped institutional religious expressions both in the United States and abroad. But amid both the historical remembrance and the present analysis, the dilemma of our theme, the tension between freedom and responsibility, is clear. Where is the center? Where lies the future of the Baptist way? Is it one way, or is it many ways? Will Baptists succeed—or fail? It is tempting to turn to the proverb credited to the sage of the American baseball diamond, Yogi Berra: "When you come to the fork in the road, take it." But a comment intended in humor contains, after all, the sharp edge of a serious question. What is the fork? Where are the significant avenues of decision? How do we maintain our legacy and at the same time be renewed for a vital future? Where is our balance?

There are, it is clear, several places where the tension is like confronting a fork in the road when it is not entirely certain where the separate avenues may take us. Still, our contributed perspectives give us the comfort of certain directions.

First, and critical to Baptist history and practice, is the question of the authority and use of the Scriptures: the central, authoritative role of the Bible. Preachers and teachers and missionaries who defined early Baptist life were unswerving in their belief that placing Bibles in the hands of men and women and teaching them to read their Bibles would provide for them the most important resource for faith. They were right. Early Baptist vitality—and balance—was the result of biblical understanding and discourse among many, not the specialized province of a few. While such an approach may have emphasized private interpretation, it nevertheless was able to build communities of faith on a universal familiarity with the Word.

Today most Baptists regard the Bible as central to their faith and to their experience in church life. Some want to read it literally, others take it seriously but not literally, still others regard it as a source of significant information or perspective. Some, to be honest, worship the Bible but neither read it nor understand it. Others, perhaps many, rarely read it but assume it provides clear authority for their most cherished tribal or cultural attitudes. Our three major contributors on scriptural interpretation have enabled us to see clearly the tension between the freedom of private interpretation and the very real limits of responsibility imposed when the interpretation of Scripture becomes a part of life in the community of faith. What emerges is that the Bible serves a very different purpose when it is consulted as a private document than when it becomes a reference for public, communal consideration. Their analyses and suggestions provide significant help in shaping our future dialogue.

It is also clear that Baptists need once again to become a biblically literate people. Historically, Baptists relied on the Bible for general wisdom and for spiritual insight. In the introduction, I suggested that one result of the late-eighteenth-century explosion of scholarship and the multiplication of scientific disciplines that focused on understanding the universe and the role of humankind within it in was a reduction in the perceived significance of the Bible. Persons outside the church abandoned it altogether. But Christians, and among them Baptists, also reduced its role. I also suggested that even those who were professionally familiar with its message failed to interpret its message for a new day and a new time.

We are again in a new day and a new time. Baptists need to maintain the Bible at the center of their experience, not merely as a cherished source for private devotions or as a reference tool for theological specialists whose opinions we seek, but as a deep well of personal knowledge and resource for every Baptist person. Only then might it serve a more public, communal role in shaping our communities of faith for the future. How can we even discuss its authority unless we know what it says, how it says it, and the circumstances in which it was first spoken? How can we maintain the priesthood of every believer as an operating principle if every believer does not immerse him- or herself in a greater understanding of the wisdom of the Word that guides our priestly acts? And how can the Bible serve as our communal reference until God's people are familiar with the Word?

Second, and critical to every expression of Baptist institutional life, our contributors urge that we must focus on the biblical, theological, and practical affirmation of the covenants that bind us together. Nearly every contribution in this volume included a significant reference to the dynamic challenge of our relationships: relationships to one another in churches, relationships between churches in association and organization, and relationships between organizations—and every permutation or combination of these. These relationships are informed by theological and biblical understanding and have powerful and practical implications for mission and ministry. Baptists have always avoided creeds to define their unity and are right to remain uncomfortable with them. Instead, we have covenants. They describe and define our relationships in community as God's people. These covenants are sometimes carefully crafted, formal, articulate, and explicit documents describing both opportunities and responsibilities. Other times they are informally expressed assumptions, such as the phrase that proved to be the enduring foundation for much of Baptist associational connection: "We do together that which we cannot do separately."

But many of the covenants that have formally and informally bound Baptists together for doing God's work in contexts larger than any single church or organization could accomplish are now forgotten, misunderstood, or ignored. Even at the risk that some of these covenants may need to be revised or even dismantled, it is time for them to be reviewed and revitalized.

Third, and essential to the survival of every Baptist church, denomination, agency, or program, we must find the balance between our expectations and our support of leadership. Baptist churches exhibit increasing dissatisfaction with pastoral leadership, and in remarkable numbers pastors are being terminated from positions. The leadership of the laity, once the great strength of Baptist churches, seems frequently to be evidenced in political and organizational activity, rather than in pastoral and spiritual expression and the work of mission. Likewise, denominational and agency leadership is almost constantly under attack for failure to fulfill programmatic, mission, administrative, or personal expectations. Major reasons for this self-destructive phenomenon included the following.

Baptist churches and denominations seem more often to reflect the conditions of the world around them than to transform them. They aspire to achieve standards of worldly recognition more often than faithful service. Specifically, churches and denominations have set a high priority on success defined by numbers of participants, financial prosperity, and community recognition, rather than on servanthood and faithful witness.

Church members, themselves challenged and stressed by a changing and demanding cultural context, seem to seek personal fulfillment and happiness and expect church leadership to provide it. Less often are church members committed to the happiness or well-being of others.

Church and denominational supporters seem unwilling or unable to engage in selfless giving to the greater good of a Baptist purpose. Churches and their representatives expect results from denominational connections and affiliations that are parallel to what church members expect from their leaders. That is, they expect to be served rather than to serve. When service is not received, leadership is criticized or canceled.

Church and denominational structures have become increasingly corporate and bureaucratic in style and, in doing so, seem to have adapted corporate values and standards. In place of spiritual fellowship, they often encourage strategic agendas, and in place of trusting in God's time, they demand to meet or exceed material time lines.

Finally, denominational structures and churches both seem generally confused regarding the qualities of leadership they desire: whether pastoral, spiritual, instructive, and sacramental leadership, or executive, assertive, goal-driven leadership.

To achieve balance, Baptist churches must reclaim a transforming, leading role in the communities in which they live by being effective models of servanthood, by supporting and respecting their leaders and the offices in which they serve, and by expecting participants within them to rediscover the value of servanthood also.

Fourth, Baptists must find faithful but creative ways to engage the world in which they live. Baptists must continue to be proud of their traditions but must also discover acceptable and enlivening ways to encounter different perspectives, claim new resources, and explore new directions. To do that Baptists must rethink their understanding of the roles of Scripture and their traditions primarily as fortresses against change. They might remember that the God our Baptist fathers and mothers followed was an agent of change and always at the head of it, not preventing it. The Bible's stirring witness celebrates change: "The trumpet will sound, and the dead will be raised imperishable, and we shall be changed," said the apostle Paul (1 Cor. 15:52 NASB). The Bible is a record of God's Word in the past, to be sure, but it points always to the future.

Baptists live in a world of astonishing changes. More, it is a world in which once distant communities are now neighbors. When old barriers crumble, people we thought were strangers may now become friends; traditions we perceived as unfamiliar may now offer us something to claim for our own lives. When previous, once isolated old communities collide, a new community may be born from the rubble of collision. May we not be confident that God is in the midst of it and calling us to be part of it? In the swirling context of these forming new communities, nearly everyone is asking important questions of ultimate meaning and of spiritual purpose. And many have experiences and partial answers that they have found enriching and encouraging. Sometimes those experiences and answers are different from what Baptists have generally experienced until now.

Yet God is in the midst of this unbalanced and sometimes dizzying world and is a primary participant in the new community in creation. Baptists have much to teach and to share with the new neighbors with whom they suddenly share intimate connection; they also have much to learn from others. Ironically, for Baptists to maintain the balance between freedom and responsibility among themselves, they must discover it also in their relationships with others. To do so does not mean abandoning Baptist ways and biblical truths. It means enlarging them so that new encounters and new experiences might magnify old meanings and empower new experiences.

Finally, as each contributor has also in some way proposed, Baptists must, most of all, be open to new vision and new direction. For several decades it seems that Baptists have focused on definition, structure, and organization. Yet Baptists have always been at their strongest when they have been ambiguous in definition but certain in purpose. The controversies and disabling disagreements that have hampered and threatened Baptists in recent decades are the result of quarreling among themselves and not the result of an adversarial relationship with the world's ills and evils. Therefore, we risk future judgment for having squandered our inheritance and wasted our resources. In short, Baptists must organize their forces and focus their energies beyond the myopic agenda of merely being Baptist and toward the long hope of being more fully God's people and more specifically Christ's commissioned servants. In the end, Baptists shall find their true balance in the One who calls us to new life and new creation, in the purposes of the One who calls all men and women to himself, and in the accomplishment of the Kingdom beyond principalities and in the victory beyond any war. As Matthew records Jesus' own final word to the church, it was neither in language of aggression nor of retreat. It was instead a counsel to invite, to welcome, to engage: "Go into all the world and make disciples." Baptize them. Teach them. Invite them to be disciples. "And be assured that I am with you always, to the end of time" (see Matt. 28:19-20).

Baptists have extended a great gift to the world of faith. It is the gift of freedom in the Spirit. Yet that gift is worth little if it is considered to be personal only and without reference to the greater gift God has promised in new communities. Baptists are fond of proclaiming the reality of the victorious, risen Christ. And yet that reality had its true origin in the remarkable moments when Christ gave up personal freedom in preference for a greater responsibility. In the great narrative of the Temptation, Jesus turned aside the extraordinary freedoms offered to him by Satan: freedom from hunger, the freedom granted by power, the freedom granted by security (Luke 4:1-13). Instead of freedom, he chose the responsibility of trust in God. Later, during his final moments of human freedom, Jesus was in the garden called Gethsemane. While the disciples slept, Jesus prayed. And in his prayer he said, "My Father, if it is possible, let this cup pass from Me" (Matt. 26:39 NASB). It reminds us that, like the rest of us, Jesus would have preferred the freedom to continue life, to exercise choice, reject external influences. But that was not his final word: "Yet not as I will, but as thou wilt" (v. 39 NASB) It was, therefore, in defining the balance between his personal freedom and his greater responsibility to God's new community that Jesus demonstrated his true character and calling as the Christ.

As we strive to be faithful as the church that bears Christ's name, we are called to define that same balance. We define it in our lives—as individuals and as the gathered churches, communities, and organizations of God's people called Baptists. That balance is found in the forceful expression of living in the freedom to which we have been born of the Spirit and also in the willingness to die in the purpose to which Christ has called us. It is, in the end, not so much the tension between freedom and responsibility as it is the transformation from life in the self to life in the Spirit.

Appendix:
The Recent Denominational Development of the American Baptist Churches in the U.S.A.

(The following brief summary of developments leading to the present ABC/USA denominational structure is presented because none of the articles in this volume specifically addresses this topic, which may be informative in considering current Baptist issues.)

In 1950 the old Northern Baptist Convention changed its name to the American Baptist Convention, a move involving more than mere public representation. First, the societies affiliated with the convention (the American Baptist Home Mission Society and others) had historically used the name *American,* and by the change, the national structure drew closer and conformed more naturally to its already established societal identities. Second, since World War II, the Southern Baptists had aggressively engaged in establishing churches in the North. The change in name allowed American Baptists to claim a national identity as well. In 1959 the Home Mission Society Board board authorized sending a general missionary into the South to facilitate affiliation with existing churches (especially minority congregations) and to encourage the establishment of new American Baptist churches.[1]

The decades of the 1950s and 1960s proved to be an introspective time of renewed awareness of Baptist history and purpose in denominational life. A general consensus emerged that the new denominational organization should project a more biblical vision of the church, an enlarged concept of its mission both in evangelism and in social justice, a greater awareness and comfort regarding racial and ethnic diversity, and perhaps most of all, more effective structures for fulfilling the mission of the church. The commitment to local and individual independence had not disappeared. But during these decades a fascination with the concept of the whole church began to develop, and Baptists became more self-conscious about their unique, collective participation in the church universal. It became an age of theological conferences, theological dialogue, and heightened awareness of the role of the church in accomplishing God's vision for Baptists. Many of these formal conferences and conversations were enabled by the new programming and fellowship opportunities made possible by the acquisition and development of the American Baptist Assembly (later renamed as a conference center) in Green Lake, Wisconsin. Indeed, acquiring the assembly itself was a move toward a greater national denominational awareness.

Publications during this period reflect this powerful impulse toward reflection and reformulation. A new journal, *Foundations: A Baptist Journal of History and Theology,* was founded, a new *History of the Baptists* was commissioned and provided by Robert G. Torbet, and a wide variety of articles reviewing the church in the perspective of Scripture and theology were published.[2] In particular, a book by Winthrop S. Hudson entitled *Baptist Concepts of the Church* made available several studies of Baptist theology and practice.[3] Its purpose was to review the established traditions of individualism and local church autonomy in contrast to the possibilities of a widened understanding of the church.[4]

Denominational programs of this period, in name, purpose, and content, also sought to enable a broader understanding of church life and to effect a corporate mission. Programs to develop churches and missions within the United States included the Crusade for Christ (1946-1951), the America for Christ annual offering, Churches for New Frontiers (1953), The Baptist Jubilee Advance (1959-1964), and the American Baptist Extension Corporation (1959), established to enable funding for church development and extension. Beyond the United States, programs included the World Mission Crusade program (1946), a new annual World Fellowship Offering (1950), and the initiation or reestablishment of mission work in several countries. In a step toward greater unity, both the Home and Foreign Mission Boards voted in 1955 to integrate the Woman's American Baptist Home Mission Society and the Woman's American Baptist Foreign Mission Society into the ABHMS and ABFMS respectively (though neither process was fully completed until 1968). In education the Year of Baptist Achievement (1955) focused on church school growth and reflected a new commitment to developing resources for teachers, church leaders, and educators in secondary and collegiate institutions.

This same era witnessed broad development of institutional and administrative programs. Examples include a Committee on Chaplains (1965), which was established to develop standards and provide endorsement for military and institutional chaplains; the American Baptist Personnel Services (1971), which was created to assist churches in finding professional church leaders; and a wide variety of programs established to develop aspects of church life from architecture to stewardship to mission support programs. Programs to represent American Baptist policy concerns were initiated and established in Washington, D.C., and greater involvement with the National and World Councils of Churches was initiated by many of the denomination's leaders.[5]

An attempt to integrate individuals, churches, and the mission societies underlay much of the activity of these decades. For example, Jitsuo Morikawa, who became secretary for evangelism in 1956, gave active leadership to the perspective that evangelism had to be joined with issues of social justice and practical mission. It was his view that the church was God's agent for activity in the world, and he sought to enlarge the vision of Baptist churches to become part of the church universal at work in the world. Morikawa called Baptists to exemplify concerns for social justice and ministry to the poor and disenfranchised while also engaging in the more familiar "call to Christian life" that evangelism had always meant to Baptists. His proposals cut across many familiar habits and were therefore controversial. The peace and freedom movements encompassing civil rights, poverty, military engagement in Vietnam, and a broad variety of social justice concerns in the 1960s provided an immediate laboratory for effecting this view of the church in mission. The compelling, preoccupying, immediate, and frequently polarizing character of these broad social movements caused Morikawa's strategy to have divisive as well as transforming results for American Baptist churches.

Ultimately, two institutional actions of American Baptist corporate life both demonstrated the spirit of denominational development and helped to accomplish it. The first was a decision in 1958 to move the societies (agencies) from scattered locations in New York City and Philadelphia to a central headquarters facility at Valley Forge, Pennsylvania. The decision was controversial because various factions advocated alternative plans to physically consolidate but remain in New York or to build a new headquarters facility on land offered on the campus of the University of Chicago. In the end, while the consolidation was accomplished at Valley Forge, it was not complete. The Ministers and Missionaries Benefit Board (retirement and insurance support) remained in New York, and the collections of the Historical Society remained in

Rochester, although both organizations established offices in the new facility in Valley Forge.

The second action was a reorganizational strategy initiated in 1961, expanding the General Council of the denomination to a total of ninety-six, more than doubling its former size. The new council had forty-six voting members elected by the convention and fifty nonvoting members drawn from the incorporated boards, cooperating societies, and affiliating organizations. The intention was to bring the entire leadership of the denomination into structural conversation in order to improve communication, coordination, and policy development. Administrative heads of program boards (Foreign and Home Missions, Education, and others) became associate general secretaries of the whole American Baptist Convention. The Council itself began several aspects of study to develop and implement convention-wide systems of administration and program development. Several commissions subsequently offered organizational reforms, which, to greater or lesser degrees, effected stronger denominational unity, particularly between the former societies, agencies, and affiliating organizations.

The first commission was the Commission for the Study of Administrative Areas and Relationships Project (SAAR). This commission, initiated in 1962, issued a report recommending that the convention reorganize by dividing into fifteen geographic regions, further subdivided into areas, each with a staff of specialists and area ministers whose work it would be to provide resources and support to churches and also to encourage churches to become more effective in corporate relationship to the whole denomination. Ultimately, several mergers were effected between former associations and societies resulting in new regions. Many state, regional, or city associations and societies resisted the proposal, however, and continued their traditional boundaries and structures.

The second commission was appointed in 1968 as the Study Commission on Denominational Structure (SCODS). At the heart of its work was the issue of freedom and order among Baptists in denominational relationships. A Statement of Purpose adopted in 1969 for the commission's work directly confronted some of these long-standing concerns. On the one hand, it described the American Baptist Convention as a "manifestation of the church universal," but it also reaffirmed the belief that God's work and purpose could be identified and followed "in local congregations . . . and in associational, regional, national and world bodies." It clearly moved, however, to affirm the ecclesial nature of structures that were broader and larger than the local church. It declared an intention to "seek such a balance of freedom and order as will keep all parts of the Convention open to the guidance of the Holy Spirit and at the same time enable them to work responsibly to carry out the common task of mission and ministry." As it viewed the issues of freedom and order in the wider church, it identified four issues especially for American Baptists:

1. To bear witness to the gospel of Jesus Christ in the world and to lead persons to Christ.

2. To seek the mind of Christ on moral, spiritual, political, economic, social, denominational and ecumenical matters, and to express to the rest of society, on behalf of American Baptists, their convictions as to the mind of Christ on these matters.

3. To guide, unify and assist American Baptists in their witness in the world, in preparing members for the work of ministry, and in serving both those within and outside the fellowship of Christ.

4. To promote closer relations among American Baptist churches and groups within the whole body of Christ and to promote understanding with other religious bodies.[6]

It was, in short, a comprehensive plan for the full establishment of a national denomination—and nearly a national church—far beyond anything yet proposed among Baptists.

The report of SCODS was received and implemented following the 1972 convention. The changes moved American Baptists from convention to denomination in many respects.

For one, the official name was changed from American Baptist Convention to American Baptist Churches in the U.S.A. It was generally felt that the word *convention* reflected a meeting, while the word *church* was ecclesiologically and theologically more positive. There was significant support for using the name American Baptist Church, but the traditional fear of connectional implications and loss of independence again became a major consideration, and the word *Churches,* though somewhat less corporate, was retained as a compromise.

Also, a general board was created composed of representatives from the churches through election districts composed of from forty to sixty churches in geographic proximity. Representatives were not elected directly by churches, nor by the association, region, or society structures with which the churches were already affiliated. In this sense the proposal again skirted the issue of independence in building its denominational connections. It also left somewhat ambiguous the question regarding whether churches were affiliated with the ABC/USA directly, through their region or association, or through the constitutional device of the election district. More recently, however, election districts have been revised to be more congruent with regional associations or units.

Further, to ensure that men and women, clergy and laity, ethnic groups, youth, and other minorities and/or special interests would be represented on the General Board, provisions specified what categories of candidates could be posted for election. In addition, one-fourth of the General Board would be elected at large at the Biennial Meeting (a change from annual conventions). These were to be chosen for nomination in order to bring racial, ethnic, gender, and geographic balance, and also to arrange for persons with special expertise needed by the General Board or the program boards. In creating the General Board, it was clearly the plan of the SCODS members to emphasize interdependence and to affirm corporate action among churches. The General Board was also effectively empowered to establish and implement policy for the American Baptist Churches, a major change from previous practices of requiring votes of representatives at annual convention meetings.

SCODS also implemented a new method for providing members to the national boards of the societies (now program boards) of the convention. Rather than by separate elections, the members of the related program boards were now to be chosen from the membership of the General Board. Therefore, members of the boards of educational, national, and international ministries were congruent with the constituency of the General Board. The Ministers and Missionaries Benefit Board was treated as an exception, allowing for some of its members not to be members of the General Board in recognition of its special needs and purposes.

Further, the general secretary was empowered with greater authority and responsibility as the administrative head of the entire denomination, particularly regarding the coordination of the program boards, as the leader of denominational ecumenical relations, and as a guide in the process of personnel selection for denominational professionals and employees.

The third commission, the Study Commission on Relationships (SCOR), was appointed by the General Board in 1974 to propose how greater integration of denominational structures could be effected, especially in light of the SCODS changes. Its 1977 proposals effectively completed the process of implementing the proposals first established by SAAR and SCODS—namely, to fashion the American Baptist Churches as a national, inclusive Baptist body, encompassing national, regional, and local organizational structures. Its proposals were required because the national denominational structure was created and empowered by representatives elected and sent by local election districts, which, as we have noted, had no official connection with regional associations. Therefore, the ABC/USA technically existed without official relationships with the associations, societies, and regional bodies around which its constituent churches were organized. For that matter, it had no direct "official" connection with its churches.

Therefore, SCOR provided that these regional bodies would themselves become constituent members of the denomination and would send representatives to the biennial meetings and to the General Board. But, despite the appearance of a "dual constituency," in reality SCOR provided that representatives elected in local election districts would also serve to represent their respective society, region, or association, and also maintained that these associational bodies could send representatives to the election district elections. In a sense, these regional bodies assumed a three-way identity as a result: First, they were created by local churches in association to serve their needs and to encourage their common mission; second, they represented the national denomination to the local churches to encourage church support of national programs; and third, they increasingly became intermediary agencies that were challenged to communicate and facilitate relationships between local churches and the national denomination. It is not surprising, therefore, that much of the tension in contemporary Baptist life is discovered at the regional, associational, or society level among American Baptists.

Several other aspects of denominational relationships were changed as a result of the SCOR proposals. For example, two national councils were created. One was composed of the chief administrative officer of the regional associations, normally titled executive minister, along with the general secretary of the ABC/USA, and named the Regional Executive Ministers Council. Also created was a larger General Executive Council comprised of the general secretary, the National Executive Council, Regional Executive Ministers Council, associate national secretaries, and the executive directors of such agencies as the American Baptist Assembly, American Baptist Historical Society, American Baptist Men, the Commission on the Ministry, and the Ministers Council. Through these gathered councils of leaders, the varied perspectives and interests of regions, societies, agencies, and others are represented to the General Board, which retains the constitutional power to make most decisions.

With SCOR, a new, more formal concept of interdependence was articulated. It was specifically reflected in the concept of covenants, which sought to define relationships. A Common Budget Covenant, for example, defined the protocols for raising funds for the support of both regional and national mission programs. A Covenant of Relationships defined the basis for relating regions to the national organization, and Statements of Agreement were devised to unite former affiliating organizations with general, national, and regional boards. What SCOR did not provide for directly, although it was implied, was a more explicit covenant between local churches and the denomination. In effect, SCOR completed a process whereby the local, regional, and national organizational structures had entered into an ecclesial relationship, which, for all practical purposes, was binding and corporate. (It took until 1990, however, for all regional boards to complete the process of endorsing the covenants.) But even the prevailing desire for unity and effectiveness that led to this remarkable achievement could not effectively require local churches to abandon the principal of independence.

While the SCOR report and the several covenants defining relationships between institutions and between institutions and churches contained biblical and theological support for the relationship of churches to national and regional organizations, it recognized the authority of local congregations to order and practice their own church affairs. Its hope and intent, however, was clear: "The freedom of the congregation is genuine, but not absolute, since the nature of the body of Christ calls for interdependence between congregations in association, regional, national, denomination-wide, or international expressions of the church." To effect a closer connection between churches and the regional association or organization to which they relate, and thereby the national denomination, many regions have strived to develop covenants between the local churches in their constituency and the regional structures. These, however, lack corporate, legal implications in nearly all cases and do not fundamentally alter the continuing independence of the local church. The matter of corporate relationships remains one of the most challenging aspects of denominational life for American Baptists.

Notes

1. One purpose of this action was to develop relationships especially with African American congregations during the conflict and controversy of civil rights reform and as churches struggled to become racially integrated.

2. Robert G. Torbet, *A History of the Baptists*, 3d ed. (Valley Forge, Pa.: Judson Press, 1973).

3. Winthrop S. Hudson, *Baptist Concepts of the Church* (Valley Forge, Pa.: Judson Press, 1959).

4. It was, interestingly, a proposal to republish this volume that led to the development of the present volume as an alternative. Ultimately, Judson Press and I agreed that *Baptist Concepts of the Church* remained a valuable contribution as published, containing scholarly articles of high quality and, at the same time, presenting its material in light of the American Baptist conversations as of 1950. Hudson's own material in that volume, as noted in the preface, became the basis for much of the discussion in the earlier sections of the introduction to this volume.

5. An ABC/USA Chronology developed at the request of the American Baptist Historical Society is available in the American Baptist Archives Center, ABC/USA, Valley Forge, Pennsylvania. Although it lists actions of the society boards separately, a brief perusal in each program area will demonstrate the amazing denominational impulse of the twenty years roughly between 1950 and 1970.

6. Final Report of Study Commission on Denominational Structure of the American Baptist Convention, May 1972. See also Norman H. Maring and Winthrop S. Hudson, *A Baptist Manual of Polity and Practice,* rev. ed., Norman Maring, ed. (Valley Forge, Pa.: Judson Press, 1991), 210-15.

7. For a more detailed discussion of the provisions of SCODS and SCOR see Maring and Hudson, *Polity*, 208-17, and the final reports of the commissions as well as the official minutes of the 1968 and 1972 meetings of the ABC/USA, available at the Archives Center, American Baptist Historical Society, Valley Forge, Pennsylvania.

Baptist History and Identity Resources

The following resources are representative of available materials on Baptists, their development, and their circumstances. It is not an exhaustive compilation or a complete Baptist bibliography. Readers are directed to the notes of many of the articles included in this volume where more extensive resources related to specific themes are noted.

I. Books

Nancy Tatom Ammerman, *Baptist Battles: Social Change and Religious Conflict in the Southern Baptist Convention* (New Brunswick, N.J.: Rutgers University Press, 1990).

Gene Bartlett, *The Authentic Pastor* (Valley Forge, Pa.: Judson Press, 1978).

William H. Brackney, ed., *Baptist Life and Thought: 1600-1980* (Valley Forge, Pa.: Judson Press, 1983).

L. R. Bush and T. J. Nettles, *Baptists and the Bible* (Chicago: Moody Press, 1980).

LeRoy Fitts, *A History of Black Baptists* (Nashville: Broadman Press, 1984).

Edwin S. Gaustad, ed., *Baptists, the Bible, Church Order, and the Churches: Essays from Foundations* (New York: Arno Press, 1980).

Everett C. Goodwin, *The New Hiscox Guide to Baptist Churches* (Valley Forge, Pa.: Judson Press, 1995).

Stanley J. Grenz, *The Baptist Congregation: A Guide to Baptist Belief and Practice* (Valley Forge, Pa.: Judson Press, 1985).

Paul M. Harrison, *Authority and Power in the Free Church Tradition: A Social Case Study of the American Baptist Convention* (Princeton: Princeton University Press, 1959).

Evelyn Brooks Higginbotham, *Righteous Discontent: The Women's Movement in the Black Baptist Church, 1880-1920* (Cambridge: Harvard University Press, 1993).

Herschel H. Hobbs and E. Y. Mullins, *The Axioms of Religion* (Nashville: Broadman Press, 1978) (a revision).

Sloan S. Hodges, *Black Baptists in America and the Origin of Their Conventions* (Washington, D.C.: Progressive National Baptist Convention, Inc., 1969).

Winthrop S. Hudson, *Baptists in Transition: Individualism and Christian Responsibility* (Valley Forge, Pa.: Judson Press, 1979).

Winthrop S. Hudson, ed., *Baptist Concepts of the Church* (Valley Forge, Pa.: Judson Press, 1959).

Joseph H. Jackson, *A Story of Christian Activism: The History of the National Baptist Convention U.S.A., Inc.* (Nashville: Townsend Press, 1980).

Lewis G. Jordon, *Negro Baptist History, U.S.A.* (Nashville: The Sunday School Board of the National Baptist Convention, 1930).

William L. Lumpkin, *Baptist Confessions of Faith* (Valley Forge, Pa.: Judson Press, 1969) (a revision).

Norman Maring and Winthrop S. Hudson, *A Baptist Manual of Polity and Practice* (Valley Forge, Pa.: Judson Press, 1991) (a revision).

H. Leon McBeth, *The Baptist Heritage: Four Centuries of Baptist Witness* (Nashville: Broadman Press, 1987).

William G. McLoughlin, *New England Dissent: 1630-1833: The Baptists and the Separation of Church and State.* 2 vols. (Cambridge: Harvard University Press, 1971).

Henry H. Mitchell, *Black Belief* (San Francisco: Harper & Row, 1975).

Alan Neely, ed., *Being Baptist Means Freedom* (Charlotte: Southern Baptist Alliance, 1988).

Stewart A. Newman, *A Free Church Perspective* (Stevens Book Press, 1986).

Peter J. Paris, *The Social Teaching of the Black Churches* (Philadelphia: Fortress Press, 1985).

Owen D. Pelt and Ralph Lee Smith, *The Story of the National Baptists* (New York: Vantage Press, 1960).

H. Wheeler Robinson, *Baptist Principles* (London: Carey Kingsgate Press, 1960).

Walter B. Shurden, *Associationalism among Baptists in America, 1707-1814* (New York: Arno Press, 1980).

Walter B. Shurden, *The Baptist Identity: Four Fragile Freedoms* (Macon, Ga.: Smyth & Helwys, 1993).

Walter B. Shurden, ed., *Proclaiming the Baptist Vision: The Bible* (Macon, Ga.: Smyth & Helwys, 1994).

Walter B. Shurden, ed., *Proclaiming the Baptist Vision: The Priesthood of All Believers* (Macon, Ga.: Smyth & Helwys, 1993).

John E. Skoglund, *The Baptists* (Valley Forge, Pa.: Judson Press, 1967).

Elliott Smith, *The Advance of Baptist Associations Across America* (Nashville: Broadman Press, 1979).

Howard R. Stewart, *Baptists and Local Autonomy* (New York: Exposition Press, 1974).

Robert G. Torbet, *A History of the Baptists*, 3d ed. (Valley Forge, Pa.: Judson Press, 1973).

William P. Tuck, *One Baptist Tradition* (Macon, Ga.: Smyth & Helwys, 1993).

James M. Washington, *Frustrated Fellowship* (Macon, Ga.: Mercer University Press, 1986).

James Wood, ed., *Baptists and the American Experience* (Valley Forge, Pa.: Judson Press, 1976).

Norman A. Yance, *Religion Southern Style: Southern Baptists and Society in Historical Perspective* (Macon, Ga.: Mercer University Press, 1978).

II. Articles

Glenn H. Asquith Jr., "Moving Toward Harmony," *Foundations* 15 (Jan.-March 1972): 26-41.

Gerald L. Borchert, "The Nature of the Church: A Baptist Perspective," *American Baptist Quarterly* 1 (Dec. 1982): 160-69.

William H. Brackney, "Commonly (Though Falsely) Called. . . : Reflections on the Search for Baptist Identity," *Perspectives in Religious Studies* 13 (Fall 1986): 67-82.

Ralph H. Elliott, ed., "American Baptist Identity," *American Baptist Quarterly* 6, no. 2 (June 1987).

C. Welton Gaddy, "Religious Freedom: Achievements and Challenges," *Baptist History and Heritage* 25 (Jan. 1990): 23-31.

Robert T. Handy, "American Baptist Polity: What's Happening and Why?" *Baptist History and Heritage* 14 (July 1979): 12-21.

D. R. Harris, "The Gradual Separation of Southern Baptists and Northern Baptists," *Foundations* (April 1964): 130-44.

Leland D. Hine, "A Second Look at the Baptist Vision," *American Baptist Quarterly* 4 (June 1985): 118-30.

Winthrop S. Hudson, "The Associational Principle among Baptists," *Foundations* 1 (Jan. 1958): 10-23.

Winthrop S. Hudson, "Documents on the Association of Churches," *Foundations* 4 (Oct. 1961): 332-39.

Winthrop S. Hudson, "The Quest for Freedom within the Church in Colonial America," *Journal of Church and State* 3 (May 1961): 6-15.

Bill J. Leonard, "Varieties of Freedom in the Baptist Experience," *Baptist History and Heritage* 25 (Jan. 1990): 3-12.

Norman Maring, "Baptists and Changing Views of the Bible," *Foundations* 1 (July 1958): 52-75.

David O. Moberg, "Baptists in a Pluralistic Society," *Foundations* 21 (July- Sept. 1978): 196-210.

Lawrence A. Nelson, "The Associational Principle, 1707-1814: Its Rationale," *Foundations* 21 (July-Sept. 1978): 221-24.

Eric H. Ohlmann, "The Essence of Baptists: A Reexamination," *Perspectives in Religious Studies* 13 (Fall 1986): 83-104.

Lawrence Slaght, "An Appraisal of the Grand Rapids Affirmation of Faith," *Foundations* 6 (July 1963): 218-32.

James E. Taulman, "Freedom and Responsibility in Baptist Life," *Baptist History and Heritage* 25 (Jan. 1990): 13-22.

Robert G. Torbet, "Options for a Viable Church Order," *Foundations* 13 (July-Sept. 1970): 237-47.

Hugh Wamble, "The Beginnings of Associationalism among English Baptists," *Review and Expositor*, Oct. 1957, 554-59.

III. Video Series, Brochures, and Workshops

"American Baptists: A Unifying Vision," study document and leader's guide produced by the Commission on Denominational Identity, published by the Office of Communication, ABC/USA.

"Baptist Basics," ten brochures produced by the Baptist Union of Great Britain.

"Our American Baptist Heritage," four tapes: The First Baptists; Baptists in Early America; Unity and Diversity in the American Baptist Movement; American Baptists Come of Age. Available from Educational Ministries, ABC/USA.

Workshops for local church leaders: "American Baptists—Our Historical Roots"; "The Church School and American Baptist Identity." Available from Educational Ministries, ABC/USA.

Index

Abernathy, Ralph David, 46, 112
Abolitionists, 97, 333. *See also* Slavery
Abortion, 47, 48, 132, 226, 322
Abyssinian Baptist Church (New York), 102, 103
Achan, 345
Act of Toleration (1689), 6
Adams, C. C., 113
Adams, John, 71 n.1
Adams, John Quincy, 279
Adventist movement. *See* Millerite movement
African American Baptists, 40, 41, 42, 45, 46, 59, 60, 97-121, 204, 280
  communions/conventions, 98.
    See also under individual names
  development of in Virginia, 1867-1882, 333-40
African Baptist Missionary Society, 103, 105
  of Richmond, 120
AIDS/HIV, 49, 226, 355
Alabama Baptist Convention, 238, 239
Aleshire, Daniel, 234
Alliance of Baptists. *See* Southern Baptist Alliance
American and Foreign Bible Society, 205
American Baptist Churches of the South, 98
American Baptist Churches in the U.S.A., 40, 44, 50, 51, 98, 197, 199, 206, 376, 378, 387-95
  biennial meetings, 392

  headquarters, 389-90
  name change, 391
  programs of, 388, 389, 392, 393
American Baptist Home Mission Society, 100, 106, 200, 207
American Baptist Magazine, The, 251
American Baptist Missionary Convention, 103, 200
American Baptist Missionary Union, 100
American Baptist Publication Society, 14, 100, 110, 200
American Baptist Seminary of the West (Berkeley Baptist Divinity School), 207, 210, 211
American Baptist Theological Seminary, 106, 109
American Baptist Union, 103
American Bible Society, 205
American Colonization Society, 121
American Mainline Religion: Its Changing Shape and Future, 350
American National Baptist Convention, 104
Ames, William, 10
Amherstburg Association (Canada and Michigan), 103
Ammerman, Nancy T., 133, 134, 196, 260
Ammons, Edsel, 352
Amphictyony, 244. *See also* Associationalism; Associations
Anabaptism, Anabaptists, 3, 64, 72, 75, 79, 85, 87, 91, 92, 99, 143, 277
  Munsterites, 73, 76
Anderson, Frederick L., 17

Andover Theological Seminary, 179
Anglicans, 62, 65, 72, 73, 78, 80, 281,
    282, 306
Anti-intellectualism, 124
Antimagistracy, 73
Antinomianism, Antinomians, 73, 76,
    77, 79, 81
Antipedobaptists, 72-96
Archer, Peter, 335
Armey, Dick, 303, 304
Arminianism, 73, 80. *See also*
    Calvinism
Arminius, Jacobus, 5, 122 n.4
Armstrong, Annie, 314
Ashcraft, Morris, 129
Associated Baptist Press, 228
Association of Theological Schools,
    234
Associationalism, 36, 51, 102, 243-57
Associations, 13, 36, 38, 51, 102,
    115-16, 117, 265-70
    etymology of the word *association*,
        247, 254-57
    future of, 253-56
    principle of, 243-57
    regional, 376
    See also names of individual
        associations; Associationalism
Atonement
    general, 3. *See also* General Baptists
    limited, 3. *See also* Particular Baptists
    particular, 3. *See also* Particular
        Baptists
Augustine, 366
*Authority and Power in the Free
    Church Tradition,* 252
Autonomy
    for Virginia's Negro Baptists, 335-38
    of local churches, 50, 51, 52, 56 n.52,
        119-21, 127, 241, 260, 359, 375-77,
        388

Babcock, William Smythe, 185-86
Backus, Isaac, 13, 14, 32, 66, 67, 68,
    69, 70, 71 n.1, 93 n.3, 94 n.14, 95
    n.22, 280, 281, 282, 283, 293, 294,
    300, 301

Bailyn, Bernard, 289, 292
Baker, Ella, 119
Baker, William, 95 n.21
Baldwin, Thomas, 37, 71
Baptism, 4, 23, 77, 143, 177-78, 183,
    189, 205, 319
    believers', 16, 142, 325
    by immersion, 63, 64, 73, 74, 79, 87,
        99, 200, 201, 206, 212 n.1, 213 n.8
    by sprinkling, 63, 73
    infant, 60, 63, 64, 74, 76, 79, 84, 85,
        87, 88, 89, 90, 92, 200, 213 n.8
    legislation regarding, 91-92
    See also Antipedobaptists
Baptist, the name, 17
Baptist Center for Ethics, 228
Baptist College (Warren, Rhode
    Island), 67
Baptist Concepts of the Church, xiii,
    xvii, 374
Baptist General Association of
    Virginia, 338-40
Baptist General Conference, 40, 44
Baptist General Convention of
    Oklahoma, 129
Baptist General Convention of Texas,
    236-37
*Baptist Identity: Four Fragile
    Freedoms, The,* 343
Baptist Joint Committee on Public
    Affairs (SBC), 130, 132, 133, 237,
    308, 309
Baptist Jubilee Advance, 201
*Baptist Manual of Polity and Practice,
    A,* xvii, 255-56
Baptist Ministers Conference
    (Baltimore), 120
Baptist Missionary Convention. *See*
    Triennial Convention
Baptist Missionary Training School,
    202
Baptist Theological Seminary
    (Richmond), 228, 234
Baptist World Alliance, 206, 237, 312,
    354
Baptistification, xii, 17, 219

Baptists and the National Centenary, The, 205
Baptists Committed, 228
Baptists Concerned, 56 n.51
Baptists Today, 228
Barbour, Clarence A., 18
Barnes, Elizabeth B., 144
Barth, Karl, 144, 155
Barth, Trevisa, 247
Barton, John, 141
Baylor University, 136 n.9, 235, 238
Beeson Divinity School, 228, 235
Bellah, Robert, 152, 153
Bellevue Baptist Church (Memphis, Tennessee), 132, 229
Benedict College, 106
Benedict, David, 205, 206
Bennett, F. Russell, 247, 253
Berkeley Baptist Divinity School. *See* American Baptist Seminary of the West
Berra, Yogi, 302, 381
Bible. *See* Biblical authority; Biblical interpretation
Bible Institute of Los Angeles, 202
Biblical authority, 23, 24-27, 35, 45, 127, 144, 145, 146, 151-70, 174-90, 252, 374, 375, 376, 377
Biblical interpretation, xii, 18-19, 24-27, 33, 50, 139-40, 151, 152, 157, 164-65, 166-69, 360, 368
    dogmatic hermeneutics, 160-61
    fundamentalist view, 35, 127
    hermeneutics, power of, 158-60
    heteronomous view, 374-75, 378
    historical-critical method, 24, 25, 124, 156, 186
    inerrant view, 35, 132
    private, 141-49, 174-90
    theonomous reading, 377-79
    See also Biblical authority; Inerrancy, biblical; Theology, challenges to
Biblical Recorder, The, 236
Bill for Establishing Religious Freedom, 284
Bill of Rights, 284, 285, 286-96,

298-304, 307. *See also* Constitution, U.S.; First Amendment
Bishop, Josiah, 101
Bitting, William C., 18
Black Baptists. *See* African American Baptists
Black, Hugo, 286, 301
Black power movement, 113
Blackmun, Harry, 290
Bloudy Tenent of Persecution, for Cause of Conscience, The, 277, 278
Bluestone (African Baptist) Church, 100
Boardman, George Dana, 18
Booth, L. Venchael, 113
Bork, Robert, 133
Bowditch (Bowdish), Mrs. William, 88, 95 n.24
Bowers, Benanual, 86, 87, 91, 95 n.19
Bowers, George, 86
Boyd, Henry Allen, 110
Boyd, R. H., 110
Boyd, T. B. Jr., 110
Boyd, T. B. III, 111
Brackney, William H., 143, 255
Brauch, Manfred, 145
Brewster, William, 93 n.1
Bridges, Robert, 88
Bristol Baptist College, 247, 253
Broadus, Andrew, 340
Brown University (Rhode Island College), 14, 36, 70, 279, 280
Brownists, 73
Brueggemann, Walter, 262, 263, 265
Bryan, Andrew, 101
Bunyan, John 314
Burger, Warren E., 294
Burroughs, Nannie, 119
Burrows, John L., 339
Burton, Ernest De Witt, 17
Bush, George, 132
Bush Run Church, 180, 181
Busher, Leonard, 293
Byrd, William, 100

Cainites, 177, 178
Calvin, John, 2, 73
Calvinism, 3, 5, 65, 66, 67, 73, 74, 75,
    77, 81, 100, 280
    hyper-Calvinism, 3, 6, 200
Calvinists, Five Principle, 80
Cambridge Platform, 12, 82, 83, 92,
    93 n.2
Cambridge University, 89, 280
Campbell, Alexander, 180-82
Campbell, Benjamin, 16
Campbell, Robert C., 211
Campbellites. See Restoration
    movement
Candler School of Theology (Emory
    University), 235
Carey, Lott, 103, 120, 121
Carey, William, 314
Carneado, Jose Felipe, 354
Case, Shirley Jackson, 17
Castellio, 292
Cavaliers, 277
Chafin, Ken, 222
Chambers, T. M., 113
Champion, L. G., 253
Chapman, Morris, 237
Charles I, 276, 277
Charles II, 64
Charleston (South Carolina), 8
Charleston Baptist Association, 9
Chauncy, Charles, 63, 79, 96 n.30
Childe, Robert, 83
Childs, Brevard, 176
Christian Church (Disciples of Christ).
    See Restoration movement
Christian Coalition, 302, 309
Christian Connection, 16, 185
Christian Life Commission, 133
Christian Right, 222
Church and state, separation of, 68, 70,
    74, 78, 81, 99, 127, 133, 198, 273,
    289, 292, 295, 298-304
Church as a Social Institution, The,
    245
Church attendance, 70
Church of Christ, 16

Church of England, 4, 75, 275, 282,
    300
Church order. See Polity
Church universal, 28, 374
Civil disobedience, 309
Civil punishment. See Punishment,
    civil
Civil rights movement, 46, 107, 113,
    119, 309, 375
Civil War, 103, 200, 205, 334, 335
Clarendon Code, 6, 76
Clarke, John, 8, 81, 83, 85, 88, 89, 91,
    95 nn.23,24,26, 99, 293
Clarke, William Newton, 17, 26, 27
Clegg, Stewart, 267
Clifford, John, 6
Clinton, Bill, 222, 311, 317
Cobbett, Thomas, 82, 87, 88
Coke, Sir Edward, 287
Coker, Daniel, 121
Colby College, 70
Cold Spring (Pennsylvania), 8, 9
Colgate Rochester Divinity School,
    202, 203, 204, 371
Colgate University, xii, 17
Colley, W. W., 104
Colored Baptist Convention, 340
Colored Baptist Home Missionary
    Society, 103
Commager, Henry Steele, 209
Commission for the Study of
    Administrative Areas and
    Relationships Project (SAAR), 390,
    392
Commission on Denominational
    Identity, 211
Committee on Nominations (SBC),
    133
Committee on Resolutions (SBC),
    127, 128
Communion, 5, 10, 23, 26, 75, 76, 88,
    197, 200, 203, 212
Communism, 73
Community, 263-65, 320, 321, 332,
    371, 374, 378, 381. See also
    Diversity

Community Renewal Act of 1996, 302, 303, 304
Compassion, 154-55. *See also* Good Samaritan, parable of the
Confession of Faith of 1644, The, 249
Confessions of faith, 175
  primary roles of, 249
Congregationalism;
  Congregationalists, 4, 6, 10, 12, 61, 62, 64, 65, 66, 69, 70, 75, 76, 80, 90, 280, 282
    New Lights, 66, 280
    Old Lights, 66
    Separate, 13, 66
Conservative Baptist Association, 40, 41, 44, 197
Conservative Baptist Fellowship, 228
Conservative Baptist Foreign Mission Society, 41
Conservative Baptist Home Mission Society, 41
Consolidated American Baptist Missionary Convention, 104
Constantine, 292
Constitution, U.S., 280, 284, 285, 298-304, 306 *See also* Bill of Rights; First Amendment
Constitutional Convention, 14, 299, 300
Continental Congress, 14, 307
Conventions. *See* Associations; Polity
Conwell, Russell H., 18, 21
Cooperative Baptist Fellowship, 45, 228, 232, 233, 234, 235
Cooperative Program (SBC), 39, 231, 236, 237, 239
Corpew, E. G., 335
Cotton, John, 63, 82
Council for National Policy, 132
Covenant Church, 182-84
Covenant theology, 3, *See also* Theology
Cox, Harvey, 315
Craddock, Fred, 148
Crandall, John, 88, 89, 96 n.26
Crane, William, 120

Creed, J. Bradley, 294
Criswell College, 129, 234
Criswell, W. A., 125, 234
Cromwell, Oliver, 6, 8, 74, 225, 277, 287
Crozer Theological Seminary, 17, 26, 33, 252
Cuius regio, eius religio, 74
Cunningham, Henry, 102
Curry, Thomas J., 292

Daniel, W. Harrison, 336, 337, 338, 340
Darwin, Charles, 18, 186
David C. Cook Publishing Company, 234
Davids, John, 94 n.14
Davies, G. Benton, 125
Davis, John, 67, 68
De Padua, Marsilius, 292
Deacons, 117, 118. *See also* Polity
Declaration of Independence, 284
Denominational organization, 40, 41-46, 47, 103, 119-21, 265-70. *See also* individual names of denominations; Polity
Department of Education, U.S., 308
DePuy, Norman, 251
Dilday, Russell, 221, 235
Disciples of Christ (Campbellites). *See* Restoration movement
Discipline, 23. *See also* Punishment
Diversity, among Baptists, 208, 209, 210, 211, 212, 219, 221, 262, 263, 347, 353
Divorce, 48
Doctrine, 53 n.10
Donatus, 380
Donne, John, 256
Douglas, Frederick, 331
Draper, James T., 132
Drummond, Lewis, 129
Du Bois, W. E. B., 107, 331, 334
Duke University Divinity School, 235
Dungan, Thomas, 8, 9

Dunn, James M., 132, 133, 195, 219,
  273, 286, 316
Dunster, Henry, 64, 79, 83, 89, 90, 91,
  96 n.30

Eastern Baptist Theological Seminary,
  145
Ebenezer Baptist Church (Richmond),
  335
Ecclesiastical taxes. *See* Taxation,
  religious
Ecumenism, 10, 20
Edelman, Marianne Wright, 119
Edwards, Jonathan, 65, 66
Edwards, Morgan, 36,
Eisenhower, Dwight, 198
Elder, Lloyd, 130
Elliot, Ralph, 45, 125
Ellison, Ralph, 346
Employment Division v. Smith, 307
Endecott, John, 88
English Civil War, 6, 275
Enlightenment, the, 22, 165, 260, 293,
  295
Episcopalians, 83, 341 n.8
Equal Employment Opportunity
  Commission, 308
Erastianism, 82
Ernst, Eldon G., 195, 197
Ervin, Sam J. Jr., 295, 314
Establishment Clause. *See* First
  Amendment, Establishment Clause
Estep, William R., 291, 293
Euthanasia, 132, 322
Evangelical Covenant Church, 183
Evangelical Revival, 6
Evangelicalism; Evangelicals, 5, 6, 11,
  14, 15, 16, 17, 19, 21, 23, 27, 31,
  295
Evans, James H. Jr., 312, 371
Evans, Milton G., 17
Everett, Harvey, 251

Faith healing, 73
Falwell, Jerry, 132, 209
Familism; Familists, 73, 76

Farrakhan, Louis, 301
Faubus, Orval, 314
Faunce, W. H. P., 18
Federal Council of Churches of Christ
  in America, 206
First African Baptist Church
  (Philadelphia), 102
First African Baptist Church of
  Richmond, 101, 335
First African Church of Savannah,
  101, 102
First Amendment, xi, 206, 285, 286,
  287, 289, 290, 292, 294, 295, 296,
  298-304, 375
    Establishment Clause, 298-304, 377
    Free Exercise Clause, 298, 302, 306-9
    See also Bill of Rights; Constitution,
    U.S.
First Baptist Church (Austin, Texas),
  226
First Baptist Church (Berkeley), 209
First Baptist Church (Boston,
  Massachusetts), 79, 100
First Baptist Church (Charlestown,
  Massachusetts), 83
First Baptist Church (Chicago's south
  side), 202
First Baptist Church (Dallas, Texas),
  234
First Baptist Church (Kingston,
  Jamaica), 121
First Baptist Church (Monrovia,
  Liberia), 103
First Baptist Church (Newport, Rhode
  Island), 81
First Baptist Church (Philadelphia,
  Pennsylvania), 185
First Baptist Church (Providence,
  Rhode Island), 80
First Baptist Church (Rochester, New
  York), 18
First Baptist Church (Seattle,
  Washington), 201
Fisher, Miles Mark, 98, 101
Floyd, John, 333
Ford, G. R., 247

Foreign Mission Board (SBC), 129, 229-30
Foreign missions. *See* Missions, foreign
Fosdick, Harry Emerson, xii, 53 n.9
Foster, George Burman, 17
Foucault, Michel, 153, 154
Foundations, 251, 388
Franciscan School of Theology, 209
Free for All Missionary Baptist Church, Inc., 98
Freedom, xiii, 1, 24, 31, 52, 220, 225, 252, 271, 287, 327, 385
    Bible, 343
    church, 343
    from slavery, 336
    of private interpretation of the Scriptures, 141-49, 155, 188, 190
    political, 68
    religious, 9, 68, 78, 79, 189, 198, 260, 277, 286, 288, 289, 293, 295, 298-304, 306-9, 343, 377, 381
    responsible, 275-85
    soul, 33, 50, 53 n.10, 63, 65, 67, 77, 127, 153, 162, 174, 211, 219, 221, 276, 343
    See also Responsibility
Freewill Baptists, 6, 16
Freud, Sigmund, 18
Fundamentalism, Fundamentalists, 21, 127, 233, 266, 375
Furman University, 238

Gaines, J. H., 335
Galphin, Jesse (Peters), 101
Gardner-Webb School of Theology, 228, 235
Gaustad, Edwin S., 7, 273, 275, 291, 294
Gay caucuses, 49, 56 n.51. *See also* Homosexuality
Geertz, Clifford, 221
General Baptists, 3, 4, 5, 6, 7, 8, 36, 75, 99, 253
    New Connexion, 6
General History of the Baptist Denomination in America and Other Parts of the World, A, 205

General Missionary Convention of the Baptist Denomination in the United States of America for Foreign Missions. *See* American Baptist Missionary Union
Genovese, Eugene D., 334, 335
George W. Truett Theological Seminary, 228
Gingrich, Newt, 222
Glossolalia, 181
Gnosticism, 26
Goldingay, John, 153
Good Samaritan, parable of the, 154
Goodspeed, Edgar J., 17
Goodwin, Everett, 225
Goodwin, Thomas, 10
Goodwine, Christopher, 86, 87
Goold, Thomas, 8, 63, 64, 94 n.14
Gore, Al, 222, 311, 317
Gottwald, Norman, 344
Graduate Theological Union, 209
Graham, Billy, 198, 308
Grant, Marse, 236
Graves, James R., 15
Great Awakening, 9, 10, 11, 16, 65, 66, 67, 79, 80, 99, 100, 204, 279, 280
Green, Joel B., 140, 151
Green, Thomas, 66

Haizlip, Shirlee Taylor, 312, 330
Haldane, James, 180
Haldane, Robert, 180
Hall, Robert, 5
Hamer, Fannie Lou, 119
Hamilton College, 37, 70
Hamilton Missionary Society, 37
Hancock, Loni, 209
Handy, Robert T., 205
Hannibal-LaGrange College, 129
Hardin-Simmons School of Theology, 235
Harper, William Rainey, 17, 21, 53 n.9
Harrison, Paul, 252

Harrison Street Baptist Church
  (Petersburg, Virginia), 335
Hart, Oliver, 9
Harvard University, 64, 65, 89, 90, 186
Hastey, Stan, 60, 124
Hasting, Brownlow, 316
Hatch, Nathan O., 184
Hatfield, Mark, 198
Hauerwas, Stanley, 161, 162
Havel, Vaclav, 317, 318 n.3
Hays, Brooks, 314-15, 318
Hays, Marion, 314
Hazel, John, 96 n.28
Helms, Jesse, 1, 315
Helwys, Thomas, 74, 75, 248, 293
Henderson, Charles R., 17
Henry, Patrick, 69, 282, 283, 288, 306
Henson, P. S., 18
Henson, Thomas, 335
Heterodoxy, 67
Heteronomy, 373, 374-75
Himes, Joshua V., 179
Hinson, Glenn, 225
Hippolytus, 178
Hiscox, E. S., 34, 38, 55 n.36, 225
History of Baptists, A, 249
HIV/AIDS. *See* AIDS/HIV
Hobart, Alvah S., 17
Hobbes, Thomas, 145
Hochma, 317
Hocking, William Ernest, 318
Holiness, 358
Holland, 99, 248
Holliman, Ezekiel, 80
Holmes, James, H., 335
Holmes, Obadiah, 83, 88, 89, 91, 96
  n.26
Home Mission Board (SBC), 129,
  229-30
Homosexuality, 48, 49, 50, 51, 56
  n.50, 165, 222, 226, 266, 322, 372,
  373
Honeycutt, Roy L., 129
Hooker, Thomas, 10
Hovey, Alvah, 17, 25, 27, 32, 34
Howard, A. E. Dick, 295

Howard College. *See* Samford
  University
Howell, David, 67
Höyem, Isak, 183
Hubbard, William, 76
Hubmaier, Balthasar, 293
Hudson, Winthrop S., xiii, xvii, 15, 27,
  29, 33, 37, 203, 251, 255, 388
Hughes, Richard T., 181
Human Genome Project, 165
Hume, David, 292-93
Hunt, W. Holman, 256
Hurse, J. W., 111
Hutchinson, Anne, 79, 80, 83, 90, 94
  n.7

Identity, Baptist, 195-212, 219, 240,
  241, 260-71
Ill-Newes from New England, 89, 95
  n.23
Independency, 5, 75
Individualism, 12, 18, 22, 32-35,
  151-52, 163, 343, 372, 375-77, 388
Inerrancy, biblical, 25, 35, 125, 126,
  127, 130, 132, 151, 223. *See also*
  Biblical authority; Biblical
  interpretation
Infant baptism. *See* Baptism, infant.
  See also Antipaedobaptists
Intellectualism, 19, 20, 22
Internal Revenue Service, 308, 309

Jackson, Jesse, 1, 209, 301, 315
Jackson, Joseph H., 46, 107, 112, 113
Jacksonian populism, 23
Jacob, Henry, 5, 7, 8, 75, 93 n.7
Jaffree case, 289, 290
James, Rob, 141
James, William, 19, 362
Jefferson, Thomas, 14, 62, 69, 282,
  283, 284, 285, 288-90, 293
Jeffersonian democracy, 22, 31-32
Jemison, D. V., 107
Jemison, Theodore J., 107, 109
Jessey, Henry, 75
Jeter, Jeremiah B., 338, 339, 340

Johnson, Bernice Reagon, 119
Johnson, Elias, H., 17, 25, 26
Johnson, Gustaf F., 183
Johnson, Lyndon, 314, 315
Johnson, Norman S. Sr., 312, 343
Johnson, W. Bishop, 105
Jones, Abner, 16
Jones, E. E., 111
Jones, E. P., 111
Joshua, 345
Joy Street Church (African Baptist Church, Boston), 102
Judson, Adoniram, 205, 314
Judson, Ann, 205
Judson, Edward, 18
Justification by faith, doctrine of, 160-61

Keach, Benjamin, 8, 10
Keach, Elias, 8, 9
Kelsey, David, 158
Ketocton Baptist Association, 9
Kiffin, William, 8, 75
Killingworth, Thomas, 8, 9
King, D. E., 113
King, Martin Luther Jr., 46, 107, 112, 113, 119, 204, 207, 314
King, Martin Luther Sr., 112, 113
Kingdom theology, 2,1 See also Theology
Knollys, Hanserd, 75
Knox, John, 2
Kraft, xii
Kristlig troslära (Teachings on Christian Faith), 182
Kuralt, Charles, 287

Lake Avenue Baptist Church (Rochester), 18
Lance, H. Darrell, 372
Landmarkist movement, 15, 200, 251
Latourette, Kenneth Scott, 205
Laud, William, 276
Laying on of hands, 80, 81, 117, 249, 280
Lectio Divina, 146

Leland, John, 14, 32, 284, 286, 292-94, 300, 301,
Lemon, William, 101
Lenox, David, 200
Leonard, Bill J., 39, 133, 134, 135, 195, 228
Levellers, 73
Lewis, C. S., 223
Lewis, Larry, 129
Liele, George, 100, 101, 121
Light of the World, The, 256
Lincoln, C. Eric, 60, 97
Linfield College, 198, 199, 201
Lobby Disclosure Act, 309
Localism, 18, 47, 135
Locke, John, 292
Lolley, W. Randall, 129
London Confession, 10, 35, 143, 223
Lord's Supper. See Communion
Lorimer, George C., 18
Los Angeles Baptist City Mission Society, 210
Lott Carey Baptist Foreign Mission, 98
Lott Carey Foreign Missionary Convention, 105, 110
Lotz, Denton, 312, 326
Lucar, Mark, 8
Lukar, Henry, 81
Luke, Gospel of, 165-66
Lumpkin, William L., 128
Lund, Nils, 183
Luther, Martin, 2, 73
Luther Rice Seminary, 231, 234
Lynn, Massachusetts, 83, 87, 88

MacArthur, R. S., 18
Macquarrie, John, 142
Madison, James, 69, 282, 283, 284, 285, 286, 288, 290-91, 293, 296, 306, 309
Magisterium, Roman Catholic, 175, 189
Malina, Bruce J., 190
Mamiya, Lawrence H., 97

Manning, James, 12, 36, 62, 67, 71 n.1
Manual of Christian Theology, 32
Maring, Norman, xvii, 37, 251, 255
Marsden, George, 132
Marshall, Molly T., 139, 141
Martin, Dan, 130
Marty, Martin, xi, 17, 219, 221, 223
Mason, George, 288, 306
Massachusetts Bay, 74, 77, 81, 83, 90,
    91, 99, 299
Massachusetts state constitution, 68, 70
Mather, Cotton, 76, 90, 93 n.2
Mather, Increase, 76, 77, 82
Mather, John, 93 n.2
Mathews, Shailer, 17, 27
Mays, Benjamin, 46, 112
McAteer, E. E. (Ed), 132
McBeth, H. Leon, 219, 248
McClendon, James, 143
McKinney, William, 350
McKnight, Edgar, 160
McLarry, Newman, 316
McLoughlin, William G., 59, 61, 72,
    281
McNutt, William R., 33, 34, 251, 252
Megachurches, 240
Megatrends, 254
Melanchthon, Philipp, 2
Membership, church, 6, 200, 241, 260,
    320, 351
Mennonites, 74, 143, 249, 283
Mercer University, 235, 246
Message of Genesis, The, 125
Methodism; Methodists, 15, 16, 17,
    79, 99, 103, 117, 283, 334
Meyer, Ben, 146
Mid-America Baptist Theological
    Seminary, 228, 231, 234
Middle District Association, 336
Midwestern Baptist Theological
    Seminary, 125, 129
Miller, Perry, 287
Miller, William, 179-80
Miller, William Lee, 290
Millerite movement, 179-80
Million Man March, 301

Milton, John, 80, 287, 314
Missio dei, 142
Missions, 23, 39
    foreign, 37, 70, 120-21
    home, 70
    See also individual names of
        mission societies
Mississippi College, 238, 239
Mitchell, Jonathan, 89
Moberg, David O., 244
Modalism, 178
Moltmann, Jürgen, 378
Monroe Association, 203
Montgomery, Helen Barrett, 202
Moody, Lady Deborah, 85, 91
Moore, David O., 333
Moral Majority, 132, 209
Morehouse College, 106
Morehouse, Henry L., 210
Morgan, Robert, 156
Morikawa, Jitsuo, 201, 202, 205, 375
Morris, E. C., 105, 106, 107, 109, 110
Moses, 344, 345, 348, 349
Mount Zion First Baptist Church
    (Baton Rouge), 109
Movements, 41, 352
Moyers, Bill, xi, 132, 311, 314
Mullins, E. Y., 32, 144, 314
Murton, John, 74, 75
Myers, Cortland, 18
Myles, John, 8, 76

Naisbitt, John, 254, 255
Nash, Diane, 119
National Association for the
    Advancement of Colored People
    (NAACP), 107
National Association of Evangelicals,
    354
National Baptist Convention of
    America, 98, 106, 109-12, 120
National Baptist Convention, U.S.A.,
    Inc., 46, 98, 100-109, 111, 120
National Baptist Educational
    Convention, 104
National Baptist Evangelical Life and

Soul Saving Assembly of the U.S.A., 98
National Baptist Publishing Board, 110, 111
National Baptist World Center, 109
National Conference of Catholic Bishops, 309
National Council of Churches, 309, 375
National Council of Churches in Christ, 354
National Labor Relations Act, 309
National Missionary Baptist Convention of America, 112
National Primitive Baptist Convention, U.S.A., 98
Neely, Alan, 231
Negro Baptists. See African American Baptists
Neo-orthodoxy, 124
Networking, 244, 254, 255. See also Associationalism; Associations
Nevin, John W., 184
New Christian Right, 132
New Connexion General Baptists. See General Baptists, New Connexion
New Hampshire Association, 67
New Hampshire Confession of Faith, 14
New Jersey College. See Princeton
New York State Constitution, 306-7
Newport (Rhode Island), 8
Newton Theological Institution, 17
Newton Theological Seminary, 70
Nicholson, John, 249
Niebuhr, Reinhold, 62, 318
Nixon, Richard, 314
Noetus, 178
Noninstrumentalists, 181
Non-Separatists, 4, 5, 7, 10, 75, 76
Norris, Kathleen, 146
North American Baptist Conference, 40, 44
North Carolina Baptist Convention, 238

North Carolina General Baptist State Convention, 115
Northern Baptist College (Manchester, England), 248
Northern Baptist Convention, 16, 41, 42, 43, 197, 200, 201, 202, 204, 206, 387. See also American Baptist Churches/USA
Northern Baptist Theological Seminary, 201
Northwestern and Southern Baptist Convention, 103
Noyes, John Humphrey, 178-79
Nyvall, David, 182-84

O'Connor, Elizabeth, 146
Oneida Community, 178-79
Operation Rescue, 309
Oregon Territory, Baptist churches on, 199-201
Owen, John, 10
Oxford University, 280

Pacific Coast Theological Society, 209, 210
Pacifism, 73
Padilla, C. René, 164
Paine, Robert Treat, 71 n.1
Painter, Thomas, 85, 87, 91
Papists, 73
Parks, R. Keith, 129, 134
Parks, W. G., 107
Particular Baptist Confession of Faith, 10
Particular Baptists, 3, 4, 5, 6, 7, 8, 10, 12, 14, 15, 40, 75, 99, 253
Patterson, Paige, 125, 129, 131, 132, 134, 136 n.9
Patton, George, 317
Paul, the apostle, 245, 246, 263, 264, 351
Paul, Thomas, 102
Peace Committee (SBC), 127, 128, 129
Peace Fellowship, 56 n.51, 208
Pedobaptism. See Baptism, infant
Pelagius, 380

Pembroke College, 287
Penn, William, 8
People of the Book, 141
Perfectionism, 67, 178, 179
Peters, Jesse. *See* Galphin, Jesse
   (Peters)
Peterson, Merrill, 291
Pettaway, C. D., 111
Philadelphia Baptist Association, 9,
   10, 12, 13, 36, 99, 100, 250, 254,
   279
Philadelphia Confession of Faith, 10,
   11. *See also* Particular Baptist
   Confession of Faith
Phinehas, 345, 346
Pietism, 222-23
Piscataway (New Jersey), 9
Plan of Union Committees, 104
Plato, 244
Plessy v. Ferguson, 105
Pluralism, 211, 221, 222, 261. *See also*
   Diversity, among Baptists
Plymouth Colony, 90
Politics and religion, 13
Polity, 28-31, 32, 33, 34, 102, 115-19,
   224-25, 268. *See also*
   Associationalism, Associations
*Polity and Practice in Baptist
   Churches,* 33
Polygamy, 64
Postmodernist organization, 264, 265,
   266, 267-68
Poston Relocation Center, 202
Prelacy, 82
Presbyterianism, Presbyterians, 11, 75,
   76, 78, 80, 83, 277, 280, 283
Pressler, Paul, 124, 125, 130, 131, 132,
   133, 134, 136 n.9
Price, Bill, 316
Price, Ira M., 17
Price, Nelson, 126
Priesthood of all believers, 52, 73,
   127, 144, 220, 264
Prince, G. L., 111
Princeton (New Jersey College), 291
Progressive National Baptist

Convention, Inc., 46, 98, 106, 107,
   111, 112-15, 120
Prosser, Gabriel, 102
Protestant Reformation, 2, 3, 99, 165,
   175, 292, 357, 366
Providence (Rhode Island), 7, 8, 276,
   278
Providence Association (Ohio), 103
Providence Plantations, 75, 78
Public Affairs Television, Inc., 132,
   314
Publications, 70, *See also* individual
   names of publications
Punishment, civil, 64, 80, 84, 85, 86,
   87, 88-89, 90, 92, 95 n.21
Puritanism; Puritans, 64, 66, 72, 73,
   76, 77, 78, 79, 80, 81, 82, 83, 84,
   85, 89, 90, 91, 92, 99, 277
Putney Bible School, 179

Quakerism; Quakers, 6, 63, 65, 73, 76,
   77, 78, 80, 81, 83, 85, 86, 87, 90, 93
   n.4, 283, 307, 321-22, 333
Quassey, 100
Qur'an, 141

Rabinove, Sam, 290
Race relations, 52, 105, 106-7, 339,
   See also Racism
Racism, 46, 105, 106, 326-29, 337
Ramm, Bernard, 224
Ranterism, 76
Rappahanock Association, 336
Rathbun, Valentine, 69
Rauschenbusch, Walter, 17, 202, 324,
   325
Reagan, Ronald, 132, 133, 209
Reavis, Ralph, 312, 333
Reconstruction era, 98
Reconstruction Movement, 346
Redstone Baptist Association, 181
Reed, Ralph, 302
Regular Baptists, 11, 16, 100
Rehnquist, William, 289, 290, 295
Religious Equality Amendment, 303
Religious Freedom Restoration Act
   (RFRA), 298, 307, 308

Religious Herald, 338, 339
Religious liberty. *See* Freedom,
 religious
Religious Roundtable, 132
Responsibility, 1, 24, 31, 52, 225,
 260, 275-85, 316, 382, 385. *See
 also* Freedom; Soul competency
Restoration movement, 180-82
Revolutionary War, 68, 281, 282,
 283, 291, 292, 300
Rhode Island, 7, 63, 78, 80, 99, 277
Rhode Island College. *See* Brown
 University
Rice, Luther, 37
Ridgecrest Conference on Biblical
 Inerrancy (1987), 126
Ringe, Sharon, 145, 148
Riverside Church (New York), 56
 n.47, 204
Robertson, M. G. (Pat), 132, 209, 301
Robinson, John, 4, 75
Rochester University, 17
Rockefeller, John D., xii, 21, 43, 44,
 53 n.9, 56 n.47, 204
Rogers, Adrian, 125, 126, 135, 229
Rogers, Melissa, 273, 298
Roman Catholics, 2, 70, 208, 264
Roof, Wade Clark, 350
Rosseau, Jean-Jacques, 293
Roundheads, 277
Rushdoony, Rousas J., 223
Ryland, Garnett, 338
Ryland, Robert, 101

Sacerdotalism, 82
Salem, Massachusetts, 83, 84, 85, 87,
 88
Salvation by grace, doctrine of, 12, 19
Samaritan, parable of the good. *See*
 Good Samaritan, parable of the
Samford University (Howard
 College), 235, 238, 239
Sams, J. C., 111
Sandy Creek Association, 11, 14, 125
Savoy Declaration, 10
Scalia, Antonin, 295

Schism, 15, 24, 106, 240, 279, 316
Schmidt, Nathaniel, 18
Scholer, David M., 140, 174
School prayer, 47, 128, 132
Scientism, 20
Scott, Harrison, 335
Scott, Mrs. Richard, 80, 93 n.4
Scripture, authority of. *See* Biblical
 authority
Seekerism, 76
Segregation, 46, 105, 106, 144, *See
 also* Racism
Selective Service, 309
Sellers, Ian, 248
Separate Baptists, 11, 12, 66, 67, 68,
 100
 Connecticut, 12
 Massachusetts, 12, 13, 14
 Virginia, 14
Separatism; Separatists, 4, 11, 75, 78,
 79, 81, 99
 Lincolnshire, 4
Seventh-day Adventist denomination,
 180
Seventh Day Baptists, 40, 81, 280
Sexuality, 48, 226, 322. *See also*
 Homosexuality
Shackleford, Alvin C., 126, 130
Shaftesbury, Vermont, Association, 67
Shakers, 69
Shaw University, 106
Shepard, Marshall L., 113
Sherman, Lawrence W., 311, 319
Shotwell, Malcolm G., 196, 243
Shurden, Walter B., 125, 246, 248,
 343, 344
Silver Bluff Baptist Church, 100, 101
Simmons, William J., 104
Simons, Menno, 293
Six Principle Baptist churches, 80,
 250, 280
Skoglund, John, 203
Slater, Philip, 320
Slavery, 38, 42, 60, 97, 100, 101,
 103, 144, 222, 280, 281, 330, 332,
 333, 334
Smith, Abby, 180

Smith, Chileab, 71 n.1
Smith, Ebenezer, 66, 280, 281
Smith, Elias, 184-85, 186
Smith, Gerald Birney, 17
Smith, Hezekiah, 12, 66
Smith, J. M. P., 17
Smith, Julia Evelina, 180
Smyth & Helwys Publishers, 228, 233, 234
Smyth, John, 4, 248, 293
Soares, Theodore G., 17
Social Security, 309
Society of Universalist Baptists, 185
Socinianism, 78
Sola Christi, 142, 379
Sola fidei, 142, 224, 376
Sola scriptura, 141, 164, 175, 184, 190, 224, 360-61
Soul competency, 32, 33, 144, 153, 220, 316
Soul freedom. *See* Freedom, soul
Southeastern Baptist Theological Seminary, 129
Southern Baptist Advocate, 231
Southern Baptist Alliance (Alliance of Baptists), 45, 135, 228, 231, 232, 234
Southern Baptist Conservatives of Virginia, 237
Southern Baptist Convention (SBC), xi, 39, 40, 44, 45, 51, 59, 60, 98, 103, 106, 124-35, 228-42, 267, 314, 375, 378
    educational institutions, 234-36
    internal control, 128-31
    local issues, 239-42
    national politics, 131-35
    network of organizations, 228-42, 244
    regional transitions, 236-39
    revolt, 266
    theological disputes, 124-28
Southern Baptist Journal, 231
Southern Baptist Theological Seminary, 186, 202
Southern Christian Leadership Conference, 107

Southern Seminary, 129
Southwark, England, 5, 7, 75
Southwestern Baptist Theological Seminary, 235, 314
Sparkman, G. Temp, 129
Spelman College, 106
Spilsbury, John, 5, 7, 8, 75, 94 n.7
Springfield Baptist Church (Augusta, Georgia), 101
Spur, John, 96 n.28
Spurgeon, Charles, H., 5
Stamp Act, 280
Standing Order of New England Congregationalism, 11. *See also* Congregationalism; Congregationalists
Statement of Concern, 49. *See also* Homosexuality
Statute of Virginia for Religious Freedom, 284
Stearns, Shubal, 11
Stetson University, 21, 238
Stevens, John Paul, 295
Stewart, J. W. A., 18
Stiles, Ezra, 61, 71 n.1
Stillman, Samuel, 67, 294
Stone, Barton W., 181
Stonington, Connecticut, Association, 67
Straus, Oscar S., 287
Strong, Augustus Hopkins, 17, 21, 24, 25, 26, 28, 29, 30, 31, 32, 34
Stuart monarchy, 6
Study Commission on Denominational Structure (SCODS), 206, 251, 253, 254, 255, 390, 391, 392
Study Commission on Regions (SCOR), 254, 255, 378, 379, 380
Sunday School Board (SBC), 130, 132, 229, 234, 239
Sunday School Publishing Board of the National Baptist Convention, 106, 109, 120
Supreme Court, 289, 295, 307, 308
Swansea, 8
Swedish (Evangelical) Mission

Covenant Church. *See* Covenant Church
Sweetser, Benjamin, 94 n.14
Sweetser, Seth, 94 n.14

Tanner, William G., 129
Taxation, 281
religious, 9, 64, 65, 66, 68, 69, 79, 287, 300, 303
Taylor, Alrutheus, 334, 335, 336, 340
Taylor, Gardner C., 46, 112, 113
Teague, Collin, 120
Temptation of Jesus, 158-59
Tennent, Gilbert, 11, 66
Tertullian, 177-78
Theodosius the Great, 292
Theology, 47, 155, 156
Baptist, 324, 371-80
challenges to, 18-24
systematic, 155, 171 n.14
See also Biblical authority; Biblical interpretation; Covenant theology; Kingdom theology
Theonomy, 373, 377-79
Thomas, Oliver, 273
Thurman, Howard, 378
Tiffany, Frederick, 145, 148
Tillich, Paul, 373
Tindall, George Brown, 335
Toleration, 74, 80, 89, 91, 92, 306
Toleration Act, 65
Tombes, John, 75
Torbet, Robert G., 249, 250, 251, 374
Toy, Crawford Howell, 186, 187, 188
Transubstantiation, 77
Triennial Convention (Baptist Missionary Convention), 37, 39, 70, 202
Trinity, doctrine of the, 16, 300
Truett, George, W., 220, 235, 301, 314
Truman, Harry S., xii, 198, 224
Turner, Nat, 98, 102, 333
Tuskegee Institute, 106
Underground Railroad, 103, 155
Union Association (Ohio), 103

Unitarian Baptists, 16
Unitarianism, 3, 6, 253
United Free Will Baptist Church, 98
United Methodism, 163. *See also* Methodism; Methodists
Universalism; Universalists, 26, 79, 185
Universalist General Convention, 185
University of Chicago, 17, 21, 27, 53 n.9, 56 n.47, 201
University of Richmond, 238

Vane, Harry, 80
Vanhoozer, Kevin, 157
Varieties of Religious Experience, The, 19
Vedder, Henry C., 10, 17
Vesey, Denmark, 102
Vietnam War, 113, 206, 207, 208, 375
Virginia Assembly, 283, 333
Virginia Baptist State Convention, 335, 337, 338-40
Virginia Declaration of Rights, 306
Virginia Union University, 106
Voltaire, François-Marie Arouet, 292
Volunteer Committee for the Formation of a New National Baptist Convention, 113
Voting Rights Act, 307

Wake Forest University, 235, 238
Waldenström, Paul Peter, 182-84
Walker, Brent, 308
Wallis, Jim, 315
War for Independence. *See* Revolutionary War
Ward, Nathaniel, 74
Ware, Browning, 226
Warner, Stephen, 264
Warren Association, 9, 13, 67, 68, 281
Grievance Committee, 68, 69
Washington, Booker T., 106, 107
Washington, George, 62, 284, 291
Wayland, Francis, 14, 15, 32, 71, 144
Weiss, Daniel E., 212, 225, 312, 348
Wells, Richard H., 335, 339

Welsh Tract Church, 9
Werden, Peter, 67
Wesley, John, 142, 163
Wesleyan Quadrilateral, 163-64
Wesleyan theology, 6, 16
West Country, The (Western
    Association), 249
West, Morris, 247
Western Association. *See* West
    Country, The
Western Colored Baptist Convention,
    103
Westminster catechism, 70
Westminster Confession of Faith, 10,
    12
Westminster Standards, 3
Westmoreland-White, Michael, 144
Weston, Henry G., 17, 26, 28, 30, 31,
    32, 34
Wheeler, Osgood Church, 207
Whibley, Leonard, 244
Whipping. *See* Punishment
White, Esther, 68
Whitefield, George, 65-66
Whitley, W. T., 248
Wickenden, William, 84
Willamette Association, 200-201
Williams, Henry Jr., 335
Williams, L. K., 107
Williams, Leighton, 18
Williams, Roger, 7, 63, 68, 76, 77, 78,
    79, 80, 83, 90, 91, 93 n.1, 93 n.5,
    99, 142, 276, 277, 278, 279, 283,
    287-88, 290, 292, 293, 299, 314
Wilson, John, 88
Wimbush, Vincent L., 357
Winchester, Elhanan, 185, 186
Winthrop, John, 77, 80, 85, 91, 93 n.5,
    94 n.17, 96 n.32, 276
Witter, William, 87, 88, 91, 95
    nn.22,24
Woelfkin, Cornelius, 18
Wolcott, William, 84
Women, role of, 47, 48, 119, 120, 128,
    144, 222, 249, 266, 353
Wood River Association (Illinois), 103

Woods, E., 111
Word of God. *See* Biblical
    interpretation
World Council of Churches, 203, 354,
    389
Wright, Wendy, 147
Wuthnow, Robert, 154, 155, 165

Yale Divinity School, 61, 179, 204, 207
Yoder, Edwin M. Jr., 296
Young, Edwin, 135

Zion Baptist Church (Cincinnati), 113
Zion Baptist Church (Portsmouth), 335